THE EARLY SWISS AND GERMAN MISSION IN JAPAN

The Early Swiss and German Mission in Japan

Paradoxes of Liberal Theology

ESBEN PETERSEN

CHISOKUDŌ

Cover photograph: Thies Matzen

Copyright © 2021, Chisokudō Publications

ISBN: 979-8541073171

Nagoya, Japan
http://ChisokudoPublications.com

Contents

Introduction 1

PART I HISTORICAL BACKGROUND

1. Universal Religion from the Swiss Highlands:
   Ernst Buss and the Liberal Christian Mission 25
2. The Emergence of Liberal Christianity in Japan:
   The Rise and Fall of the AEPM 49

PART II PARADOXES OF THE MISSION IN JAPAN

3. Internal Conflicts and External Challenges The Failure of
   Missionary Educational Projects in Meiji Japan 81
4. A Class Dispute: Japanese Students and the
   Discordant Nature of Religious Conversion 113
5. Christian Magazines and the Identification
   of Religion in Meiji Japan 141
6. Buddhist Exposures to Liberal Christianity 187
7. Educating Youth at Home: Swiss and German Youth
   Missionary Literature 218

Conclusion 241

Notes 245

Acknowledgments 287

Bibliography 289

General Index 321

v

Introduction

Two hundred meters east of Tokyo University in a rather unremarkable corner of the city, crowded with residential homes and newly built parking lots exists the ruins of what once was a picturesque little stone church. It stands today forgotten, hidden by the wild flowers, which especially during the long summer months fully covers the remaining ruins of the once so quaint church. In spite of its current dolorous state, the church conceals a remarkable history, one that represent the dynamic convergence of human and historical trajectories behind the seemingly presumptuous and foolhardy attempt by Christian missionaries in the late nineteenth century to transform Japan into a Christian nation.

Just like the church, its owners, the German-speaking mission society of the *Allgemeinen Evangelisch Protestantischen Missionsvereins* (henceforth AEPM),[1] seems today to have become a forgotten part of Japan's modern religious history. Yet, in this book, I argue, the Swiss and German missionaries belonging to the AEPM introduced a new type of Christianity, i.e., Liberal Christianity, which became prevalent in Japanese Christianity during the period between the late nineteenth century and through the early twentieth century. The prominence of Liberal Christianity spanned Japan's modern periods and manifested in a wide-ranging variety of contexts even outside of theological circles.[2] Some examples of the AEPM's influence from the Meiji period can be found within the theology of Ebina Danjō 海老名弾正 (1856–1937); the establishment of Kyoto University's Center for Christian Studies under Hatano Seiichi 波多野精一 (1877–1950); and the influence of modern Buddhist scholars such as Murakami Senshō 村上専精 (1851–

1929). During the Meiji (1868–1912) and Taishō (1912–1926) periods, popular intellectual magazines, such as the *Meirokū zasshi* 明六雑誌 and *Shinri* 眞理 was inspired by Liberal Christianity or *jiyūshūgi shingaku* 自由主義神学 as it is called in Japan. As these examples show, the influence of Liberal Christianity in Japanese society appeared in different contexts and often were not linked to one another. Moreover, the concept of Liberal Christianity itself carried different meaning over time. Yet, starting in the late nineteenth century, the arrival of the Swiss and German missionaries as agents of Liberal Christianity in Japan constituted a recurring and pervasive pattern in Japan's modern religious society that is worth studying.

This book focuses on the aspect of the reception and appropriation of Liberal Christianity in modern Japan. In more concrete terms, it presents the history of the first Liberal Christian mission movement in Japan, the AEPM, during the Meiji and Taishō periods. It explores the dynamic networks—both religious and academic that developed around it and asks how Liberal Christian ideas emerging from the fold of the Swiss and German missionaries' work in Japan were contested, disputed, and ultimately changed through its encounter with the Japanese people. Although the theme of the AEPM occupies a central place in the historiography of nineteenth century mission movement to Japan, no more than a handful of studies, perhaps most noteworthy of these being that by Suzuki Norihase (1979) and Heyo Hamer (2002), has focused on this particular mission movement.[3] This is partly because, little trace of the many educational and social projects initiated by the AEPM remains today.[4] This book is a modest attempt to understand the consequences of the first Swiss and German mission's presence in Japan; its aim is to see whether this particular episode in Japan's history can yield any new insights to the intellectual and religious processes that took place in Japan around the turn of the century. To this end, this study utilizes a variety of documents that are explicitly related to the missionaries, such as missionary records, mission publications, personal letters, diaries, and memoirs.[5]

The German Evangelical Church in Tokyo, ca. 1890. Photo: Zentralarchiv der Ev. Kirche der Pfalz.

Furthermore, I argue, that the work of the AEPM missionaries in Japan highlights several paradoxes within the Liberal Christian mission itself. These paradoxes will be the center of the investigation, as several micro-historical case studies will demonstrate, how the ambiguous ideas of a "Liberal Christian mission" were imported by the missionaries with their own cultural and ethnocentric agendas, and how these ideas which emerged from the fold of Christianity was assimilated and reformulated in the Japanese context. This approach begs the question of whether the ideas of a "Liberal Christianity" introduced by the Swiss and German missionaries, in fact were as "liberal" or "*allgemein*" as they claimed, and many missionaries still claim. Or, on the contrary, if they were culturally determined. Without anticipating the solution to these questions raised in the following chapters and in spite of claims made by missionaries and followers of the belief, we may already recognize like Michel Mohr reminds us, "that as soon as the word "universality" is uttered in a particular language, it inevitably loses its universal aspect and falls into the relative realm of differentiations."[6]

This book examines the contradictions of Liberal Christianity from the outset of the history of the AEPM. It attempts to move beyond the explicit line of division often drawn between mission studies and religious studies while taking seriously the historical development of the concept of Liberal Christianity throughout the last half of the nineteenth and early part of the twentieth century. Through this analysis, it will try to explain why the initially, so promising Liberal Christian mission of the AEPM in Japan ended up becoming nothing more than a forgotten church among Tokyo's many skyscrapers.

WHAT IS LIBERAL CHRISTIANITY?

The expression *Liberal Christianity* consists of two basic elements. The word *liberal* can mean free, tolerant, progressive, humanistic, enlightened, or rational, among other possibilities. The noun Christianity is much plainer and simpler, it can mean the faith, the doctrine, or belief in Christ. Of course, Christianity is not simple, like liberal, it covers a lot of subjects. The combination of these two components produces a number of possible meanings and connotations which has made a definition hard to pin down, leading scholars to use such definitions as: "Critically Theology," "modern Theology," "Free Theology," "Culture Protestantism" and "Liberal Theology."[7] In this book, I will adopt the usage *Liberal Christianity*, the most common rendition, and refer to the AEPM as a "Liberal Christian mission" as the basic translation of this religious movement.

Many associate the expression "Liberal Christianity" with the nineteenth century in particular, but it has a longer history, dating back to at least the late eighteenth century and the first publication of Schleiermacher's Speeches (*Reden*) in 1799. In fact, the expression *theologia liberalis* finds mention in several texts connected to the

Rationalists movement of Immanuel Kant.[8] Although it is difficult to grasp the precise definition of "Liberal Christianity" from these eighteen-century texts—Schleiermacher for example never called himself "liberal" or "free theologian'—these early representatives of Liberal Christianity functioned in two ways: (1) as a movement that fought for doctrinal freedom from the church; and (2) sought to replace the faith in original sin and predestination with a rational faith in God and the moral autonomy of the individual.

Although in many ways different to late nineteenth century Liberal Christianity, these early references reveal that the concept of Liberal Christianity conveyed a sense of a new beginning and a desire to change the situation of the church for the better (or to free it from a dangerous condition). In Schleiermacher's writings, however, the language of Liberal Christianity did not yet function as a framework through which to interpret concrete social events, like the argumentation for a world mission. This changed in the last half of the nineteenth century. Coeval with the appearance of a philological and historical critical understanding of the Bible was the practice led on by David Friedrich Strauss of interpreting "Liberal Christianity" as the transformation of the old obsolete Christianity into a new rational religion of humanity or faith in the divinity of the human being.[9] Accordingly, Liberal Christianity became a universal instrument which appeared in diverse circumstances, from political protests, democratic nationalism, and in the formation of an imperial church. The prominence of Liberal Christianity continued throughout the nineteenth century and early twentieth century. Despite the rapid social and demographic changes, theologians continued to utilize the language of Liberal Christianity for interpretive purposes and upheld it for its universal values.

Before further discussing the history of Liberal Christianity's grounding in its proposed universalism, it is necessary to delineate the ways in which scholars of Church History and Religious Studies have approached the study of Liberal Christianity in their own technical and analytical ways. Scholars typically use the term Liberal Christianity as a historiographical category through which they refer to a variety of nineteenth and twentieth century movements or characters, such as the Tübingen School and its establishment of "the Protestant Union"(*Deutscher Protestantverein*) in 1863, or Albrecht Ritschl and the "History of Religions School"(*Religionsgeschichtliche Schule*). Driven largely by political critical methods, scholars have paid particular attention to the last half of the nineteenth century, during Germany's transition from small city states to a modern empire, and have attempted to find the source of tolerance exhibited by the theological liberals there.[10] Based on the fact that only a few contemporaneous church circles employed the language of tolerance, dialogue, and openness in theology, scholars have designated a number of nineteenth century movements that fulfill the criteria as Liberal Christians. Scholars such as Johannes Zachuber, Otto Gerhard Oexle, Matthias Wolfes, Hans-Joachim Birkner and Friedrich Wilhelm Graf, for example, have utilized the category of Liberal Christianity to refer to the following "classical" characteristics:

1. "scientific theology," in the sense that it increasingly adopted a critical approach to the study of history and not just the Bible;
2. anti-dogmatic, in the sense that it refused dogma and instead argued for the rational inquiry of human actions;
3. non-denominational, in the sense that they accepted religious pluralism within their churches;
4. and focuses on individual religious experience as the basis for the definition of all truth. [11]

Scholars have largely qualified these broad definitions, but suggested the need to also emphasize the explicitly anti-liberal nature of the liberal Christian movement.[12] Jennifer Jenkins (2003), based on her social-historic research on the Protestant and liberal cultural projects in Imperial Germany, for example, argues that the liberal Christian movement in Imperial Germany was an authoritarian project who thought to construct a "moral community of citizens."[13] I nonetheless prefer the above mentioned "core" characterizations of Liberal Christianity as the main definition with an emphasis on the new historical approach to the Bible and the significance of the personal religious experience, both of which are crucial elements for the understanding of the historic developments which happened around the Swiss and German missionaries belonging to the AEPM in Japan.

Furthermore, scholars with a more direct interest in theology and philosophy, such as Richard Crouter, developed the lens of systematic theology to describe the universal validity of Liberal Christianity.[14] From the 1970s, we find numerous books and articles worldwide on German Cultural Protestantism and German Liberal Christianity. For example, there exist countless publications about Schleiermacher and his theology.[15] In Japan alone, the number of recent Schleiermacher publications is overwhelming.[16] There are also works and translations of key figures such as Ferdinand Christian Baur, Albrecht Ritschl, Wilhelm Hermann, Adolf von Harnack and in particular Ernst Troeltsch and Tillich, both of whom not only have had a significant influence on the theological developments of Japanese Christianity in the twentieth century at the Kyoto School of Christian Studies but throughout the whole world.[17]

The use of Liberal Christianity as a universal category, while sometimes serving meaningful analytical purposes, has led to problematic consequences. First, despite the prevalence of scholarship that references the term Liberal Christianity, surprisingly little has been done to examine the actual claim of its "universality" when put outside its Western-speaking context. Liberal Christianity was initially a local category based loosely on a few instances in which historical actors themselves employed the expression to express concrete theological circumstances in eighteenth and nineteenth century Germany.[18] However, the term Liberal Christianity gradually took a life of its own and has come to function as a blanket term that includes numerous movements and writers who had very little in common except the belief that theology should be open to modernity, that Protestantism is the more modern religions, and that other religion (in most cases Catholics) are morally worse.[19] In other words, some scholars have uncritically designated a number of local social phenomena and movements based on criteria such as tolerance and faith and ascribed to them a universal validity, but in doing so they have not examined in any systematic way the history of the concept Liberal Christianity when put out of its local environment.

This book touches on the question of Liberal Christianity in its practical framework. In other words, what are the consequences of Liberal Christianity when it is transplanted into another (non-Christian) culture? To the best of my knowledge, this question has not yet been examined. To put it another way: what is understood as Liberal Christianity in this book is not a Liberal Christianity as understood in the works of Schleiermacher, Harnack or Troeltsch, which can be critically examined by theologians, but rather a Liberal Christianity as it was understood by the missionaries and who brought it to Japan and mixing it with ideas from the other academic disciplines, local philosophies, and current intellectual movements of the time. This book, to put it more precisely, does not ask: what specific form of Liberal Christianity did Swiss and German missionaries bring to Japan?[20] Rather, it examines the historical cases and the acts of transferring these liberal Christian ideas to Japan itself.

That being said, this book does not oppose the idea of universalism suggested in the works of Schleiermacher, Troeltsch, and so on. Such studies are necessary in order to highlight the salient patters of the state of mind of people at the time, and I use a number of these categories in this book myself. Furthermore, frameworks such as liberal and tolerant have helped me illuminate the agency of the Swiss and German missionaries. The newly proposed approach is necessary in order to highlight the development of Liberal Christianity in cultures different from the European, and at the same time, account for the prevalence of Liberal Christianity in the Japanese society from the late 1800s to the early 1900s from a broader analytical standpoint. The examination of the history of the liberal Christian missionaries of the AEPM will serve as an effective way to accomplish this.

The AEPM: The First Liberal Christian Mission in Japan

It was in the mid-1880s that the first liberal Christian missionaries began to enter Japan. The introduction of this new group of missionaries in the Japanese Christian landscape constituted a significant change in which the discourse of religion permeated Japanese society from the time. When referring to *liberal Christian missions* in Japan, I refer specifically to the actions and institutions as expressed by the historical actors related to the Swiss and German AEPM, unless otherwise noted. In this study, I will take into consideration closely related variations of the liberal Christian missions in Japan, such as the two American missions, the Universalists and the Unitarians,[21] but will analyse the framework of liberal Christian mission in Japan from the perspective of the AEPM. An examination of the rise (and fall) of Liberal Christianity related to the AEPM will highlight the significance Liberal Christianity played within the various religious and intellectual movements in Japan between 1885–1929. Rather than presume the applicability of the universal approach to Liberal Christianity, this study's approach offers a unique analytical angle by looking into the integration of a liberal Christian discourse in Japanese society.

In this book, I analyse the reception and appreciation of liberal Christianity in modern Japan through a series of case studies that focus on the outset of the mission work of the AEPM. Based on these case studies, I argue, it is possible to outline here some general characteristics of the liberal Christian mission in Japan. During the Meiji and Taishō periods, the Swiss and German missionaries of the AEPM, in essence, served as agents of Liberal Christianity. Through the AEPM mission and its networks, the first missionary Wilfried Spinner was responsible for the establishment of the Fukyū Fukuin Kyōkai 普及福音教会, a Japanese Christian community, in 1886, which developed into a place for lectures and discussions on Liberal Christianity in Japan. Spinner also founded, in 1888 the Shinkyō Shingakkō 新教神学校 or Theological Seminary, a center for liberal theological studies and training of local Japanese pastors. However, in the course of the 1890s the mission increasingly lost native Japanese support. In its early days it depended on the encouragement and support of Aoki Shūzō 青木周藏 (1844–1914)[22] and others, such as the Christian profile Hiromachi Kozaki 小崎弘道 (1856–1938).[23] The drawback of the mission in Japan, however, was an outcome of the specific anti-western intellectual context that developed following the promulgation of the Imperial Rescript on Education (*Kyōiku chokugo* 教育勅語) in 1890.

The AEPM in the late Meiji and Taishō years did not, in their mission work, aim to bring a radical and dogmatic transformation of the Japanese religious society with them. Instead, they focused on solving, what they deemed to be, specific moral and social problems in the Japanese society by suggesting solutions found in the ideas of Liberal Christianity. The missionaries of the AEPM were not dismissing the learnings of the Japanese religions such as Shinto and Buddhism, but instead aimed on building their own Christian teaching on the Japanese religious traditions by pointing on their elements of truth. In some cases, the missionaries, primarily through their literary publications, did serve as vehicles through which social critique was expressed and specific adverse conditions from which different communities suffered were highlighted, but they never directly challenged the prevailing world order of State Shinto and the Emperor rule. In the numbers of Japanese members, the mission was also not making any radical notion of itself. In the year 1907, the mission numbered 234 Japanese members making it insignificant compared to the overall Christian landscape of 60.000 Japanese Christians at the time.[24] One can ask oneself, was the mission of the AEPM unsuccessful? Here it is necessary to clearly separate the quantitively low numbers of members from the discourses on Liberal Christianity that developed around the scholarly work of the missionaries and influenced the establishment of Japanese Christianity.

What the AEPM achieved up until the late 1920s is better understood as a form of "Cultural Transfer," a process in which Liberal Christian ideas and concepts were introduced into a new cultural setting. Here they were followed by a process of negotiations, before eventually being transformed and adopted into its new cultural settings of Japan. The theory of *Kulturtransfer* or Cultural Transfer, proposed by the historians Michel Espange, Micheal Werner and Wolfgang Schmale, explains how new ideas and knowledge eventually lead to perceptible and sustainable changes to a society's collective values.[25] The scope of Liberal Christianity in Japan initially did not extend beyond the immediate mission community of AEPM, but was gradually introduced to the Japanese intellectual society through the missionary's publications. In this, we see a link to the theory of Cultural Transfer from the beginning of the work of the AEPM in Japan, allowing this book to go beyond the limits of a plain history of the mission in Japan and into an exploration of how Liberal Christian ideas themselves influenced a far broader range of Meiji-era religionists. First, with the emergence of Liberal Christianity, we see how Michitomo Kanamori 金森通倫 (1857–1945)[26] and Ebina Danjō, both highly significant actors in contemporary Japanese Christianity, were influenced by the ideas "historical theology" introduced to Japan by the AEPM.[27] The idea of historical theology, for example, would later become one of the tenets of Ebina Danjō's theology of *Religious Essence* (*Shūkyō no honshitsu* 宗教の本質), one of the most momentous ideas of Japanese theology in early twentieth century.[28] Second, the impact of AEPM away from Christianity, and into the wider intellectual and educational circles through missionary Carl Munzinger's introduction of the discipline of Religious Studies (*shūkyōgaku* 宗教学) in Meiji Japan with his article "On the Necessity of Religious Studies" (*Shūkyōgaku no hitsuyo o ronzu* 宗教学の必要を論ず, 1890). Finally, Liberal Christianity, also found itself in the writings of some of the leading figures of Modern Buddhism which benefited from Liberal Christian ideas in developing its response in its doctrinal fight against State Shinto (*kōkka shintō* 国家神道) in the late nineteenth century. These observations become possible by tracing the history of the missionaries of the AEPM from their arrival in Japan to this process of reception and appropriation of Liberal Christianity into larger spheres of the Japanese society.

Field of Research

Scholars have long valued the significance of Christianity in the modern history of Japan. The historian Mikio Sumiya, has for example, pointed to the role that Christianity played during the last decades of the nineteenth century in the fields of literature and politics.[29] Other Japanese historians, such as Maruyama Masao, have identified the early Christian movement's important role—particular as a social critic—in Japan's transition from a traditional to industrial society.[30]

As is clear from this short list alone, Christianity and the Western missionaries in Japan has been a fairly consistent theme in Japanese's modern religious history. However, many scholars look to the nineteenth century as a time in which the indigenous movement of Japanese Christians became especially prominent in the Japanese society and thus often neglect the foreign mission movement in their research. Examples often raised in support of this claim include the emergence of indigenous attempts to combine Christianity with the indigenous traditions such as Confucianism that came about in the late nineteenth century. "Japanese Christianity" writes Kyoto University scholar Ashina Sadamichi, "became an effort to preserve Christian values while giving them a concrete form in relation to the situation in Japan."[31] Scholars, in other words, typically contextualized these developments within the socioeconomic and political upheavals of the nineteenth century as a story largely in terms of the Japanese people's own acceptance of Christianity. They have been unable to pay sufficient attention to the Western missionaries who communicated the new ideas, or even to examine accurately the ideas themselves.

While I generally that the importance of the indigenous Christian movement of the nineteenth century played an important role in the modern history of religious thought in Japan, I maintain that much can still be learned about the modern history of Christianity in Japan by taking a closer look at missionary sources. Within the last decades there has been a shift in the approach to missionary studies. Post-colonial studies, for example, have revealed the importance of missionary sources in attaining the insight into the encounter between the expanding European culture and the countries which were forced to accept the "white man."[32]

Recently, this academic direction has led to several publications that attempt to give the modern idea of religion a historical basis from different perspectiives. Many scholars have begun to examine the idea that Western or Christian influence either was "transplanted" (Isomae), "invented" (Josephson), or "percolated into the non-Occidental cultural worlds" (Osterhammel).[33] This scholarly application, however, should not obfuscate the fact that missionaries ideas and discourses was just one of many religious discourses that emerged in nineteenth-century Japan and that, as the history of the AEPM will suggest, the discourse changed over time, developing into several versions of Christianity in twentieth century.[34] Being aware of this allows us to better appreciate the situation of the nineteenth century Japan as a place of competition where a diversity of ideas and discourses, which historic actors—the AEPM being one of them—utilized to articulate their own religious agendas, rather than simply to lump them all together under simple categories of "Western missionaries" or "Japanese Christianity."

If one moves further into the field of study and looks at the literature specifically in relation to the history of the AEPM, the picture becomes different from the research highlighted above. Where there exist a wealth of research on Christianity in Japan, there has so far been very little in-depth research done on the topic of the AEPM in Japan aside from the missionaries' own accounts.[35] In fact, the sole book, to date, devoted to the history of the AEPM is the work *Mission und Politik* (2002), written by the German church historian Heyo Hamer.[36] Hamer's book offers an in-depth study of Swiss missionary Wilfried Spinner's personal diary and provides a great analysis of the tension between the mission enterprise and German colonial politics. But it is limited in its temporal range as it only covers the years of the mission from 1885 to 1892. Aside from this work, only a few other publications mention the work of the AEPM in Japan: Otto Marbach's *50 Jahre Ostasien-mission, ihr Werden und Wachsen* (1934) focuses mainly on the founder of the AEPM, Ernst Buss, and pays almost no attention to the subject of Japan; Theodore Devaranne's *50 Jahre Evangelische Arbeit im Fernen Osten* (1934) offers some bibliographical sketches of some of the first missionaries and the most important Japanese converts, but does not incorporate any Japanese material. This is also the case for Johannes Bielfeldt's *75 Jahre Ostasienmission* (1962) and Ferdinand Hahn's *Spuren: Festschrift zum hundertjährigen Bestehen der Ostasien-Mission* (1984). All these historiographical studies have in common that they are either works paid by the mission or written by authors connected to the mission society. Thus, they sometimes tend to ignore the less successful events in their depiction of the history of the AEPM in Japan.[37]

Otherwise, there exist only a few critical or even descriptive studies in German that report the work of the AEPM in the Japanese mission field, and fewer still in English.[38] This is best signified by the Handbook of Christianity in Japan (2003) entirely leaving out the subject of the AEPM.[39] Only a few English language books about the Protestant missionary movement in Japan mentions the mission work of the AEPM. The earliest book is *A History of Protestant Missions in Japan*, (1898) written by the German theologian Karl Heinrich Ritter. This was originally published in German in 1890 under the title *Dreißig Jahre protestantische Mission in Japan* and translated eight years later into English.[40] A more recent publication is Yasuo Furaya's A *History of Japanese Theology* from 1997, which shortly discusses the influence of the AEPM and German Theology on Japanese Theology.[41] These two books, however, are exceptions. Most studies in the English language on Christianity in Meiji Japan—if they make a reference to the Swiss and German missionaries' enterprise at all—swiftly summarize what they seem to regard mostly as an unimportant historical endeavour.

Notto Thelle's important study of *Buddhism and Christianity in Japan: From Conflict to Dialogue, 1852–1899* (1987), for example, looks at the contact of Buddhism and Christianity through the study of periodicals from the period. Yet he only mentions the work of the AEPM in a few pages under the subheading: "Liberal Theology." The topic is summarized with the hurried conclusion that while "Liberal Theology was certainly a significant factor for establishing a positive relationship to other religions.... It facilitated compromise with reactionary forces, introducing an active support of nationalism and of burgeoning Japanese imperialism."[42]

Another book, *Protestant Beginnings in Japan*, written by Winburn T. Thomas, entirely passes over the subject of the AEPM.[43] In a similar manner the monographs of Charles W. Iglehart (1959), Otis Cary(1982), Aasulv Lande (1989) and Richard H. Drummond (1971), all authors of more recent and broader histories of Christianity in Japan, only mention the AEPM in connection with the church of American Unitarians and Universalists under the subtitles "liberal denominations" without much further comment.[44]

Japanese publications, in contrast to the English and German publications, do offer more abundant sources for research with several books referring to the work of the AEPM. Harada Tamao's edited *Nihon ni okeru jiyū kirisitokyō to sono senkusha* 日本に於ける自由基督教と其先駆者 (*The Free Christianity and its Pioneers*), published in 1935, is a transcript of the memoir of Minami Hajime 三並 良 (1869–1940),[45] a student of the first missionary Wilfried Spinner, and a significant member of the Japanese church Fukyū Fukuin Kyōkai. Minami worked as an editor of the Christian propaganda journal *Shinri* 眞

理 and his memoir provides valuable samples of the correspondences between the missionaries and the Japanese members of the Church, making it an important source for this study.

Another important contribution is Saba Wataru's chapter "*Nihon ni okeru Doitsu shingaku no eikyō*" 日本におけるドイツ神学の影響 (Influence on German Theology in Japan).[46] It sensitively describes the relationship that the missionaries had with the Japanese in Europe. Saba draws heavily on Japanese language sources (including that of Harada), and investigates the first introductory contacts of several Japanese individuals with the German missionaries. A third source written in Japanese that touches the history of the AEPM in Japan is the influential *Meiji shūkyō shichō no kenkyū: Shūkyōgaku kotohajime* 明治宗教思潮の研究：宗教学事始 (Studies on the Religious Trends of the Meiji Period: The Beginning of Religious Studies) from 1979, by Suzuki Norihase.[47] In his semantic study on the various religious trends surrounding the early formation of religious studies in Japan, three chapters are devoted solely to the work and influence of the AEPM. Although Suzuki draws mainly on Japanese language sources, his work stands out as the only effort so far to look at the history of the AEPM beyond a purely Christian frame of reference. Instead, he embeds and relates the AEPM to the larger context of the religious discussion occurring at the time in Japan. Suzuki's work therefore offers a great inspiration to this study. Yet the specific interactions of the liberal missionaries with their Japanese church members, and the struggles that emerged in the process, do not draw his attention. Still, because one of this book's major interests is the missionaries' contribution to the study of Japanese religions, all interactions between the AEPM and Japanese religious traditions are of interest; emphasizing these interactions will be on of this study's contribution to the overall field.

Lastly, the historical work of the AEPM's publication written in the Japanese language needs mentioning here. One of the central figures here is Mizutani Makoto, in the book *Nihon ni okeru Doitsu: Doitsu senkyōshi hyaku nijūgo nen* 日本におけるドイツ：ドイツ宣教史百二十

五年 (*Germany in Japan: 125 Years of the German Mission*) Mizutani writes about the historical relationship between Japanese Protestantism and German Evangelism, both before and after the Second World War. In his research he devotes most of his attention to the Japanese church member Minami Hajime and his work for Japanese language Christian journals.[48] Although it is important to recognize the editorial work of Minami in spreading liberal Christian ideas in Japan, Mizutani totally omits his personal relationship to the missionaries and the influence they sanctioned over Minami during his time as an editor and church member of the AEPM. As this book's case studies on the relationship between the Swiss and German missionaries and their Japanese students will show, the missionaries acted as involving agents actively contributing and engaging in the work of their Japanese students.

Overview

The following case studies highlight the paradoxes in the practical reality of the early Swiss and German missionaries attempt to transfer Liberal Christianity to the Japanese society between the late nineteenth and early twentieth centuries. As stressed earlier, the network of missionaries allowed for Liberal Christianity to appear in a variety of social contexts. As a result, this study collates and examines independent historical cases, not usually discussed alongside one another. Furthermore, although the first chapter of the analysis begins in the 1880s and the last chapter ends in the late 1920s, the chapters do not follow a chronological order. Instead, the structure of these chapters is thematically defined, and each chapter revolves around a special historical incident. This avoids asking identical questions in relation to each examined period. The reasoning behind this structure is grounded in the following rationale: (1) there is no suggestion that any analytical benefit could be derived from asking identical questions in relation to each period of investigation throughout the book. (2)

in particular circumstances and settings some questions and issues are considered to be more relevant than in others. And (3), by not being reliant on a set number of questions, this study is able to cover developments that otherwise might have been overlooked. Furthermore, this structure is founded on the premise that cultural logic often extends from one social situation to another, and that it may be transformed, changed, or even forgotten over time. The thematic structure of the book, in summary, reflects an analytical desire to examine changes and transformations beyond spatial, social, and temporal boundaries.

The book is divided into two parts. Part 1 (Chapters 1 and 2) supplies the necessary context and is of an introductory character. It offers a historical perspective on the development of the AEPM and their operations in Japan. Chapter 1 focuses on the founder of the AEPM, Swiss pastor Ernst Buss (1843–1928) and his attempt to combine the theology of Liberal Christianity with the mission idea. By examining the work of Buss, this chapter analyses the ways in which the universal claim of Liberal Christianity was interpreted in the 1870s and early 1880s and how they came to be adopted in a missionary context. To the best of my knowledge, Buss's writings represent the first successful attempt at combining Liberal Christianity and missionology. It thus marks an important turning point in German mission history. The examination of Buss's writings also set a basic pattern for the emergence of the missionaries' practical approach to Liberal Christianity in Japanese society.

Chapter 2 expands the story, with a description of the first years of the AEPM in Japan. It tells a familiar story of an ultimately failed Christian mission whose basic outline will be recognizable to other historians of mission history in Japan: an initial period of excitement and growth, ambitious projects and institution building alongside a few setbacks, the emergence of indigenous sympathizers and converts, but then increasing tensions between these indigenous converts and the foreign leadership that, combined with a shift in national sentiment, let to an eventual split and an end to the official mission.

The details of this case—which in a sense provide the manifest of a narrative of the Swiss and German mission in a competitive religious environment in Meiji and Taishō Japan will be scrutinized further in Part II. By navigating the missionary journals and personal diaries, each of the following chapters (3 to 7) encompasses its own separate subject, theme, or narrative, yet remains inextricably intertwined with the others. All of them represent reveal particular examples of the paradoxes that entangled the Swiss and German mission work in Japan.

Chapter 3 focuses on the direct trans-cultural exchange of the mission society with the local Japanese. Here the challenges and struggles faced by the missionaries in the founding and running of schools for Japanese children and students are the central themes. These difficulties prevailed right from the start of their mission enterprise in the mid–1880s and persisted all the way to the first decade of the twentieth century. For example, the missionaries often blamed the collapse of their educational projects on the lack of finances yet conveniently abstained from recognizing the role of their own internal conflicts as being part of the problem. The changeability of their short-lived schools can be seen as an indication of the disputed nature of their authority in Japan, as well as of the generally low level of local interest in what these schools had to offer. The chapter thus reveals the highly insecure nature of their control and power, and of the influence the missionaries actually retained. Even more so, it demonstrates the discrepancy between the Swiss and German mission discourse apparent in their publications compared with the reality on the ground.

Chapter 4 examines the missionaries' interactions with its Japanese students and analyses the missionary perception of the Japanese people by looking at the norms and practices by which Christians and non-Christians were governed in the first years of the AEPM mission enterprise in Japan. The chapter challenges the characterization often given in scholarship of mission societies being a coherent organization founded on a clear goal by demonstrating the missionaries' ambiguous relationship to their Japanese students. On the one hand the missionaries invested much of themselves in order to convert and educate their Japanese students, yet, at the same time, they had profound doubts as to whether the Japanese students could ever become truly independent Christians. Even Japanese who had been converted were considered "insufficient" Christians. Based on this observation, I argue that that the missionaries, through these kinds of practices, created a social disparity that supported a discourse of cultural superiority that on one side legitimized their own existence in Japan, but on the other pushed the Japanese Church members away from the missionaries who had educated them.

Chapter 5 examines the mission journal *Zeitschrift für Missionskunde und Religionswissenschaft*. Historians have claimed that Protestant Missions generally were hostile toward Japanese religions during the last decades of the nineteenth and early twentieth century. However, by attempting a close reading of the German-language journal, I make the claim that this was not much the case. In fact, inter-religious relations were continuously being redefined by transnational factors from the 1880s to the 1920s. Taking a "tolerant" position, many writers claimed that "all religions were all different expressions of the same truth" encouraging some of the earliest religious studies of Japanese religions. On the same time, however, the articles also took a "inclusivist" position, as writers also would claim that only Christianity embodied all the truths. By demonstrating these contradictions between "tolerance" and "inclusivism," I show, how the ambiguous nature of the liberal Christian Mission infused the literal mission of the AEPM.

Chapter 6 uses the mission materials as a stepping-off point from which it tries to contextualize the contested debate amongst the missionaries and Buddhist intellectuals, especially related to the attitudes and statements of two key persons involved. The chapter highlights the continuing relevance of the discourse of religious truth in the Meiji and Taishō periods and analyses how the Buddhist intellectuals connected the language of Liberal Christianity with their own religious agendas. This chapter also problematizes the agency of the Swiss and

German missionaries in this historical event and shows that the intellectual discussions surrounding "religious truth" was a complex event involving actors with differing motives and, at times, contradictory visions of the world.

Finally, Chapter 7 takes up the case of the Swiss and German missionaries' youth literature and examines the message the missionaries conveyed to the youth in Switzerland and Germany. The chapter postulates that the missionaries became highly influential as educators, not so much in Japan but rather at home in Switzerland and Germany where the youth literature nursed a feeling of sympathy in their young readers for Japanese children of the same age in a way that was concurrent with a modern, cultivated Protestant Christian identity.

As can be seen, the following chapters will be exploring the nature of the early Swiss and German mission activities in Japan from a myriad of angles. It will, however, begin its story in Switzerland, looking further into the circumstances that initially led Liberal Christianity to Japan.

PART I
Historical Background

1

A Universal Religion from the Swiss Highlands

Ernst Buss and the Liberal Christian Mission

A short hike to the North-East of the Wildrubels Glacier and the Wildhorn Mountains in the Berner Highlands of Switzerland leads one to the less conspicuous mountain town of Glarus, where hidden away between steep mountains and winding hiking trails lies the grave of Ernst Buss (1843–1928). Remarkably, this remote place was once the site of a reformation within the mission landscape of the German-speaking world. Influenced by the radical criticism on contemporary mission policy suggested by the Swiss theologian Ernst Friedrich Langhans (1829–1880) in his work "Pietism and Christianity in Relation to the Foreign Mission" (*Pietismus und Christentum im Spiegel der äußern Mission,* 1864),[1] and the Tübinger Historian of Religion Poul Rudolf von Roth (1820–1892), Buss became a key figure in the 1880's movement of the *"Neuorientierung der evangelischen missionen"* i.e., "the repositioning of the evangelical missions." In his texts, Buss argues for the establishment of a new mission society, one that transcends differences between denominations or church parties and instead ties elements of the truth of the non-Christian religions to the ideas of Christianity.

But who was Ernst Buss? Why did he feel a need to reform the German mission landscape? And more importantly, why were German and Swiss liberals so eager to support his new mission ideas? The ennoblement of Buss's ideas among Swiss and Wilhelmian German liberal-Protestants represents a pivotal moment for this study as it marked the beginning and the rise of the first liberal Christian mission society in the German-speaking world. An analysis of pertinent primary sources reveals that liberal Protestants who supported Buss's ideas were the product of two important factors: (1) the change in global structures as new discoveries from the networks of European colonies demanded acknowledgement and answers from the church,[2] which (2) temporarily created an opening and opportunity for alternative political and theological models to flourish. The work of Ernst Buss and the subsequent establishment of the *Allgemeinen Evangelisch-Protestantischer Missionsverein* in Weimar on June 4, 1884 can be seen as the event where these two factors overlapped.

The question now is: from what perspective should this new intellectual movement, represented in Buss's writings, be studied, and in what way can it add to this book's study on the AEPM in Japan. There are many considerations to be made to answer such a question, and it will likely be difficult to reach consensus among researchers. Scholars typically use a historiographical approach to refer to the variety of late nineteenth century Christian mission movements that dealt with the early efforts of globalization and the establishments of various interconnected networks. Jürgen Osterhammel and Niels P. Petersson, for example, utilized the concept of *Interacktionsraüme* or "spaces of interactions," to refer to the cultural contact, transfer and exchange that happened within the global mission field of the nineteenth century.[3] Furthermore, scholars with a more direct interest in Liberal Christianity, such as Johannes Zachhuber and Emanuel Hirsch, use the lens of historical theology to describe the liberal theologians' inner yearning for a *Neuorientierung* of the evangelical mission. According to these scholars, the liberal theological movement manifested itself as a variety of historical phenomena, including the so-called "scientific" theologians.[4] These scholars also made a fairly liberal application of the category of Liberal Christianity, going beyond the temporal context of the nineteenth century and far further into post-modernity. Gavin Hayman and Paul D. Murray, for example, both see manifestations of a liberal Christian theological mindset in today's post-liberal movement.[5]

In short, scholars have employed different approaches to the study of the new intellectual movement of Liberal Christianity in Germany as a historiographical category to highlight the intellectual and social qualities of the movement. The use of Liberal Christianity as a scholarly category, while serving a meaningful analytical purpose, has also led to problematic consequences. For example, despite the prevalence of scholarship that references the term Liberal Christianity, it is mostly listed as a generic keyword. The historiographical category, which is also mentioned in the introduction of this book, was initially based loosely on a few ambivalent keywords, which historical actors themselves employed to serve their objectives. However, the category of Liberal Christianity began to take a life of its own and has become a blanket term for a myriad of intellectual movements, the mission movement of the AEPM being one of them.

I am not necessarily against the use of Liberal Christianity as a generic category per se. Generic categories like these are required in order to highlight salient historical patterns of Liberal Christianity, and I adopt a number of like terms throughout this book myself. Furthermore, critical approaches to Liberal Christianity have helped clarify the agency of the liberal theologians, rather than simply generalizing them to the status of tolerant Christians.[6] Nevertheless, it is precarious, that the category of Liberal Christianity lacks a clear conceptual boundary. A new approach is necessary to emphasize the limits of Liberal Christianity, while accounting for its prevalence in the *Neuorientierung* of the mission discourse in the German-speaking landscape of the late 1800s from a broader analytical perspective. By scrutinizing Ernst Buss's mission ideas in relation to Liberal Christianity, this chapter begins to tackle this issue.

In the first section of this chapter, I situate the writings of the mission founder Ernst Buss and compare the characteristics of his Christian thought with some of the leading figures of Liberal Christianity. Next, I analyze how Buss integrated these liberal Christian thoughts in a mission context. In the final section, I look at how the ideas were received among both liberal and conservative circles in nineteenth century Germany. The chapter is summed up with some perspective thoughts on why Buss succeeded in creating a new mission society based on Liberal Christianity.

Reconsidering pluralism: Ernst Buss and Liberal Christianity

The conceptualization of Liberal Christianity outlined above serves as the basis for the portrayal of Ernst Buss's mission ideas. Through his 1876 published book *Die christliche Mission, ihre principelle Berechtigung und practische Durchfüuhrung* (The Christian Mission, its Principle Authorization and Practical Implementation), it becomes evident how liberal Christian ideas of non-dogmatical church policies and the focus of personal faith underpinned the mission idea of Buss. The book, in many ways, represents an attempt to incorporate the "modern" ideas of Liberal Christianity into a new modern mission discourse which would eventually lead to the establishment of the AEPM in 1884. For example, in his book, Buss highlights the problems of the contemporary mission and the need to reform the German-speaking mission world from within, by focusing on the constitution of individual faith, the acceptance of religious pluralism, and the proclamation of a world conquering mission. Although the book's relationship to Liberal Christianity is more or less forgotten in contemporary research circles, it nonetheless represents an early and unique instance of a link between Liberal Christianity and world mission.

One point that becomes obvious when reading the book is that Buss discusses Christianity through the perspective of modern academic research and the newly developed field of Comparative Religion. Of course, although Buss does not go through the formal procedures used in modern academic research in the assessment and evaluation of previous research or in quoting other texts, one can sense that he was inspired by the discussions which took place in the academic circles of the time. At one place, for example, Buss replaces the legalistic understanding of the content of doctrine with the wish for reflection based on one's own religious experiences and praises lived religion instead of dogma, stating:

> Christianity should be just as dogmatically broad and simple as it is spiritually high and fruitful.... Christianity should respect the deepest introspection, the highest spirituality, and the warmest outward-reaching love, Christianity at once of freedom, reason, and of moral vigor.... In other words, the true missionary stance should be the Christianity of Christ.[7]

In this passage, the individual religious experience is treated as a full-fledged legitime religion. It is seen as the only possible way to describe the doctrine of faith. The personality of the life of Christ, which signifies the essence of Christianity, can, Buss claims, only be understood as a matter of internal experiences. This passage makes explicit the religious experience "broad and simple." Characteristics of modern German Liberal Christianity as established by Schleiermacher can thus also be seen as reminiscent in Buss's text by his main theological focus, at least in the quote, being grounded in the "religious feeling", i.e., in the "warm and outward reaching love" of Christ. Another Buss quote found in the essay titled "Mission as the responsibility of the Nation" (*Die Mission als nationale Aufgabe*, 1886) offers a similar example. Two themes reoccur in this essay: (1) the "non-confessional church" is defined as the "essence of Christianity." In other words, Christianity is the universal concept of religion replacing dogma and ceasing all indifference among all confessions of faith. And (2) using this "essence" concept, the particularities of Christianity are shown to be in fundamental agreement with all other religions. Consequently, Buss, in his book, attempts to open the dogmatic claims to the absoluteness of one's own faith community to other confessions and religions. More precisely, he attempts to free the Christian message from any culturally defined subjectivity and teaches the Christian religious life in its original sense of Jesus and the Apostles. In the article, Buss is quoted as saying:

> [Christianity] should not necessarily be tied to any certain ecclesiastical archetypal and specific cultural systems of the West but must go hand in hand with the universal ethical advancement of the individual as well as all people, whose collective fruit is a higher civilization and culture.[8]

This passage exemplifies Buss's liberal approach to other religions and how closely his ideas of mission politic and Liberal Christianity intertwined. It is tempting, as scholars often do, to associate Liberal Christianity with an "autonomous religion." Theologian Friedrich Wilhelm Graf, for example, in a talk he gave at Kyoto University in 2019, described some common threads in the understanding of the autonomous self among liberal theologians such as: "self-reflexive subjectivity, liberation from the immaturity of traditional forms of authority, the formation of personal identity through strong self-discipline, the growth into a personality in consciousness of the bondage to God, and the call for a concrete form of freedom which was bound up with values and ideals" as some of the key common points among others.[9] However, this interpretation is inadequate; the morality of the individual in Liberal Christianity was also intricately linked to the social reality. This observation becomes clear by tracing Buss's understanding of the "Kingdom of God." The quoted passage above shows that the emic concept of Christian culture was not static but rather changeable. Buss differs between what he describes as "Christian culture" and "Christian religion." To him, "culture" should be understood as a locally developed phenomenon that differs among societies and nations. This, furthermore, leads to the acceptance of culturally diverse interpretations of Christianity. But while there exists a German Christianity, a British Christianity, or even a Japanese Christianity, there can only ever be one Christian "religion." To Buss, the essence of religion is universal and unbounded by national or cultural characteristics. The Christian religion, he states, always remains the same no matter which culture it spreads to. It is therefore essential when propagating Christian religion "to take the message of Jesus seriously by freely allowing the missionaries to spread the message of Christian life."[10] On the other side, Buss, like most German protestant liberals, argued for a practical cultural superiority of Christianity (or Protestantism) above other religions. Since Protestantism is understood as the religion of freedom and personality, it has to be regarded as the universal religion of the modern culture of individuality. As Friedrich Willhelm Graf points out, there were only very few liberal theologians who called into question this claim of superiority.[11]

Ernst Buss's *Die christliche Mission, ihre principelle Berechtigung und practische Durchfüuhrung* was written initially as a response to the Haager Gesellschaft's wish to "defend the Christian religion.[12] In the book, Buss combines new academic fields, such as the cutting-edge critical Bible studies, which was prominent in Ferdinand Christian Baur's Tübingen School as well as in Albrecht Ritschl's historical theology.[13] Reflecting both authors—but without referring to them—Buss outlines the need for Christianity to be understood in relationship to its history:

> Due to its entire preceding religious development, Christianity has been evidently called upon to unite within itself all religious hopes and endeavors of the old world, to fill and complete them, and thereby to take on a historical duty of universal significance.[14]

Buss thus sets the tone for what he, and later the AEPM, would be striving to accomplish. His work consolidated two central points; First, he advocated "tolerance" as being necessary to properly approach any foreign religion. In other words, an open-mindedness beyond the solidification of dogma and apologia. Second, he emphasized a core belief of Liberal Christianity: that there exists an essential unity and sameness in all religions when approached in such manner, and this essence is revealed in their irreducible connection to the truth.

The development of buss's idea of mission

The concept of dogmatic "inclusiveness" rather than "exclusiveness" is central to Liberal Christian thoughts and signifies a revitalization of nineteenth century theologians by rectifying the dogmatic battles between orthodox and liberals in the German speaking world. Ernst Buss was born in the Swiss Canton of Bern as the son of a pastor. From an early age, he had expressed a wish to become a missionary. However, the ideological battles between liberal and conservative forces, which in Switzerland was particularly dominated by the more conservative Basler Mission, initially led the more liberal Buss to give up his dream of becoming a missionary.[15] Instead, after completing his studies in Bern, he became a parish priest, first taking over the parish of his home Canton, followed by a period in Aagau and finally in Glarus, Switzerland.[16] His devotion to questions concerning the meaning and purpose of Christian missions, however, remained with him and his 1876 publication of *Die christliche Mission, ihre principelle Berechtigung und practische Durchfüuhrung* was in many ways, an attempt to revitalize a mission based on liberal Christian values. Two important themes underpinned this process of revitalization: (1) because Liberal Christianity since Schleiermacher had been based on individual religious experience, liberal descriptions of the doctrines of faith had so far been unable to incorporate an adequate understanding of the unified identity in churches or mission communities,[17] and (2) as liberal theologians found it difficult to develop any strong understanding of the church, many liberals privileged other forms of reintegration of the individual into the community. In the midst of these intellectual reforms, liberal theologians roamed free without the constrains imposed by dogma and church teachings. It was, as Tomoko Masuzawa also explicates, within this setting that liberal Christians began to accept a religious pluralism within their churches, formulating visions of the religious life guided not by dogma, but by moral action and practical reason.[18] In other words, religious life itself became the unique sphere which defined the uniqueness of Christianity. Consequently, this discourse of religious pluralism developed models of religious self-determination or religious freedom of the individual.

This reintegration often happened, as we have also briefly seen above, through the argumentation of "culture." As scholars have argued, liberal theologians essentially saw themselves as "Theologien der Kultur" or "theologies of culture."[19] They spoke rather often of their concern to integrate a modern pluralist society within their religious framework, rather than establishing a uniformity of their own confessional churches. To use the metaphor of the German socio-historical theologian Ernst Troeltsch, as modern society "collapsed" into competing "Weltanschauungen" or world views, establishing a fundamental consensus on Christian culture became ever more pressing. Buss, for example, at a preparatory meeting for the establishment of the AEPM on 4 June 1884, joined this spirited debate about culture and its place in theology by laying out his plan on how to defend "Christian culture" in an ever pluralizing society. His solution was simple: a new mission society should not be founded on dogma or denominational creeds, but rather on the basis of a rational, universally acceptable faith in humanity and Jesus Christ. As he stressed:

> The Missionary Society [should] regard missionary work in the non-Christian world as something founded on the directive and vow of Jesus, as well as being an unavoidable duty of all of Christendom, and it therefore assigns itself the task of helping to ensure that the salvation through Jesus Christ, and the blessings of a Christian understanding of God, a Christian way of life, and a more humane Christian culture become ever more the common heritage of all societies.[20]

This optimism is also present in Buss's writings in his editorial essay "Programm," published in the first edition of the mission journal *Zeitschrift für Missionskunde und Religionswissenschaft* in 1886. Buss begins here to assert how he intends to lead and reorganize the mission movement into the modern era based on liberal and universal values. The Mission Society, he asserts,

> must be an authority that represents the missionary idea—it must stand independently and recognize all lines of thought. It does justice to the free-thinking circles and is capable of carrying the mission idea for those [theologian] circles which do not show support to the more orthodox interpretations.[21]

Tolerance and acceptance toward other people and religions, in other words, was the basic tool to reintegrate a pluralist society into a community of Christ, and as Ferdinand Hahn (1984) puts it, "Buss did not want to stand against other mission endeavors, but next to them… and starts from the premise that the ability to pursue mission is not a right belonging to only one religion."[22]

While I agree that there existed a tolerant approach to other groups of faiths, in Buss's text, I want to be careful not to conflate his approach to total acceptance of other religions. As the preceding example from Buss will demonstrate, tolerance towards other religions did not always involve acceptance. In stark contrast, while in the language of Buss there was an emphasis on the universal "Gemeinschaft," open to all beliefs, he and the AEPM—like most other liberals at the time—developed models of society which, in fact, left little room for religious minorities. The reason for this is simple: if the liberal Mission accepts all religious faith, then it loses its reason to missionize. The following text gives a glimpse of the kind of religious hierarchy Buss envisioned among the religions of his time. On the first page of his 1876 book *Die christliche Mission, ihre principelle Berechtigung und practische Durchfüuhrung,* he states:

> Mission can only arise among religions, which to their own awareness are based on *Allgemeingültigkeit* or universal principles and in which the religious consciousness among the people is stronger than any national. Only then can people safely put down their walls of fear and embrace

the all-encompassing religious community, which extends over national borders and possibly to all humans.[23]

In other words, missionary work can only be realized as a result of a religion's awareness of its own "Allgemeingültigkeit" or "universal validity." We have to separate the means from the end and keep in mind that the concept of tolerance itself does not necessarily or always signify a universal acceptance of other faiths. Christianity was, in Buss's and many liberal theologian's worldview, the only "universal" and its universal validity was used to justify the spread of Christian culture through the mission. This is a subtle but important distinction to remember as we analyze the ways in which the missionaries employ the language of Liberal Christianity to highlights its tolerant stance towards other faith systems.

As one may expect, Buss, in his analysis paid particular attention to the historical conditions of each of the great religions and concludes: "The most preeminent mission-religion is and remains Christianity," as "truth and morality are most perfectly represented in it."[24] Here, it is possible to consider the historical theology of Buss from the idea of "Christian essence," or in other words, the idea that the true meaning of Christianity is the life of the Christian and rather than doctrine of belief. Buss surveys the historical development of religion starting from the so-called theistic *Urreligionen* of humankind, to the polytheistic religions, up to monotheism exemplified by Moses the later establishment of Christianity, and concludes his description with:[25]

> Christianity was through its entire religious development evidently called upon, to unite within itself all religious hopes and aspirations of the ancient world, to fulfil and complete them, and thereby as the religion of fulfilment and completion demonstrate its universal validity and perfection.[26]

The above passage, in its entirety, established the primacy in which Buss held Christianity in his *Die christliche Mission, ihre principelle Berechtigung und practische Durchfüuhrung,* and although this is merely a short summary of the content of Buss's understanding of Christian history, it allows us to confirm Buss's connection to the movement of historical theology and, not at least, German idealism.

It is worth reiterating here that, on the one hand, Buss's understanding of history correlates with the idea of the Logos; that is, a belief that a Logos developed through all things, making it possible to see various phenomena of world history as developing along a unified thread. This may seem contradictory, especially when thinking of Buss's claim above, in which he argued for the sovereignty of Christian culture over other religions. However, by sustaining the preconception that "universal validity" is an explicitly Christian feature, it becomes quite easy to see his logic. The authority of Christianity, Buss goes on to argue, lays in its clear awareness of its world-wide destiny. Christianity's destiny, however, for various reasons throughout history remained hidden and only now, in his time, and with the help of its own historical awareness, was it rediscovered, giving Christianity the impetus for the realization of its universal validity. The life of Christ should stand as the standard for all individuals and communities of the world. The Christian church, as it existed in Western Europe, should be model to all cultures of the world; And, "the true meaning of Christianity [should be] the life of the Christian, not the doctrine."[27]

The early reception of the aepm

So far, this chapter has analyzed the core characteristics of German Liberal Christianity, the relationship between Buss and the liberal Christian movement, and his mission ideas, which shared stark associations with historical theology and the concept of Logos. This background already gives to give an idea of why the aepm gained such wide support among liberals in early 1880s Germany. Ernst Buss, was, of course, not the only liberal theologian active specifically in association with reforming the idea of a Christian mission. The following sections will illuminate some of the historical actors involved in the establishment of the AEPM in 1884.

A variety of people supported Buss's manuscript *Die christliche Mission, ihre principelle Berechtigung und practische Durchführung*, when it first came out in 1876. It initially attracted the attention of politically conscious theologians, but in the early 1880s, the movement also began to appeal to unpretentious church communities in Switzerland and southern Germany. Liberal theologians, however, became the focal point for the AEPM.[28] Friedrich Nippold (1838–1918), a German church historian at the University of Bern, was one of the first to react to Buss's work. In a series of letter exchanges between him and Buss, Nippold expressed his belief that Buss's ideas could be used as an opportunity to start a revolution within the German-speaking mission landscape. Reacting euphorically to Buss's text, Nippold reported back: "Es ist gerade das, was man heute braucht" or "It is just what we need today."[29] Nippold recognized Buss's text as a part of a greater effort to restart the orthodox dominated mission field of Germany and Switzerland. This revolutionary zeal was reverberated in Nippold's following letter to Buss. Here he encouraged Buss to send a copy of his text to his close friend, the then already famous religious scholar Friedrich Max Müller, in Oxford.[30] This revolutionary enthusiasm, also resonated with Müller. After a longer period of correspondence Müller encouraged Buss form a mission society based on his mission ideas.[31]

In general, the early group of members can be categorized into a model of three groups, each divided by the varied motives and objectives of the participants. Discernable in primary sources, I categorize the members of the early movement of the AEPM into the following groups: (1) those who adhered to reforming the mission movement such as Nippold and Müller; (2) those who saw the mission as a way to remedy the dire cultural situation of the world, but did not necessarily share the political objectives of group 1; and (3) those who did not support the mission and fought against its establishment. Needless to say, this model is an expedient means for displaying general differences, and the boundary, especially between group 1 and 2, is not explicit. Nonetheless, this model reflects the complexity of the members associated to the AEPM.

Group 1, by far the smallest, but also the most prominent, consisted of mainly liberal theologians and of course the religious scholar Max Müller. At the time of the establishment of the AEPM in 1884, this group was by no means enormous, numbering no more than thirty-three members, but this group included individuals who also served as core organizers, such as Max Müller, as well as the theologians Otto Pfleiderer, and Karl Heinrich Kesselring, who in addition to Ernst Buss, were key member throughout the whole process.[32] Not all early members of the AEPM were liberal theologians, but the above individuals embraced the new mission idea of Buss. On January 3, 1883, a select group of four people (Buss, Nippold, Kesselring and the later missionary to Japan, Wilfried Spinner), formed the so-called "Initiative Committee," in Olten, Switzerland. One of the objectives of this meeting was to build a network among the AEPM members scattered in different parts of Switzerland and Germany. According to primary sources, this attempt was, by and large, successful. On April 11, 1883, only four months later, all thirty-three members of this group met in Frankfurt am Main.[33] According to a handwritten letter from the meeting, a plan by this group to "author the Program for the establishment of the AEPM" was established with the aim to build "a stronger emphasis on the cultural meaning of the foreign mission."[34] At the same meeting, Buss would reveal a list of 300 new members across Germany and Switzerland who supported the cause.[35]

These official AEPM members of group 1, with their ambitious agenda of forming a mission based on Buss's book, constituted the core of the AEPM leadership. Surrounding them were an additional 300 members, so called "Liberals" who were also part of the AEPM leadership and shared the objectives of group 1. The Grand Duke Carl Alexandre v. Saxony-Weimar-Eisenach is one example. Recognized locally as an AEPM member, the Duke of Saxony-Weimar saw the potential for the AEPM to send missionaries abroad "to bring the highest culture which exists in Christianity to the civilized pagans of the world."[36] Here we sense a clear ideological connection to the members of group 1. The revolutionary zeal at the core of the AEPM members of group 1 also resonated with the members in group 2. However, evidence suggests that the vast majority the of AEPM membership had different motivations to join the new missionary society than those held by the members of group 1. For the members that comprised group 2, the largest constituent of the AEPM, the rejection of the dogmatically divided mission landscape and the wish for uniformity was what led them to join the AEPM. Unlike group 1, they had little interest in a nationwide revolution within the German-speaking mission field. This ideological divide between groups 1 and 2 was visible even within the leadership itself. For example, Bernhard E. Hesse, a member of the church council of Saxony, who witnessed the formation of the AEPM in Weimar in 1884 left a record of it in his memoir, writing how "unavoidably necessary it is, first of all to uniform the Protestant Germans into one community."[37] The disconnect between the groups was also evident for Buss at a talk entitled "Confidential invitation to form a general mission association" (*Konfidentielle Einladung zur Bildung eines Allgemeinen Missions Vereins*) held in April 1883, where he tried to reach a reconciliation between the two groups by stating:

> Since we regard the mission as a common matter of the entire Protestant Church, which should remain unaffected by special religious-ecclesiastical agendas, we would like the association to be formed from the outset of the broadest shared Evangelical-Protestant consciousness, one which accepts every sincere Christian belief and is based on a basis above and apart from any dividing difference. By simply keeping the big common goal in mind we want to shape our activities freely and independently to the best of our knowledge and discretion. We will therefore gladly welcome the participation of everyone who in this broad-hearted sense wishes to practice his love in the service of the kingdom of Christ, regardless of the religious orientation, denomination, or ecclesiastical party he otherwise belongs to.[38]

This quote reveals why the mission policy as of the AEPM between the late-nineteenth and early-twentieth centuries became defined explicitly as "liberal" or "tolerant." Buss reflected the attitude of the majority of the members of the AEPM, who, primary sources suggest, understood themselves to be taking part in a protest as opposed to a revolution against the contemporary mission landscape of the German-speaking world. This comes as no surprise given that Buss had maintained that the AEPM saw themselves as righteous saviors of communities, and the specific improvements that its missionaries realized were conceived not only to be religious but also culturally and morally justified and necessary for the survival of all humankind. In another talk for a preparatory meeting of the founding asseMBLy of the AEPM held in Weimar in 1884, Buss expressed the objectives of the AEPM to the attendees as follows:

> The Missionary Society regards missionary work in the non-Christian world as something founded on the directives and vows of Jesus, as well as being an unavoidable duty of all of Christendom, and it therefore assigns itself the task of helping to ensure that the salvation through Jesus Christ, and the blessings of a Christian understanding of God, a Christian way of life, and a more humane Christian culture become ever more the common heritage of all societies.[39]

Such a consensus was to be established on the basis of a rational, universally acceptable faith in humanity, and this quote of Buss shows how he, from an early point, seemed determined to seek ways to consolidate the presence of the AEPM and to propagate tolerance of non-denominational Christianity.

Finally, we turn to group 3, which consisted of individuals who either did not support the claims of Ernst Buss or fought against the establishment of the AEPM. Although Buss received a lot of praise from contemporary liberals due to his advocation of a total freedom of belief and openness towards other faiths, his ideas were not met with open arms everywhere. At times, the idea of a new liberal mission society was looked at with great suspicion, criticized, and even laughed at within conservative-orthodox circles of the Protestant Church. To these communities, the AEPM presented an immediate concern. These individuals maintained a reserved attitude toward the AEPM and had a lukewarm attitude towards the AEPM members and their ambitions, an attitude that was quick to take hold. Even before the establishment of the AEPM in Weimar in 1884, critics published a variety of news article and editorial comments exposing the flaws of Buss's new mission idea. For example, in the Protestant journal *Allgemeine Conservative Monatsschrift für das Christliche Deutschland*, the editor observed the following about the inaugural committee meeting of the AEPM 1883:

> On 23 July in Frankfurt am Main, German delegates agreed with Swiss reformers on statutes for the formation of a new mission association. Of the negotiated outcome we only want to call attention to one sentence, which highlights the absurdity and ridiculousness of these scholars" affairs: "In non-Christian religions exist sounds of the divine truth, whose development and completion are to be tied to the Christian religion." One should only try to develop the ideas of King Musa or Dahorney and Ashanti.[40]

Although there was critique and a lack of interest from other religious societies in Germany, the initial popularity of the AEPM nevertheless reflected a common undercurrent in 1880s Germany in which people derived religious authority, in part, through scientific currents that dominated during that time. For example, in comparison to the conservative German mission enterprises, the AEPM, in its initial years, seemed to offer a new and positive answer to contemporary problems which justification for its existence allowed it to gain interest from liberal church societies around Switzerland and Germany at the time. This explains why the ridiculing and criticism from more conservative communities was unable to stop the establishment or harm the attractiveness of a new liberal mission society. Unlike the more conservative mission societies in the German-speaking landscape, such as the Halle and Herrnhut-missions and the Basler Mission, the AEPM did not merely see themselves as bringers of the Scripture of God, but as bringers of modern culture.[41]

Yet, despite their widespread support, the AEPM itself, as this analysis shows, was not in unanimous agreement on how to best lead the mission and how to best overcome their difficulties. Many supported a total revolution of the mission field, but others clearly did not. This suggests that the AEPM may have been prone to internal problems and calling into question the popular notion that it was a rather uniform movement. Scholars of Mission Studies often characterize the European mission to the East as a united movement and tend understate the presence of internal coercion. Yet, we must take this aspect seriously in order to understand the work of the Swiss and German missionaries' encounter with the Japanese people in its full complexity.

It is a mischaracterization of the AEPM to claim that the members shared the same unifying goal. Some groups within the AEPM leadership, such as Buss, Nippold, Müller and Kesselring were well aligned and played a leading role in organizing the mission. Yet there was still friction and disagreement on vision even among the leadership of group 1, as will become evident in the following section.

The purpose of this analysis has not been to dismiss the significance of the AEPM as an organized mission society but to refine current understanding of the nature of their involvement. Many members of the AEPM supported Buss's new mission ideas, not because they identified with them themselves, but more as an external force that conveniently addressed their localized problems. Exploring the differences between various groups that made up the AEPM deepens our understanding of the AEPM and may help us explain the reasons behind some of the troubles that occurred in the Japanese mission field.

Defining the mission field

An analysis of the letters and protocols and other related primary documents located at the ZASP reveals that the formation of the organizational structure of the AEPM was determined and agreed upon at the Foundational Meeting of the AEPM or *Die inaugural Sitzung für die AEPM* in Weimar in 1884. For example, a text entitled "Mission Decrees of 4 June 1884" was signed by 93 prominent theologians and religious scholars, including well-known theologians such as Adolf von Harnack, Otto Pfleiderer, Richard Lipsius, Heinrich Bassermann, Gustav Emil Lisco, and not least Max Müller, who was mentioned above.[42]

In the years that followed the *Inaugural Sitzung* of 1884, the AEPM leadership frequently articulated their understanding of their own position in the world. One of the primary conceptual tools they employed for this was that of *Kulturmission* or "Culture mission," which allowed them to highlight their own Christian superiority to other religions and countries, which led them to situate Liberal Christianity at the epicenter of all religions. Not surprisingly, Buss played a leading role in systematically developing this viewpoint.

In 1886, Buss published an essay in the AEPM's journal *Zeitschrift für Missionskunde und Religionswissenschaft* (Journal for Mission and Religious Studies) in which he declares "We [the AEPM] do not want to spread Christian culture, but Christian religion. That is the first object of our mission society, to spread Christian religious life in the sense of Jesus and the Apostles."[43] In it he explains that in contrast to other missions, the AEPM wished "not to transfer our church organization to the foreign soil with the purpose of alienating the heathens from their previous social structures;" instead, the focus remained on "sending the Gospel of Jesus to the heathen people in a variety of ways without pressure or force, but through calm and patient work, spread the message to deeper and wider circles of the society which will lead to evangelization on a larger scale"[44] In the same essay he highlights the correlations between all religions. Within this article, he acknowledges that all religions do not match perfectly, as they have changed considerably since the time of Logos. However, Buss believes that with the "modern tools of science," it was for the first time in human history possible to unearth the *Anknüpfungspunkte* or "points of contact" between the religions of the world. It was in these years that the AEPM took an explicitly scientific and modern ideological turn. Similarly, the formation of the AEPM expressed an ever-increasing interest in exploring the relationship between the Christian faith and other religious cultures and shows us both the systematic and historically complex relationship between these two fields in the 1880s. In their literary praxis, they engaged in an exhaustive study of the religions of East Asia. An important point made by the AEPM was that a critical study of world religions would not lead to a rejection of their own Christian faith; rather, they were convinced that people's faith would only be strengthened by subjecting religion to the strict tools of modern science, as they would support the ultimate truths of Christianity.[45] Buss in his essay envisioned the process of this project in these sweeping terms: "We [the AEPM] aim at removing the incomprehensible covers [of other religions], from under which the truth (*Wahrheit*) can emerge and shine even more brightly."[46]

Although scholars tend to associate the nineteenth century mission movement with aggressively subversive and colonial sentiments, the AEPM exhibited less aggressive characteristics than other missions by establishing itself on the scientifically proven pillars of universal truth. Still, this cross-fertilization of liberal Protestant ideas that occurred in the mission writings of the AEPM was far from balanced, and the ideas of a "universal truth" more often reflected the missionaries' own cultural and ethnocentric agendas than a coherent or conclusive belief or dogma. Thus, although the ideals of "tolerance" and "acceptance of other religions" was on the lips of everyone, as will be shown, the German missionaries in Japan more often than not displayed an attitude that revealed their condescension towards their own Japanese co-workers' beliefs. Such incidents beg the question of how far the "tolerant" attitudes of the German missionaries actually stretched or whether these attitudes exclusively were "fine words" disguising a Christian-colonial agenda.

Lastly, a brief comment on the choice of Japan as the first mission field of the AEPM may be of interest, as it provides a fascinating example of one of the many inter-cultural networks already at place in the late-nineteenth century. As elaborated above, the confidence of the liberal theologians peaked in the 1880s, and they aimed to settle their first mission among what they considered to be "Hochkulturen" or "high cultures" and not among the "Kulturlose Völker" i.e. the culture-less people.[47] High cultures were countries that, according to the members of the AEPM, already had a level of culture, which allowed them to understand the "contemporary Western powers."[48] The importance placed on culturally "developed" countries constitutes another aspect of the religious confidence in the "universal" validity of their theology in salvaging all people from their cultural predicaments.

The geographic focus was directed towards the ancient "Kulturländer Asiens;" India, Japan, and China. In the leadership's eyes, these three countries still held on to their morally underdeveloped traditions and could culturally be "improved" through exposure to the truths of Christianity.[49] Early on, the AEPM leaned towards choosing India as the first mission field. The two board members Max Müller and Heinrich Kesselring had, for several years, been in correspondence with the new religious leader Brahmo Somaj, the founder of a syncretistic movement that worked towards unifying the two religions of Christianity and Hinduism.[50] The success of Brahmo Somaj in India seems to have convinced Müller and Kesselring that India would be an ideal mission field for the AEPM. That India was to become the first mission field of the AEPM is also evidenced by that the first missionary to Japan, Swiss missionary Wilfried Spinner, beginning an intensive study of Sanskrit as a part of his preparation. Spinner had visited Max Müller in Oxford as early as 1882 to improve his study of Sanskrit, with the intention of studying it further in preparation for his future work in India. However, as destiny would have it, once in Oxford, Spinner happened to encounter two Japanese Buddhist students, Nanjō Bunyū (南条文雄 (1849–1927) and Kasawara Kenjū (笠原研寿 1852–

1883). Nanjō and Kasawara might not be familiar to all readers, but to scholars of Japanese Buddhism, both occupy a central place in the establishment of Modern Buddhism (近代仏教, *kindai bukkyō*), a Buddhist movement that from the 1880s held significant influence over the religious landscape of Japan.[51]

Nanjō and Kasawara were the first Japanese Buddhists to spend an extended period of time studying in Europe. They both had been sent to Europe by the Jōdo-Shinshū sect in order to study Sanskrit at Oxford under Max Müller and to help him translate the Buddhist sutra Tripitaka. According to Müller, both had become accomplished scholars in Sanskrit; in fact, they were so skilled that they could "read the canonical books of Buddhism in its original."[52] Whether it was Spinner's meeting with these two bright Japanese Buddhists in Oxford that caused the initial mission field to become Japan and not India, the letters and documents at the ZASP archive do not say, but in a letter from June 1884 sent out to the board members of the AEPM, it was suddenly announced that, "the AEPM will not direct its activity towards India, as some members fear too much involvement from Brahma Somaj, and instead they will focus on Japan."[53] Furthermore, in a notification called "Announcement No. 1 of January 1884; The principles and goals of the Allgemeiner Evangelisch-Protetantischer Missionsverein," addressed to the founding committee of the AEPM, the board member Karl-Heinrich Ritter discussed the question of the future mission field. According to Ritter, the mission board had now finally agreed "to make Japan the first country for the mission," thus making Japan and not India the first mission field of the AEPM.[54]

With the decision to make Japan "the first [country] to be introduced to our mission," and the rejection of India and China as the future mission field,[55] the AEPM became conscious that it could not initially become an officially supported colonial mission society.[56] Still, seen from a church-historical perspective, the AEPM kept its close connection to the German State through the relationship with the Grand Duke Alexander of Saxony-Weimar. The Grand Duke, writes church historian Hayo Hamer, functioned as the patron for the AEPM and symbolized the close link between the German missionary movement and the German Protestant Church, and gave the mission endeavor of the AEPM both political and diplomatic authority in Japan.[57]

Conclusion

This chapter asked how Buss and the AEPM managed to establish a mission society in Japan based on Liberal Christianity. In response, it laid out some of the early, pre–1886 political and religious factors which led to the founding of the AEPM, and the initial forces that led to a liberal-Christian mission starting in Japan. As this chapter reveals, the establishment of a liberal mission society was not as straight forward as one might think, as there exist within Liberal Christianity several contradictions. The two German historians Friedrich Wilhelm Graf and Thomas Nipperdey, for example, both point to liberal theology's structural illiberality in forming church-organizations as one of the main problems of the movement.[58] So how was Buss and the AEPM able to establish a liberal mission society?

Given this chapter's exploration of Buss's writings, one explanation seems to be as follows: Buss and the AEPM formed their mission decrees following "the footsteps of the finest traditions of German idealism."[59] They were considered an alternative to the established and often more conservative mission societies. Not holding on to a set of specific articles of beliefs, they found themselves compatible with the modern Western transformations of the time. In applying the latest ideas of "historical theology," Buss and the AEPM recognized the historical development and manifestations of "true religion" throughout the entire history of humankind and asserted that the realization of this truth was possible all over the world and even recognizable in other religions. Of course, Buss was aware that the Christian religion did not simply equate to all cultures. As the quotes scattered throughout this chapter reveal, Buss believed that different cultures could develop a unique form of Christian cultures, while still being of the same Christian *religion*. The point he emphasized was that the Kingdom of God transcended all cultures and ethnicities and was being realized on the backside of the process of modernization. This assumption allowed Buss and the AEPM to see the spread of Christianity as a justified realization of its destiny, and therefore a religion to be missionized.

In its theoretical form, the liberal protestant mission of the AEPM intended to work towards the "Christianizing of the heathen people" while "freeing the poor and superstitious heathens from their inner and outer sufferings."[60] With the establishment of the AEPM, the first German-speaking mission society in Japan, the ideas of Liberal Christianity were finally applied in the real world. However, as we shall see, the optimistic belief in the "universalism" of Christianity, as suggested in Buss's writings, quickly faced difficult challenges as the AEPM encountered a difficult and contested reality in Japan, as it want to occur when theory turns into praxis. This brings forth the question also asked in the introduction of whether the "universal" ideas of Schleiermacher, Harnack, Troeltsch are indeed really "universal" when put into a new cultural setting such as Japan. To answer this question, the following chapter will examine the practical realities the theoretical ideas of Mission Director Ernst Buss and the missionaries of AEPM faced in Japan after 1886 by looking at the countless obstacles and challenges they met there, challenges which Ernst Buss and the liberal theologians could not have foreseen.

2

The Emergence of Liberal Christianity in Japan

The Rise and Fall of the AEPM

Exactly one year and five months after the establishment of the Allgemeiner Evangelisch-Protestantischer Missionsverein in Weimar, the first missionary of the AEPM stepped ashore the harbor-city of Yokohama.[1] His arrival on 4 June, 1884, marked the start of one of the most significant religious discourses in modern Japanese history, commonly referred to as *jiyushugi shingaku* 自由主義神学 or "Liberal Theology." The AEPM's effort in Japan were led by Wilfried Spinner, a Swiss theologian from Bern who was a central member of the newly formed AEPM. In November 1885, Spinner formed the first church community for Japanese Christians in the Kanda-district of Tokyo called Fukyū Fukuin Kyōkai 普及福音教会. This began Liberal Christianity in Japan, a movement that would quickly stand in opposition to the "absolutist" approach of most American and British mission societies at the time. The movement gained momentum in the mid–1880s, and in 1887 it successfully established a theological seminary to educate liberal-minded Japanese. Two years later, Spinner created *Shinri* 『眞理』, which became the first liberal Christian journal in Japan.

A variety of people supported the AEPM in its early stages. Initially, it attracted politically-conscious former samurai and liberal reformers, but in the early 1890s, Japanese supporters began to appeal for more self-control. Independence became the focal point for a faction of Japanese Christian community members of the Fukyū Fukuin Kyōkai members, who, against the wishes of the Swiss and German missionaries, advocated for more autonomy. This faction was involved in a series of protests in the late 1890s and early 1900s, with protests against the missionaries' pro-government attitude during the Russo-Japanese War in 1904 and 1905 being among the most prominent.

As one can see, the story of the AEPM in Japan, with its interactions with local traditions, local politics, and other foreign missions, forms a convoluted narrative. This chapter examines the path of the first liberal Christian mission in Japan from its initial acceptance to its repeated rejection. Scholars typically study nineteenth century mission movements through a framework that centers around a single significant personality who achieved something extraordinarily within social welfare or education, but I adopt a different analytical angle by contextualizing the AEPM within the nationalization movement of the late-Meiji period. Focusing on the struggles of the Swiss and German missionaries allows, I argue, for a discussion of the reality of this tradition in the late nineteenth century and early twentieth century.

Furthermore, we gain new insights into the mission movement by shifting the focus away from prominent individuals. By examining the ways in which the AEPM interacted with its Japanese church members, it is evident that the mission movement was a complex organization involving historical actors with differing agendas. Those who rely on a biographical framework tend to present a one-dimensional view based on the objectives of individual missionaries or Japanese Christian 'activists,' dismissing the myriad of voices and opinions that constituted the whole movement. I utilize a nuanced multilayered approach in this chapter to analyze the highs and lows of the history of the AEPM in Japan and to illuminate its oft-neglected aspects.

Early Japanese Support

The establishment of the Fukyū Fukuin Kyōkai in November 1885 marked the beginning of Liberal Christianity in Japan, but its very establishment begs the question: How was it possible for a foreign missionary unfamiliar with Japan to congregate a Japanese Christian community and build up a church society within one month of his arrival? Surprisingly, the answer takes us to Berlin where two consequential actors Aoki Shūzō 青木周藏 (1844–1914) and Wadagaki Kenzō 和田垣謙三 (1860–1919) found themselves. Aoki and Wadagaki were both Japanese nationals born to samurai families. However, their similarities end there. Aoki Shūzō was born in 1844 and raised in Yamaguchi-prefecture where his family served under the Chōshū domain. His father was a physician and Aoki himself went to study Western medicine in Nagasaki before being sent by the Chōshū domain to Germany, where he studied medicine and then law at Berlin University in 1868. After his initial stay in Germany from 1868 to 1874, he returned to Japan. However, in 1880, he returned to Germany (1880–1884), this time as the ambassador of the Japanese Empire.[2]

Wadagaki Kenzō, on the other hand, was born into an elite family that served the Toyooka clan in Tajima (Hyogo Prefecture). Following a largely predestined path, Wadagaki completed his undergraduate studies at Tokyo Imperial University, and was then sent abroad for his studies in law, first at Cambridge University and then at Berlin University, before returning to Japan in 1883 to a position as a professor of law at Tokyo Imperial University.[3]

In particular, Aoki Shūzō was instrumental in establishing an early connection between the AEPM and Japan. In 1872, during his first stay in the Prussian capital, Aoki was introduced to the ideas of Liberal Christianity through visits him and his fellow Japanese students made to liberal theologian and later member of the AEPM, Gustav Emil Lisco.[4] Here they learned about Liberal Christianity and actively began to disseminate their knowledge about the relationship between state and religion.⁵ Aoki was convinced of the potential for Liberal Christianity to enrich Japan and believed Christianity was a moral religion exceptionally well suited to aid in the modernization of Japan. In a section concerning the Iwakura mission to Europe, Aoki, for example, reflects on a conversation between him and two prominent politicians and high-ranking members of the mission, Kido Takayoshi 木戸孝允 (1833–1877) and Itō Hirobumi 伊藤博文 (1841–1909) in 1873. According to Aoki, the three of them, for purely pragmatic reasons, considered "to petition the emperor so that he and all the government could convert to Christianity, based on the idea that all countrymen would follow suit to the immense benefit of our diplomatic relations with the greater powers."⁶

In 1882, Aoki's enthusiasm for Liberal Christianity led him to entreat the board members of the AEPM to send a representative of liberal Protestantism to Japan. The three persons who played a central role in organizing this request were liberal theologians Karl Heinrich Ritter and Gustav Emil Lisco, and the Japanese, Wadagaki Kenzō. They made their first appeal to the mission board in December 1883, followed by a series of appeals in 1884. Despite their tremendous involvement, few sources acknowledge the active role Aoki and Wadagaki played in promoting Japan as an attractive mission field. The later chancellor of Germany, Georg Michaelis (1857–1936), for example, mentions Aoki and Wadagaki as the "initiative takers," and Karl Heinrich Ritter acknowledged the role of "the two excellent Japanese who we have come to know," referring to Aoki and Wadagaki.⁷ Furthermore, in the *Misssionsblatt* of the AEPM from 1894, they wrote that it was: "the Japanese representative Aoki who [drew] the attention of the mission members towards Japan, and it is thanks to him that the young association [chose] Japan as its first field of work."⁸

By following these developments, it is not hard to recognize Aoki's fundamental role for the initial success of Spinner in Japan. Even the arrival of Spinner in Yokohama in September 1885 was carefully organized by Aoki.⁹ Shortly after his arrival, Aoki introduced Spinner to the already established German community in Yokohama, and arranged that Spinner was introduced to Dr. Otto Bernhard Hering (1859–1929) immediately after his arrival.[10] Hering, at that time, was a so-called *Oyatoi*—a foreign teacher—hired to work at the German Studies Society School (Doitsugaku Kyōkai Gakkō 獨逸學協會學校). The school itself had been founded in 1881 by a group of liberal Japanese connected to Germany, including the Japanese philosopher Nishi Amane 西 周, the Japanese Christian Kato Hiroyuki 加藤弘之, and of course, Aoki himself.[11] For the next month, Spinner stayed with the Hering family, who had been ordered by Aoki to give Spinner a quick but thorough introduction to Japanese culture before setting him free to establish his first church community in Japan.[12]

Throughout the initial phase of his work in Japan, Spinner profited enormously from the strong support of Aoki, who maintained an influential relationship to the Japanese political and intellectual elite— among them the royal family members Prince Arisugawa Takehito 有栖川宮威仁親王 (1862–1913) and Prince Kitashirakawa Yoshihisa 北白川宮能久親王 (1847–1895)—as well as the network of Meiji-Germans living in the foreign colonies of Yokohama and Tsukiji in Tokyo.[13] Under such favorable circumstances, Spinner set out to address educated and urban Japanese people, mainly originating from high standing former samurai families. The reason being that a conversion of members at this spectrum of society was believed to serve as a social and moral model for the rest of Japanese society.[14] Spinner's interest was primarily directed at the circle of students belonging to Doitsugaku Kyōkai Gakkō, which had been recommended to him by Aoki and Dr. Hering as conductive first contacts for the mission.[15]

Support for Spinner's mission enterprise also came from other parts of the Japanese elite. Well-known Japanese Christians such as the Heidelberg University graduate Hirata Tōsuke 平田東助 (1849–1925), a member of the famous Iwakura-mission to Europe in 1873, and Doitsugaku Kyōkai Gakkō board member, Kozaki Hiromichi 小崎弘道 (1856–1938), the to be later author of the book *Jiyūshingaku* 『自由

神学』 or "Liberal Christianity" (1892), and also president of Dōshisha University, were both early supporters of Liberal Christian ideas and the AEPM.[16] At the Parliament of World Religions in 1893, Kozaki Hiromichi commented on the work of Spinner and the reception of Liberal Theology in Japan, which provides a glimpse of the warm reception Liberal Christianity had during its first years in Japan:

> [Response to "Christianity in Japan: Its Present Condition and Future Prospects," 1893]
>
> While missionaries are both preaching and teaching the so-called orthodox doctrines, Japanese Christians are eagerly studying the most liberal theology. Not only are they studying, but they are diffusing these liberal thoughts with zeal and diligence, and so I believe that with a small exception most of the Japanese pastors and evangelists are quite liberal in their theology.[17]

Kozaki's emphasis on Japanese Christians' intent to study Liberal Christianity accentuates AEPM's relationship with these early Japanese supporters and symbolizes the early positive atmosphere that existed between the AEPM and these Japanese intellectuals. Aoki Shūzō loyalty to the AEPM during this time cannot be overstated. Throughout the period, he ardently occupied a key position and succeeded in building the foundation for the establishment of a liberal Christian church in Japan. Moreover, throughout his political career, he was influenced by liberal theology and tried, one way or another to build a bridge between Germany and Japan. It was only through the extraordinary support and effort of Japanese locals that, as Japanese church-historian Mizutani Makoto points out, the missionaries of the AEPM came to play the important role they did in the birth of Japanese Liberal Christianity.[18]

WILFRIED SPINNER, CENTRAL FIGURE OF THE MISSION

Wilfried Spinner is an intriguing person whose character will be examined throughout this book because he instantly became inextricably linked to the future of the AEPM. Although his stay of six years (1885–1891) was relatively short, Spinner, by the strength of his spirit, functioned as the central figure of the mission for many years even after his return to Switzerland.

Spinner was born in Bonstetten, Zürich as the first son of the Deacon Johannes Heinrich Spinner. Although the precise year is unknown, Spinner joined the theology studies department at Zürich University in 1873, where he trained under the church historian and later AEPM board member Heinrich Kesselring. Kesselring was significant in that he imparted in Spinner an interest in religious studies, strongly encouraging Spinner to travel around universities all around Europe to collect material on the Reformation in Switzerland.[19] It was during his travels around Europe that Spinner was introduced to Japan and its religions. His later personal encounter with the two Japanese Buddhist students, Nanjō Bunyū and Kasawara Kenju, while visiting Oxford University in 1882, would further strengthen his interest in Japanese Buddhism. In the following years, the study of the religions of Japan remained close to his heart, and utilizing the new tools developed in comparative religious studies, Spinner initiated some of the first German-language accounts of Shintoism.

Spinner's three essays on the *Gion-matsuri* in Kyoto from 1888 are cases in point. In the reports, with the help of detailed drawings, Spinner explains nature and purpose of the festival: how the festival is held to purify and appease the gods in order to protect the city against fires, earthquakes, and floods. It is clear that observing the festival was an important experience for Spinner, as he mentions it in his diary several times during his visit to Kyoto in 1888.[20] Spinner's study of the *Gion-matsuri* had been made possible by two students, Kayama Shinjirō and Nakarai Sunao.[21] They provided an excellent viewing location from which Spinner could watch the festival, and made every effort to answer and explain in detail what Spinner saw.[22] The mission journal *Zeitschrift für Missionskunde und Religionswissenschaft* would later publish these essays.[23] He could be certain that Ernst Buss, the director and editor of the journal, would welcome the results of his inquiry into Japanese religions and would gladly publish them in the mission journal, especially as the AEPM was firmly promoting the study of non-Christian religions as one of the mission society's main tasks.[24]

Still, Spinner was not always pleased with what he saw among the Japanese religions. There was, Spinner believed, a need for radical change among the Japanese. Spinner's evaluation of Japanese Buddhism often revealed a lack of substantive engagement with its ideas and followers. Throughout his notes, Spinner's writings on Japanese Buddhism, for example, only described it in negative terms; when he compared it to his own Christianity, Spinner only focused on the deficiencies and flaws of Japanese Buddhism.[25] This particular negative assessment of Buddhism is reflected in a letter sent by Spinner from Kyoto in 1888 to Ernst Buss. In the letter, Spinner reports his disappointment in his encounters with Buddhist monks in the old capital. What follows is a translation of this short letter:

> Here in the Rome of Japan, it is teeming with monks from all sects which have their center in the great monasteries and temples of Kyoto.... I have learned how diminutive the education of the Kyoto Buddhists is; the best people of the *Zen* and *Shinshū* sects[26] have no more than what I would call a Buddhist scholastic education, which in its method reseMBLes our medieval practices.... As degenerated as Buddhism is at present, it would be impossible to think Christianity to be situated in contact with it. The Buddhism of Japan is not the Buddhism, which we, after reading the Tripitaka and the values of the later Hindu forms, recognize as its ideal image.[27]

This description of Japanese Buddhism reveals how Spinner lacked any intent to engage with Buddhism. His refusal also contrasts sharply with the sentiment espoused by Buss in his writings mentioned in the previous chapter, and exposes a clear schism between the expressed attitudes of promoting tolerance and openness towards other religious beliefs preeminent in Liberal Christianity and the actual behavior of its missionaries, who consistently recited the liberal mantra in order to preserve the mission's own identity as a denomination. The contradictory pattern in which the AEPM presented itself as a liberal and tolerant mission society will be further investigated in Part II of this book.

Establishment of the church community

Spinner's relatively critical view of Buddhism and other Japanese faith communities caused him to urgently seek ways to consolidate the Liberal Protestant presence of the AEPM and to propagate the ideal of a "tolerant" Christianity. He initiated several projects at an early point during his stay in Japan, shortly after he had arrived in Yokohama in September 1885, to accomplish this end. However, before we go into those projects, it will be helpful outline the objectives of the AEPM in Japan, as they rationalize much of Spinner's work in those early years. Before leaving Europe, Spinner had been given three objectives by the Home Board of the AEPM:

1. To organize the German and Swiss Protestant living in Japan under one church community;
2. to establish a Japanese Christian community; and
3. to create educational facilities for the propagation of Liberal Christianity.

Given the challenges at the time, it is impressive that Spinner completed each one of these tasks within the first two years of his stay. In 1885, he first created the German church for Germans staying in Tokyo and Yokohama.[28] Spinner cracked down on existing quarrels between the Swiss and German nationals by stressing the importance of forming a German Protestant community whose members would act as Christian role models for the Japanese, both in business and in daily life.[29] Spinner reportedly practiced a pious private life himself, to the point that he managed to fall-out with his fellow missionary Otto Schmiedel, due to the latter's socializing conduct.[30] In the end, Spinner's attempt to develop role models failed, mainly because the majority of Swiss and Germans stationed in Japan, according to the highly vocal criticism of Spinner, were indifferent to religious life.[31]

Spinner paid particular attention to the creation of a Japanese church community. In the eleventh month of the seventeenth year of Meiji (1885), only a month after Spinner had arrived in Japan, he established Fukyū Fukuin Kyōkai, a church for liberal Christianity. The church acted as an independent community with a core made up of mostly young students from Doitsugaku Kyōkai Gakkō. In 1886, six months after its inception, the Japanese church community numbered 33 members. A year later, in the spring of 1887, the number had doubled to 73. It was at this point that Spinner began entertaining the possibility of building his own church. Initially, Spinner had responded swiftly to the high demand for his services and rented the American Union Hall in Tokyo for the first few years.[32] But in 1886, he complained in a letter back to Switzerland: "When will we get our own church here?" asking for financial assistance. Nonetheless, the Fukyū Fukuin Kyōkai had been a success from day one, attracting many Japanese students, who through their life in the community, all maintained a close contact with Spinner and with German language and culture. An independent church for the Fukyū Fukuin Kyōkai in the well-located area of Kanda in Tokyo would first be built after Spinner's return to Switzerland in 1891.[33]

Following these developments, Spinner set out to fulfil the third objective of setting up several distinctive educational institutions. Usually, both church and school were under the same roof in order to meet the rising demand of the Japanese public for Western education while simultaneously allowing the missionaries to proselytize their students. After serving as an instructor at the Doitsugaku Kyōkai Gakkō for a few months, Spinner began to formulate his own plan of founding his own theological school. In September 1886, Spinner wrote a letter addressed directly to mission director Ernst Buss describing the atmosphere of the rapidly developing mission field of Japan and outlining his ideas for a future theological academy. This letter gives a glimpse of the kind of school Spinner envisioned to be the center of AEPM's educational activities in Japan:

> In Japan, time flies even faster than in Europe; I am always so busy with projects and there is no time at all. I envy my successors, who can walk accordingly on the well-kept paths. Within a year I want to begin my new project: The founding of a theological seminary, perhaps it shall be done in collaboration with and under the same roof as the Society of German Studies.[34]

Shortly after this letter was sent to Buss, Spinner established the Theological Seminary, or in Japanese, Shinkyō Shingakkō 新教神学校. Its establishment in 1887 quickly became, as Rolf Wippich and others had remarked, Spinner's "favorite project."[35] It was the culmination of his ambitious plan to make the Hongo community in Kanda, Tokyo the heart of all the activities of the AEPM. Aside from the church, Spinner aimed at establishing the Shinkyō Shingakkō as a distinctive educational institution that would offer public lectures, publications, and the training for future pastors, which would be housed in a single building.[36]

In 1891, Spinner compiled an 18-page long pamphlet with pictures, entitled "Our Duty in East and South Asia" (*Unsere Aufgabe in Ost- und Südasien*), in which he explained the mission's priorities and encouraged donors to contribute to his dearest project, the theological seminary. An excerpt reveals his passion and enthusiasm for the seminary:

> Support with all your willpower our Theological Seminary! Its purpose is to teach liberal theology. This institution is already becoming widely known and attractive. Its unique character and its excellence [in teaching] will provide the means for higher education.[37]

Evidently, and opportune for Spinner, contemporaneous public opinion was particularly well-disposed to the ideas of the AEPM and like-minded groups. Thus Spinner's fundraising activities received a favorable response. With the help of donations from Germany as well as from liberal-minded Christians such as Aoki Shūzō and Kozaki

Hiromichi, the Shinkyō Shingakkō opened its doors in the beginning of 1888.[38] Spinner's ambitious plan to create a liberal Christian center in the heart of Tokyo which could be used as a headquarters for all the activities of the AEPM were successfully achieved. The first students of the seminary were the Japanese Christians Minami Hajime 三並 良 (1865–1940) and Mukō Gunji 向軍治 (1865–1945). In the following semester of 1888, after his baptism, Maruyama Michikazu 丸山 通一 (1869–1938), a student from the Doitsugaku Kyōkai Gakkō, joined as the third student of the academy.[39] Unfortunately, running the Shinkyō Shingakkō soon proved a significant financial burden for the modest enterprise of the AEPM. Because the admission of a student often included a contractual guarantee for later employment in the service of the AEPM, the missionaries following Spinner often had to walk a fine line between keeping the enterprise financially afloat and expanding the activities of the seminary.[40]

Though some were successful, Shinkyō Shingakkō and the other educational and religious institutions of the AEPM did not always bear fruit, and the continual financial difficulties were a worrying indication. As will be shown in the following chapters, the schools often served as the venue for internal quarrels over authority and power among the missionaries, the Japanese Christians, and the Japanese government. This had a decisive dampening impact on the Swiss and German missionaries' attempt to educate and work in Japan.[41]

Internal protests

Despite the prevailing belief that the AEPM's initial foray into Japan was a success, several protests and disturbances of varying intensity took place within the AEPM. One notable development was the emergence of Japanese supporters who protested or rejected some missionary practice or ideas. Between the early 1890s and the 1910s, the number of incidents of internal protest from Japanese church members proliferated in various parts of the missions, marking what Michel

2. The Emergence of Liberal Christianity in Japan | 61

Shinkyō Shingakkō in Koishikawa.
Tokyo, 1908–1912. Photo: Zentralarchiv der Ev. Kirche der Pfalz.

Missionary Wilfried Spinner and Carl Munzinger with Japanese Christians.
Tokyo, 1890–1891. Photo: Zentralarchiv der Ev. Kirche der Pfalz.

Mohr has coined, the period of "wavering Japanese support," which I will borrow.[42] In what follows, I address two incidents of wavering support which amounted to uprisings within the AEPM.

The first record of an internal protest occurred in 1889. This incident could be called the "Article 28 Protest" because it revolved around the missionaries' pro-governmental reaction to Article 28 (*Teikoku kenpō dai 28-jō* 帝国憲法第 28 条) of the renewed Meiji Constitution. Article 28 was important for the missionaries because its guarantee of freedom of religion or *shinkyō no jiyū* 信教の自由, for the first time in Japanese history granted Christianity the same status as the two larger religions, Buddhism and Shintoism.

On February 18, 1889, Spinner, together with the second missionary of the AEPM in Japan Otto Moritz Schmiedel, expressed their gratitude for the new reform and took the occasion to congratulate the Meiji Emperor in a personal letter:[43]

> As representatives of Christianity and preachers of its peaceful message in Japan, we join the jubilation of the Christians of this nation and Christians all over the world, praising Your Imperial Majesty's wisdom and justice.[44]

The letter was presented to the Foreign Minister Okuma Shigenobu 大隈重信 (1838–1922) to an official audience. Shortly after, the two missionaries received a letter in return from the emperor in which he thanked the two missionaries for their peaceful work in Japan. This is recorded in a letter from 8 March, 1889 submitted by Okuma himself to the two missionaries. Below is a translated quote of the emperor's letter in which he stated:

> The fact that you as Christians, through your letter of thanks, have shown the religious spirit of peace and harmony has given me great joy.[45]

What is intriguing about this quote—and the reason for the protest from the Fukyū Fukuin Kyōkai church members—is the ambiguity of the Emperor's words "religious spirit of peace and harmony." Spinner, Schmiedel, and the AEPM surmised that this statement referred to the emperor's acceptance of Christianity and thus an indication of a promising future for Christianity in Japan. This is certainly a possible interpretation of the letter, and if true, the letter could be seen as the concrete indication of the influence of Christianity in Japan at the time. Indeed, the AEPM was so grateful for the letter, that they published it in its entirety in both of their German-language journals at the time.[46]

On the contrary, the willingness of the missionaries to accept the letter of the emperor at face value was seen by many in the local Christian community as an act of demonstrative submissiveness to authority. Several members of the church protested the missionaries' response to the letter and demanded a clearer rejection of the emperor's Shintō rule. As a consequence, eight members withdrew themselves from the church.[47] The anti-governmental protests within the Fukyū Fukuin Kyōkai Christian community was in line with many other Japanese Christians at the time. Although outside of the influence of the AEPM, the famous incident of the Japanese Christian Uchimura Kenzo in 1891 reflects the strong anti-regime mood among Japanese Christians at the time. With his refusal to shake hands with an authority representing the emperor, Uchimura conveyed a Christian autonomy and independence from the Shinto State. Scholars have later termed this event the "Uchimura Incident," as a reflection of Japanese Christians' resistance against the Shinto State in the late nineteenth century.[48]

The Swiss-German missionaries, as a smaller foreign enterprise in Japan, could not please its church members by taking a strong stand against the Shinto State. Instead, they managed to differentiate between a religious and a political allegiance and interpreted the submission to the emperor as a political necessity and not as a religious stance. In the end, however, this balancing act between pleasing the government and pleasing the community members of Fukyū Fukuin Kyōkai proved quite difficult, and several conflicts aroused in subsequent years.[49]

One example of these later conflicts occurred around the years 1905 and 1906. The protest started among Japanese Christian churches and triggered similar protests within many mission churches. Collectively, these protests are known as the "Unified Church Protest."[50] In contrast to the "Article 28 Protest," in 1889, the "Unified Church Protest" occurred in response to the pro-war movement rising among Japanese Christians following the success of the Russo-Japanese War of 1904–1905. The missionaries' stance towards the Japanese government remained unchanged throughout the period, quietly affirming the Japanese government's increasingly nationalistic and militaristic actions while being careful not to offend the Japanese among which they lived. Already during the Sino-Japanese War of 1894–1895, but mainly during the Russo-Japanese War, arguably all Japanese Christians whole-heartedly supported Japan's war efforts. Even Uchimura Kanzō, who in 1891 had been anti-regime, published in the Japan Daily Mail an editorial article defending the war with China as a rightful war to liberate Korea from the uncivilized and savage influence.[51]

Thus, the passive attitude of the German missionaries during these years received a lot of criticism from the Fukyū Fukuin Kyōkai members because they, in contrast to some independent Japanese preachers, did not verbally approve the government's war efforts. The central figure in supporting the Japanese war effort was the Japanese Congressionalist Ebina Danjō. Strongly influenced by German and American interpretations of Liberal Christianity, the theological similarities between him and the AEPM are rather striking and worth a brief note.[52] He worked hard to install in his congregants a specific understanding of God, Christ, and Christian behaviour, calling for a transformation of Japan through faith. The precise contours of his definition of Christian belief, and the transformation it could accomplish, drew the attention of many Fukyū Fukuin Kyōkai members. Established in 1900, Ebina's Hongō church was only located 500 meters away from the Fukyū Fukuin Kyōkai and the AEPM. Ebina offered "strong, politically inspired sermons," in which he evoked the biographies and theological or philosophical arguments of the German liberal tradition—Ferdinand Christian Baur, Johan Gottfried, and especially Friedrich Schleiermacher—were some of his favourite points of reference.[53] Ebina's popularity grew year by year. In 1905, just as the Russo-Japanese War was drawing to an end, the missionaries would report how "the hall Ebina preaches in holds more than 500 people and stands directly next to our church. His church has now become too small again, so he wants to extend it to the street."[54]

Ebina was attractive to the Fukyū Fukuin Kyōkai members because he, like the missionaries, wished to unite the churches of Japan and transform Japan into God's kingdom. The only difference was that Ebina was a much better communicator than any of the Swiss and German missionaries in Japan.

Ebina's Hongō church had a massive influence over the AEPM and the Fukyū Fukuin Kyōkai. In the Annual Report (*Jahresbericht*) of 1906, there was an incident at the Fukyū Fukuin Kyōkai church where several members who were in protest against the AEPM "joined the neighbour church in Hongō run by Ebina Danjō," marking the first of what would become a common occurrence.[55] Only three years later, in 1909, the missionaries had to close Fukyū Fukuin Kyōkai due to unremitting loss of congregants.

These two examples show that during the twenty-year period from 1889 to 1909, a series of protests manifested within the AEPM and served as potent destabilizing forces for the relationship between the Swiss and German missionaries and the Japanese Church members of the Fukyū Fukuin Kyōkai. The protests within the AEPM were not unique, but rather a part of a larger trend. The autonomic sentiment spreading through Japan's churches affected various mission societies. The biggest losses in membership were recorded by the largest Christian societies (Congregationalist and Presbyterian), whereas smaller ones, like the AEPM, managed to keep the losses within acceptable limits. It was common for Japanese Christians to characterize their protests as both righteous and necessary in order to protest the government failure to implement the ideals of "benevolent rule." The significant shift occurred in the thinking of Japanese Christians: from the early 1980s onwards, Japanese Christians started to break away from the mission-led churches and thus began questioning the missionaries' religious authority. The question of whether the protests within the AEPM were otherwise qualitatively different from other protests within the Japanese mission landscape must await a separate analysis. However, it is a compelling fact that Japanese Christians throughout the Christian landscape utilized their difference of being Japanese Christians as a source of religiously sanctioning their protest not only against the Shinto State rule but also the missionaries' authority.

Furthermore, it is intriguing that rather than supporting its Japanese church members and Ebina Danjō's Hongō community themselves, the missionaries throughout the period upheld an indifferent attitude towards Japanese-led churches. In this sense, the discourse within the Japanese Christian's protests can be understood as a window for self-empowerment, as opposed to an unquestioning faith in missionaries as religious authorities. As Ann Lee Stoler (2002a) has also shown in the case of Indonesia, there were competing visions of community and prosperity between the indigenous Christians and the missionaries.[56] The protests within the AEPM showed the former's actual authority in Japan to be real and prominent.

Being german in japan: a life of solitude.

There are several reasons for the relationship between the missionaries and the Japanese Church members of Fukyū Fukuin Kyōkai being so unstable. These reasons can be categorized into three types: (1) the missionaries' inability to relate themselves to their Japanese church members' needs; (2) the missionaries' inability to live outside their own Western culture; and (3) their inadequacy in negotiating and finding a balance between the two. According to letters and missionary records, the way the missionaries lived reflected their desire to preserve and uphold their German and Swiss cultural identity, a way of life that was, in many ways, detached from the lives of their Japanese converts. The life of a missionary in Japan mirrored the secluded clerical life at home in Germany or Switzerland and didn't offer points of contact with the Japanese society and culture surrounding them in any dialectical way. With only a few exceptions, the Swiss and German missionaries kept to their Western lifestyle while in Japan. Most of them taught in Japanese schools and lived in Western style houses.[57] Wilfried Spinner is a noteworthy exception. The first few years in Tokyo, he lived in what was described as a "very huMBLe" Japanese house with "paper walls and doors… without a second floor."[58] Another option for the missionaries was to live in homes that were "half Japanese and half European." Missionary Otto Schmiedel's home in Tokyo, for example, was typical for those built by foreigners in Japan in the early Meiji period: A two story, wood-frame structure. Although the house had been "quite neglected by its previous owners," the location in the Kanda area, was according to Schmiedel, "bright and peaceful."[59]

It is possible to trace the daily life of the German missionary Otto Schmiedel and his family during his six years in Tokyo (1887–1892), as it has been well documented by Schmiedel himself in his book *Die Deutschen in Japan* (1920). In the book, Schmiedel provides a detailed account of a missionary's life in metropolitan Japan in the late nineteenth century. Their lifestyle was Western, right down to the details of their daily diet. Although it was difficult to obtain Western food locally, various items could be easily ordered from the foreign shops in Yokohama. An evening dinner at the Schmiedel's consisted of caviar, meat, fried vegetables and potatoes, poultry, cheese, fruit, ice cream, and coffee.[60] Otto Schmiedel enjoyed German beer and often bought *Flensburger Pils,* the only obtainable German beer in Japan at the time, at the exorbitant price of one Deutschmark a bottle. For the more frugal, German merchants had started their own local brewery called *Kirin*, whose beer proved agreeable to even the most critical German.[61]

Most of the Swiss and German missionaries consumed Western food. While they were not unaccustomed to the occasional Japanese dish, they never learned to embrace the local cuisine. It only rarely appeared on the dinner table and when it did, it hardly ever seemed a culinary delight. This can, among other things, be seen in the descriptions of a summer trip to Mt. Fuji. Here, the Schmiedel family stopped at a local Japanese restaurant that served "unappetizing food, with finger-like fish, poor quality rice, and bitter green tea."[62]

The problem around particular eating habits was joined by another, more penetrating issue: isolation. Just after 1900, the German community in Kyoto, for example, consisted of only a single family: the missionary Emil Schiller, his wife, his three daughters and their Japanese helper, Okubo. The German merchants, diplomats, and other Germans closest to them lived in the coastal city of Kobe, approximately 80 km away. "It is a lonely, silent life which we live here," Schiller wrote around the turn of the century, and added, "in Europe, one can hardly understand how it is to be next to the Japanese people year after year without getting any closer to them."[63] Forming close relationships with the Japanese people was felt to be almost impossible. This may ultimately have been due to the missionaries' own profound cultural and psychological barriers which inhibited a real familiarity with Japanese affairs, but this should also be seen in light of the Japanese character of withholding closeness. To the Schiller family, as well as to many others, the spiritual and moral life of the Japanese people remained a puzzle, described by the missionary Carl Munzinger in the following words: "to be fully lord [over the Japanese way of thinking]… is an impossibility for the white man."[64] Responding to their solitude in Kyoto, the Schiller family would once a month take a three and a half hour train ride to Kobe in order to socialize with the German community, known as "*der Deutsche Club.*" The club was described as "the only place for the encounter and maintenance of familiar customs for the Germans living here."[65]

The "maintenance of familiar customs" seems to have been more important for German parents than their children. In general, missionary children were less effected than their parents by the sense of isolation. Missionary Emil Schillers' three daughters—Erna, Margret, and Liselotte—had all been born in Japan after the family moved to Kyoto and never seemed to experience the extreme sense of isolation that their parents did.[66] In their young years, the Schiller girls would play with the Japanese children in the kindergarten belonging to the Kyoto mission, which was administered by their mother, Astrid Schiller. When they grew older, they would join their Japanese friends at the Sunday school run by their father, Emil Schiller.[67] Unlike the older generation of their parents, born in Germany, the children growing up in Japan quickly perfected their spoken Japanese, which they learned through close contact with their Japanese friends.

Missionaries did not usually send their children to Japanese schools out of a fear that they would not learn the necessary habits and attitudes that German parents felt would be essential for the future approval and re-assimilation of their own families and back home, where they and their children eventually had to return. Amongst the missionaries, the education of their own children was an important issue, which in as early as 1888 led Spinner to establish the German Boys School (*Knabenschule*) in Tokyo. For many years, this Knabenschule provided a German education for male children of missionaries and German language residents in Japan.[68] This meant that there was no longer a need to send children to Germany or Switzerland until they were ready to enter high school.

The goal of the Knabenschule was to give "European boys in Japan thorough instruction in all German subjects."[69] The school covered eight scholastic years. Boys from the age of six could enter the first class if they were of European or American nationality and possessed knowledge of German, English, or French.[70] From an early age, the pupils were encouraged to participate in so called "instruction lessons," so that with time they would grow into a linguistically homogenous class and be capable of following lessons taught only in German.[71] In this setting, the missionaries were able to inculcate in their own children, growing up in a non-Christian society, their own favorable Wilhelminian bourgeois understanding of the German Christian culture.

Unlike the Schiller family in Kyoto, the missionaries in the metropolitan areas of Tokyo and Yokohama—although equally removed from Japanese cultural life—were never truly isolated from Western society. Otto Schmiedel, for instance, was much involved with other Western Protestant denominations in Japan through his close contact with the American Universalists, especially the Perin family.[72] The relationship developed through work, but easily reached the level of a personal friendship, with private parties often held at the home of the Schmiedel family.[73] Besides Schmiedel, Spinner also became close to the Perin family attending a missionary conference together with American Universalist George L. Perin in 1890.[74]

Amongst the Protestants it was common for groups of missionaries—especially of the Anglo-Saxon missions—to meet at large inter-regional missionary gatherings in Tokyo. On May 4, 1886, Spinner mentions in his diary the first time he participated in a regional missionary convention in Tokyo. It was a gathering of voluntary representatives from different American and British denominations and missionary societies. What bound these denominations together was their mutual appreciation of the obstacles they all faced in Japan. Looking past their differing mission methods and their theological orientation, they formed a homogeneous group able to devote time and resources to attack problems common to all denominations.[75]

The summer holidays offered further opportunities for foreigners living in Japan to socialize. For many foreigners, staying in Japan during the intolerably hot and humid summer months was often unbearable, and the Swiss and German missionaries were no exception. In the hottest months, they would often leave their metropolitan lives behind and relocate to the much cooler mountain and sea resorts.[76] The summer holidays served as an important change to their otherwise monotonous daily life in the cities. For Schmiedel, the holidays gave him the opportunity to meet people and see the country:

> The land and people outside of Tokyo and to learn about the interior of Japan, *inaka* as the Japanese say: to get to know peasants, fishermen, carriers, and packers, Shinto and Buddhist priests.[77]

Thus, the summer holidays proved favorable in bringing missionaries from all over Japan into social contact. For the Swiss and German missionaries in Tokyo, the sea resorts of Oiso and Atami, both located southwest of Tokyo and referred to as "the Karlsbad of Japan,"[78] became the most visited. The ocean climate there was attractive, while activities such as swimming, picnicking at the beach, and bathing in hot springs with Western style hotels served as excellent escapes for the missionaries. As an interesting cultural by product, the holidays even performed the function of introducing German leisure culture to the Japanese, as happened when Otto Schmiedel, to the great curiosity of the Japanese bystanders, introduced them to the German bathing suit.[79]

While the missionaries of the AEPM espoused their intention to reach the Japanese people, their writings tell us of their self-made difficulties to do so and underscore the highly paradoxical nature of the mission situation. Like most Protestant missions in Japan at the time, the great majority of the missionaries lived a life isolated from the Japanese society they strove to change. On one hand, there was a real impetus amongst the missionaries towards converting the Japanese, but on the other hand, the missionary's hands-off approach to Japanese culture in the name of retaining their own hurt their chances of successfully bringing in Japanese converts. In their private lives, the missionaries purposely stood aloof from the Japanese, seeking to preserve their cultural identity in the face of the unfamiliar culture that surrounded them.

The mission in numbers

For the more quantitative, the isolation of the missionaries can be reflected in numerical terms as well—the low number of Japanese church members. The number of Japanese Protestants belonging to the Fukyū Fukuin Kyōkai remained comparatively nominal throughout its whole history: as few as 296 members at its peak (.02% of the total Christian population of Japan). And with only seven people baptized in 1900, the number was not increasing much.[80] However, the influence of liberal theology on Japanese society was far greater than these statistics might suggest and can be traced largely to the impact of outstanding Japanese Christians, such as Ebina Danjō, rather than to a pervasive appeal of the Christian message conveyed by the Swiss and German missionaries.[81] Around the turn of the century, there were noticeable signs of recovery in the Christian churches, and after the hard and problematic years of the 1890s, Japanese Protestantism went through what Japanese scholars have since called the "second phase of revival."[82] This extended to the AEPM; The 16th Annual Report for 1899–1900 displayed a newfound optimism for the future of Christianity in Japan, when it proclaimed:

> The victory of Christianity is only a matter of time, it may still be in a distant future, and we may not live to see it, but it is destined to come.[83]

This missionary optimism, although carefully worded, was only partially justified. From the late 1890s onward, Japanese Christian communities developed an interest to free themselves from the paternalism of Western missionaries and began to reinterpret the Christian message to suit an independent Japanese church. Already in 1894, the missionaries Carl Munzinger and Max Christlieb sensed this shift in tide and recognized that their time as missionaries may come to an end rather soon:

> The Japanese are no longer content with the mere organizational leadership of their churches but believe that the entire spirit of the Christian churches should be led by their hands.[84]

This tendency towards indigenization, which intensified at the beginning of the twentieth century, spread rapidly and deliberately attached itself to national traditions, while simultaneously emphasizing a Christianity unique to Japan. Its Japanese distinctiveness opposed the occidental character of the Gospel as proclaimed by the missionaries.[85] In light of these new tendencies, Carl Munzinger stressed that the missionaries were obliged, just like a puppeteer, "to stay in the background and keep the threads in the hand and to lead the community in such a way that they stay in the belief of controlling it themselves."[86] He saw "the church community [as] a family in which the priest is the guiding father and the community members are the children."[87] Beyond rhetorical moves, the mission work of the AEPM was also restructured and concessions were made in sensitive areas of the church organization, such as faith practices, giving greater control to their Japanese members. The Japanese officials (pastors, evangelists) increasingly dominated most of the church activities and decision-making functions. Theological education at Shinkyō Shingakkō, however, stayed under the influence of the German missionaries. Still, as the above quote from Munzinger shows, the missionaries nevertheless maintain a role in which they watched over the Japanese Christians to ensure that their practiced Christianity was not completely "Japanized." The mission's three main concerns were that: (1) the syncretism of Christian doctrines with ancestor and emperor worship had to be prevented under all circumstances;[88] (2) any recognition of the Christian faith through Buddhism and in particular the adoption of Christianity into a pantheistic religion should be watched and counteracted;[89] and (3) Christianity had to be safeguarded against any of the supernatural characteristics of Confucianism.[90]

To the missionaries, the alleged paternalism was no more than a delusion of the self-conscious Japanese Christian communities who asked for full autonomy, equality, and liberation from Western culture. The missionaries failed to grasp that this reaction was a direct result of their own shortcomings, namely, their inability to motivate and install a quality in their Japanese employees in a way that these would contribute to Christianity's "rightful development" as defined by them. This failure brought much criticism because the success of the "rightful" Christianity largely depended on the Japanese pastors: "We especially lack suitable Japanese who are able to gather and influence their compatriots," complained, for example, missionary Emil Schiller around the turn of the century.[91] The few Japanese pastors who were trained and ordained by the theological school seemed, according to the missionary Emil Schroeder, hardly worthy of their job. In 1913, he criticized the Japanese pastors of the Fukyū Fukuin Kyōkai by stating:

> Our Japanese pastors lack knowledge of the Kingdom of God. They do not value education and their teaching is poor.[92]

Christlieb and Munzinger also regretted that no "great, apostolic Japanese personality" had emerged within the AEPM to continue the work Spinner had begun and to give new impetus to the mission work. The two most likely Japanese candidates, Minami Hajime and Maruyama Michikazu of the Shinkyō Shingakkō, who worked as pastors for the Japanese Christian community in Hongo, were considered to lack essential qualities to warrant faith in them. Minami was described as being too soft and kind, while Maruyama, in contrast, was seen as tending to be too passionate and too independent.[93] For Christlieb, it was quite clear that "any form of progress of our mission is impossible as long as these two have the decisive influence on our work and plans."[94]

Thus, it is not surprising that most prominent leaders of the Japanese Christian society proved to come from church societies that had little contact with the missionaries of the AEPM, mainly because the AEPM just did not produce any influential figures for the new and developing Japanese Christian movement. The AEPM entered the twentieth century on unsure footing: it was clear that their ambitious mission work and the realization of this struggle put a strain on continued efforts. Criticism from within the AEPM's own ranks accused the mission of neglecting work in their Japanese communities. In 1907, the German translator Karl Vogt noted in his lengthy essay *Lage des Christentums in Japan* (*The situation of Christianity in Japan*) that the AEPM with its 234 members belonging to Fukyū Fukuin Kyōkai, was of little or no significance in the Christian landscape of Japan.[95]

Two years later, in 1909, this reality was felt when the Japanese church community Fukyū Fukuin Kyōkai closed due to the lack of visitors.[96] According to Kozaki Hiromichi, this was the result of the Japanese community alienating themselves more and more from the AEPM establishment. Finally, the remaining members of the former Fukyū Fukuin Kyōkai church joined other newly established Japanese liberal church communities outside the influence of the AEPM's missionaries.[97] From then on, contact between the AEPM and the Japanese Christian movement remained centered on evangelical and social pedagogic campaigns.[98]

In the case of the missionaries Johannes Martin Ostwald and Georg Würfel, their frustration with their daily life as missionaries was obvious. Both of their contracts with the AEPM terminated on 1908 after they had declared that there was nothing to gain from practical missionary work in Japan. They wanted to focus on academic and literary work instead. But an emphasis on the practical mission work was stipulated from home and was an important factor for the AEPM's economic support as these donations essentially meant either the demise or survival for the mission in Japan.

Given the increasing indigenization of Christianity and the emergence of a confident group of dedicated Japanese church leaders, the only path to survival for the AEPM was to cooperate with theologically-related denominations. This was indeed the path they took, marked by when the AEPM established a collaboration with the Congregational church of Nihon Kumiai Kirisuto Kyōkai (Japanese Unification Church). By cooperating with the second largest Protestant denomination in Japan, the education policies of both organizations merged, enabling the AEPM to maintain a restructured version of their theological education at Shinkyō Shingakkō under the scientific influence of Dōshisha University in Kyoto. Thus, from then on, the activities of the Swiss-German missionaries were removed from those of the Japanese Christian and instead came to function within the confines of their own mission and educational institutions. Therefore, by the early 1920s the missionaries reluctantly and with little choice obtained a role as observers of, rather than participants in, the twentieth century Japanese Christian movement.

CONCLUSION

Norman Etherington commented on the nineteenth century global missionary movement, stating:

> The most important late twentieth century scholarly insight into the growth of Christianity... was that European missionaries accomplished very little in the way of conversion.[99]

As in other parts of the world, the Protestant missions in Japan were generally reluctant to adapt to the local cultural and religious environment. This is one of the reasons why the AEPM's missionaries' success in terms of formal conversions was limited.[100] But whether the number of conversions defines the success of a mission society depends on one's expectations. The objective for this chapter was not to trivialize the work of the Swiss and German missionaries in Japan for not being successful in attracting large crowds of Japanese to their churches, or for lacking certain cultural qualities when it comes to understanding the Japanese. The goal, rather, was to evaluate critically and without exaggeration what the AEPM sought to achieve in their encounter with their Japanese congregates. The analysis reveals a story about promising beginnings and a rapid decline. It has mentioned the missionaries' personal lack of flexibility in adapting to a time of escalating social changes in the Japanese society as one of the reasons why the missionaries had difficulty gaining a foothold among Japanese congregates.

Still, this chapter has also revealed that the AEPM and Liberal Christianity successfully extended its influence outside the mission compounds. We saw that the Theological Seminary had to be abandoned in 1909 due to financial reasons, but later integrated under new settings at the Theological Institute of the congressional Dōshisha University, which eventually became one of the centers for Japanese theology in the twentieth century. Its structure with public lectures, publications and educational facilities left enduring traces in Japan. From the beginning of the twentieth century, German became the predominant foreign language within Japanese theology. All of the so-called great Japanese theologians of the twentieth century such as Satō Shigehiko 佐藤繁彦 (1887–1935), Ishihara Ken 石原謙 (1882–1976) and not least Hatano Seiichi 波多野精一 (1877–1950) went to Germany to study philosophy and theology. Hatano went to Berlin and Heidelberg in 1904 and is said to have attended lectures of liberal theologians such as Otto Pfleiderer, Adolf von Harnack, Johannes Weiss, and Ernst Troeltsch, before returning to Japan in 1906. It is after this trip that he established the Center for Christian Studies at Kyoto University, embracing Liberal Christianity as an academic discipline.[101]

The publication activities of Shinri is another example of the missionaries' influence reaching outside its mission compounds. Shinri, which was briefly mentioned in the introduction of this chapter, launched in 1889 and quickly gained popularity both inside and outside the Christian circles of Japanese readers.[102]

Though, as the following chapters will show, the missionaries themselves often complained about the quality of their converts, and faced a multitude of obstacles which caused them to question their role and purpose in Japan, the above examples exemplify how the missionaries managed to sow seeds of Liberal Christianity in Japan.

PART II

Paradoxes of the Mission in Japan

3

Internal Conflicts and External Challenges

The Failure of Missionary Educational Projects in Meiji Japan

Until about 1891, the German mission of the *Allgemeiner Evangelisch-Protestantischer Missionsverein* had been expanding at a steady pace with Wilfried Spinner's opening of Shinkyō Shingakkō 新教神学校 in 1889, marking the peak of this development. However, from 1892 onward, this promising trend slowed and eventually ceased completely. An event that occurred in April of 1892 conveniently marks this turning point. The female missionary Auguste Diercks (1862–1921)[1] who was responsible for the main Swiss-German female mission, wrote to the Home Mission Board to report an incident that had taken place in a mission school for girls in the nearby district of Hongō, where missionaries had recently opened a school for poor children:

> The most troublesome experience this year was the visit from five of our best students. The purpose of their visit was to ask the foreign board members to stop their work and give over the control of the school to Japanese hands. They were influenced by a group of Japanese counselors, who themselves did not belong to the school.[2]

Beyond Auguste Diercks initial shock, this incident also led her to ask whether she could continue her missionary work as a teacher if the school came under Japanese control.[3] The five girls promptly were expelled from the school after the event, with the motives behind the girls' action being blamed on a sese of Japanese patriotism that was on the rise at that time, not just among the non-Christians, but also among the Christian Japanese. Diercks reported that Japanese people were interested in the education they received, but still distrustful of her, both as a foreigner and as a Christian:

> We are here in an exceedingly difficult time of repudiation; Christianity is being attacked on many sides, and only a few Japanese, under the present circumstances, have the courage to convert to our mission.[4]

While this incident was extraordinary, the anti-Christian sentiments expressed by the Japanese and felt by Diercks, in many ways characterize the challenges the Swiss-German missions' educational projects in general would face in the last few decades of the nineteenth century. From 1885, when the AEPM's first missionary Wilfried Spinner started his mission work in Japan, to 1912, between twenty and twenty-five educational projects ranging from kindergartens to theological academies were established in and around Tokyo, Yokohama, and Kyoto. Missionary writings and available statistical accounts, on which this chapter's data is based, do not provide a clear or comprehensive picture of the educational developments established in the period, nor an account of the exact number of schools established. Indeed, the attempt at forming a chronology of the schools has been at times frustrating and often unsuccessful, until it became clear to me that I was trying to reconstruct a system that basically did not exist. The mission newsletters of the AEPM would proudly mention the establishment of new schools and educational projects, but at the same time, they would *not* record these projects' closings. But the educational projects of the AEPM did close. In some occasions, the termination of a mission school was first mentioned years after it had taken place. In other cases, the closing of a school can only be assumed because it simply stopped being mentioned in the missionary journals. Thus, the organization of the mission schools in Japan was as muddled as the missionaries' own accounts about them. Furthermore, we must keep in mind that missionaries' writings often functioned, among other things, to collect financial support from their German and Swiss readers.[5] Therefore, there existed an apparent reticence and financial incentive not to report any failures of their school projects and ambitions.

Due to the dearth of systematic material, many scholars have experienced similar obstacles in writing about the missionaries' educational efforts, both in Japan and elsewhere. In her research of Christian education for girls by American missionaries in Kobe, Ishii Noriko Kawamura focuses mostly on prosperous mission schools, but she also makes references to some of the many failures and unsuccessful educational projects of the missionaries, particularly in the late nineteenth and early twentieth centuries.[6]

But why were the efforts of founding and running local mission schools so unstructured and, as we will see, so ineffective? What does this tell us about the balance of power between the missionaries and their Japanese students? And what role did education play in this Swiss-German/Japanese experience? This chapter examines the causes behind the failure of the educational projects of the AEPM. Most work on the history of education typically approach its subject rather narrowly, as the more or less institutionalized schooling of children or youth.[7] In this chapter, I adopt a broader analytical scope by understanding education as a process which can (and often does) take place both inside and outside of formal educational institutions. By contextualizing the educational projects of the AEPM within the environment of the Meiji period, this chapter is able to expound the actual role of mission schools in modern Japan and will highlight the tenuous footing of these projects at the time.

Furthermore, we gain new insights into the mission schools of the AEPM by shifting the focus away from the schools themselves. By examining the ways in which various groups attached their own ideas to the mission schools, it becomes evident that the missionary education projects were more multi-faceted, involving actors with differing agendas. From the beginning, the educational effort of the AEPM attracted support from a variety of people, most of them being politically conscious students and families of former samurais (*shizoku* 氏族). But by the early 1890s, the educational project—as shown in the incident of Auguste Diercks—began to draw the attention of other groups of Japanese society. The educational enterprise of the mission movement became the focal point of several groups within Japanese society who advocated directly against the educational efforts of the missionaries. The Japanese government itself became involved in a series of educational law modifications in the early to mid-1890s. The formation of the Educational Association in 1896 was among the most prominent. Christian education was banned, and foreigners were placed under Japanese law. Accordingly, as Carol Gluck (1985) has already noted, these laws added considerably to the degree of control the government could exercise over the activities of the mission schools.[8]

The debates and disagreements surrounding the missionaries' schooling projects demonstrates that education was a contentious issue in Japan at the time. The government, who organized the new laws, perceived education as vital to bringing about and maintaining social order, and indigenous groups perceived Christian education as harmful to the Japanese identity. On the other hand, the missionaries preoccupied with finding solutions to their immediate problems of running economically challenged schools. Furthermore, several other groups, such as Shin Buddhist sects, also began to engage in educational efforts, which further added to the instability of mission schools in Japan.

Education at the turn of the late nineteenth century and early twentieth century was a highly contested field with multilayered agendas, yet those who rely on the framework of exploring either the history of government educational laws or the history of the mission schools tend to present a one-dimensional view of the field based on the objectives of government bureaucrats or sole missionaries, and thus dismiss the diversity of voices that constituted the educational field in

Japan around the turn of the century. Richard Rubinger, for example, in his work, "Education from One Room to One System," (1984) solely describes the government's motives behind the educational reforms throughout the Meiji period. On the other side, Heyo Hamer (2002), in a similar fashion, wrote a comprehensive account of the Swiss-German missionary schools, educational projects, their students, etc., but without investigating the world of outside the mission compounds. This chapter takes a more nuanced, multi-layered approach to analyze the many motives behind the missionaries' educational projects and to illuminate the controversies surrounding them. The example of the AEPM's mission schools and projects emphasizes that instead of just being in binary opposition, the power relations of the Swiss-German missionaries and the Japanese were complex, multifaceted, and very difficult for the missionaries to maneuver in, let alone change.

Just as different agendas led to the incident that occurred at Auguste Dierck's at the girl-school, competing visions informed the educational projects of the AEPM throughout the whole period. While the missionaries of the AEPM continued to uphold the Christian character of their schools and had a set of specific goals in mind, the Japanese government and their close supporters increasingly, throughout the 1890s, waged their war against the mission schools on the battlefield of education. For the government, as will be demonstrated, the educational field came to serve as a symbol of control. To explicate this rift between the missionaries' educational projects and the Japanese government and its supporters, the following section will first outline some of the characteristics of the mission schools belonging to the AEPM in the late Meiji period and will then examine the motives of various actors included in these projects.

The Educational Projects of the AEPM

Despite the difficulties surrounding the sources, this chapter has tried to define and establish what can be documented with certainty about the AEPM's mission schools and projects in nineteenth and early twentieth century Japan. During the mission's early years in the 1880s and 1890s, the missionaries concentrated their energy and resources on the institutions of higher education. This is best reflected in Wilfried Spinner's and Otto Schmiedel's lecturing at the German Studies Society School (Doitsugaku Kyōkai Gakkō 獨逸學協會學校), but also in the establishment of the Shinkyō Shingakkō, the theological academy for students, from 1889 onward.[9] Later, during the 1890s and into the early part of the 1900s, the type of schools run by the AEPM changed. A Sunday School, which Wilfried Spinner established in 1887 at the Hongō community in Tokyo and which was the only mission school in the 1880s that could also be joined by children, seems to have been shut down or changed into an *Armenschule*—a school for poor children—just after Spinner's return to Zürich in 1891.[10] From 1894, a significant increase of so-called "voluntary" schools run by the mission can be seen: evening schools, Bible schools, schools for the poor, and kindergartens all emerged around this time.[11] These schools developed into the most common types of schooling projects in the Swiss-German mission field right up to the end of the Meiji period in 1912.[12]

A lot of the schools were short lived and would close down within a few years, only for another school to be opened under a new name at the same location, usually with the same group of students. Some Bible and Sunday schools were located in the outskirts of Tokyo in branches of the Swiss-German Mission and run by local ministers and volunteers.[13] Most schools, however, were situated in the mission compound itself and were attended mostly by students from higher education centers or by Japanese who were in one way or another associated with German culture. The quantity of pupils in the educational institutions varied from three to a hundred or more.[14] The number of students not only changed from school to school, but also on a monthly or daily basis in the same school. Some school projects were separated by gender, others were not.[15]

The teachers were either the missionaries or Japanese converts. Most of these had been former or current students in the mission schools themselves and had never received any formal training as teachers, apart from some tutorial sessions available within the local Christian community. The language of instruction in all schools was either Japanese or German; German was mostly used in classes with higher-level students who already spoke German to some degree. In a few cases, missionaries also mentioned teaching in English to students with an interest in missionary work, but unable to yet understand German.[16] The subjects being taught seemed to have varied somewhat, and to the great dissatisfaction of the missionaries, may have even been irrelevant at times. Students, they complained, only attended classes in order to learn a foreign language.[17] An introduction to Christianity was included in the curricula of the majority of the schools, but due to governmental restrictions, not in all of them.

From the mid–1890s to the beginning of the twentieth century, the Swiss-German missionaries sought governmental recognition for most of their schools. The positive attitudes toward Western education in Japan that had existed since the opening of Japan in 1858 had turned to the opposite by the beginning of the 1890s. According to historian Thomas Rohlen, a "reaction to the extremes of foreign influence surfaced in the 1890s."[18] A series of education laws issued in Japan during the 1890s marked the shift from the mere importation of Western learning to the development of a national educational ideology.[19] Not only did they link the ethical system taught in schools to notions of loyalty and patriotism, but they also underlined the role of the emperor as the head of the state.[20] It was argued that the Japanese people were "mystically" bound to the emperor. And it is precisely this view that was believed to have been threatened to become undermined by any thought about independence and autonomy that the Christian schools taught and wished for their subjects in Japan.[21]

As Japanese nationalist sentiment grew, education became the field in which the large chasm between the objectives of the missionaries and the Japanese government began to become visible. The conflict between the religious independence of the Christian schools and the Japanese government was perhaps best exemplified by the sustained attack by Inoue Tetsujirō 井上哲次郎 (1855–1944) on Uchimura Kanzō 内村鑑三 (1861–1930) in 1893. Uchimura Kanzō, a Christian high school teacher, refused to bow before a photograph of the Meiji Emperor in a school ceremony. This incident, which was attributed to his Christian faith of rejecting the divinity of the emperor, was attacked by Inoue in his 1893 essay titled "Kyōiku to Shūkyō no shōtotsu" 教育と宗教の衝突 (The Collision of Education and Religion), a work which would be republished in over thirty different journals, including a German translation published in the AEPM journal *Zeitschrift für Missionskunde und Religionswissenschaft*.[22] Christianity, so Inoue stated in his essay, was, by choosing the Kingdom of God over the Imperial Nation, the most dangerous religion in Japan. Inoue questioned the compatibility of Christianity and the Imperial Rescript on Education and in his view, Christian schools needed to be subjected under the laws of the emperor and the Japanese state.[23]

In the process, missionaries, such as the Swiss-German missionaries, therefore, may have been welcomed in the schools for their expertise, but at the same time were marginalized for their foreignness. According to Richard Rubinger, an expert on the history of education in Japan, the new national education policy raised standards, minimized class inequities, and broadened access to schooling, but also weakened the private sector, which until then had been controlled predominately by the Christian mission societies. Rubinger elaborates:

> The centralized bureaucracy of the 1890s inevitably brought with it diminishing possibilities for individual and local influence in the control and practice of education.... The private schools were no longer outside the system but were appendages of it.[24]

With the Imperial Rescript on Education (*kyōiku chokugo* 教育勅語) in 1890, the Vocational Supplementary School Regulations (*jitsu-*

gyō hoshū gaku 実業補習学)in 1893, the formation of the Educational Association in 1896, and the Vocational School Order (*jitsugyō gakkō rei* 実業学校令)in 1899, the Japanese government slowly increased its control over the education field. The new education laws meant that the government could—or could not—award schools a certificate to permit teaching. The government's approval was of considerable financial significance for the running of schools and gave them greater prestige, improving their chances of attracting new students. The enhanced financial support as a positive consequence of the government's approval was an important inducement, as most AEPM mission schools offered their services for free. On the other hand, an official certificate gave the Japanese government leverage to influence the missionaries' educational priorities and—to the missionaries' dismay—prohibited religious instruction in the schools. For many mission schools in Japan, the new educational laws had a direct negative effect. German missionary Emil Schiller mentioned the new cabinet law of 1899 in a newsletter published in the ZMR, that:

> Since the news [concerning the centralization of education] has been released in the Japan Daily Mail at the beginning of November [1899], 25–30 Christian Schools have been forced to close and the cessation of others lies ahead.[25]

In response to this dire situation, some missionaries of the AEPM appealed to the local authorities to withdraw these strict rules. Amongst the Swiss and German missionaries, discussion was internally raised whether they should let their schools continue under the new law or close them down, and whether it would still be beneficial for the mission society to run their schools when religious education wasn't allowed. Emil Schiller played a central role in organizing this appeal. In December of 1899, he and the AEPM made their first appeal to the local authorities, but to no avail.

In the spring of 1900, Schiller commented again on the situation of the mission schools in a newsletter in the ZMR. To him, the educational laws could be understood as nothing less than a conspiracy organized by the three indigenous religions of Japan in order to dismiss the "foreigners":

> One is not wrong to deem these actions of the Ministry of Education as having less to do with anti-religious tendencies than with chauvinistic undercurrents in the educational circles that want to get rid of the missionaries' influence on the school activities. The newspapers have divided views on this topic.... Worst of them all is the newspaper called *Sangen*, (i.e., The Three Eyes, namely Shintoism, Buddhism, and Confucianism), which incites the tree ancient religions to unite and fight against Christianity. This happens because Christianity today, and ever since the time of the old Portuguese mission, follows political goals in Japan and therefore is regarded as a national enemy.[26]

Schiller's quote is interesting because it points a finger towards the contested nature that surrounded the field of education at the turn of the century. It clearly supports the scholars of history in their claim that the mission schools of the nineteenth century were often meant to achieve more than just reproduce an order of society; they were generally designed with the purpose of changing it. Students at the mission schools were enrolled in inclusive and comprehensive educational regimes designed to teach them a particular Christian moral and faith.[27] This politically-charged nature of education frequently made the schools a site of material and symbolic battles over social identities; a battle that the mission schools often had a hard time adjusting to, hence the massive numbers of school closures.[28]

It became obvious that due to the new regulations within the educational field, the mission schools of the AEPM could not continue as they were. In the spring of 1900, Schiller and the AEPM finally gave in to the government's education laws. In a rather somber and straightforward newsletter sent to the Home Board in Germany, he accepted the new reality while noting: "From the perspective of the Mission, we are determined to get rid of our religious education rather than to let the school deteriorate. The fate of our *Armenschule* has not yet been determined."²⁹ The Armenschule was different because, just like the above-mentioned lace school, it served a more profane role by helping children in need, with Christian education playing a secondary role in these schools.

Rather surprisingly, the activity of AEPM's mission schools was reinvigorated in the following summer of 1901. The mission schools received renewed interest, especially from the poorer parts of east Tokyo, and its network spread, including the entrance a dozen of new students. In 1901, missionary Adolf Wendt reported that a practical agreement was reached between the AEPM and the local-city government, which allowed the schools to teach religious education on a voluntary basis, after school hours, for those children and students who wished to participate. This also applied for the Armenschule, which could continue its work as it previously had.³⁰

In some way or another, most of the missionary schools run by the AEPM managed to provide some form of Christian education. The mission journals, for example, inform us that the kindergarteners

Children at the Armenshule in Tokyo, before 1901.
Photo: Zentralarchiv der Ev. Kirche der Pfalz.

sang Christian songs every morning and had Christian plays during Christmas.[31] Furthermore, the girls' schools of the AEPM, similar to the Armenschule, also offered voluntary Bible lessons after school, which, according to Auguste Dierks, most of her students joined.[32]

It is clear that at the most fundamental level, harsh competition from different religious groups and unfavorable governmental law made the life of the mission schools very unstable. By the first decade of the twentieth century, hardly any of the schools started by Spinner in the late 1880s were still in operation, and by the end of the Meiji period in 1912, only the Doitsugaku Kyōkai Gakkō and a couple of preschool institutions continued to exist. Other schools had either ceased to exist or been restructured. While the reason for the short-lived nature of the schools can be blamed on the government laws, a close analysis of primary documents also reveals that the missionaries running the schools did not necessarily share a common objective. As the following section will illustrate, understanding the layers of agendas surrounding the mission schools is a necessary step towards grasping the real reason of the failures of the missionary educational projects in Meiji Japan.

Multilayered agenda

The primary factor complicating the success of the AEPM educational projects can, according to the missionary sources highlighted above, thus be explained by outside factors such as strict governmental laws and an unfavorable environment that made it difficult to run the schools. But this was not always the whole answer. Scholars such as Karen Vallgårda have relativized the role of the missionaries themselves by placing more emphasis on local and internal issues immediately connected to the mission schools. Vallgårda, for example, has illustrated how "an important cause of the instability of the schooling regimes is to be found with the missionaries themselves."[33] In the following section, I contend that these two perspectives can be reconciled by considering the multiplicity of viewpoints that surrounded the mission schools of the AEPM. To this end, I propose a new model that sheds light on the reason for the instability of the mission schools. I categorize these instabilities into two different groups: (1) *Internal Conflicts*, understood as instabilities ascribed to the missionaries themselves; and (2) *External Challenges*, understood as instabilities afflicted on the mission schools due to outside pressure. Needless to say, this model is created for convenient means, and the boundary between external and internal conflicts is not always explicit. However, this model does reflect the complexity surrounding the schools as a place with multilayered agendas.

Internal Conflicts

From the time the AEPM established the first mission school in Tokyo in the late 1880s, and throughout the next several decades, the education of Japanese students was a highly contested subject, and in 1891, the first conflict regarding the educational projects broke out. The conflict erupted when the German missionologist Gustav Warneck published the essay "Kultur- und Missionsbilder aus Japan" (Images of the Culture and Mission in Japan) in the journal *Allgemeine Missions-Zeitschrift*. Here Warneck criticized the AEPM's schools and practical mission work for its lack of success in converting Christians and attracting large amounts of students. Warneck stressed repeatedly that the blame could only be faulted on the missionaries' soft attitude towards conversion.[34]

It is difficult to tell how much Warneck's criticism had to do with substantial ideological differences. But the AEPM responded promptly by publishing the article "Antwort auf Dr. Warnecks Urteil über unsere Missionare" (Reply to Dr. Warneck's Critique of our Missionaries) in their own journal the ZMR. In the article written by the missionary Otto Schmiedel, they argued:

If anybody is careful not to brag about finished results, it is me and my colleagues. Reciting pre-produced results and memorizing them is an English-American custom, whereas a theologian educated in Germany will teach his students to work out their own results by presenting and discussing diverse and opposing views. We have never deviated from this method, which is particularly well established in our biblical scholarship.[35]

Schmiedel's comment alluded to a core belief among the liberal theologians: the idea that the teaching of Christ could not be hurried or forced. According to Schmiedel, a real and deep-rooted faith could only be encouraged in the schools and could only be brought to fruition through free will. Unlike many of the Anglo-Saxon missions in Japan, Schmiedel and the missionaries of the AEPM refused any method of mass conversion and valued the personal and individual conversion through persuasion and free will.[36]

The disconnect between Warneck and the missionaries of the AEPM made evident the various internal agendas of the people connected to the mission. The missionaries in Japan maintained a reserved attitude toward any criticism from abroad, and the lukewarm critique from Warneck was a source of frustration. The disparity in the attitudes between the missionaries and their followers back home in Germany and Switzerland resurfaced very quickly. Shortly after the episode involving Warneck and Schmiedel, another conflict regarding the mission schools reoccurred within the AEPM. This time, the criticism was voiced by the German missionary Herman Dalton. Dalton had visited the mission of the AEPM in Tokyo in 1894, and after his return to Germany, he published a book about his experiences in Japan. In the book, titled *Auf Missionspfaden in Japan* (*On Mission Paths in Japan*, 1895), Dalton strongly advised friends of the AEPM against making donation which directly supported "the upbringing and education of individual Japanese." Instead, he recommended a strengthening of "the actual mission work" through the donation of funds which supported the education of future missionaries at home.[37] According to Dalton, the gain from the schools was so low that the educational efforts of the AEPM could be seen as nothing less than a waste of money.

It is difficult to establish how Dalton arrived at his conclusion. Some members of the AEPM believed that it was based on an overall dissatisfaction with the treatment he received during his stay in Tokyo.[38] But the missionaries recognized the gravity of the criticism and responded instantly with several essays published in the ZMR, expressing: "the schools are not the least important part of the mission." From the view of the missionaries, their schools helped to educate and develop real Christians who, they asserted, would be the building blocks of future Japan's Christianity.[39] However, what the AEPM had originally envisioned as an opportunity to show the positive sites of their mission to a fellow missionary had quickly escalated into a direct confrontation with other mission societies at home. From the perspective of the missionaries, the mission schools functioned as the main gate through which new supporters were recruited to their church society. This is also suggested in an article published in the periodical *Das Missionsblatt* in 1897. Once more, the AEPM conveyed that their focus on upbringing and education was indeed a valuable cause, not least because the young Japanese functioned as "sourdough" in the heathen society of Japan. In the missionaries' view, young Japanese were more impressionable and less corrupted than the adults. Thus, it made good sense to give their education a high priority in the evangelizing efforts of the AEPM. This guaranteed a more secure and sincere impact than could be expected from any other kind of mission work, such as preaching in the streets.[40]

A number of contemporaneous writers around the mission supported the viewpoint that the schools were a Christian obligation and closing the educational efforts of the AEPM would be abandonment of the Japanese youth. Otto Hering, while contemplating the significant work of the Armenschule, for example, stated in 1897: "Lead the children to me and do not repel them, for such is the Kingdom of God."[41] Education, in other words, especially of the Japanese youth, remained an integral part of AEPM's mission projects. Hering pointed out that many other mission societies in Japan, considered the education even of non-baptized children to be the only effective path to conversion and encouraged the mission board to keep following this path. For, so he postulated: "It is the task of our schools to lead the young souls to Jesus." Therefore, the AEPM "should be determined on continuing their educational work among the young Japanese."[42] Yet, despite the conviction with which he expressed his viewpoint, Hering neither specified nor indicated what role the schools were to play in the overall work of the AEPM in Japan, nor did he draw up a structured plan for a continuous improvement of the mission schools. Instead, rather than being founded on a punctilious plan laid out by a set of decrees agreed upon by the Mission Board, the proliferation of mission schools in the 1890s seems to have been the product of individual missionaries' initiatives, which received the support from the Mission Board back in Germany only after having been established.[43] Thus, the instability of the many mission schools run by the AEPM can be ascribed to the simple reason that the mission board simply fell short in developing a clear and constant set of goals and applying their policy in the form of regular and reliable instructions. Instead, from the time the AEPM created its first mission station and school in 1886 until the end of the century, the schooling of Japanese students continued to be an internally highly disputed matter.

Finally, we turn to a third example, which in contrast to the two previous cases consist of individuals who were actually employed by the AEPM as missionaries, but whose discontent with the nature of the mission schools led them to participate in a protest against the AEPM and the other missionaries stationed in Japan. In 1907, the two missionaries Martin Ostwald and Georg Würfel sent a letter to the Mission Board refusing to contribute to any teaching related to the mission schools of the AEPM. In their letter, they articulated their displeasure with the futility of the practical work in the schools. These, they claimed in the letter, were ineffectual and gained Christianity nothing. Instead, it would be more fulfilling to allow them to focus exclusively on their job as pastors for the German Christian community.[44] While both Ostwald and Würfel, on a mere human level, supported the school projects—because they operated as civilizing institutions—they doubted their efficiency as a means for spreading Christianity in Japan. A literary rather than a practice-based mission was, they believed, the only way to win genuine converts. The methodological discussion of a practical mission versus a literary mission grew into a full-blown personal conflict between the four missionaries stationed in Japan at the time. The missionaries Hans Haas and Emil Schiller argued the one side, Martin Ostwald and Georg Würfel the other, and by 1908, the bad atmosphere between the two sides culminated in an extraordinary conference in which the Mission Board of the AEPM back in Germany declared:

> In a letter from December, Schiller writes that he does not see any possibility of working on with Ostwald and Würfel; the two do not even exchange greetings with Haas anymore. The only possible way to regain peace in our society is to terminate their contracts.[45]

Both Ostwald and Würfel were subsequently expelled from the AEPM in the same year in which their criticism was published.[46] While the majority of the Board members remained in favor of the educational mission projects, their numbers with regard to conversions continued to be rather small.[47] But, as has been said earlier, there may have been more pragmatic reasons for the strong emphasis on keeping the schools running: they continuously provided the mission journals with stories of success. These, again, were indispensable for the economic support which they attracted in the form of donations. And, naturally, donations were vitally important for the running of the mission society.[48]

As can be seen from this short analysis, it would be a mischaracterization of the educational projects of the AEPM to claim that the agendas related to the mission schools served as a unifying objective. Some elements within AEPM leadership and their core supporters upheld one agenda, articulated their motives accordingly, and played a leading role in organizing and running the schools. Yet there was discord and incoherence of vision even among the missionaries in Japan themselves, as was most evident in the case of the two missionaries Ostwald and Würfel. Most of the missionaries seemed to have pursued their own interests, which were not dictated by the Home Board. It is difficult to reconstruct fully how actors with different motives interacted with one another and maintained a certain kind of unity throughout the whole period, and it goes someway to explain why so many of the educational projects of the AEPM had to close down. As an *obiter dictum*, this short investigation into the missionaries' schools also serves as a reminder that while the missionaries are often portrayed in literature as a unified group comprehensively supporting a clear set of ideas, they were not so in reality. Here they proved to be a frictional group of individuals who, although sharing specific religious beliefs and norms, differed on many issues and not seldom would disagree on the transformations of policies into practice. As a result, the absence of a clear structure generated highly unstable schooling projects that were undermined by internal disputes, lack of initiative, and as we will see, external challenges.

External Challenges

Of the external challenges faced by the AEPM's educational projects, the main ones were, as mentioned, presented by the Japanese government. Since the first introduction of Catholicism by the Jesuits to Japan in the sixteenth century, Christianity had, in Japanese society, been regarded as an invasive religion.[49] Therefore, like most foreign mission societies, the Swiss-German missionaries were met with great resistance and general mistrust, sometimes with violent consequences. From the start of the 1890s, this mistrust extended to their mission schools. The mission journals cannot be read uncritically due to their one-sided reports, but in general they provide an interesting point of view into the violent and hostile attitudes that existed towards the Christian societies in

Japan at the time. In 1892, the AEPM published in their periodical the ZMR Karl Heinrich Rittter's report of the Christian landscape after the assassination attempt on the Russian heir in Tokyo. The so-called Ōtsu incident (Ōtsu jiken 大津事件) was a failed assassination attempt on Nicholas Alexandrovich (later Emperor Nicholas II of Russia) which occurred on April 29, 1891. In the report titled "After the failed assassination attempt on the Russian Heir" (*Nach dem Attentat auf dem russischen Thronfolger*), Ritter reported how the failed attempt by a local policeman to assassinate the Russian successor to the throne had subsequently led to several violent persecutions of foreign Christians and missionaries. The story suggested that the hostility was rooted in national chauvinism, which expressed itself in "irrational, misguided, and often ill-considered actions towards Christians."[50]

The persecution of non-Japanese Christians, such as portrayed by Ritter, depicted the Japanese people's overall unfriendly attitude towards Christianity in the late nineteenth century. Regarding the Swiss German mission schools, none of the incidents appear to have been devastating. Still, they were written about and published as reports in the missionary journals. Many were incidents of small protests similar to the one experienced by Auguste Dierks above. How many of the details might be truth or fiction is difficult to judge. Yet, the missionary literature supports the existence of the Swiss and German missionaries' conviction that the "Japanese hated Christianity."[51] In the reports, the missionaries' sympathies lay unambiguously on the Christian side. What seems to be indisputable, however, is that the mission schools and their personnel were subjected to a growing mistrust by the Japanese public. In 1890, for example, Wilfried Spinner mentioned that Aoki Shūzō had received death threats.[52] Harassment of Christians had become widespread in Japan. In 1900, the missionary Emil Schiller painted this general hostile picture of the situation:

> In a small-town north of Tokyo, the houses of Greek Christians were attacked and some of the residents were dragged through the streets. In Nagoya, a thriving commercial and industrial city west of Tokyo with

200,000 inhabitants, the Buddhist priests have so far succeeded to stir the hatred of the masses and to prevent public lecture meetings by the missionaries. In the latest attempt, a missionary was injured by stones thrown by the masses. In some schools, especially in those training teachers and cadets, Christian students are bullied by their classmates and forced to resign.[53]

The simple fact that these men and their families were Christians may have been reason enough for some Japanese groups to attack them. The fact that many Christians were teachers working at the mission schools is likely to have exacerbated the situation. There was, it appears, a general resentment among various parts of Japanese society towards the missionaries' activities in Japan, especially their plans to educate Japanese youth. In 1891, missionary Otto Schmiedel reported the incident of a baptized Japanese Christian member of the AEPM who was afraid to confess his religion because of the consequences his family might be subjected to by local Buddhist sects who warned against the Christians:

> One day a Japanese student came to me highly alarmed. He told of a friend from his youth who had become a Christian in Tokyo and had returned home to preach the gospel with enthusiasm. Immediately after his arrival, Buddhists attacked him, and the inhabitants of his native city punished his family by forcing his father to abandon his medical practice. The student was now afraid that the same would happen to him and his family.[54]

As this quote by Schmiedel indicates, being Christian in Japan in the 1890s was by no means safe and it did not matter whether the Christians were foreigners or Japanese. Preaching and openly declaring one's faith could not only endanger oneself, but also one's family.[55] Buddhist sects were disapproving of Christian influence in society in general, but they were, as has been pointed out by Japanese historian Tanigawa Yukata, particularly concerned about Christian involvement in the education of the youth.[56] The Buddhists therefore set out to lead an anti-Christian campaign discouraging the Japanese to join Christian communities. The campaign must have been successful, at least based on the report of female missionary Auguste Diercks in the ZMR. In 1893, she wrote that the missionaries had to work twice as much just to keep up the number of their communities. And the Japanese church community "hardly won over any new souls to Christianity anymore."[57]

Japanese bigotry and hostility aimed at mission schools has to my knowledge not yet been studied in any detail, but the missionary literature suggests that the AEPM's experiences matched those of other Christian missions and denominations. Roberta Wollons mentions interruptions in and hostility towards mission kindergartens in the Tokyo of Meiji era Japan.[58] Ishii Noriko, in her survey of the American missionaries in Kobe, in fact notes opposition from both Christians and non-Christians to the opening of a Christian girls' school in the 1870s.[59] And Anna Johnston states that the London Missionary Society in general met an "intense native resistance to European forms of education" in the second half of the nineteenth century.[60] Thus, the hostility and resentment on the part of Buddhist priests directed at mission schools in the Swiss-German mission field reflects a larger social battle that took place in Japan at the time. The hostilities reveal that education was a seriously "contested arena," one reaching beyond the usually stressed binary antagonisms of the European missionaries and the indigenous religious elites. This time, the battle included the more common strata of Japanese society as well.[61]

It cannot be stressed enough that the hostilities towards Christianity shown especially by the indigenous religions were directed at anyone who even in the most general way showed an interest in Christianity, affecting far more people than just the foreign Christians and their Japanese Christian converts.[62] Sometimes violence was used, and at other times different tactics were applied. A Japanese national who decided to convert to Christianity could not do this without fearing severe consequences to his or her self or even the family's public and social life. Missionary Johannes Witte, for example, writes about a young Japanese girl who had converted to Christianity, and at the same time, lost contact with her family:

> A young Japanese girl had, for her baptism, chosen to put on her best dress. Paper flowers sparkled from her shiny black hair. Her narrow face was pale. It was obvious to see that she was deeply grateful and moved; now she was a real Christian, and now she was glad. It had not been easy for her to be baptized. Her parents had allowed it, but they lived far away. She lived with her old aunt who hated Christianity. The aunt had told her: "if you get baptized, I will make sure that much evil will harm you" But the young Japanese girl was not afraid; God was with her, so she left her family. She has been chased out of the house by her aunt, and no one from her family wishes to talk to her anymore. Look how brave you have to be if you want to become a Christian in Japan. They [the Japanese Christians] really love God above all things, such is God's will.[63]

The report from missionary Witte, while rather one-sided and obviously manipulated for the Swiss and German readers, portrays the cultural context of the Japanese Christians very well. In the Japanese cultural context, approaching and accepting Christianity was often seen as a sign of insubordination and disobedience towards your family. The fear with regards to Christianity thus existed not only among the religious groups but was also conspicuous in all layers of Japanese society as well as deep into the family.

It is difficult to say what the main reason for the hostile response by the indigenous religions was, but it seems clear that missionaries' influence on the Japanese youth, in the eyes of many Buddhist institutions, offered an impending threat to the social order; and a threatened social order meant a threat to their privileged position. Scholars have argued that conversion can be an effective tool for cultural critique.[64] As religious scholar Isomae Jun'ichi and others have implied: Christian conversions in Japan were used by young students to demonstrate "their discontent with the profane measures" of the modern state.[65] As was the case with many, the Christian converts may have deliberately used their conversion either as a mode of political contestation or as a medium to enhance their position within the rapidly changing social hierarchy of late Meiji Japan.

It is in this context that we need to see the indigenous religions' persecution of the Christian schools and their students. These were only harassed because they were the concrete proof of Christian intrusion. In other words, Christians and their schools became the arena of larger sociopolitical battles about power in which newly evolving groups of elites fought for their promotion over others who sought to deny them that claim.

Ultimately, there was a more comprehensive factor that made the Christians and their schools such a disputed issue in Japan: the essential character of education itself. As the historian of education Paula Fass has noted, education is an area in which "each society tries to protect its own identity."[66] There is an undeniable truth in this, as it is through the results of education that a society reproduces itself. The Japanese youth were educated to take their predetermined seats within the "social hierarchy," which formed the foundation of future economic and social relations.[67] The Japanese government of the 1890s was fully aware of this fact and made the institution of schools a national battleground for the protection of Japanese identity. As discussed earlier, the AEPM sought to transfer Christianity into Japanese society with the help of education precisely because they judged the Japanese youth to be more impressionable to new Christian ideas. And, because the missionaries did not acknowledge the Japanese government's desire for educational autonomy, their continuous emphasis on Christian education was consequently highly disputed.

Competition for cultural power

It would seem that resentment towards the missionaries and their Christian schools, their teachers, students, and potential converts developed as it did because of the relative weakness of the AEPM's position in Japanese society. While the missionaries, in some situations, were able to offer help and support to intimidated individuals, this was more the exception than the norm. More often than not, the missionaries had no simple way to prevent or avoid actions against them or their Christian community members. When, for example, the house of a Christian Orthodox was set on fire and the local authorities did not interfere, the Christian groups and their converts could not necessarily rely on the help of the local Japanese. German missionary Adolf Wendt perfectly describes the situation of the missionaries as he tells of an incident in a town of Kyoto prefecture where a group of young Japanese was harassing him and his wife:

> Now many of you think, "Why didn't the missionary get angry?" Had he scolded them, then the young kids would have turned away.... but we cannot get angry; as foreigners we attract the hatred of the people even though we do not want that.[68]

As can be seen, Christian groups were not particularly welcome in the 1890s and 1900s, and their potential to interfere with the social structures of the Japanese people was remarkably limited. When the missionaries moved outside their "normal" mission zones to come face to face with the locals, they were often, as in the case of Adolf Wendt, met with distrust and dislike. Eugene Irshick has come to the same conclusion. In his study *Dialogue and History* (1994), he questions the actual knowledge and cultural identity generated in the missionary projects of the nineteenth century as he points to the inconsistency of the Western cultural influence: "There were large areas", he writes, "where authority was altogether lacking or uncertain." Compared to other mission fields in Asia at the time, the missionaries in Japan had to accept that in crucial spheres of Japanese society, "local governments exercised greater dominance than did the Western powers."[69] The absence of an obvious and dominant Western presence had a bearing on the field of education in which the missionaries sought to establish themselves. For the missionaries, a strong Japanese government represented the most powerful antagonistic section of the society.

The opposition towards the Christian missionaries by the Japanese society can be argued to have been grounded on fear: the fear of losing power and control over their own social identity. The hostility from some groups in Japan was a means to counter this fear. This proposition is supported by historian Irwin Scheiner's argument that the Japanese people in the nineteenth century interpreted the work of the Western missionaries as symbolizing a risk against social stability in Japan. Even more so, he asserts, the missionaries were, through their work, "dramatically altering local configurations of domination."[70] The Swiss and German missionaries certainly aspired to change the social settings of Japan, but their attempts to do so through the mission schools were often unsuccessful. At some localities and for limited periods of time—like at the Shinkyō Shingakkō and to some degree the Armenschule in the Hongō community—the missionaries did manage to create relatively controlled, if not necessarily hegemonic environments, but generally this was not the case. Instead, their assumed authority as educators was highly challenged, their educational projects were opened and closed, the Christian education harassed. Thus, falling short of the necessary alliances with the indigenous religions and national elites, the missionaries occupied a peripheral place in Japanese society.

Theoretical analyses of the history of missionary projects in many parts of the world more often than not have crossed paths with colonial frameworks of power that encompassed everything in the socio-economic landscape.[71] The Japanese mission field of the AEPM, however, proves different. Though not officially representing a colonial power—geographically and politically Japan had never been colonized—the missionaries have often been seen as representatives of the same kind of colonial framework. In the above literature about missionaries' projects, hostilities and conflicts seldom threatened the domination of the missionaries' power. On the contrary, they helped to strengthen it, as even the resilience and the ability to withstand them was based upon colonial rationalities.[72]

Still, with regard to Japan, such an interpretation may first unrealistically overemphasize the authority and power of the missionaries' role as agents in the wrangling for cultural dominance, and second may misjudge the ability of the Japanese or other indigenous people to either reject, creatively adapt, or even transform Christian ideas for their own purposes.

Examining the central ideas offered by Jean and John Comaroff, who state that missionaries with great success transferred "a coherent, rationalizing, globalizing system that taught one universal truth", Elizabeth Elbourne has astutely questioned "the capacity of Christianity to convey as effectively as it would have liked a message of unifying orthodoxy, or indeed the overall ability of missionaries to accomplish their objectives."[73] The external challenges that the Swiss-German missionaries faced in their attempts to teach Christian values in their schools in Japan support Elbourne's skepticism. Not only, as shown in this chapter, were the mission schools of the AEPM weak, they were also unable to effectively sustain themselves vis-à-vis the Japanese society. This had specific consequences for their ability to successfully run Christian schools in Japan.

Lack of attractiviness

The missionaries' internal conflicts and external challenges from various groups within Japanese society remain some of the central explanations for the lack of success of the Christian schools and institutions of the AEPM's mission throughout the 1890s and early 1900s. Another, perhaps even more significant cause will have to be added: the general hesitation of common Japanese to join the missionary community and schools.

While the missionaries in their published journals painted a joyful and untroubled picture—parents happily sending their children to the kindergartens and mission schools, students on their own initiative asking for guidance and teachings—it bore no resemblance to the truth.[74] The fact was, as explored in the previous chapter, that the Swiss-German missionaries and their Japanese teachers usually were uncapable of attracting and sustaining a high number of students in most of their schools.[75]

When it came to the discussion regarding low school attendance, the missionaries blamed it on external events, not their own flaws. Naturally, they were motivated to portray their engagement in Japan as important, and themselves as indispensable for reaching the mission's goals. And in "News from our Mission in Japan," a subsection of the mission journal ZMR, they never came even close to considering themselves as part of any problem. There they presented a variety of explanations for the Japanese motivation to stay away from their Christian schools. The governmental policy of the period, as we saw above, was blamed the most, as it decreased the autonomy of the Christian schools. At other times, the criticism would be directed at the nature of the Japanese people. Sometimes, so the missionaries declared, Japanese parents were absurdly afraid of them. Scornful of their superstitious and emotionally driven fears, missionaries described incidents where mothers had withdrawn their children due to the fear of misfortune.[76] Other missionaries, like the female missionary Agnes Heydenreich, who worked in the Hongō community in Tokyo, argued that Japanese people were either indifferent or outright hostile towards the offered education.[77] In a newsletter to the ZMR, she commented that some Japanese parents even feared that "their children would learn too much Christianity."[78]

It seems more likely that in their reluctance to join the Christian schools in the 1890s and 1900s, the Japanese were motivated especially by two factors: by an uncertainty about the benefit of a Christian education versus a public education, and by a suspiciousness and unease about the influence that the missionaries and their Japanese Christian employees would exert on them. Because, whether deliberately or not, the overall refutation was also a rejection of the missionaries' efforts in placing themselves in a position of moral and spiritual authority.

Indeed, what the missionaries understood as an "indifference" by the Japanese might have been a cautious form of resistance.

With their Christian schooling projects, the Swiss-German missionaries sought to challenge the Japanese government's authority. They cheered when their students showed any type of rebelliousness towards Japanese customs and norms, which they considered depraved and outdated. Wilfried Spinner, for example, wrote in his accounts about his work among young Japanese students:

> I believe it would be a pleasure for you readers to see my Japanese followers, who regularly come to me and embarrass themselves to tell me their feelings.... the young people do not seem to tire in coming here to hear something else than the outdated morality of their venerable Kōshi (Confucius).[79]

What he expresses is the missionaries' high expectation and confidence in the young Japanese to renounce Japanese customs and norms. Getting students to tread a different path, one leading away from their family's authority, inspired missionary hope and optimism. Only then would the Japanese people, in a distant future, become a Christian nation. As concluded by Ondina González, missionaries were often determined to educate students of indigenous Christian households to become different from their parents.[80] This intention was also present among the missionaries of the AEPM in Japan. The missionary Max Christlieb recounted in the 1890s that once the students had studied with him for a certain period of time, their Japanese families would demand that they to drop out of the school and join a public school or university instead. In his article, "Young Samurai" (*Junger Samurai*), he focused attention on this problem in *Das Missionsblatt*:

> Japanese who grow up in their old environment and are hardened by the old ways do not gain the gospel as easily as the youth, who still have a receptive heart. If one were able to win these young men over to Christianity, they could ideally, after a series of years, return home, take prestigious and influential positions, and hopefully continue their work within their Christian circles. Unfortunately, however, many of them,

after returning home, also return to their old heathen ways influenced by their heathen surroundings or the faith of their families.[81]

In other words, the missionaries hoped for more than merely teaching Christianity to the Japanese. By changing their spiritual beliefs, they intended to cultivate a new set of "modern" ideas in their students. They wanted to provide a different social imagination, but like Christlieb shows, the results fell short of what was hoped for and they were often disappointed.

There exists evidence that the Japanese deliberately and openly resisted the missionaries in this regard. Roberta Wollons has described how families took their girls away from school because they were taught to sing Christian songs.[82] In other cases, Japanese parents explicitly sought to avoid the evangelizing facets of the mission school. A critic of the AEPM pointed out "Nothing comes of the schools. The people are only interested in enlightenment and non-spiritual help."[83] The majority of the Japanese people, in other words, simply did not seem interested in having their youth converted to Christianity.

The message that the missionaries took home was unmistakable: a clear repudiation of their attempts to exert religious influence over the Japanese youth. Yet, while the Japanese youth were indifferent to a real Christian education, many were interested in receiving an education from a Western school. However, they did not expect to be conditioned by the missionaries in such a way that they would no longer share their families' worldview, nor respect their moral and spiritual authority.

This, once more, points to the weak nature of the missionaries' power in the Japanese mission field. As representatives of a religious institution, rather than of a nation state, the missionaries did not possess the political muscle and political support to force their Japanese students into compliance. They had to rely on their ability of persuasion, which was inadequate.[84] Their attraction of converts was ineffective and unsuccessful, which impeded their efforts to transfer German Christian worldviews to Japan. By staying away from the mission schools, the Japanese resisted the missionaries' aspiration for control.

Summing up the reasons for the failure of the educational projects of the AEPM

The considerable variety of mission schools and educationally inspired projects established in the Swiss-German mission field during the 1880s, 1890s, and 1900s clearly indicates a profound desire among the missionaries of the AEPM to educate the Japanese youth. But since the missionaries' approach to their mission schools was anything but systematic, logical, and consistent, they were unstable, disordered, and chaotic institutions. Instead of being a story of unprecedented educational triumph, they tell one of disappointments, and this chapter has endeavored to identify the reasons for that.

First of all, much of the school's failing was of the missionaries' own making. They disagreed habitually: on whether precedence should be given to the schools, about who should teach what, about what subjects should be taught under which conditions. They failed to communicate and implement a consistent policy with regard to the education of Japanese children and youth. As a result, the educational projects of the AEPM perennially suffered from a lack of funds.

The source of their challenged can also be traced to the resistance they met from numerous Japanese groups. As the Japanese government's interest in education grew, the missionaries' educational projects became a place of heightened scrutiny and controversy. Therefore, a second reason for their failure was their difficulty in gaining local approval, as the missionaries' schooling projects were increasingly taken by many Japanese as a threat to the Japanese government's social and moral authority. Articles and newsletters published in the missionary journals indicate that local nationalist groups attacked converts or were in other ways hostile towards the Christian schools. They feared that the schools would stimulate rebelliousness against the Japanese state.

Third, there was a general hesitancy among the Japanese to enter mission schools, often only doing so only sporadically or for a short period of time to obtain foreign language skills. The Christian schools also lacked recognition and authorization from the state, rendering them meaningless as steppingstones for further education. Another reason may well have been the fear of a Buddhist or Shinto-National persecution, or at least religious discrimination. Within a wider societal context and in the micro units of families, one central question was repeatedly asked, "Is it desirable to let the missionaries and Japanese Christian teachers become established as the moral and religious authorities over the Japanese youth?" Most Japanese families answered: "No."

The purpose of this analysis has not been to dismiss the AEPM's and its educational projects' significance, but to refine our understanding of the highly contested environment that surrounded them. Many Japanese rejected the schools, not because they disagreed with their teaching or even refuted the religious character of the schools, but because the mission schools represented an external force that challenged the local social hegemony. Many in Japan were not interested in defying the social order and establishing disintegrating communities. There was a significant gap between the missionaries' agenda and what the people in Japan hoped the missionaries would do for them, and the latter is much more important for understanding why so many of the AEPM educational projects failed.

For this study of the AEPM in Japan, the mission school's failure is significant in that it shows how missionaries during this time carried little authority outside their confined Through the study of the educational projects of the AEPM, we see that the government of Meiji Japan begin to take education seriously, making the space an arena with multilayered agendas.

The transfer of liberal Christian ideas through educational efforts had not taken off as the missionaries anticipated. The next chapter will analyze how the framework of Liberal Christianity took a decidedly important turn in the late nineteenth and early twentieth centuries, when directed directly at the students of the Shinkyō Shingakkō.

4

A Class Dispute

Japanese Students and the Discordant Nature of Religious Conversion

One morning in Tokyo in 1887, during the second period at the German Studies Society School or Doitsugaku Kyōkai Gakkō 獨逸學協會學校, a young Christian student named Minami Hajime 三並 良 was involved in an incident that he recalled fifty years later.[1] Like his fellow classmates, he enjoyed school, but despised that second period, botany, taught by the Japanese teacher Fujiyama; They simply couldn't understand the grades their teacher gave them. Their dissatisfaction increased during a particular session, and in the end, their frustrations escalated into an open dispute, first with the teacher and eventually with the whole school administration. As the conflict unraveled, the students agreed to remained united as they feared somebody might be unfairly punished.[2] However, Minami and his classmate Mukō Gunji 向軍治 were singled out by the school administration as having been particularly radical in their protest and were swiftly expelled from the school.[3]

The protest was one of the most intriguing events that took place within the educational activities of the AEPM during the 1880s and 1890s. We know from primary sources that missionary Wilfried Spinner, since arriving in Japan in 1885, had planned to build a theological academy for Japanese students to train Christian pastors in Liberal Christianity.[4] The exclusion of Minami and Mukō from Doitsugaku

Kyōkai Gakkō allowed Spinner to bring the two promising Japanese students under his own wing where he could cultivate them as he wished.[5] Scholars within mission literature typically highlight the significance of mission schools as the only place where missionaries were able to operate as "conscious agents of cultural transformation."[6] Furthermore, scholars also characterize the mission schools as "total institutions" through which students attained social knowledge that challenged the existing discourse.[7] The Home Board of the AEPM supported Spinner's decision of adopting Minami and Mukō and saw his work in establishing a theological academy as a "great starting point for the Mission," which had the potential to allow Spinner to instigate changes on a larger social scale in the Japanese society.

Here, the phenomenon of mission education will be approached from a new analytical angle. Rather than considering the mission schools to be manifestations of social transformations, as was done in the previous chapter, this chapter will examine the personal encounter of the missionaries and their students. An analysis of relevant sources reveals that the missionaries' work with the Japanese students evolved into a seemingly contradictory state. On the one side, the missionaries devoted a great amount of resources and time in educating their Japanese subjects into what they perceived to be true Christians—mainly so that they themselves could be seen as the "legitimization and authority for the development of Japanese Christianity."[8] On the other side, they repeatedly expressed deep doubts about their students' potential to become the type of Christians they envisioned, a sentiment they never wavered from. Even students who had been converted were considered "insufficient" Christians and given less respect. These extraneous complaints are often glossed over when examining the history of mission schools, but they are critical to understanding the nature of the Swiss and German mission field. Furthermore, the doubt and mistrust towards Christian converts expressed by the Swiss and German missionaries were by no means unique; rather, they exhibited the same bias of other missionaries in Japan at the time. Irwin Scheiner, has for example, shown how both missionaries and Japanese converts began to doubt the sincerity of the efforts of their fellow Christian coverts as Japan developed during the Meiji period.[9]

These observations problematize the prevailing characterization, within mission literature, of mission schools as being structured entities who had great control of their surroundings. They also allow for a more nuanced understanding of the relationship between the actors involved in and around the mission schools. Furthermore, the characterization of mission schools as purely a place of "social transformation" has led to a somewhat exaggerated interpretation of the missionaries' position in the mission field. Rather, this chapter looks at the juxtaposition of these intense missionary efforts at educating "real Christians" and the continuous missionary doubts related to these efforts. I argue, the constant tension between both proved fruitful in that it helped create a notion amongst the missionaries that the Japanese students were in constant need for help and guidance, a notion that was supported by a discourse on cultural superiority, continuously legitimized the missionaries' educational engagements in Japan.[10] On the other hand, it at the same time distanced the missionaries from their Japanese converts. In other words, similar to the contemporaneous examples provided in the preceding chapter, the missionaries maintained their strong and unerring belief in the education of the Japanese youth and pursued it despite their other doubts.

Reaching the youth: the driving force of the missionaries

Apart from their intrinsic Christian responsibility of bringing "the gospel of Jesus Christ, the joyous message of redemption [and] the love and grace of God" to the Japanese,"[11] Wilfried Spinner had numerous practical reasons to involve the AEPM in the education of the Japanese youth.[12] The main reason may have been the great resistance he and other missionaries met in their efforts to reach non-Christian adults. For even if Japanese adults wanted to convert to Christianity, their reasoning was sometimes, as the following text will demonstrate, peculiar:

> I encountered a Japanese man who wanted to become a Christian. Due to a bad translator, he had heard a missionary preach: "Convert to Christianity and you will be released from your debts." He requested [from me]: "Convert me and pay off my debts!" The following day, a lawyer—who seemed to oppose Christianity—approached me and offered to be active for Christianity, if he were paid. He acted surprised that I rejected him, since he honestly intended to offer his services.[13]

Spinner's encounter with the Japanese adults was often a complicated one because these—in the missionaries' eyes—often seemed more concerned with improving their economic situation than redeeming their soul. In the missionary publications, Japanese adults were more often than not portrayed as materialistic and shallow, seeking only material riches. In another account, this time published in the missionary journal ZMR, Spinner conveys how their yearning for riches led to rather curious creations like the religious doctrine of *haikinshū* 拝金宗 (the worship of almighty money):

> It calls itself *haikinshū* or *shōbai no susume*, the religion that worships money. Its Japanese founder is sadly unknown, but is absolutely serious about his devotion to mammon, which he rationally justifies as follows: "Nothing is more necessary than money. Nothing reigns more supreme in the world than money. It is placed above any divine and human authority; t therefore deserves religious admiration, yes almost worship.[14]

Spinner interpreted such articulations of—in his view—indifferent, contradictory, and almost ridiculous attitudes towards materialism as a sign of mammonism and corrupt heathenism, and of an amorality within the Japanese society which was corrupting the nature of Japanese adults. He suggested that pure greed and materialistic longing had to be a part of their native religions and culture, "I fear that the old religions still have a huge influence. Our mission is to find a way to cut down the mountains of idolatry and to fill out the deep holes of religious materialism in Japan," he wrote in *Das Missionsblatt* in 1886.[15] To him and other mission contemporaries, the resistance of Japanese adults towards Christianity was an indication of a "moral decay" among the indigenous religions. Hence, he and the AEPM preferred to Christianize the youth of Japan rather than its adults. This was partly based on a deep distrust of the religious nature of Japanese adults and of Japanese religious customs. This distrust was not just confined to missionary compounds but was also widespread amongst Western settlers in Japan during the Meiji era. A conversation with a German trader in Yokohama led Spinner to describe the Japanese people as a "race with ineradicable falsity," as he wrote down in his diary:

> Intellectually the Japanese are very highly developed, otherwise not. The total Christianizing of the nation cannot happen fast enough; the superstition is rooted so deeply in these people, and they can easily be led to fanaticism by the Buddhist priesthood or the opposition parties.[16]

Siding with other missionaries, Spinner claimed that in order for the Japanese people to become real Christians, they had to relinquish their former beliefs, dispositions, and social practices. Like for many other evangelical missions in the late nineteenth and early twentieth centuries, a genuine conversion entailed a complete transformation of the mind and soul.[17] Wilfried Spinner repeatedly voiced his concerns about the authenticity of adult conversions in letters to the mission board in Switzerland and in his own diary. In fact, he noted: "True belief, as one finds it among Christians, cannot be expected in the Japanese people."[18]

Throughout the whole investigated period, the missionaries comprehended the difficulties of drawing adults to the church and in attaining what they considered to be true conversions and decided to turn their attention to the Japanese youth almost right from the start. The youth seemed to be more profitable recipients of God's word: "If one wins over the youth... one should be hopeful that they continue to serve Christianity," German missionary Max Christlieb, for example, would write in *Das Missionsblatt* 1898.[19]

Through their educational projects, the missionaries tried to influence the youth before their Japanese character was fully developed. The sooner the AEPM could start their guidance of how individuals were to live as enlightened Christians, the better the chances that a conversion would be permanent, that the immoral deterioration through the "Japanese religious materialism" would be removed, and that the proper ideological system could be cultivated.[20] A meeting with a Japanese student prompted the German missionary Carl Munzinger, for example, to write in the mission journal ZMR:

> The individual wholesomeness in which the actual power of the teaching of Christ exists throughout eternity must firstly be emphasized in Japan. He who in agony and suffering personally has felt the help of Christ; he will forever be deeply connected to him.[21]

Similarly, Missionary Emil Schiller added, "he who has the youth—he has the future" in an essay in "Missionsarbeit unter der Jugend" from 1922.[22] Clearly, to the AEPM, educating the youth of Japan was a future-oriented strategy and a natural stage in guaranteeing the progression of a flourishing and appropriately organized Japanese liberal Christian society. Establishing schools to expose young Japanese students to Christianity was the first step in the Christianization of Japan—this belief did not waver at any point of the AEPM's engagement in Japan.[23] A statement by Albrecht Lipsius, a board member of the AEPM, in *Das Missionsblatt* 1898, supports this interpretation:

> Our messengers have already shown the way towards Christ by drawing quite a few celestial citizens to the Kingdom of Heaven. Shouldn't we be allowed to celebrate the success of our schools in Tokyo whose purpose it is to educate the Japanese youth in Christianity so that they themselves will be able to carry the Gospel to their people.[24]

Lipsius and the missionaries profoundly believed that the Christianization of the Japanese youth would cause Japan to become a Christian nation in the future. But at the same time, this belief did not obliterate the reality at the schools and the daily frustrations over their students' failure in progressing towards what the missionaries described as a "true" Christian subjectivity.

Cultivating true Christian cubjects: the Shinkyō Shingakkō

There is no way of knowing what was in Minami Hajime and Mukō Gunji's minds and how they might have felt when they started their protest during the botany class at the Doitsugaku Kyōkai Gakkō in 1887; whether they felt excited about their youth protest against the school, whether it was founded on a feeling of injustice, even whether they anticipated or feared a possibly harsh response and reaction by the school. It may have just been a wish to get away from a dull and repetitious life at the German school.

What we do know with certainty, however, is that Minami Hajime and his fellow "rebel" Mukō Gunji were just two of four-hundred-and-seventy students attending the classes at the Doitsugaku Kyōkai Gakkō in 1887.[25] The school had been established in 1881 modeled after the Prussian model by a group of progressive and reform-friendly Japanese. Among them were the Japanese Christians Hirata Tōsuke 平田東助 (1849–1925), Katō Hiroyuki 加藤弘之 (1836–1916), the Japanese philosopher Nishi Amane 西周 (1829–1897), and the AEPM supporter Aoki Shūzō. What all these men had in common was the fact that they had all spent several years in Germany studying abroad.

The school had originally been given the name *Verein für deutsche Wissenschaften* or Doitsugaku Kyōkai 獨逸學協會 but changed its name to Doitsugaku Kyōkai Gakkō in 1883.[26]

The students at the Doitsugaku Kyōkai Gakkō were given lessons in German, Japanese, and English. They were taught in general history, Japanese history, ethics (incl. religion and bible teaching), arithmetic, geometry, geography, and botany—the subject taught when the students initiated the dispute.[27] The students were taught to write and speak German and occasionally, drawing and music lessons were added. The curriculum was composed of elements typical of a German and particularly Christian education, but also contained subjects obligatory in schools in Japan, such as Japanese and classical Chinese.

As was the case for many foreign schools in Japan at the time, much of the funding came from private individuals or groups of donors. The German Empire, however, was also interested in sponsoring an education that would "transfer German values and norms" to Japanese subjects. From 1883 to 1891, around 100,000 yen was donated from various German state institutions.[28] Transferring German values and norms was a central element of most education program run or supported by the AEPM at the time, and the transfer of norms was incorporated into efforts to foster and develop a particular set of Christian competences in the young students' minds. From the perspective of the AEPM, the financial support from the German Empire was seen as a helpful contribution to their project of cultivating "individual Christian identities" (*christliche Persönlichkeiten*).[29]

Scholars and postcolonial theorists have often stated that the protestant missionaries' striving to educate and improve non-Christian people was representative of a particular modern phenomenon of colonial power. By attempting to shape their students according to the norms and practices of their own Christian background, the missionaries practiced what Homi Bhabha has described as "a desire for a reformed, recognizable other."[30] In the course of the transformation of colonialism, the particular nature of it shifted from what Michel Foucault has identified as "pre-modern" colonialization—a system reliant on intimidation and physical domination—to a seemingly softer "modern" form of colonialism, which was dependent on a multifarious system of development, education, and welfare, etc.[31] According to the missiologist David Scott, the modern expression of missionary power was less about punishing and disciplining than about regulating and determining certain forms of behavior and activities.[32] Drawing upon such a distinction between old and new colonial mentalities, anthropologist Nicholas Thomas has argued that:

> The distinct character of nineteenth century Protestant missionary activity is itself an index of this change that seeks a kind of wilful inner rebirth on the part of the colonialized individual, ... a relation of hegemony and compliance rather than brute dominance.[33]

The mission methods of the Swiss-German missionaries in many ways symbolize this change within the nineteenth century missionary movement. The general goal, so the Home Board stated in a protocol letter from 1886, was to "spread Christianity with maximum impact... to the individuals and the nation as a whole," by combining it with the objective of establishing a system of liberal social reforms in education and welfare.[34] To accomplish this, Spinner believed that his students had to be placed in a different schooling system than that of Doitsugaku Kyōkai Gakkō. To Spinner it was important to provide a schooling regime which could enable the development of liberal Christian identities. He stated that he did not aim at a complete remake of the Japanese character, but rather, through a Christian education, intended to intervene with the Japanese way of thinking and thereby develop "strong Christian subjects" for the mission. Spinner expressed his ideas of forming a theological academy for the training of theologians in a letter back to Mission Director Ernst Buss in 1887. Here, he states that:

> In this school a specific type of student must be educated. He has, on the one hand, to live up to the demands of the common Japanese educational system, but, at the same time, meet the levels of our philosophical and theological education in Germany as well. This is necessary in order to equip the student with sufficient legitimacy and authority to allow him to develop a Japanese-Christianity.[35]

Spinner wished to combine Japanese culture and education with the newest developments of German Liberal Christianity in a schooling regime, thereby prompting a specific Christian individuality and liberal character in his students. To him, the education of his Japanese subjects had to be understood in a broader sense: as a process which could affect how an individual understands the world and behaves in it, as one which could become the leader of the Japanese Christian community both inside and outside of the formal walls of the mission institution. The shaping of strong Christian individuals, however, could not only be formed in the schools but needed to also be informed by the experience and support of the Christian community. This was particularly reflected in a letter to the Home Board in 1886:

> Real religious education, the development of Christian personalities, can neither be acquired by a single person, nor by the school. The individual student depends on a congregation, so that he stays within the experience of religious warmth in the union of like-minded people and eventually becomes an active upholder and advocate of his own belief.[36]

Spinner recognized that it was not possible to educate Christian subjects within the school environment of the Doitsugaku Kyōkai Gakkō alone. Instead, he encouraged the coexistence and cooperation of the schools and the local Christian community, where the "equal minded" would be able to receive its "religious warmth."[37]

Through his own teaching at Doitsugaku Kyōkai Gakkō, Spinner had known the two Japanese students, Minami and Mukō, from as early as 1885 and must have been aware of their frustrations at the school.[38] Minami especially had given Spinner the impression of having a "pure Johannes nature," referring to John, the author of the Book of Revelation.[39]

Interestingly, he seemed to have supported the young protestors' course against the school at which he himself taught, and hints towards the reason in his diary. Once Minami and Mukō had been expelled, he noted that he wished "to educate Minami and Mukō for a theological profession."[40] That Spinner wanted to educate the two young Japanese for a theological profession, and not simply (like other missions) train them as their own local community clergy was based on determined reasoning. As a missionary of the AEPM, Spinner felt obligated to cultivate liberal Christian individuals in Japan. But his teaching at the Doitsugaku Kyōkai Gakkō had made him realize that a few hours of teaching during the week would not allow for a complete transformation of his students into liberal Christian individuals. To achieve this, he was undoubtedly in urgent need of employees who would understand his liberal thoughts and attitude, and who could successfully transcribe these into Japanese. In other words, he needed the assistance of local employees who, in the long run, would be able to exercise a theological profession in the community and perform the services of a qualified pastor. Therefore, with the expulsion of Minami and Mukō from the school, Spinner had suddenly been presented with two qualified and obvious candidates.

At the time, there already existed a number of theological schools in Japan that educated Christian workers; in the year 1887, we know of fourteen such schools with a total of 260 students.[41] But Spinner wanted to establish a new theology based on German liberal Christian values, and therefore was in need of assistants trained in this theology, should his mission have any chance to succeed. So, when the two young intellectually outstanding and promising Christians, Minami and Mukō, started the school protest at the Doitsugaku Kyōkai Gakkō in September 1887, it gave Spinner the impetus to establish a new school, the Shinkyō Shingakkō.[42]

Spinner quit his job as a teacher of ethics and history at Doitsugaku Kyōkai Gakkō in October 1887, and in the same month began to privately teach Minami and Mukō for four hours daily in "preparatory disciplines of theology." This establishment of Shinkyō Shingakkō coincided with the arrival of Otto Schmiedel (the second missionary sent to Japan by the AEPM) in Tokyo on October 13. Schmiedel, soon after having been introduced to the Japanese community in Hongō, placed a note on the bulletin board of the newly established Christian community center which read: "Theological, philosophical, and philological (Latin and Greek) lessons for theology students: every morning from 8:00–12:00."[43] From Spinner we know that the two missionaries shared the teaching load at the school. Spinner took care of the lessons

Missionary Otto Schmiedel(left), Carl Munzinger (center), Max Christlieb (right) with their students in front of Shinkyō Shingakkō, Tokyo, 1895.
Photo: Zentralarchiv der Ev. Kirche der Pfalz..

in philosophy and church history, while Schmiedel taught the students in Latin, Greek, and Exegesis. Dr. Otto Hering, an experienced *ōyatoi* and language teacher at Doitsugaku Kyōkai Gakkō, voluntarily gave classes in German.[44]

Spinner was well aware of the overall political environment in which he established his school. He was in no position to impose on his two students, Minami and Mukō, the full evangelical program of study he would have wished for. Instead, he had to make sure that the students of Shinkyō Shingakkō were educated within a curriculum that lived up to the expectations of Japanese society. Only then could the education of Japanese Christians, according to him, be legitimized. The students entered an educational program designed in three stages which was published in a newsletter written by Ernst Buss in the mission journal ZMR in 1888:

Stage I propaedeutic basic course of two semesters.
Stage II two semesters of basic theological studies. Completion of stage I and II with a concluding examination in philosophy.
Stage III Advanced theological studies of four semesters with a final theological exam.[45]

With the establishment of the Shinkyō Shingakkō, the educational frame for shaping strong liberal Christian personalities was in place. As the program indicates, the education of Japanese students was a long-term and future-oriented strategy based on the idea that a prosperous and properly organized Japanese Christian society could be accomplished through the strict educational regime of the Japanese youth. The aspiring objectives of the school, however, had a constraining effect on the number of students. During Spinner's time in Japan, the school constantly lacked students. The total sum of all student educated over the course of Spinner's time at the school (1889–1892) was eight.[46] This low number, however, can be considered as advantageous in that it allowed for an optimal monitoring and an intensive exertion of influence on the students, but language difficulties and cultural differences resulted in obstacles marring the daily contact. As the next section will show, these daily obstacles were not seen by the missionaries as arising from communicational and cultural misunderstandings, but as springing from "inherent flaws" in their Japanese students.

Expectations versus reality

The importance of the Shinkyō Shingakkō for the mission work of the AEPM in Japan was once more pointed out in a pamphlet titled "Our mission work in East Asia" (*Unser Missionswerk in Ostasien*), which the AEPM published after Spinner's return to Europe. In the pamphlet, Spinner vigorously stated that the school was "the future of our whole Mission."[47] But however important the school might have been for the future of the AEPM, the success of both the Shinkyō Shingakkō and the Mission depended on financial support. Already in 1889, the second year of the school, financial problems relating to the running of the school were mentioned in *Das Missionsblatt*. Here Spinner voiced his concerns of the financial situation of the school:

> Until now, it has sadly been the custom in Japan that most of those students who study theology are poor and without means. Whoever possesses wealth visits the university. The large American theological schools in Tokyo and Kyoto have huge grants at their disposal, so that the monthly income of a theologian is on average three Yen (ten Mark). What can we do in light of this?[48]

Even from its earliest beginnings, the school was constantly in need of money. Facing competition from various economically better positioned rivals, its complaints about financial hardship entered the mission publications more often than did the potential success story it was intended to be. In another article in *Das Missionsblatt* in 1891, Spinner once again continued his plea for financial help, this time highlighting the unacceptable living situations of both missionaries and students:

> Until now the missionaries have to house the penniless students, mostly coming from far away regions, in their own accommodations. In the long run this is not sustainable with growing numbers [of students].[49]

Admission for the students entering the Shinkyō Shingakkō was free, and therefore a constant supply of money needed to be secured. Such money came from local supporters, such as the schoolteacher Otto Hering, or from the Home Board back in Europe. But because the AEPM, in contrast to Doitsugaku Kyōkai Gakkō, was a small and independent mission enterprise, its finances were constantly lacking, which in consequence often led to the loss of students. One of the first students, Mukō Gunji, who had joined the school together with Minami Hajime, had to stop attending the school already in 1889 because he was financially unable to support sick family members. A year later, the third student of the school, Maruyama Michikazu, dropped out for similar reasons.

Besides the financial limitations, the gap between the missionaries' expectations and the reality in the mission field proved to be a major problem. In the mission journal ZMR from 1892, Schmiedel described the main tasks at the Shinkyō Shingakkō:

> Here we want to teach German theology and science to the Japanese youth. The ambition is both to achieve intellectual enlightenment as well as the cultivation of a spiritual and moral life [of the Japanese].[50]

In its simplicity Schmiedel's formulation represented the Mission's goals as proposed by Ernst Buss in his founding essay "Programm" written for the inaugural founding asseMBly of the AEPM in Weimar in 1885. Here Buss had stated that the mission did "not want to spread Christian culture, but Christian religion."[51] In other words, the missionaries expected more than only running a school in which they could educate theologians. By establishing and running other institutions such as Sunday schools and kindergartens, they wanted to ensure that the future students of the theological school, in addition to their theological studies, were also taught how to actively "spread the Christian faith" among the Japanese people.[52]

Already the first students at the Shinkyō Shingakkō made Spinner familiar with the discrepancy of his own expectations of the school and the reality at hand. He had two disquieting experiences. One with Mukō Gunji—the second student of the school—the other with Otatsume, a Japanese scholarship holder, who had studied abroad in Heidelberg, Germany for three years and by the Home Board in Switzerland was considered to be Spinner's future assistant for his work within the Japanese Church community in Hongō.[53]

A look into Spinner's diary tells us how much Spinner had wanted to build a special working relationship with Mukō. Particularly the fact that Spinner chose him and not Minami—the more promising candidate—as his companion during his trip to Kyoto in the summer of 1888 supports this. At the same time, he had chosen him as his language teacher for the Mission School. Yet, the several weeks they spent together in Kyoto did not lead to the deepening of their relationship that Spinner had hoped for. Even the meeting between Spinner and Mukō's blind mother towards the end of their visit in Kyoto did not further the bond.[54] While in Kyoto, Spinner had felt let down by Mukō who, according to Spinner, proved to be a "unreliable" language teacher. There is no explanation in the diary about what happened between the two, but we know that Spinner left Mukō for the rest of his stay and instead used the two students Kayama Shinjirō and Nakarai Sunao as his interpreters. The disappointment about Mukō's behavior in light of his expectations was expressed in Spinner's diary: "There is not much to be done with Mukō and his laziness."[55] Mukō, as mentioned above, would later have to drop out of the school and find a job to support his poor family. He subsequently became a German language teacher at a foster school before obtaining a position as a language teacher at the Methodist university Kwansai Gakuin in Osaka.[56] Yet, Spinner's disappointment with Mukō's work efforts highlights the cultural differences between the two. The fact that Mukō's "laziness" alone could cause such disappointment in Spinner is an indication of how a specific German-national and religious discourse manifested itself in the missionary work and influenced the way the missionaries perceived their Japanese subjects.

One way to overcome these cultural differences would perhaps have been to allow the Japanese students to be taught German culture and language in Germany or Switzerland in order to become exposed to the ideas of Liberal Christianity there. They then could have brought these ideas home and introduced them to Japan upon their return. Spinner considered this himself while he established the Shinkyō Shingakkō. In his diary, he had originally considered employees to be allowed to attend a two-year university course in Germany after their graduation from the Academy: "For our students, a two-year course at a German university should be a prospect when completing their studies."[57] In this way, the students could fully concentrate on their studies and at the same time be fully introduced to the liberal Protestant background behind the activities of the Swiss-German Mission, previously only known to them from Japan. Spinner expected that once they returned, such a stay would not only minimize the cultural differences between him and his students, but also give them further motivation and a fresh impetus for their continued work for the Mission in Japan.

These well-meaning intentions, however, were soon forgotten upon the return of the Japanese student Otatsume from one of these prolonged stays in Germany in 1889. Upon returning to Japan, after a three-year study program in Germany, he only participated—as a dismayed Spinner writes—for "a few hours" in the teaching at the school. The returnee did not even prove able "to keep up with our two other students."[58] Already within days, Spinner concluded: "For this young and supercilious person, no help is really possible."[59] Spinner's experience with Otatsume —this young Japanese Christian who during his three years in Germany had been held up as a beacon of hope and who had been recommended to Spinner by other members of the AEPM as his future employee—led Spinner to reach a devastating verdict about these "Japanese abroad." Japanese students, like Otatsume, seem to Spinner to:

> guided by the sense of adventure, without attracting sufficient means or support, playfully move to foreign countries to acquire whatever skill that will make them great men at home. In the foreign countries they turn to Christian clubs or personalities and seek all kinds of promises for financial and, above all, moral support.[60]

Spinner almost categorically felt that, due to a lack of structure in their education in Germany, the returning students were of no use as preachers or helpers to the Mission. The disillusioning experience with Otatsume caused Spinner to conclude that "Japanese theologians must first be educated in the country [Japan] and may eventually be sent abroad only after they end their studies."[61]

It is not known whether Spinner ever recommended a prolonged stay abroad to a trained Japanese theologian. Or whether he feared a negative influence from the liberal Europeans on the young Christians from Japan, or from the high living standard in Europe, which he regarded as hazardous. But as correct as Spinner's warning and cautioning against sending unqualified young Japanese (with their exaggerated opinions of themselves) to Europe may have ultimately been, he did misjudge the situation at one point. The young Otatsume's competence and aptitude may have been overestimated in Germany, but in his defense, it has to be said that Spinner may simply have been expecting too much. A liberal Christian identity is not formed within only three years, as was Spinner's expectation and subsequent source of disappointment.

The questions remain: Why would Spinner judge his young Japanese students so uncompromisingly without reflecting on their social background first? Had his impaired awareness and obliviousness to Japanese social customs and culture not been the actual cause for the disappointments he experienced with, for example, Mukō? After all, Spinner must have known of the difficult family situation Mukō found himself in, and after three years in Japan, he must have been well aware of the important role the family played for young Japanese. Why couldn't he appreciate Mukō taking care of and supporting his poor family? If Spinner felt disappointed about his students quitting their studies at the Shinkyō Shingakkō—thereby lessening the Mission's potential to recruit educated staff—the cause for this most probably has to be found in Spinner himself, or in the nature of the Shinkyō Shingakkō.

Both Mukō's and Otatsume's examples point to another interesting fact about the nature of the mission schools. The Japanese students were caught in a Christian training regime that only functioned while being based on the fundamental difference between the German and the Japanese. In the missionaries' eyes, the young Japanese students became objects of transformation. To improve on undesirable dispositions and to "cultivate" particular Christian characteristics in them were elements of an educational regime that would often lead to disappointments. Though, as the next section shows, these disappointments often proved to be positive constructs.

Constant disappointments: a positive construct?

We saw above that Wilfried Spinner was convinced that young Japanese were both more impressionable and easier to work with than adults. This did not mean that converting young students was accomplished effortlessly: "This institution [Shinkyō Shingakkō] still causes us much distress and trouble, brought about partly by the destructive tendencies of the students. I do not believe that arrogance and ambition make them suitable as theologians," he stated in his diary in 1888.[62] Yet, just a little later he added something to the contrary: "I just realized... how skillfully they work; the natural talents seem to be there, it is only necessary to make sure that they are not weakened but properly developed."[63] These two quotes demonstrate the ambivalence that marked the Swiss and German missionaries' impression of their Japanese students. The belief that nurture—education and cultivation—beats nature in the making of a human being was the underlying belief at the root of the missionaries' engagement in educative work, and indeed of all missionary work of the AEPM. It formed the core of their identity and of all they did. However different and culturally removed the Japanese youth were from them, this could be overcome with a proper Christian education.

Some of their texts maintain this notion. The German teacher and member of the AEPM church community Georg Michaelis, for example, wrote about the pleasure he enjoyed in the daily work with the students, which often concealed and even outweighed the problems. The Japanese students were good students, they worked well, they did all the work they were assigned, but their unusual interpretation of politeness concerned him. The students seemed to have a different socio-ethical background in which telling a lie rather than the truth did not matter as long as it was done in a well-mannered way. Politeness was paramount. Thus, some observations about his students and Japanese culture were appended to his initial praise:

> When my students missed a lecture, they had to give a written apology. One type of apology was that the student couldn't attend because he was *skoshi byoki*, a little sick. The second explained that a *tomodachi*, a friend, had come. The third, obviously the noblest one, said that the grandmother had died. In the beginning, I really believed that the old lady had died, and offered my sincere condolences. But it became conspicuously odd when the very same student not only lost the second grandmother as well, which at least may have been possible, but when this happened a third and even a fourth time. Obviously, this caused me to become utterly upset, and I believed it to be a brazen untruthfulness. But I later learned that all these excuses were nothing else than procedures of politeness, and that the excuse of the grandmother having died counted as the politest excuse, as if the student had wanted to say: "Your lecture is to me of such an importance, that the only reason I'd ever miss it would be the death of a close relative." … The Japanese doesn't feel obliged to give the real reason for his absence from the lecture.[64]

Michaelis' experience with his Japanese students is a good example of the socio-ethical misunderstandings the foreign teachers would often encounter. The Japanese students had been raised and educated at home in a social environment guarded by solid traditional Japanese ethics. Based on these, none of the students seemed to have found it necessary to expose the real reasons for their absence to a foreign teacher. The Swiss and German missionaries—Spinner and his colleagues—were, and remained, strangers. They were outsiders who indeed were useful and beneficial, delivering the training for the young Japanese, but remained irrelevant to their personal and social life. As disheartening as this often was, they lacked the necessary knowledge and awareness of the social rules in order to properly read and comprehend local situations. Instead, they found reconciliation by intellectually embedding their experience in a wider religious context:-

> The only tangible feature of Shintoism is a cultivated ritual; in the case of Confucianism, it is a personal and political ethic, and also Buddhism is no teaching of God, but instead an apotheosizing of humans and of ideas. Therefore, a cold scepticism is the predominating approach amongst my students with whom I try to talk about God and divine matters. They face the questions of ethics and morals, and consider them as a matter of fact as seen in natural science. It is in this way they also meet Christianity, with this very same cold and guarded attitude.[65]

After having reconciled themselves to their situation in such a way, the missionaries still maintained an optimism. They asserted that the two major flaws they had identified in their Japanese students, namely the inclination to lie with great skill and audacity, and their tendency not to reflect deeply on religious subjects, were not permanent. Even if these shortcomings, as Spinner reminded, were deeply rooted in the Japanese mentality, they were learnt and could therefore be unlearnt. They could be eliminated if the students would receive the right and properly, methodically implemented education. Spinner criticized the other mission stations in not doing so and warned, "As long as the incoherent prattle-worship (*Plappergebet*) of *Namu Omidha butsu* [Amida Buddha] is heard in Japan, Christianity has not fulfilled its duty among these seeking and highly-intellectual people."[66]

According to Spinner, the fundamental differences between Europeans and Japanese were expressed in their social behavior. But an even more distinguishing feature of the Japanese was, to him, the inability of the Japanese to thoroughly understand religious and moral ideas. Just as impressed as the missionaries were by their students' willingness to learn European theories and ideas, equally strongly did they doubt their students' ability and aptitude to learn them properly.[67] This teacher-student relationship shaped an almost dialectical process within the missionary himself, which served as recognizing the missionaries' work in Japan with (unceasing) approval, also at home. In

1891, for example, Spinner encouraged his Swiss and German readers to contribute to the boundless and ever-ready willingness of the Japanese to learn by sending books and money in order to build a library at the missionary station in Tokyo.[68]

Differences between Japanese and Europeans related to moral, social, and intellectual characteristics. Missionary Otto Schmiedel noted how Japanese students were just as interested in Bible lessons as their European counterparts, hence their moral behavior could be just as good.[69] Yet, there existed significant differences; in fact, in Japan everything seemed to be quite "the opposite" to Germany.[70] On their capability of independent thinking, Carl Munzinger observed in 1898 in his book *Die Japanern*: "What they shall learn by heart comes easily to them. By contrast, what they shall think about and learn by way of their intellect is more difficult to them."[71] In a programmatic approach, he listed the dissimilarities in several categories, describing the nature of the Japanese student as follows:

> In its form, his [the Japanese] thinking is impulsive and intermittent. He does not like to immerse himself into something in great detail, he detests the quiet and continuous study of a subject. He willingly adopts the results but avoids the effort of thinking. The German professors are always complaining how difficult it is to teach the Japanese students the terms and notions of development—this basis of all scientific understanding. Yet, why is it so difficult? Because the way of Japanese thinking is not that of a calm and slow development of thought, not that of a clear and logical conclusion, but an impulsive way, one of sudden realizations. Japanese knowledge is less of a logical nature than of being guided by premonitions.[72]

Munzinger clearly interpreted the differences in a bigoted vein. The failures were inherent in the "nature of the Japanese." In contrast to a European student endowed with positively valued qualities, like intellectual superiority and independence, the Japanese student was notoriously effete and had distinctly negative traits such as deceptiveness. The ostensible dishonesty of the Japanese supported the notion of them being "snake-people" (*Schlangenmenschen*).[73] Munzinger noted: "The Japanese people are known as Schlangenmenschen in the sense of being excellent acrobats and jugglers, but they are also Schlangenmenschen in the figurative sense, pliable and malleable, a people lacking a fixed straight backbone."[74] Adding a further layer to the already established image of the inept Japanese student, he later predicted that, ultimately, they would not succeed in developing the kind of religious conscience he and other missionaries hoped for:

> According to his nature, the Japanese student is inclined to adopt something from all areas, a bit here and a bit there, and finally he has gathered much knowledge, but it is not digested, not processed to an organic whole.[75]

Thus, Christianity, according to Carl Munzinger, had no chance of becoming the exclusive religion of the Japanese people.

In his description of the Japanese, Munzinger, like many other European observers, consistently inflated racial/national and religious classifications. He divided "European Christians" and "Japanese Christians" into two sharply contrasting groups, indicating that the religious categorization was inflected by ideas of race, culture, and national character. He did this to a degree at which he abstained from describing already baptized Japanese simply as what they were, namely "Christians," but always called them "Japanese Christians", as if to further emphasize his point. To be an "actual" Christian was to be a European; to be a Japanese Christian was a step in the right direction, but never quite an accomplishment on the same level.

While there existed a discourse of religious tolerance towards other Christian denominations in the missionaries' writings, they still mostly emphasized the difference between the two categories of Christians. Therefore it is not just, as Karen Sánchez-Eppler has suggested, that the missionaries, through conversions, conveyed a message of universality, while in reality "fully support[ed] an ethnocentric cultural imperialism."[76] The Swiss and German missionaries in Japan, in fact, worked on the assumption that not only religion and education, but also inherent determinants—nature beside culture—counted as factors of the moral and social make-up of an individual or group. The missionaries' writings about their Japanese students thus, in other words, often reflected their utilization of an ethnocentric agenda.

Insufficient christians

The small number of converted Japanese students enrolled at Shinkyō Shingakkō and the small overall local membership could by some be considered as proof of the early missionaries' failure to convert the youth of Japan in the 1880s and early 1890s. The Swiss and German missionaries certainly voiced more frustrations than delight about the individual improvements of the AEPM's Japanese members, which could perhaps be expected in light of what they ideally wanted to achieve. The transformation of their Japanese subjects into independently thinking, righteous, and self-reflective liberal Christians, with an appropriate understanding of personal faith, was destined to remain insufficient. The young Japanese students of the AEPM were, in the words of the recognized father of postcolonial studies, Homi Bhabha, "almost the same but not quite."[77] They could, in contrast to their German colleagues, never be counted as truly Christian and thus were "not quite" good enough for the missionaries' ambitions. This mental blueprint inherent in the missionaries' schools therefore contained the reason for its own failure, but nonetheless, it added its part to the working of Western cultural superiority as a whole.

Generally, the students at the Shinkyō Shingakkō were subservient: they did what the missionaries expected of them; they acted and performed as they were supposed to, and they tolerated the high turnover of missionaries in charge. Though, whether they were compliant or not—particularly when they were not—they were subjected to the missionaries' discourse about differences. The slightest behavioral deviation from the Christian norms and values was taken as an affirmation that they indeed were different from the West. In the end, the Japanese students reached a situation in which they disputed other, opposing values. The missionaries may have had their reasons for feeling frustrated, but among the Japanese students, being compliant to their teachers' hopes and expectations ensued a dissatisfaction and frustration as well. According to the missionaries, they couldn't become "true" Christians, but on another level, the one more important to them, they at least could affect the course of their own Christian life, be it "truly" Christian or not.

The genre of mission literature was significantly permeated by the Mission's need of securing support and funding for their projects. Consequently, the missionaries had an incentive to widely elaborate in their texts on what they perceived as problematic and troublesome features of the Japanese society. Immoral behavior and religious superstition were brought to the fore, more admirable qualities or commonalities between Japanese and Swiss-German values and interests generally left out. Whether intended or not, these negative written evaluations of the Japanese helped to frame education as a domain for legitimate interference.

However, not all missionary texts of this period are homogeneously critical and judgmental of the Japanese's moral nature and learning abilities. Metaphorical descriptions about the universality of the "innocence of the child" were occasionally invoked as being a praiseworthy element in Japanese parenting.[78] And in some texts, like the ones explored above, the Japanese students were praised for being good, interested, and willing to learn.[79] On the other hand, non-Christian Japanese were regularly characterized as being morally inadequate or strange, as too superstitious, as occasionally even harmful to themselves, with a penchant for sinful talk and behavior, but also for an irrational fear guiding their behavior in relation to their heathen religion.[80] In this, a person's religious roots and belonging was indirectly linked to the racial or national disposition of the Japanese.

Even Japanese Christians often disappointed the missionaries with their lack of religious and intellectual aptitude, as well as falling short in Christian morals.[81] Spinner pleaded to avoid an overall change to the Japanese character, but rather to guide them towards Christianity by teaching a way of thinking based on Christian ethics:

> Our purpose is to train a staff of Japanese theological forces who have fully and wholly understood us. Once they possess the fullness of our hearts, have been scientifically, but above all morally and religiously trained to be missionaries with the genius similar to the apostles, with holy, gripping seriousness, then we need not to worry about their destiny and the fate of those who will be influenced by them and directed to us.[82]

The Swiss and German missionaries were not alone in their condemnation of the Japanese religious and moral habits. British, American, and Canadian missionaries in nineteenth century Japan also perceived the indigenous religions as particularly detrimental in their impact on the Japanese youth's moral development.[83] Such attitudes towards the Japanese moral code of behavior would color a central part of the missionaries' daily work and legitimized their interventions to ensure a more moral and righteous conduct, ideally by developing and encouraging their specific liberal Christian identity. Social factors such as nationality and religious identity played a role in the missionaries' personal encounters with their Japanese students. Similarly, hidden ethnocentric discourse and practice dominated the missionaries' interaction with them.

Conclusion

The story of the two Japanese students Minami and Mukō is in many ways symptomatic of the underlying difficulties of the Swiss-German schooling projects in the 1880s and 1890s. Their experience within the schools reflected the Swiss-German missionaries' intention to transfer social knowledge and to inculcate in their students a particular way—a Christian way—of thinking, behaving, and feeling. They aimed to eliminate all undesirable traits while nurturing those which they deemed desirable. They worked at delegitimizing "heathen" dispositions, instincts, and expectations in their Japanese students and replacing those "negative" attributes with positive, respectable Christian ones. To achieve this, the missionaries' employed methods that were as simple as verbal encouragement, to developing specific schooling curriculum based on Christian ethics. Yet ultimately, the racial and national views of that permeated missionary ideology also led to their projects falling short of their ambitious goals.

Just as the students were subjected missionary teachings that shifted and changed without consideration, the teachings themselves were under the influence of changing attitudes of the global sphere. In the late nineteenth century, the missionaries' aspirations were affected by a world that was becoming increasingly nationalistic and racially motivated, both at home in Europe and in Japan. Instead of helping to smooth over differences and foster assimilation, their mission their projects in Japan enforced and often strengthened the idea that differences defined by race, nationality, and religion were legitimate. The Shinkyō Shingakkō in Tokyo was just one of many places in which social and cultural dissimilarities between Europeans and Japanese, and the dichotomy between heathen and Christian, or moral and amoral, were highlighted, fostered and then used to fit the agenda of the Mission.

The missionaries' view of their students was two-sided; on the one side they self-assuredly maintained that just by being born Japanese, a student could never become a *true* Christian. Many Japanese Christians never being allowed to succeed were thus deemed failures, which again proved the missionaries' initial convictions: an exemplar of self-fulfilling fallacy. And, naturally, any insufficiency on the side of their Japanese students was proof of the continual need for missionaries in Japan, thus legitimizing their presence.

On the other side, though, they saw the students as tools to accomplish their larger aspiration to make Japan a nation of God. Day by day, ever so slightly, through work with their students in defiant battle against Japanese culture, they could and would change Japan. The students would be these agents of change that would allow them to build a Christian culture based on the already existing truths; if not now, then in the future.

In some way, the missionaries' encounter with Japanese students seems logically unacceptable and self-contradictory: here the missionaries made great investments both in money and in time in order to convert and educate their Japanese students, yet at the same time, they had deep doubts as to whether the Japanese students could even become truly independent Christians.

5

Christian Magazines and the Identification of Religion in Meiji Japan

In January 1886, in the first issue of the mission journal *Zeitschrift für Missionskunde und Religionswissenschaft* (henceforth ZMR), German scholar Karl Heinrich Ritter published an article titled "Die Religiöse Entwicklung des Japanischen Volkes im Zusammenhange mit seinen politischen Wandlungen" (The Religious Development of the Japanese People in Relation to its Political Changes). In the article, Ritter commented on the Japanese people, their political transformation towards a modern state inspired by the West, and the moral status of the indigenous religions. Given the general Christian nature of the mission journal, his conclusion was not surprising: In order to achieve the transformation into a modern state similar to that of any Western power, there had to be major changes in the religious landscape of Japan. Ritter made this clear in a statement that he ended with a question: "the imminent downfall of Buddhism, as well as Shintō, is only a matter time; Japan needs a new [religion]. What will the new religion be?" Not unexpectedly his answer was: "Christianity!"[1]

In this chapter, I will examine the missionaries' understanding of Japanese religions, by focusing on the mission journal ZMR and its identification of religions in Meiji Japan. ZMR was the first European mission journal to publish articles on Japanese religions to a German-reading audience and it contributed significantly to the understanding of Buddhism and Shintoism in Europe at the time. Still, mission journals and Christian magazines from the Meiji period remain today a relatively unexplored research field as scholars often tend to disregard this literature due to its Christian inflection. In fact, the value of religious journals and newspapers during the Meiji period have only recently been brought to our attention by scholars from Kyoto University, Bukkyō University and Ryūkoku University through their co-conducted research on Buddhist magazines *Meiji nenkan bukkyō kankei shinbunzatsushi mokuroku* 明治年間仏教関係新聞雑誌目録 (Yearbook of Meiji Buddhist-related Newspapers and Journals).[2] Yet, while the study of Buddhist magazines is slowly emerging, the study of Christian journals from the Meiji period has so far been ignored.[3] This is regrettable, as Christian Meiji journals flourished in the intellectual world around this period and achieved a wide readership. A common characteristic of these journals was that they would take a Christian position, like that of Liberal Christianity, and present it as if it were *the* religion of civilization and modernity. All magazines tried to juggle the tasks of propagating Evangelism while explaining and formulating their own particular response to the Japanese religions. In this vein, ZMR adopted a tolerant approach to Japanese religion and many of its publications embraced a comparative methodology, looking for similarities, and ultimately claiming the universal character of religion.

Japan's religions and their future became the central point of discussion in the ZMR. Besides competing for followers through their educational projects, the AEPM's missionaries also engaged in debates to discover and develop the religion that would most suit modern Japan—a task that they garnered considerable attention.[4] In other words, the competitive intellectual environment of late nineteenth century Japan led to a competition for the "fittest" religion which again permitted the appropriation of "religion" as a comparative tool to fit into a specific religious agenda.

Here, I examine in detail writings on Japanese religion written by Swiss and German missionaries' for the ZMR and offer an interpretation of the main rationales behind them. The ZMR was underpinned by a liberal Christian narrative, especially from the 1890s, where likeminded scholars like Max Müller, Adolf von Harnack, Otto Pfleiderer, Richard Lipsius, Heinrich Bassermann and Ernst Troeltsch just to name a few of the contributors, helped expand the scope of Liberal Christianity in the world. It also allowed contributors to reconcile their highly ethnocentric viewpoints with their international outlook by constructing a hierarchical yet mutually constitutive relationship between Christianity and the Japanese religions. Ernst Buss had originally created the ZMR with the purpose of contributing to "mission studies in its broadest sense,"[5] and it oscillated between being an abstract academic arena especially dedicated to the new science of

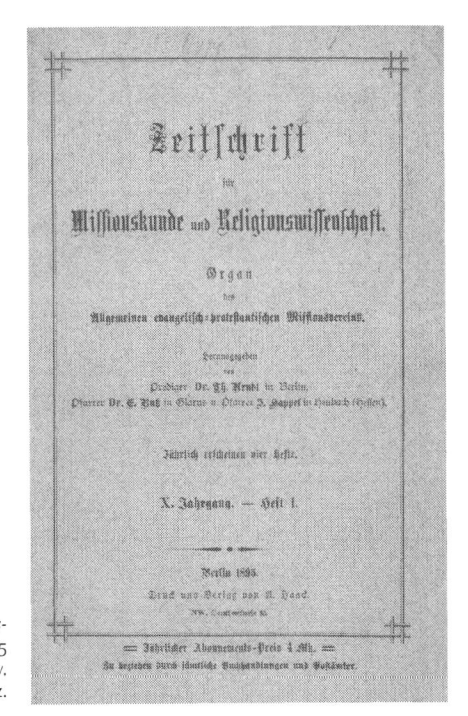

Cover page of *Zeitschrift für Missionskunde und Religionswissenscaft*, 1895
Photo: Zentralarchiv der Ev. Kirche der Pfalz.

religion and being a mouthpiece for missionary accomplishments. This two-sided character of the journal seems not to have been of any concern at the time: "What, truly, would religious studies be without the missionaries," wrote Max Müller, for example, in the ZMR, emphasizing its value and praising the important role of the missionaries for the new understanding of foreign religions.[6]

This chapter explores the conceptualization of the category "Japanese religions" as it was portrayed in the ZMR. A close examination of the contents highlights a self-contradictory character of the AEPM's approach to religion: On one side, the texts depicts a liberal Protestant "tolerant" attitude toward Japanese religions arguing for the existence of *Klänge von Wahrheit* or "sounds of truth" found in all religions, and thus consequently seeing non-Christian religions as potential sources for salvation. On the other side, the texts portray the missionaries' own cultural and ethnocentric agenda, arguing for Christianity as the absolute religion. Both arguments, in turn, will inform our examination of the ZMR's understanding of "Japanese religions" at the turn of the century.

Defining "japanese religion" in the ZMR

The phrase *Japanese religion* today functions as a scholarly category referring to a wide range of religious practices normally associated with the religions Shintō, Buddhism, and to a lesser degree, Confucianism and folk/new religions.[7] The use of *Japanese Religions* as a scholarly category, however, is as Jonathan Z Smith, Tomoko Masuzawa and Jason Ānanda Josephson have all repeatedly demonstrated not a Japanese "invention," but a historically conditioned category, which was consciously formulated to meet several agendas.[8] As has been proven repeatedly within the last decade, defining religion in Japan was a politically-charged project that extensively reclassified the inherited materials of Buddhism, Shintō, and Confucianism. All three traditions were radically changed in a way that has only recently begun to attract scholars' interests.

Scholars generally agree that *Japanese Religion* is a culturally specific category that took shape among Christian-influenced intellectuals and missionaries and spread both eastward and westward.[9] The spread of the category was gradual. *Japanese Religion* remained an intellectual word and did not spread to the wider population until the late 1910s.[10] This means that the formation of *Japanese religion* did not take place simultaneously in all parts of Japan and that the use of the concept of *Japanese religions* is best understood within the context of respective intellectuals (Meiji intellectuals and the missionaries).

Scholars have furthermore rightly contextualized the occurrences of the category *Japanese Religion* within the critical developments of the diplomatic and legal negotiations between America and the Tokugawa government in the late 1850s and early 1860s.[11] In the preceding years, the influx of Christian missionaries to Japan reached a historic high. Western styles and accoutrements became fashionable, and were a symbol of the drive towards "civilization and enlightenment" (*bunmei kaika* 文明開化). Knowledge of foreign languages and foreign experiences were seen as pathways to success, and caused texts such as Charles Darwin's *On the Origin of Species* (1859),[12] Herbert Spencer's *First Principles* (1862), and Friedrich Max Müller's *Introduction to the Science of Religion* (1873) to become very popular, and led to widespread discussions about the connection between science and religion, and—stretching even further—to far fetching theories about evolutionary developments within religions themselves.[13] The category of "Japanese religions" transpired in the midst of this epochal transition and facilitated the rise of religious comparison and categorization of what could be deemed "Western" and "Japanese" religions. Furthermore, scholars have recently emphasized how the European concept of "religion" expanded in part as a Christian universalization, but in so doing also "assimilated diverse cultural systems, which had little to do with religion's Christian formulations."[14]

All these developments were reflected in ZMR. One noticeable pattern in the Swiss and German missionaries' treatment of Japanese Religions in the ZMR, regardless of whether the evaluation is positive or negative, is that Japanese Religions were examined primarily through the lens of Christianity. While this approach helped to illuminate various aspects of Japanese religion, it also created a tendency to examine Japanese religions in terms of adverse qualities. As a result, many articles highlighted the flaws and idiosyncratic nature observable in Japanese religions as signs of denigration and underdevelopment. If Christianity was the universal embodiment of modern civilization, they stated, then this could not apply to the Japanese religious traditions like Buddhism and Shintō as well; they had to be something else. In their study of the Japanese religions, the missionaries themselves were forced to define and redefine their very own understanding of and relation to "religion." To them, "religion" became the fundamental aspect of human morality and ethical nature: "culture is impossible without religion," an author would write in the ZMR.[15]

In the ZMR, the German missionaries discussed the ethical systems of Shintō, Buddhism, and Confucianism as the foundation of the Japanese "Geistesleben" or spiritual life and compared them to Christian ethical practices they knew from home. These comparisons, however, did not mean that all four religions were regarded equally. Instead, they were measured and categorized differently.[16] Confucianism was described from the beginning as a moral philosophy, not a religion. It was contrasted—disparagingly—with contemporary currents of Western philosophy. The exclusion of Confucianism from the category of religions in the ZMR allowed the missionaries to relegate it to an outdated mode of thought—one that should be eliminated or at the very least be ignored.[17]

With Confucianism not being considered a religion worthy to a modern state, most of the publications in the ZMR discussed only the two religions, Shintō and Buddhism. Of these, Shintō was never taken seriously. Its beliefs and practices were considered superstitious, and it was by the authors of the ZMR repeatedly used as a clear example of the backwardness of Japan. Shintō, they claimed, had no future in any modern society. Only Buddhism, the missionaries concluded, was in possession of a genuine religious doctrine and hence could be deemed a completely articulated religion equipped for the modern world. It was seen as the one serious contender to challenge Christianity as the future religion of Japan. Hence it seemed only natural for the missionaries to engage in intensive studies of Buddhism to find its "seeds of truth" and then perhaps, as Heinrich Ahlers suggested in his article "Buddhismus und Christentum"(1887), enrich and expand these with Christian mission ideas. He wrote:

> Even the missionary idea [Missionsgedanke] suggests the question: What do we have to offer the non-Christian people? The personal belief that our religion belongs to the future, that it corresponds to the longing and desire of the human soul, and that it is the divine truth in its purest and most perfect form is not enough to impress people. The missionary idea calls for a fair judgement of the seeds of truth found in the religions of the non-Christian people, an emphasis on what can be offered as a supplement or can be added to their failing concepts.[18]

But even with expressing such good intentions of building their Christian mission on the "seeds of truth" found in Buddhism, other texts in the ZMR remained doubtful of the Japanese religions: Buddhism, these articles would argue, lacked a functional morality and— even more so—a functional idea of God. In other words, it failed to meet all the relevant criteria for what constituted a "good" religion.[19] In comparison to Christianity, Buddhism seemed neither perfect nor suited to being a ruling religion in any modern nation. Yet, it did contain elements of similarities that could be built upon in forming a Japanese Christian nation. In the 1880s, 1890s, and into the 1900s, the similarities between Christianity and Japan's cultural traditions were constantly being discussed in the publications of the ZMR. While comparative writings on Japanese Buddhism had the largest interest of the missionaries, the reseMBLances between Christian ethics and Confucian doctrine again gained some scholarly attention after the turn of the century. German scholars and Japanese Christians attempted to merge the two traditions in articles such as "Konfuzius und Christus nicht Feinde, sondern Freunde" (Confucius and Christ not Enemies, but Friends) (1903), and "Pfarrer Wilhelms Gespräche des Konfuzius" (Pastor Wilhelm's Discussion with Confucius) (1910).[20] In these, Confucianism was favorably viewed as being capable of assimilation into Christian faith because of its pseudo-theistic concept of God and its apparent rational moralism.[21]

Yet, all these efforts of combining Buddhism and Confucianism with Christian thought suffered from the absence of a clear and mutually agreed upon understanding of how the liberal Christian missionaries fully were to understand other Japanese religions. The missionaries tended to characterize Japanese religions as something spontaneous or instinctive explosions unfit for the modern world. In short, more attention was paid to examining what Japanese religions reflected rather than what Japanese religions was.

In the following, I pay close attention to the process through which the category of *Japanese religions* took shape within the mission discourse of the AEPM through a close reading of the mission journal ZMR. By taking this approach, it becomes clear to see how the missionaries' encounter with Japanese religion was influenced by their liberal Christian background. It also becomes evident that in many cases, the categorization of Japanese religions followed a predictable framework mirroring classic colonial classifying schemes such as universal cultural religions (like Christianity and Buddhism) and national religions (like Shintō). I will in the following attempt to highlight these aspects of the missionaries' writing on Japanese religion by looking into the writings of the two Swiss AEPM members Ernst Buss and Rudolf Rüetschi.

Ernst Buss's understanding of religion

The conceptualization of *Japanese Religions* in the ZMR outlined above serves as the basis for the portrayal of the missionaries' understanding of religion in general at the time. In looking at some of the essays published in the ZMR, it becomes evident that religion in the eyes of the missionaries was a universal concept and that Christianity enjoyed the status as the superior of them all. This attitude towards religion was both reflected in and influenced by the writings of Erns Buss. Ernst Buss, although mentioned in Chapter 1, remains one of the lesser-known figures in the nineteenth century mission and church history. Compared to his long life (1843–1928), his part in this history spans a relatively short period, but in defining "religion" in relationship to the nineteenth century mission movement, his writings significantly contributed to contemporary theological and ecclesiastical developments in his homeland Switzerland. Although his most famous book *Die christliche Mission, ihre principielle Berechtigung und praktische Durchführung* (1876) was examined in Chapter 1, it was in the publications of several editorial essays in the ZMR in which Buss first scrutinized his understanding of "religion" in relationship to modern culture.

Buss's understanding of missionary work, "religion," and its relationship to the modern world can easily be discerned especially in the opening editorial essay of the ZMR titled "Programm" from 1886. Here Buss stresses the obligation of the Church to serve as guardian of the people, qualifying religion as

> the hidden pulse of mankind. Rooted in the religious life lies the moral force and thereby the cultural ability to develop the spiritual and material welfare of men.[22]

Buss's understanding of "religion," is here closely linked to the underlying mythology centered around the myth of the Tower of Babel, a story from Genesis 11:1–9 which tells the story of an once existing unity of men. If a nation desires to become a "civilizational heaven,"

Cross under a Torii, A symbol for the Christianization of Japan, 1900-1910. Photo: Zentralarchiv der Ev. Kirche der Pfalz.

Buss stated, it should not neglect the truths of religion. Without the "beautiful characteristic nature" of religion, it would be impossible to carry out great projects or reap great benefits, as those achieved in the myth of the Tower of Babel. Religion, so argues Buss, forms the bedrock of human nature. By connecting religious experience to a universal phenomenon, Buss thus establishes a religious pluralism: all people have religious faith which originates from the same source! In this argument, Buss in many ways reflects the tolerant view of Schleiermacher in his *Reden* (Speeches). Still, while accepting the plurality of religion, Buss at the same time believed that this plurality of religious experiences could (and should) be measured. To him, religion defined the morality of culture and determined its potential for civilizational progress. Buss, in other words, sought to confirm the absoluteness of each particular religious tradition. He stated in the following section:

> It is a fact that Christianity not only denotes a higher level of religious development of humanity than other religions, but that it is the truth par excellence. That it is—although not in its current ecclesiastical forms—in its principles the absolute religion, the fulfillment and completion of all religious longing, and the hope of human hearts. It is the only religion capable of understanding all the healthy ways of faith and devotion existing among the various peoples and helping them to progress no matter their nationality or current development. Christianity is destined by God to become the universal religion of humanity.[23]

Christianity, according to Buss, is to be understood as the primordial religion that is set to become the "universal religion of humanity." In the same section of the essay, Buss continues his definition of religion and identifies what he deems as the worst types of "unworthy ideas" of the "old world", claiming that these represent a deterioration of religion as they do not allow "the essence of God, the feeling of piety, love, and seriousness to come forward and thus prevent the progression of conscience."[24] To Buss, the religious traditions of the old world seem to struggle with allowing the freedom for the individual's moral and cultural development. Buss accords Christianity as the singular leader in the world based on the identification of its historical accomplishments. To Buss, a religion should "lead not to darkness but to light," and according to Buss, only Christianity has so far throughout the human history proven capable of this. Reiterating this view, he writes in the following section of his essay:

> A religion that does justice to the demands of reason, conscience and mentality is the most powerful lever of morality, culture, and inner and outer well-being. It will allow the nation to progress. However, if the religious life fades, a nation will lose its vital nerve and every higher spiritual development will die out.[25]

While Buss revealed many of his own tolerant personal beliefs in his essay, by saying all religions were equal and suggesting that "all religions have to be understood in the context of the entire history of the religious evolution of man,"[26] he at the same time confirmed his Christian one-sidedness by demonstrating the superiority of his own religion. Although speaking in the language of ecumenical empathy, claiming to believe in the authenticity of experience and the deep unity of all religions with the aim of reaching world peace and prosperity, Buss at the same time advocated that missionaries should act as good parents and guide the ignorant away from false beliefs and toward the truth. Indeed, to Buss, the guidance towards progress—not faith—was itself the essence of the missionary's work. Once guided, he believed, people's culture and lives would reach what he termed a higher "*Geistesentwicklung*" —level of spiritual development. He argued that, "the fundamental principle of religion is to search for the truth by frustrating evil"[27] "Real religion," fundamentally for Buss, was created through the quest for and progress towards the truth, and rejection of any falsehood.

In the 1880s, all groups of German protestants who tried or wanted to be liberals developed, as German theologian Friedrich Wilhelm Graf has argued at a talk held in Kyoto in 2019, "models of thoughts which focused on the religious freedom of the individual."[28] To many liberal Christians, individual religious experience became the basis for the definition of truth. Buss also adopted this line of thought in his understanding of religion in his opening editorial essay of the ZMR. In a strict Kantian sense, Buss defined religion as a part of human nature that provides the primary system of guidance in the world.[29] Suffering, misery and anguish found among other cultures, he argued, were to be blamed on the failure of local religion's capacity in guiding it rightfully. As Buss stated:

> A poor education or a degeneration of a culture's religion is the greatest, if not the only, obstacle to spiritual progress and true human existence.[30]

Buss, like many religious scholars of the time, sought the roots of the absolute truth. A legalistic understanding of the content of religions was replaced by a focus on the religion's ability to allow for a religious experience to become a lived religion. In a non-confessional way, Buss sought to define the "essence of religion," as it had the ability, he stated, to "lead the people to a higher morality and culture."[31] His essay contended that insofar as a religion represents the will of the people and if a people's belief was lacking in morality and ethical principles, the culture itself would be reflective of this.[32] A good religion had to be committed to the enlightening of its people, and no religion did this more truthfully than Christianity. Using the essence concept, the particularities of each religious tradition could be shown to be in fundamental agreement with all the monotheistic religions. Still, Buss, like many German protestant liberals at the time, did not give up the claims for a practical cultural superiority of Christianity (or Protestantism) above other religions. While agreeing with Tiele that religion was a universal phenomenon finding various expressions in cultures throughout the world, Buss thus still believed that Christianity was superior to the rest.

In 1888, in Buss's second essay in the ZMR, "Neue Missionsbestrebungen" (New Aspirations for the Mission), he re-addressed the universalism of Christianity and the question of world religions, repeating the essential arguments of the first, but in a significantly different tone. The first article had spoken of a general "*Geistesentwicklung,*" or spiritual development among people and had praised Christianity for its moral superiority. This second article praised the virtues of Christianity also in relation to the peoples' cultural well-being and characterized the universalism of Christianity much more forcefully as something existing beyond cultural and national borders. And here, specifically, the missionaries were given the key role in freeing religion from any cultural resistance:

> The Missionary Society considers the mission in the non-Christian world to be an irrefutable duty of all Christendom, founded in the command and the promise of Jesus as well as in the divine destiny of Christianity, and therefore sets itself the task of participating in its part, that of salvation through Jesus Christ "the blessing of the Christian knowledge of God, Christian life and Christian human culture are increasingly becoming the common property of all peoples."[33]

Any nation desiring to become a "civilizational heaven", Buss argued, cannot disregard Christianity. "Christianity is and will be the one and only religion for mission, as it represents the truth and morality at its purest."[34] Though, in regard to the validity of religions other than Christianity his position was somewhat problematic. He did acknowledge their claims to the truth in principle—based on his assumption that all religious scriptures contained potential sources of salvation—but at the same time suggested that they should be appraised along the rules applied to Christianity. His book *Die christli-*

che Mission, ihre principielle Berechtigung und praktische Durchführung contained such a—consequently—paradoxical assessment of religions. The goal [of the mission enterprise] is to convert members of other religious confessions to Christianity, to convince them to give up and exchange their previous religion, and thereby lead them to a higher level of morality and inner bliss. It attempts to reach the highest possible number of people who still have no contact with Christianity, to achieve the greatest general dissemination, and ultimately to gain absolute power [*Alleinherrschaft*] over the whole world.[35]

The term "Alleinherrschaft," or "absolute power" is interesting in this context. Buss did not apply it as a political term or as a description of political dominance, nor in a negative sense. Instead, he used it to describe the truth and the moral power of Christianity. The "principielle Berechtigung," i.e the fundamental legitimization of the Christian mission, he concluded, lay in the universalism of Jesus Christ and the conception of a universal mission as it appeared in the early history of Christianity.

Buss's articles defining and outlining "religion" were some of the most influential commentaries on the subject in the ZMR. In addition to initiating a discourse on religion as being essential for human life, several of Buss's views on religion and missionizing stood out amongst the more mainstream theological interpretations of the late nineteenth century. His articles took an ethical perspective rather than a dogmatic approach in their aim to discover the most profound relationship between the world's people and God as a true revelation. While potentially placing all religions on the same footing, he claimed that Christianity morally echoed the highest point of humanity, and by maintaining its superiority to other religious systems, it ultimately could be fulfilled everywhere.

Many prominent contemporary theologians and intellectuals in the liberal circles agreed with Buss and were inspired by what he wrote. One of these was the liberal theologian Otto Pfleiderer (1839–1908). In his essay "Die Bedeutung der Religionsgeschichte in der Gegenwart" (The Significance of Religious History in the Present), published in the ZMR in 1906, he writes similar to Buss:

> Scientifically it is the age of the History of Religion, in which we are living..., not only the theologians, but also the profane historians, the philologists, and the ethnologists have increasingly focused on the studies of religions in the past decades. Everywhere one starts to understand that religion is not of minor importance for society, not a coincidental appendage for human life, but that it is salvation and the most dominant principle in the cultural history of mankind. And that the most conspicuous manifestations of differences in the development of the various cultures can only be understood in the context of their religion, which [when studied] allow us to look directly and most deeply into a people's soul.[36]

While Buss's articles instigated a modern discourse on the subject, his early writings in the ZMR influenced a whole generation of liberal Protestant theologians who focused on the ethical and moral entity of Christianity in relation to the mission project. His religious theories directly encouraged an emphasis to be placed on the relationship between the moral progression of men and God, which became the basis of many of the issues touched on by other authors in the ZMR during the following decades.

Albrecht Rudolf Rüetschi: The Comparative Study of Religion and Christianity

Buss's definition of religion successfully captured the *Zeitgeist* of the late nineteenth century and received immediate response. In 1887, just a year after Buss's "Programm," his fellow countryman, Swiss theologian Albrecht Rudolf Rüetschi (1820–1903), wrote the article "Die vergleichende Religionswissensschaft und das Christentum" (The Comparative Studies of Religion and Christianity) (1887). Rüetschi shared Buss's notion of religion being universal and significant for the improvement of humanity, but differed considerably in his focus. Whereas Buss very much discussed religion as incepted by faith and based on the faith he himself felt, Rüetschi adopted a more comparative approach. Engaging in a comparative study of the East Asian religions, he established a new system of categories to measure and compare the world religions.

Born into a teachers' family in the city of Bern, Rüetschi was by his own account destined to become a teacher of the people himself. In 1845, Rüetschi followed his father's advice and studied theology, first in Bern, then in Berlin, before being ordained in 1842 in Tübingen. At the age of twenty-five, he took up a post as pastor in Bern-Münster in the heart of the city. Here he actively engaged with liberal forces in Bern, participating, for example, in the welfare service of *Die Gesellschaft für Zimmerleute*, a group that provided social care for children and families in need.[37] From 1878 onward Rüetschi gained further prominence through taking up an instructor position at the University of Bern, teaching the Old Testament. In his lectures, Rüetschi, inspired by the critical works of the Tübingen School and especially that of Ferdinand Christian Baur, adopted the approach of higher criticism. Just like Ernst Buss above, Rüetschi incorporated these critical ideas into the studies of the world religions, establishing in the process new categories of understanding the world.

Throughout the years, Rüetschi published several articles in the ZMR, but his approach to "religion" can in particular be seen in his article "Die vergleichende Religionswissensschaft und das Christentum." Here he examined the world religions, arguing "religion" to be a necessity for the development of the modern man. Revealing his own personal understanding of "religion," Rüetschi wrote:

> [I am] of the belief that religion, i.e., the personal relationship of man to God, is one of the essential and indispensable elements; indeed, it is the only one in which man comes to find his ideal calling. We have established the Mission [AEPM] in the further belief that we in the gospel of Jesus Christ have realized the ideal nature of religion in its purest and most perfect form. Yes, the Christian principle of religion in itself is the most perfect religion of all religions.[38]

Like Buss, Rüetschi emphasized the ideality of Christianity as the "purest and most perfect form" of all religions. He perceived "religion" as something identical to the worship of God but personified in different cultural forms. According to today's outlook, this definition is flawed and archaic in its approach, in part because it so clearly parallels a Protestant understanding of religion as a personal emotional relationship to God. But such a Protestant definition of religion was still very much in place at the time. Max Müller, for example, famously introduced the new study of religion by stating "we can hear in all religions... a longing for the infinite, a love of God."[39]

Rüetschi's notion of "religion" continued along the lines of Buss's, accepting the pluralism of the term. "Religion" was something found in all humans, ergo also in non-Christians. To Rüetschi, all religions were different expressions of the same truth. He supported his claim with the evidence produced by the new science of comparative religions:

> What can we call the positive results of our young science today? It has initially established truths: that religion actually is something universal that the whole human race, with all its differences, has in common.[40]

Stronger than Buss, Rüetschi felt compelled to inform his readers that the world is a religiously diverse place full of what he categorized into *positive* and *negative* religions. Wherever there are humans and culture, there is religion. "Religion," he stressed, "really belongs to the characteristic of man as men."[41] In his text, he rejected the discussion of religious dogma and instead argued for the universality of the individual religious experience. Drawing inspiration from the "young sciences" of anthropology, ethnology, and linguistics, Rüetschi almost passionately observed:

> Man sacrifices, he prays, he prophesies, he uses magic, he folds his hands, he makes the cross across his chest, throws himself down shrouded in a holy shiver—he roars, he sings and dances in exultant joy, he complains and sighs and tortures himself for fear and remorse—and all this is done without a direct rational purpose to be seen—as it seems so it happens

even without actual compelling reasons—or the reason for it is at least not in the natural scheme of things, but in an imaginary, an invisible, spiritual power of which man like all of nature feels dependent.[42]

"Religion" had to be acknowledged as the fundamental aspect of human nature which had functioned as the central pillar in the formation of various cultures around the world. Rüetschi observed how all cultures taught men truth and righteousness and love. And although it might seem that all non-Christian religions were potential sources of salvation, they were not.

Rüetschi divided all religions into two major categories with additional subclasses. The major categories he termed: "universal religions" (*Universalreligionen*) and "national religions" (*Volksreligionen*) The latter included everything from fetishism to animism to ancestor cults. According to Rüetschi, only three religions could be classified as universal religions throughout world history: Christianity, Islam, and Buddhism.[43] The reason that these three were seen as universal rather than national religions was to be found in their superior moral "sittliche" character. Rüetschi argued:

> In [all] religions initiated by single men [Buddhism, Islam, and Christianity] there exists an undoubted, determined, definite moral character that distinguishes them from the mere Volksreligionen. And it seems just that the more a religion is inherently moral, the more it is suited to be a universal religion, a religion of humanity.... Morality is universal within humanity. Its ideal function is the same for the people of the south as of the north; what is a good ethic does not change with place or time [Wendekreisen], and the ethical code has for the Negro as for the Europeans the same immutable grandeur[44]

Here the two-sided nature of liberal theology becomes apparent. On the one side Rüetschi demonstrated a tolerant and accepting attitude expressed in the idea of a universality shared by all cultures, but on the other side he exhibited an oriental approach by categorizing the cultures according to their moral and ethical potentials. While *Volksreligionen* seemed only to function within a specific racially or nationally defined environment, universal religions, in contrast, had a uniting effect among all people and endured through time above all due to their moral superiority.

Rüetschi's analysis of the universal religions in "Die Vergleichende Religionsgeschichte und das Christentum" was in the same text followed by a historical comparison of the religious situation in Japan. According to him, Japan had since ancient times been known as a flourishing land with a feudal society ruled by the strict moral code of Confucianism and Japanese Buddhism. These religions reached the pinnacle of their development during the Tokugawa period, and the mid-nineteenth century collapse of the feudal system, having functioned well for previous centuries, had proven that there exists in these religions a "self-sacrificing holiness, and a disintegrated and corrupted world of monks, always capable of starting a reformation based on their own principles."[45] The contemporary religions of Japan had forsaken their obligation to the people, and Japan, Rüetschi argued, would be much better served relying solely on Christianity's "pillars of free and unlimited principles and thoughts."[46] Only Christianity, he summarized, could fill the void left by the "collapse" of Buddhism and Confucianism.

Rüetschi also remarked on the increasingly nationalistic climate of mid-Meiji. In the late 1880s, reports by missionaries highlighted how the patriotic credentials of Japanese followers of Christianity were under constant suspicion and frequently attacked. The ancestor cult of Shintō merged into the religion State Shintō, promoting patriotism and the national project.[47] In the formation of State Shintō, Rüetschi recognized its ability as a unifier for the nation Japan, but also warned about its limits:

> Within the confinement of these *Volksreligionen* lies their advantage, but also their disadvantage. The more nationally oriented a religion is, the more it has grown away from the natural existence of the people itself; the greater and more general will its influence be.... But these religions are only changing contours of history. They are like flowers

and fruits on the tree of mankind. They leap out with the full power of youth, but they also age, wither, and die. And religions that only have a national character can never make the claim to last forever; they arise with the people and will pass away with them. And even more so: it is the moral progress of the people that causes the demise of the national religions.[48]

Although *Volksreligionen* such as Shintō might seem gratifying at the moment, with time, only Christianity would prove rewarding. *Volksreligionen,* those religions constrained to a national path and character, on the other hand, would lead to the destruction of the nation.[49] At the same time, Rüetschi assumed that Christianity as a universal religion provided a more enduring form of civilization:

> Among the various forms of life, in the most diverse stages of civilization, even under the rule of people with quite differing views on nature and the world, Christianity has survived and repeatedly proven its resilience as the true religion.[50]

Rüetschi's articles on religion established a set of new categories by which the world religions—including the religions of Japan—could become familiar to a wider German readership. Binary categories such as "positive religions/negative religions" and "universal religions/national religions" made it easier for the readers of ZMR to classify, systematize and become acquainted with the world's religions. Rüetschi's comparative analysis of the world's religions worked along a familiar colonial frame of power. "Fetishism," "animism," and national religions were evaluated negatively when put in comparison to any universal religion. This stance was not unique and limited to his or others' articles appearing on the subject in the ZMR; it was common.

As Michal Adas discusses in his book *Machines of Measure of Man: Science, Technology, and Ideologies of Western Dominance* (1989), binary-structures such as Rüetschi's "Volksreligionen" versus "Universal Religions" emerged as a frame, as a "measure of men," in which rationality, ethical progress, and reason were rated highly and carefully measured—often to the disadvantage of non-European cultures such as the Japanese.⁵¹ And, in the comparison of the world's religions, one religion would always prevail in the ZMR: Christianity. This, simply, was because the qualifying variables assigned to the category "religion" were derived from the universal components of the Christian religion itself. A national religion like Shintō may have "risen from the people like the leaves and flowers bloom from any growing plant," but Christianity, so Rüetschi, had manifested itself "through the divine deeds of its personal founder."⁵²

JAPANESE BUDDHISM AND CHRISTIANITY: A COMPARISON WITH A HIDDEN AGENDA

The composite picture of Japanese Buddhism that emerged in the ZMR was far from uniform, but almost all published essays discussed Buddhism along Buss's and Rüetschi's universal understanding of religion, rooted in the liberal Protestant's "tolerant" attitude towards religion, which led them to declare that both religions shared the same truth. At the same time, however, they tried to expose its inherent flaws. This was not an unusual approach at the time. Danial S. Lopez, among others, has shown in his book *Curators of the Buddha: The Study of Buddhism under Colonialism* (1995) how Western works on Buddhism at the turn of the century identified apparent reseMBLances between Christianity and Buddhism.⁵³ But the publications on Japanese Buddhism in the ZMR carried a hidden agenda, which presumed that these similarities eventually could be used as building blocks for a future Japanese Christianity, allowing for the installation of a new society modeled on Christianity. The liberal theologian Otto Pfleiderer perfectly wrapped up the liberal missionaries' agenda by stating:

> An educated missionary will no longer be able to judge the heathen religion of the people under whom he works merely as a blind superstition; rather, he will have to accept and honor the relative moments of truth inherent in their religions; the seeds of the good and of truthfulness, the influence of the divine, "Logos spermatikos," as the old apologists

used to say. His tasks will be to connect [his belief] with these better seeds in order to expose the heathen religions' inherent flaws and to convincingly allow the higher and more fulfilling truth of Christianity to be planted.[54]

Here and in all other articles of the ZMR the authors found inspiration in the new comparative method to prove their beliefs in which the ideas of a religious truth were prominent. The concept of a religious truth was not a new phenomenon. For decades, works of the rediscovered romantic Friedrich Schleiermacher had been replete with ideas about a genuine survival of an archaic belief that contained seeds of an ancient truth.[55] The missionaries saw it as their responsibility to prove that this ancient truth was a conspicuous and most eminent part of their liberal interpretation of Christianity. Claims such as mission director Theodore Devaranne's: "All primitive religions were once theistic! The divine fundamental spark is the commonality to which we need to connect it all," were therefore understood in the historical context of a reemerged primeval belief existent in German romanticism.[56]. To the missionaries, it certainly seemed plausible that the seeds of truth could be found in both Christianity and in the teachings of Buddha, and that these could be used as building blocks for a future Christianity in Japan. Still, as alleged here, even in the most idealized descriptions of Japanese Buddhism, the missionary texts of the ZMR remained anchored in a colonial mindset founded on an asymmetric structure of power and reflecting an idea of European religious supremacy.

Hans Haas: searching for the sounds of truth in Japanese Buddhism

One of the most interesting and prolific thinkers to involve himself in the Buddhist-Christian comparison in the ZMR is the German missionary and Buddhologist Hans Haas (1868–1934). Although he is now largely a forgotten figure, he was very respected in his time. He is the first to translate *Sukhavati* (Pure Land) Buddhism into German, and he wrote and published on a wide range of topics, including philosophy, Buddhism, religious phenomenology, and religious poetry. Haas was equally active as a teacher; he taught and trained Japanese students at the Shinkyō Shingakkō and founded the Deutsche Schule in Yokohama in 1904, a private institute for teaching German language and culture in Japan. Haas is also known for his contribution to the religious study of poetry and songs, and in particular, his detailed studies of Buddhist poems and legends influenced the development of the study of phenomenology of religion in the early twentieth century. Through his publications on Pure Land Buddhism in the ZMR, Hass was significant in shaping the European—and especially the German peoples' understanding of Japanese Buddhism.

A detailed account of the life and work of Hans Haas can be found in the memoir "Die Bedeutung von Hans Haas für die Religionswissenschaft," published in 1969 by Kurt Rudolph. Here, Rudolph focuses on Haas's life, dividing it into three parts: his life before going to Japan (1868–1898), his time in Japan (1898–1909), and his life after returning to Germany (1909–1934). Born and raised in 1868 in the Frankian city of Donndorf near Bayreuth, Haas lived there until the age of twenty-one, when he began studying evangelical theology and classical philology at the University of Erlangen. Because it was customary to take up a parish following graduation, Haas was ordained at the Evangelical-Lutheran church in Bayern in 1895. In 1897, however, he decided to continue his studies within philology, moving first to Berlin and a year later to London to study Sanskrit, thus following in the footsteps of his countryman Max Müller (1823–1900), whose methodology made a lasting impression on him. Haas's linguistic talents were quickly noticed and in 1898, he was offered a position as pastor for the German Christian communities in Tokyo and Yokohama. Since the AEPM sponsored his time in Japan, he was expected to teach theology at the Shinkyō Shingakkō in Tokyo, and to foster relations between the German Christian community in Tokyo and the German Embassy. Haas was diplomatic enough to be able to balance his responsibilities as a missionary and his studies of Japanese Buddhism without clashing with the denominational authorities. Haas's stay in Japan gave him the opportunity to become highly acquainted with the religions of East Asia, especially the various developments within Japanese Buddhism at the time. Haas arrived in Japan at a moment when the introduction of Western philosophy and science had led to enormous intellectual changes. Japanese Buddhism was under immense social and political pressure, and questions on how to characterize it became a significant problem not only for Christian missionaries, but for Buddhist scholars as well. Inoue Enryō 井上円了 (1858–1919) and other prominent Buddhist intellectuals argued that Buddhism could no longer be described without reference to the Western categories of "philosophy," "religion," and "science."[57]. Although Buddhism today is generally regarded as a religion, for many Japanese intellectuals of Haas's time this was not self-evident, because the word "religion" was closely associated with Christianity.[58]

Haas was drawn into this spirited debate and met with Shin Buddhist thinkers such as the Honganji-ha 本願寺派 priest Akamatsu Renjō 赤松連城 (1841–1919) and Ōtani-ha 大谷派 member Tada Kanae 多田 鼎 (1875–1937), translating their works into German in his book *Amida Buddha unsere "Zuflucht." Urkunden zum Verständnis des japanischen Sukhāvatī-Buddhismus* (1910A). Both of these Buddhist thinkers wanted to draw comparisons between themselves and Protestantism. They stressed that their religion had a character that, similar to Christian Protestantism, did not contradict the developments of the modern world in any fundamental way. Haas, still in Japan at that time, was influenced by the discussion among Jōdo Shinshū Buddhist intellectuals on the formation of Japanese Buddhism and its comparable nature to Christianity, and one can clearly see in his writings on Japanese Buddhism how he borrowed ideas from these discussions.[59] In this process of understanding Japanese Buddhism, Haas redefined both Buddhism and the comparative study of religion. As such, his interpretation of Japanese Buddhism was not, as has often been argued, simply that of a condemning Christian missionary.[60] Rather, these interpretations were written by a man who was interested in establishing a dialogue between the two religious traditions; an anti-traditionalist who searched for the "original" and "pure" form of religion, not "distorted" by tradition or dogma attached to the scriptures, but one who sought to find the elements of "beauty" and "truth" in all religions.

As both a religious scholar and a scholar of religion, Haas published a significant amount of research on Japanese religions, but he held a particularly strong interest in the comparative study of Japanese Buddhism and Christianity. In 1922, Haas published the first sourcebook on the interrelationship between Buddhism and Christianity, *Bibliographie zur Frage nach den Wechselbeziehungen zwischen Buddhismus und Christentum*.

This publication not only shows Haas's awareness of East-West exchanges, but Haas himself was the author of many of the chapters in the book, many of which were first published as articles in ZMR. The chapters written by Haas in the sourcebook are as follows:

- "Das Leben Jesu und die Buddhalegende," ZMR 1898.
- "Buddhismus und Christentum in Japan," ZMR 1899.
- *Japans Zukunftsreligion*, 1907.
- "Buddhistische Texte im Johannesevangelium?", ZMR 1908.
- "Tenrikyō," ZMR, 1910.
- *Amida Buddha unsere "Zuflucht": Urkunden zum Verständnis des japanischen Sukhāvatī-Buddhismus*, 1910.
- "Christliche Klänge im japanischen Buddhismus," ZMR, 1912.
- "Die japanische Umgestaltung des Buddhismus durch Honen Shonin und Shinran Shonin," ZMR, 1912.
- *Mark. XII, 41 ff. Und Kalpanāmandinikā (IV) 22*, 1921.
- *"Das Scherflein der Witwe" und seine Entsprechung im Tripitaka*, 1922.

As we can see, with the exception of his article "Tenrikyō," all of Haas's articles are themed around the topic of Buddhist and Christian relations.[61] Regarding the content of the articles, Haas seems to have molded them as he saw fit. For example, in "Das Leben Jesu und die Buddhalegende" (1898A), he takes on the momentous task of establishing the historical connection between Buddha and Jesus, and in the second part of the same article, he settles the matter largely through an extensive investigation of Indian material regarding the era of the birth of Buddha. This work provided the seed for the elucidation of the "historical" similarities between the two religious founders in the rest of Haas's research.

While the pioneering research within Buddhist studies exemplified by people such as Müller and Hermann Oldenberg made India the focus of historical studies of Buddhism and thus the starting point of all research, Haas's research remained largely limited to the study of Japanese Buddhism. Works such as "Christliche Klänge im japanischen Buddhismus" (1912A) and "Die japanische Umgestaltung des Buddhismus durch Honen Shonin und Shinran Shonin" (1912B), both published in the ZMR, began their investigation of Buddhism from the two Japanese Buddhist sects Jōdoshū and Jōdo Shinshū. Rather than linking Japanese Buddhism with its Indian tradition, Haas attempted to discover the strong parallels between his own Protestantism and the Buddhism of the Pure Land tradition in his research. Initially, the main reason behind this particular trajectory was that of finding "the Christian message of salvation, which so lucidly resounds in Buddhism."[62] In "Christliche Klänge im japanischen Buddhismus," for example, Haas summarized the story of the old Japanese poem *Fūshi sogo*. The poem had originally been written by the Japanese Jōdoshū monk Koa Shonin 向阿聖人 (1269–1330), one of the early leaders of the *Chinzei-ha* 鎮西派 belonging to Jōdoshū). In a section of the article, he states the similarities between the two religions:

> It would be strange, had you not also clearly and movingly perceived it

as something else than the melancholy teachings of Buddhism, had you not also heard in it the fading ring of bells by a God of love, by a God who wishes for love amongst his human children.... Here would exist points of contact for the preaching of missionaries as they were hardly ever found before in the non-Jewish world.... It really cannot be otherwise than the Christian message of salvation, the one that so lucidly voices what really resounds in Buddhism as well, just less clearly.[63]

The similarity between the Pure Land tradition and Lutheranism ultimately made Haas question the Buddhist nature of Amida Buddhism. Although not included in its entirety here, Haas's understanding of Amida Buddhism can be grasped in this quote:

If one looks at these texts [of Jōdo Shinshū] critically, how then can it be that the Amitabha [Amida] religion of the Jōdoshū and the Jōdo Shinshū, which is founded on Buddhist grounds, is yet so perfectly non-Buddhist? How very strange, that principles attacking the ideas of Buddhism have gotten into [*hineingekommen*] the system of Gotama Buddha.[64]

In particular, the departure from celibacy in the Jōdo Shinshū tradition, which took its precedence from Shinran's marriage, was compared by Haas and many others to Luther deemphasizing the traditional monastic precepts in the Catholic Church.[65] To Haas, "Not only Catholicism, but also Protestantism has found its counterpart in Japanese Buddhism, a counterpart as striking as ever."[66]

To Haas the parallels between the developments of Jōdo Shinshū and the European reformation was obvious. To prove this, Haas, for example, draws attention to the text *Ryōgemon* 領解文 (Words of Realization) written by Rennyo 蓮如 (1415–1499) as a critique of the use of prayer. Here, Haas emphasizes how Luther's theory on *predestination* for Protestants means that moral conduct and ritual prayers cannot affect salvation, because that lies in the hands of God. Moral conduct, however, remains the grounds for conceiving the reality of salvation. Haas believes he has found the same argument in Rennyo's texts. For instance, in the first line of *Ryōgemon,* Rennyo writes:

Moromoro no zōgyō zasshu jiriki no kokoro o furisutete, isshin ni Amida Nyorai, warera ga kondo no ichidaiji no goshō, ontasuke sōra e to tanomi mōshite sōrō

もろもろの雑行雑修自力のこころをふりすてて、一心に阿弥陀如来、われらが今度の一大事の後生、御たすけ候へとたのみまうして候ふ

Haas's translation in German reads:

Alle sonstigen Praktiken und sonstigen Werke wie überhaupt allen Gedanken, daß ich selber mir zu helfen vermögend sei, aufgebend, setze ich mein Vertrauen von ganzem Herzen einzig darauf, daß Amida Nyorai, was mir dermalen das Wichtigste sein muß von allen Dingen, für das Leben, das da kommen wird, meine Hilfe ist.[67]

I give up all practices and works as well as all thoughts that I am able to help myself; with all my heart, I place my trust, which is the most important thing of all, in Amida Nyorai, who will help me in the life to come.

To Haas, Rennyo's *Ryōgemon* confirmed that just like Protestantism, the chanting of the *nenbutsu* should not be understood as a prayer, but rather like the Christian "Amen" in the church, should be interpreted as nothing more than a natural expression of one's faith in God.

In general, Haas's writings on Pure Land Buddhism provides fascinating documentation of a missionary's understanding of Pure Land Buddhism in the early twentieth century. One finds Haas arguing that Jōdoshū and Jōdo Shinshū, in their missionary activities, rejection of prayers, and relative monotheism, share parallels to Protestantism. It is therefore not surprising that Haas, when speaking about Pure Land Buddhism, understood it as a modernized Buddhism inspired by *hineingekommene* or "intruded" Protestant ideas.

Haas was not alone in pointing out the similarities between Jōdoshū Buddhism and Protestantism. In fact, it seems to have been a reoccurring theme throughout the existence of the ZMR.[68] But not all were as easily convinced of the similarities between the two religions as Haas. For Carl Munzinger, for example, Japanese Buddhism could not be compared to Protestantism, but more so to the Catholic faith:

In the version of the Buddha promoted by his followers today, we find icons, precepts, consecrations, the recitations of sutras, and rosaries [all similar to those of the Catholic faith]. Further, the descriptions of heaven and hell, punishment, and rebirth are almost identical to those in Christianity. But the degree to which the Buddhists have watered these down are so strong that they cannot be discussed in the same manner.[69]

Both Haas and Munzinger in their analysis of Japanese Buddhism looked for similarities through which the parallels of each religion's evolvement could be understood. Interestingly, neither Haas nor Munzinger had their focus on aspects where the comparison of Japanese Buddhism and Christianity failed, where they differed, but rather on the commonalities that the religions shared because every time a commonality was discovered, this confirmed their belief in the universal truth of religion. In 1899, this belief was perfectly summarized with missionary Max Christlieb's metaphor:

> The real gold of Christianity has been layered with all types of Greek, Roman and Germanic precious metals which we will first need to discover again through our modern theology. This is also so in Japan, where we want to introduce the real gold to Japan, and free it and make it workable again and allow it to be covered with the finest metal that exist in the Japanese earth.[70]

These interpretations of the relationship of the two religions were far from being considered vague. The missionaries tried to prove their theories of a universal truth as being based on historical facts, even if these facts often stemmed from dubious sources that laid one hypothesis over another. Even so, for Haas their arguments were coherent. The combining of "higher criticism" to historical sources known at his time supported him in his belief that *"hineingekommene"* Christian elements of truth existed within Japanese Buddhism.

That sounds of truth could be found in all religions was the backbone of Haas's theorizing. Still, Haas's interpretation of Jōdoshū's historical connection to Christianity was in a large part an ideological reaction founded on two assumptions. First, the world's religions contained various forms of expressions of the same truth. Second, although Jōdoshū's entailed a culturally specific dimension, it still attempted to express the truth of the gospel within its own particular cultural sphere. It was Haas's aim to find these "Anknüpfungspunkte," or points of contacts between the two religions to prove the universality not just of Christianity, but also of Buddhism.

A COLLECTION OF WRITINGS ON JAPANESE RELIGION AND MODERNITY

In the late 1890s and early 1900s, the post-revolutionary society of Meiji Japan had begun to transform Japan's social and political structures. During this time, the authors of the ZMR functioned to a large degree as elite cultural interpreters commenting on the formation of public attitudes and state policies. The problems surrounding efforts to define Japanese religion diversified and opened pathways to many related questions: To which extent did religions play a role in a civilization and its progress? To which measure did religions prove useful in this or not? What constituted the ideal role of religion in the modern nation state? All these questions touched on issues that became widely disputed, with one question being discussed the most: Would it be beneficial for the Japanese state to become a Christian state?

The relevance of religion in its connection to the Japanese state is the subject of the three following reflections. Each author judges its significance in a varying degree and from a different vantage point: one promotes a vaguely defined Christian modernity, the second argues for religion as a necessity for the development of human individuality, and the third advocates Christian morality as an essential requirement in the modern state. The missionaries' writings touched on all possible sides of Japan, its people, and its religions. But central to all their writing and their discussions was the one idea of the Christian religion being the foundation of modernity.

Max Christlieb: Modern Culture and the Evangelical Mission in Japan

The German missionary Max Heinrich Christlieb's (1862–1914) first contribution to the discourse on Japanese religions in the ZMR happened in 1899 when he addressed very similar issues to those raised by Buss and Rüetschi: religion is universal and significant for the improvement of humanity. And as Christlieb commented on other manifestations of Japanese religions throughout the Meiji period, his work serves as a useful barometer for changes in the discussion. Like earlier writers, he was motivated to write on the comparability of Japanese religions and offered a typology of religion similar to that of Buss and Rüetschi. Christlieb also compared Christianity and Buddhism, concluding that Christianity was the "religion of the civilized world," yet he offered more than his predecessors. He moved away from the general comparison of "good" and "bad" religions and instead relentlessly focused on Christianity's role as Japan's guide to civilization and modernity. To a larger degree than anybody else's, his writings located the missionaries' discussion of Japanese religions within the debate about religion and modernity.

Christlieb was born in Wiblingen, close to Ulm. He studied theology in Tübingen, Leipzig, Berlin, and London. Especially in Berlin, Christlieb socialized with the creative and liberal classes, and befriended the Austrian philosopher and social reformer Rudolf Steiner, who in his autobiography portrayed Christlieb as a person "who most energetically comprehended the living reality of the world of ideas."[71] From 1888–1892, after finishing his dissertation, Christlieb took up a position as a minister in Wenkheim, close to Würzburg, before he was appointed as missionary for the AEPM in 1892, taking over from the departed Otto Schmiedel. Christlieb is an often-forgotten figure in the early missionary history of the AEPM in Japan, where much more attention is given to Spinner and his successor Otto Schmiedel. In academic studies, there have only been sporadic mentions of Christlieb and his mission activities, while no major study just about him and his writings has ever been published. But, like most of the missionaries appointed by the AEPM, he was a prolific writer and contributed several articles to the ZMR. Articles such as "Moderne Missionsprobleme" (Modern Problems in the Mission, 1902A), "Der Kampf um die Sprache in der Mission" (The Fight for the Language of the Mission, 1902B), and "Politik und Mission in den Kolonien" (Politics and Mission in the Colonies, 1904A), as well as several news updates and reports from the Japanese mission field, were all important contributions.[72]

What makes Christlieb worth mentioning in the context of Japanese religion and modernity is his publication "Die moderne Kultur und die Aufgabe der evangelischen Mission in Japan" (Modern Culture and the Tasks of the Evangelical Mission in Japan) published in 1899. In "Die moderne Kultur," Christlieb attempted to reconcile the national religions of Japan with the universality of Christianity. Christlieb divided the world religions into two groups: "Kulturlose Völker" or people without culture and "Kulturvölker," people with culture. The latter were cultures with an already existing theoretical worldview based on strong principles, ideals, and virtue, and which had been formulated in a way to suit a national goal.[73]

Christlieb wrote his essay at a time when Japanese Christians were forced to find ways to reconcile their own Christian belief with a loyalty to the emperor and State Shintō. With the outbreak of the Sino-Japanese War in 1894, patriotic sentiments had come to the fore, and support for military actions was as strong among the Japanese Christian communities as it was in the rest of the public. Interestingly, Christlieb identified the major roots of this patriotic surge as a by-product of the rapid Westernization which had undercut Japan's old religious systems. It was especially modernization that exacerbated this patriotic trend. By solely promoting a materialistic scientific culture, it led to a decay of the morality and vitality of the Japanese people, leaving the society as heartless and lifeless as never before. Like many of his contemporaries, Christlieb felt that the old religions of Japan simply were not strong enough to withstand the pressing issues of modernity that Japan faced. Without turning to Christianity, Christlieb stressed, Japan would not be able to emerge as a modern nation. By introducing reference points between modern developments of the West and of Japan, Christlieb was especially interested in laying out the differences of Christianity and Buddhism with regard to their aptness to function in a modern world:

> The main difference that impacts on the whole development [of a modern nation] is that—for us—Christianity has remained an essential, if not the most influential factor in our development, and that it has in a major way assisted in the further development of the national character and of cultural elements passed down through the ages. Buddhism, on the other hand, almost completely lacks this kind of vitality.[74]

Christlieb argued that the foundation of contemporary Western power was to be found in the strength of Christianity. Buddhism was an "archaic religion," too weak to contribute to any modern development unless a great "reform of its religious world" commenced. He proposed the integration of a new ethical system that resurrected traditional ideals and combined them with—what he supposed to be—proven elements of Western civilization. After a close scrutiny of which traditional ideals precisely were adequate, Christlieb dismissed a wide range of religious traditions in Japan.

Much attention was given to the "merkwürdige," or "peculiar" co-existence of Shintō and Buddhism, which, according to Christlieb, constituted the main beliefs of the Japanese people. Shintō was described as "a religion at its most primitive stage, a nature and ancestor worship that has never undergone any development."[75] The emperor cult of Shintō received little notice but was discussed as an absurd form of national religion that hindered the cultural development of Japan. Buddhism, on the other hand—similar to Haas's view above—merited a thorough analysis. In this context, Christlieb presented a new typology in which he distinguished between "old Buddhism" and "reform-Buddhism."[76] "Old Buddhism" was controlled by "immoral and ignorant Buddhist priests and monks."[77] In contrast, he was more positive towards reform-Buddhism. Concerning modern-Buddhism, Christlieb stated: "It copies the forms and activities of Christianity (the preaching, the providing of "Seelsorge," "spiritual support" and the establishment of clubs for the youth) to support its shaky power."[78] Even though these reforms were certainly helpful, Christlieb stressed, they would not sufficiently alleviate Buddhism unless a real reform "von innen heraus," or from within, was achieved.[79]

Christlieb did not consider the indigenous religions the sole hindrance for Japan's moral progress and development to modernity. He warned of a further obstacle: the strong chauvinism among contemporary Japanese. "Can the exaggerated chauvinism be overcome?" he asked, "it constitutes a direct obstacle to the progress of Japan, especially in the moral and religious fields."[80] He criticized the contemporary chauvinistic discourse among the Japanese. Not only did it lead to the rejection of Western ideals which supported and legitimized the modern state, but it also restrained a modern state's all-important link to Christianity.

The unrelenting focus on civilization and modernity in his writings on Japanese religions sets Christlieb apart from Buss, Rüetschi, and Haas, though his aim and motivations were consistent with the early religious discourse portrayed above. All four writers reassessed Japan's religions in relationship to Christianity, and in their comparisons followed the pattern of an occidental gauge in attributing qualities and labeling the parameters of a religion. Still, Christlieb's assessment of the Japanese religions shows that he was well aware of the intellectual trends of modernity and nationalism in Japan at the time, and actively sought to participate in the debates about the "modern culture" of Japan and its people. He questioned contemporary Buddhism by pointing out its corrupted teachings, and advocated Christianity as the most civilized religion instead. Rationality as expressed in the achievements of Western science and philosophy had to be a key ingredient of any religion that wanted to be seen as compatible with a civilized nation.

Accordingly, Christlieb's theories were read primarily by German Christians, and his analysis has to be seen in this light. In addition to being an early promoter of Japanese religions in Germany, Christlieb would over the years monitor the developing discourse in Japan and remain one of a small number of informed critical voices willing to criticize the chauvinistic currents taking place in the late 1890s and beyond.

Carl Munzinger: On Individuality and Religion

Just like Christlieb, the German missionary Carl Munzinger (1864–1938) also placed contemporary Japan in the discussion of modernity. Yet, in contrast to Christlieb, whose emphasis was on defining a Christian modernity, Munzinger focused on the individual's right to a religion. His book *Japan und die Japaner* (Japan and the Japanese) (1906A) was written following the first Sino-Japanese War (1894–1895) and the Russo-Japanese War (1904–1905), which had both invoked an increased chauvinism as well as promoted a militaristic expansionism in East Asia. Given the background of these iconoclastic events, it is perhaps not a coincidence that Munzinger's discussion of Japanese religion occurs at a point when he is defining religion in relationship to freedom and the individual's right.

Munzinger was born in 1864 in Quirnbach, Pfalz, and his background provides an insight into his motivations for writing *Japan und die Japaner*. He studied theology in Munich, Strasburg, Heidelberg, and later in Berlin before taking his exam in theology in Speyer in 1889. The following year, he joined Spinner and Schmiedel as the third missionary of the AEPM in Japan. Being younger than Spinner, Schmiedel, and Christlieb when he arrived as a missionary in Japan—he was just 26—he was criticized by Spinner for being "too young" to work as a pastor in Tokyo.[81] His young age, however, soon proved an advantage in his work among the young Christian community of

Japanese students. In 1891, Munzinger wrote the article "Die Missionsgemeinde und ihr inneres Leben" (The Mission Church and its Inner Life) in the ZMR, an essay attesting to his interest in the individual faith of the Japanese community members.[82] Displaying the curiosity of youth, Munzinger developed an idealistic approach to religion and continuously explored the relationship between the *Geistesleben* of the Japanese people and the universality of their Christian faith.

Munzinger's personal background and experiences in Japan, combined with his interest in the "Geistesleben," or "spiritual life" of the Japanese people, make him an interesting observer of the political and social changes in Japan in the 1890s and 1900s.[83] Following the Japanese victory over China in the Sino-Japanese war of 1894–1895, Munzinger wrote his debut article in the ZMR, "Das Geistesleben des Japaners und die christliche Mission" (The Spiritual Life of the Japanese and the Christian Mission) (1897), and in the following year, the book *Die Japaner. Wanderungen durch das geistige, soziale und religiöse Leben des japanischen Volkes* (The Japanese, Explorations along the Spiritual, Social, and Religious Life of the Japanese People) (1898). In both works one can sense in Munzinger's writing a disillusionment caused by the increasing chauvinism among the Japanese people and the Japanese Christian communities.[84] While respecting Japan's cultural and historical accomplishments, Munzinger eyed the contemporary developments critically. The increasing pressure of nationalism among the youth not only made the work of the missionaries more difficult, it inhibited the free and individual practice of religion as well.[85]

Similarly, *Japan und die Japaner* (1906A) was a reaction to the broader social trends following the Russo-Japanese War. Like in his earlier works, Munzinger in much of his book criticized the Japanese people and their inclination to shallow nationalistic and ill-tempered actions. But in his description of the spiritual life of the Japanese people, Munzinger also took a new approach in the discussion of the State's role in protecting the individual's right to practice his or her religious belief. To illustrate this, Munzinger, for example in the chapter "Japan as a Modern Cultural State," argued that in the formation of any modern state, laws were needed to regulate, guard, and prohibit, but more importantly, laws were created to guarantee the basic freedom and rights of the people. Regrettably, so he stated, the introduction of the Educational Rescript in 1899 had led to restrictions towards the practice of Christianity—and this was despite the existing article 28 of 1889, which was supposed to guarantee the freedom of religion.[86]

For Munzinger, the neglect of the Japanese government to protect the individual's freedom to practice his or her own religious belief was unfortunate, as the influence of Christianity and its set of principles and guidelines had never been as prominent as then. In a chapter called "The Successes of Christianity," Munzinger emphasized the radical changes that had occurred in Japan during the last twenty years:

> The traditional social basis of the [Japanese] society has undergone a radical change. Not only are the important and positive effects of the creation of a new Christian system of thought popular among the Japanese youth, but so are the destruction of the old and negative mindsets. Individualism is today setting the trend.[87]

To Munzinger, the growth of individualism amongst the Japanese people was seen as proof of the installment of Christian practices in Japanese society. And although the situation following the two wars had contributed to an increased atmosphere of chauvinism, Munzinger asserted "today, Christianity is no longer a foreign body, but a necessary foundation of modern Japanese culture."[88] Similarly, he pointed out that:

> Today's ethical thoughts are more suffused with Christianity than with any other religion. If I would be asked to name the sources of the main ethical way of thinking in Japan, I would say that Confucianism and Buddhism together constitute forty or fifty percent, but Christianity constitutes fifty or sixty percent of the elements of all ethical thought.[89]

The discussion about the modern state could not be concluded without engaging in a comparative discussion of the religions of Japan and their vitality in a modern state. Also, Munzinger, like Christlieb and Haas, compared Japanese Buddhism to Christianity from the perspective of his own Christian civilization. But while Christlieb and Haas discussed the parallels between the two religions, Munzinger intended to provide a rationale for the Japanese religions' failure to develop culturally along Western lines, while at the same time present a rationale for Christianity's superiority. In this context, he committed to a comparative historical analysis of religion's role in the development of civilization, first in the Western world and later in Japan. At the end, Munzinger concluded: "The Japanese have failed to apprehend religion and religious freedom." Munzinger's historical analysis included extended discussions on both Shintō and Buddhism.[90] He judged Shintō negatively, as did most missionaries. To him, it was a nature religion in its simplest stages with no fully formed religious doctrine, leading its priests to practice magical nonsense in order to keep their followers satisfied:

> The priests call on humbug and superstitions to help them maintain their importance, for otherwise there would be nothing supporting its position. Shintō has no church services, pastoral care is something completely unknown to it, and even for funerals their services are in low demand.... Furthermore, its priests cannot give lessons in religious education because Shintō possess no moral philosophy.[91]

This quote is interesting for two reasons. Firstly, it probes the bias and the difficulties the missionaries faced in understanding Japanese religions. And secondly, it shows how Munzinger, like many other authors in the ZMR, employed Protestant etymologies such as communion services, soul-healing, and moral teachings to describe what they themselves believed to be essential religious deeds. It does not come as a surprise that within this Protestant scheme of comparison Shintō was never favorably received.

In contrast to Shintō, Munzinger's analysis of Japanese Buddhism was much more meticulous. Summarizing the history of Buddhism in Japan, he insisted to have found historical precedents for its contemporary decline. Although Buddhism had originated as a religion guiding the life of individuals in Japan, during the Tokugawa period it had become deeply embedded in the fabric of the Japanese state. It had begun to lack true "religious authority" and, so he argued, transformed into a belief dominated by political authorities. It was used by the government for propaganda, and no longer allowed the individual choice of the believer. Buddhism, as Munzinger concluded,

> may have suited the past—but it does not fit the new times. It is incompatible with the zeitgeist; it is too old to adapt. It was the star, which lit up the night, but now that daylight has come, the morning star disappears. We gladly accept Buddha as a predecessor of Christ, but he will not be able to hold his place beside Him for any length of time.[92]

Overall, several discoursal trends intersected in Munzinger's *Japan und die Japaner*. He shared his Protestant background with many, but his youthful and idealistic focus on the individual's right to faith, which emerged just after the two Japanese wars, separated him from those seeking a more general approach. Munzinger insisted that religion was the core of the individual's life. His firm belief in individual faith, however, also made him judge the Japanese religions critically. Throughout the texts one senses Munzinger's Protestant background: To Munzinger, the proper sphere of religion was an exclusively personal and (intensely) private one. Religion was understood as an inner conscience that could not be forced or controlled in any way. Faith had to be freely chosen and not be affected by outside conditions. In the end, only God himself had a role to play. Choosing one's own faith represented the free choice that was liberated from the external control of the Japanese government. For Munzinger, the religious models of contemporary Japan seemed outmoded, and "the individualism" on which Munzinger had put so much faith seemed to have "no place in the old Japan."[93] Similar to Haas and Christlieb, Munzinger engaged in the comparative studies of Japanese religions, but instead of searching for similarities in the religions, he sought to distance their faith as much as possible from his own Christianity. Munzinger's stay in Japan lasted five years (1890–1895), but the link between religion and the individual right to faith which he explored in his book *Japan und die Japaner* inspired several Christian circles in Japan far into our times. In 1976, his book was republished in a translated version entitled *Doitsu senkyōshi no mita Meiji shakai* ドイツ宣教師の見た明治社会 (Meiji Society as Seen by a German missionary).[94]

Hans Haas: Modernity and the Spiritual Life of the Japanese Soul

One of the later, yet the more interesting contribution to the debate about Japan and its modern development is found in the writings of Hans Haas. In the second annual issue of the ZMR, published in 1907, Haas also engaged in a discussion of Japan's transit to a modern state. In his essay "Das Seelenleben der Japaner" (The Spiritual Life of the Japanese),[95] he assumed the reader's commitment to the larger project of Christianizing Japan, and then began to distinguish the boundary of modernity and progress itself. To Haas:

> The process through which the old Japan became the new Japan should be understood as a revolution, rather than an evolution.... The tree of the old civilization has been chopped down and burnt in the fire. A new tree from the West has been imported and planted in Japanese soil. And this new tree is the modern Japan.[96]

Haas here echoed the same occidental distinctions deployed by other missionaries as part of a rhetorical strategy to promote everything that was Western as modern, and everything Japanese as outdated. For the modern Japanese, the term "Fortschritt," or "progress" itself had become a goal worth striving for, and the traditional religions of Shintō and Buddhism were struggling to adjust.[97] Haas argued that these traditional beliefs did not contribute any useful knowledge towards the advancement of civilization; they were obstacles in the path of progress and modernity. To prove this, Hass described how the Meiji government had implemented laws against immoral and superstitious rituals:

> Religious customs that still existed fifty years ago have almost completely disappeared today. For example, the former extraordinarily pop-

ular devotion to phallicism has since the first instigation by foreigners been banned by the Meiji government. And this is good![98]

The prohibition of several popular religious rituals, including the practice of phallicism, was by the missionaries interpreted as a victory, not only for the progress of Japanese religions, but also for the success of Christianity. Although progress could be observed in Japanese society, Haas was aware of the fact that the traditional religious systems hindered the full integration of Christianity in Japan. Christian concepts like "God" and "sin" (*Sünde*) did not exist in the Japanese vocabulary, making it "practically impossible to talk about Christianity with the Japanese."[99] The traditional Japanese belief systems were to blame for this, as they did not contribute any useful knowledge or epistemological development. They were, he stated, "obstacles" to the progress of Christianity in Japan.

Similarly, Haas rejected the Japanese ethical system. "Religion" to Haas had to work both as a vector for public morality and as a conduit through which currents of enlightenment could flow. "The object of religion," he wrote, "is to lead the unenlightened so that they will advance along the good path."[100] In this sense, Haas's conclusion on the ethical systems existing in Japan followed the same pattern as other articles published in the ZMR; Japan needed to embrace Christianity:

> It is not to be doubted that the Japanese will ultimately have to adopt Christianity. With its higher intellectual culture, it will outgrow the old religions. Only the most developed religious form will be able to satisfy the modern Japanese.[101]

One might ask whether the discussion of modernity and religion as portrayed within the pages of the ZMR was solely a German discussion. If this were so, one might even be tempted to dismiss the missionaries' intellectual efforts merely as little else than thoughts representing an Occidental discussion of the Orient. Their insistence on a wide-scale conversion of Japanese religions to Christianity because it was deemed indispensable for the initiation of a modernization process would be irrelevant. The diary of AEPM member Aoki Shūzō (1844–1914), however, proves otherwise. As early as August 1872, he recorded a discussion on the subject of Japan's future religion taking place between two high-ranking members of the famous Iwakura missions, Kido Takayoshi (1833–1877) and Itō Hirobumi (1841–1909).[102] According to Aoki's account, Kido mentioned that some of his fellow delegates, for purely pragmatic reasons, considered to "petition the emperor so that he and all the government could convert to Christianity; their idea is that all countrymen would follow suit, to the immense benefit of our diplomatic relations with the great powers."[103] Conversion to Christianity seemed for some members of the Japanese government's administration a way of transforming the nation's status in the perception of the West. It is impossible to assert today how earnestly this idea was being considered, yet, as Aoki Shūzō's diary entry suggests, conversion on the grounds of secular reasoning, at least at the time, remained a distinct possibility.[104]

The basic structure of missionary thought as set out by Christlieb, Munzinger, and Haas would be repeated by many other authors in the ZMR over the years to come. Here, the distinction between a positive and rational religion, Christianity, and the negative, archaic, and irrational superstitions of the Japanese people was continually discussed. "Religion," "morality," and "civilization" on the one side, and "superstitions," "corruptness," and "irrationality" on the other. Constructing the differences and attaching opposing qualities allowed the missionaries to define a version of Japanese religion that would fit into their overall scheme of cultural and religious dominance.

Ending the Conversation

Haas's article was not the final word to appear in the ZMR on the subject of Japan and its religions; the understanding of "religion" and "modernity" continued to be widely discussed.[105] In the article "Unser Recht und unsere Pflicht zur Mission" (Our Right and our Duty towards Mission, 1906B) published in ZMR in 1906, Carl Munzinger summarized the debate on "religion" and defined it as: "the innate belief in God that compels man to virtuous conduct." Munzinger juxtaposed the concept of religion with the virtue of man, defining it as a moral term guiding man to good ethical behavior.[106] He believed that religion as a concept was fundamentally good, something positive, something ethical, and contributing to society. Yet, if not nurtured correctly, religion could potentially be harmful for a society. Just like Buss twenty years before him, Munzinger dichotomized religions into a "good religion," a positive version improving peoples' behavior, or a "bad religion," an ethically negative version stopping people from progressing. He stated that "good religion is when it focuses on morality, righteousness, and God." On the other side "bad religion" included *Aberglauben* or "superstition," which according to Munzinger was harmful to any society.[107]

Munzinger's ethical use of "religion" demonstrated that the categories used to compare religions were beginning to acquire legitimacy, even among scholars of a more historical approach. The two approaches of conducting a "higher historical" research (Haas) and creating a prescriptive ethical system (Buss, Munzinger) often conflated in the ZMR. They did so in missionary Emil Schiller's 1902 article "Berührungspunkte und Gegensätze zwischen Christentum und japanischem Charakter" (Similarities and Dissimilarities Between Christianity and the Japanese People's Character). Here Schiller attempted to treat Shintō historically while relating to its present situation. He defined Shintō as the manifestation of Japan's spirit and traced its history back to Amaterasu and the Age of the Gods. He referred to Shintō as a religion, which could not be related to modern Japan, but which had still managed to contribute central elements to the society, although completely lacking an ethical doctrine.[108]

The countless editorials and articles published on Japanese religion in the ZMR at the turn of the century reflected the missionaries' growing interest in other religions. They compared the strengths and weaknesses of the Japanese religions, and should there be progress to modernity, made their case for a new moral system, and altogether for the installation of a better religious system.

Far from offering an inert discussion of the religious conditions of Japan, these texts reflected a liberal protestant worldview which sparked three significant changes to the conception of "religion" overall. Firstly, their authors accepted a religious pluralism and formulated visions of religious life which were defined not by dogma or church teachings, but by moral or practical reasons defined by modern methodological instruments of research. Secondly, by enforcing the categorical division between universal/national religions vs. cultural/uncivilized religions, they served the crucial purpose of excluding seemingly delusional beliefs and indigenous practices. Their systematic organization and classifications of Buddhism, Shintō, Confucianism, and Christianity shows just how "far" the liberal theologians were willing to go in their "tolerant" approach towards other religions, as they were not ready to give up the claims of the practical superiority of Christianity. Thirdly, by praising "religion" as the essential part of the modern state and stressing its social function in encouraging moral and ethical behavior, they managed to incorporate "religion" (Protestantism) into a discourse of modernity. For the missionaries, Protestantism was to be understood as the religion of freedom and personality. It had to be regarded as the universal religion of the modern culture of individuality. To them, the Christian religion was the finest tool to gain access and control the hearts of the people and to unify the morale of a modern nation.

Conclusion

The main subject of this chapter has been the large role liberal Protestant authors of the *Zeitschrift für Missionskunde und Religionswissenschaft* played in objectifying Japanese religion The journal took a Protestant stance and presented Protestantism as the religion of civilization and modernity. Its texts articulated shifting definitions of history, nationhood and morality and served to spark the attempt to define the term "religion" itself.

On a theoretical level, an interesting insight of this investigation of the journal's central tension between what can be described as the liberal Protestants' "tolerant" attitudes towards the Japanese religions and their not so tolerance views of their own unique superiority. The former, led them to claim that "all religions were different expressions of the same truth [Wahrheit]" (Buss, Rüetschi, Haas), while because of the latter, liberal missionaries assumed that Christianity held the special key to a more enlightened form of civilization destined to spread worldwide. To them "Christianity [was] not only a higher developed religion for humanity, it [was] the truth, ... the principle and the absolute religion. (Christlieb, Munzinger).[109] Their belief in both a universality of the truth and in its own privileged position is a paradox and led to many interesting articles in the ZMR in which Buddhism, Shintō and Confucianism were given much historical scrutiny.

Ernst Buss's book *Die christliche Mission, ihre principielle Berechtigung und praktische Durchführung* (1876) is situated at the beginning of a long line of discussions that AEPM held on religions in Japan. In his book, the founder stated that "all names that divide religion are to us of little consequence," and he advocated to honor "all inspiring scriptures" side by side with the Bible and described a reverence for Jesus as a prophet next to "all holy souls that have taught men truth."[110] Statements such as these seem to have implied that non-Christian religions were potential sources of salvation. And while some circles of the German mission society resisted what they saw as the de-Christianization of the church's mission, the texts by Haas and Rüetschi explored in this chapter prove that the institutional leadership was at least nominally committed to potentially placing all religions on the same footing. And while this tolerant attitude towards other religions might seem to have rendered missionary activity unnecessary, it interestingly did not. Indeed, the AEPM in Japan embraced both Christian evangelism and a commitment to the assertion that all religions shared access to the truth. In other words, it was salvation directed toward the already saved. It is a paradox which seems not only to have infused the missionaries' practical activities in Japan, but is, as this chapter has proven, a paradox which permeated the literary production of the *Zeitschrift für Missionskunde und Religionswissenschaft* as well.

6

Buddhist Exposures to Liberal Christianity

On the warm summer day of 2 July, 1888 the Swiss missionary Wilfried Spinner sat in a "magnificent painted parlor" of the Nishi Honganji temple of the Jōdo Shinshū sect in Kyoto.[1] He was sharing the company of the Buddhist upper-priest Akamatsu Renjō 赤松 連城 (1842–1919).[2] Spinner was offered green tea and Japanese rice snacks, and the two conversed about Akamatsu's impressions of European culture during his visit to Europe a few years earlier.[3] As the conversation progressed, their dialogue shifted from European culture to matters of science, morality, and religion in Japan. When Spinner stated that he wanted to bring enlightenment and modernity to Japan by way of the Christian gospel, Akamatsu responded firmly:

> You are right, [modernity] is what I want too, and it is basically what Buddhism wants, we have all the same goals, and it is not necessary that you come here with your Christianity. You also seem to be bad politicians; you forget that the Japanese nation is the most patriotic in the world and only learns from foreigners in order to be able to maintain independence and withstand the pressure of European culture. It is not merely imitation that urges us to learn from foreigners, it is our interest in the independence of Japan, and it is therefore not good if you Christians, as foreigners, directly influence our people.[4]

Spinner, perhaps due to the strain of Kyoto's sultry weather, was unable to muster a counter to Akamatsu's claims and left the meeting discontented.[5] To him, Akamatsu already had a solidly negative opinion of Christianity and its missionaries and had no intention of changing that view.[6] Akamatsu, Spinner claimed later in his diary, introduced his Shinshū school in Kyoto to many foreigners as a form of Buddhist Protestantism. Moreover, in several of his works Akamatsu spoke of a "reformed" or "Protestant" character of Shinshū Buddhism.[7] Writing about his meeting with Akamatsu in his diary, Spinner, however, described Akamatsu as an unreliable collaborator:

> [Akamatsu] dislikes when we missionaries write simplified reports on Buddhism. When missionaries are too narrow minded, he himself becomes narrow minded, when too liberal, he becomes liberal.[8]

The meeting between Spinner and Akamatsu represents a pivotal moment for this study, as it was the first face-to-face meeting between a missionary of the AEPM and an official representative of the Shinshū sect. Akamatsu Renjō and other "modern Buddhists" represented a new kind of Buddhism in terms of their scope.[9] Before the Meiji Reformation, Japanese Buddhists, for the most part, were divided into several sects that sought to rectify specific problems in order to salvage their immediate communities. These sects, in contrast to the missionaries, did not claim to change the existing world in a fundamental sense, nor did they ever become politically active. Akamatsu Renjō, on the other hand, was part of a novel group of so-called "Buddhist intellectuals."[10] These Buddhist intellectuals differed from previous Buddhist generations in that they actively attempted to conform their nationalistic beliefs to their religious ideology by borrowing ideas and insights derived from western science, philosophy and Christianity, ideas they picked up through their travels abroad. They involved themselves in politics, education, and public discourse in order to defend their Buddhist faith.

The "modern Buddhist" movement has been studied by many and is lauded as having provided an important foundation for Japan's modern religious society.[11] Lesser known, however, is Liberal Christianity's impact on this movement.

To make sense of Wilfried Spinner's meeting with Akamatsu Renjō, this chapter takes a 180-degree turn from the last by focusing on cases in which historical actors tried to make Buddhism the paradigm and center of Japan's religious world. These Buddhist intellectuals confirmed their own position in the religious hierarchy by adjusting to liberal Christian ideas. Liberal Christianity ideals, as this chapter will argue, underpinned many Buddhist intellectuals' narratives, especially in the 1890s and 1900s, and thus played a critical role in expanding the scope of Liberal Christianity from "foreign" to "indigenous." Interestingly, this process of transfer allowed Buddhist intellectuals to reconcile the highly nationalistic yet mutually constitutive relationship between Japan and their religion.

Two Buddhist intellectuals, Murakami Senshō and Tada Kanae, will serve as examples in this chapter. As evident from a variety of contemporaneous documents and historical periodicals, these two Buddhists implemented various ideas related to Liberal Christianity into their own work on Japanese Buddhism. Murakami and Tada will be treated in separate sections, with a biographical overview provided for each before commencing an investigation of the missionaries' roles as agents of Liberal Christianity in their specific context.

Murakami senshō: Searching for truth in Buddhism

The Jōdo Shinshū Buddhist scholar Murakami Senshō 村上專精 (1851–1929) will serve as the first case for illustrating the Buddhist intellectual's response to Christianity and its proselytizing efforts in Japan. Murakami lived through a tumultuous period in Japanese history and was a contemporary of famous intellectual Buddhists such as Inoue Enryō and Shimaji Mokurai that were prominent during the late decades of the nineteenth century. Murakami was born Hirozaki Senshō 広崎專精 into the Kakuji temple of the Ōtani-branch in the Tanba-province of today's Hyōgo prefecture. From a young age, Murakami entered a scholastic education program, which was normal for Buddhists at the time. He was sent to study Chinese in Niigata Prefecture and quickly showed promising talents.

When Murakami was 23, in 1874, he became adopted by the Nyukuji temple in Mikawa (today's Aichi prefecture) and changed his name to Murakami and served as a head priest. In the thirteenth year of Meiji (1880), Murakami moved to Kyoto and started teaching at the Higashi Hongangi Temple, before beginning lecturing at the Shinshū University (Ōtani University) two years later.

Murakami, like many Buddhist intellectuals at the time, was consistently anti-Christian. Ever since the Meiji Restoration, the activities of missionaries and Christians had flourished in Japan, sweeping through the world of intellectuals. Murakami had, as a Jōdo Shinshū Priest, witnessed the invasion of Christian missionaries and the persecution of Buddhism with a deep sense of crisis. Indeed, the last decades of the twentieth century were, as the two historians Yusakata Toshimasa and Mark Blum have noted independently from each other, "a period in which Buddhism in Japan faced its greatest challenge."[12] He was concerned with Buddhism being divided into various sects with no common interests and relationships and felt the need to unify it. It shall be noted, as Ōtani Eiichi and many others have shown, that the concept of a unified "Buddhism" or "Bukkyō 仏教 " in Japanese, in nineteenth century Japan in many ways was a construct, and the idea of a unified Buddhism, to a large degree, very much was a product of its time.[13] It was first in the latter half of the 1880s, so Orion Klautau claims, that Buddhist sects adopted the religious discourse of universalism and "combined the discourse of "religion" or *shūkyō* with universalism." As a result, traditional Buddhist doctrines such as "*kyōzen gokoku* 興禅護国," "*Ōbōihon* 王法為本" or "*Ritsusho ankoku* 立正安国" were all collected under the umbrella category "Japanese Buddhism."[14]

While lecturing in Kyoto, Murakami began his research into Buddhist texts and eventually was invited in 1887 to teach at Soto-Shū University in Tokyo. Murakami's move to Tokyo was an eye-opening experience; for the first time, he saw for himself the energy of the Christian missions in the 1880s. He remarked, "Christianity has towering churches everywhere, and on Saturday and Sunday they bring together young men and women and preach to them…, I saw this situation and could not endure to lament alone."[15] Missions from abroad had been multiplying since the 1870s and 1880s, and by 1890, no less than forty-four foreign Christian societies—including the AEPM—were actively involved in missionary activities in Tokyo alone.[16] Alarmed, but at the same time inspired by the work of the Christian missionaries, Murakami began to imitate the Christian societies and established a Buddhist learning center in which he gave lectures on weekends.

Shortly after, the prominent Buddhist philosopher Inoue Enryō appointed Murakami as a member of his Philosophical Academy (Tetsugakkan 哲学館) and about a year later, Murakami was placed in charge of Indian Philosophy at Tokyo Imperial University, although as Japanese scholar Sueki Fumihiko has fascinatingly noted, he had no knowledge of Sanskrit.[17]

Another major project Murakami oversaw was the publication of the periodicals *Bukkyō shirin* 仏教史林 (*Forest of Buddhist History*) from 1897 and later *Dai Nippon bukkyō-shi* 大日本仏教史 (*Greater Japan's Buddhist history*). Both periodicals were designed to endorse historical research on Buddhism and most importantly endorsed the idea that "Mahayana Buddhism was not taught by the Buddha," a statement which Friedrich Max Müller had stated in his work *Books of the East*, but which at the time provoked an outcry among the Shinshū clergy. Although the leadership of the Shinshū elite were not always pleased with Murakami's progressive views, it could no longer deny the threat that Christianity posed to Buddhism and agreed with Murakami's idea of presenting their Buddhist faith as a unity comparable to modernity.[18]

Much of Murakami's work focused on enhancing Buddhism's readiness to face encroaching foreign threats, like Christianity. At the same time, he was an avid reader of anything, and his eclectic mind led him to explore many facets of Christianity and religion itself. Not all aspects of Murakami's life can be elaborated here, but suffice it is to say that his accomplishments have led some to dub him the father of "Critical Buddhism."[19] The following section will illuminate an aspect that is less frequently discussed: his exposure to liberal Christian ideas.

Critical buddhism and unity

During the 1890s and 1900s, Buddhist intellectuals frequently articulated their understanding of Buddhism's position in the world, shadowing many of the international developments within historical research in the 1900s. One of the primary conceptual tools they employed for this was *historicismus or* "higher criticism," which allowed them to highlight Japanese Buddhism's superiority as a legitimate religion and to situate it as the epicentre of Japan's world transformation narrative, underpinned by nationalistic ideology. Murakami Senshō played a leading role in systematically developing this new movement of "Critical Buddhism" or *Hihan bukkyō* 批判仏教 as it has later been termed.

In 1901, Murakami published the first volume of his magnus opus called *An Attempt of Unifying Buddhism (Bukkyō tōitsuron* 仏教統一論) in which he declared:

> The situation of social progress never stops. There are other things that make me feel the need to do this important research. Somehow, according to Atsushi, each research is based on previous research. The trend of comparative religion in early modern Europe has not yet arrived in Japan. Thus, looking at the current Buddhist world in Japan, the doctrine is divided into many parts, but there is no one who wants to unify it. Although each sect is in a state of crisis, there is no one who wishes to harmonize it as one. Therefore, I feel the need while listening to the trends of comparative religions to make a comparative study of each Buddhist sect.[20]

In this passage, is almost astonishing how much Murakami's ideas of unifying Buddhism seemed to be inspired by the rhetoric of the AEPM and Liberal Christianity, which itself had formulated its wish and intention to search for common points (*Anknüpfungspunkte*) of truth in religion by the tool of comparative studies.[21] In *Bukkyō tōitsuron*, Murakami explained, similar to Akamatsu above, that the teaching of the original Buddha, Śākyamuni, was in perfect harmony with the modernization project of the Meiji government. He criticized Christian literature which questioned the historical truthfulness of the Japanese interpretation of Śākyamuni and his teaching inspired from the Mahāyāna tradition. Up until the late-nineteenth century, people in Japan had uncritically believed that Mahāyāna Buddhism and its teachings, which had arrived in Japan from China, had been the unspoiled words of the first Buddha Śākyamuni. However, works of European Indologists, most famously Max Müller, had proven that even in its most apotheosized texts, the Mahāyāna had been written at least five-hundred years after the historical Buddha had died. This realization brought a wave of existential crisis across the Buddhist sects in Japan, and they began themselves to research the history of Buddha. It was Anesaki Masaharu 姉崎正治 (1873–1949) who with *A Historiography of the Sacred Texts of Buddhism* (*Bukkyō seiten shiron* 佛教聖典史論, 1899) was the first to describe the historical development of Buddhism in an effort to prove the connection between the original Buddha Śākyamuni and the Japanese tradition.[22] Just two years later, Murakami published his work *Bukkyō tōitsuron*, highlighting the correlation between the Mahāyāna tradition and its historical trueness. Within this book he acknowledged that the Mahāyāna tradition and the historical Buddha did not match perfectly, but explained that this was not a problem:

> Śākyamuni Buddha is a historical figure. He is the only Buddha who existed historically. Mahāyāna Buddhism is not the original teaching of Buddha; however, it reflects the "intention" of the Buddha. It is a natu-

ral conclusion of scientific study to view the Buddha as a historical figure and it is foolish to regard him as a supernatural being.[23]

Murakami, in other words, overcame the attack on Japanese Buddhism's historical legitimacy by stressing the philosophical side of Buddhism. It seemed almost self-evident for him that his Mahāyāna Buddhism, like any other Buddhism, could be unified under one universal category. In *Bukkyō tōitsuron*, he then declared that he wanted to promote a "unified research" on Buddhism. While each of the various sects of Japanese Buddhism held its own doctrine and biographical story, Murakami conceived of a meta-level "Japanese Buddhism." He presented a brief description of the similarities of each of the various Japanese sects and hinted to a common kinship between them, which, as he argued, should form the ingredients for a unified Japanese Buddhism.

As Michel Mohr and others have already demonstrated, Murakami's vision of a unified Buddhism was aptly inspired by the "modern European trend of comparative religious studies."[24] At the same time, while acknowledging the usefulness of the new modern tools of comparative religious studies, he questioned its capability in grasping the essence of religious faith:

> As for the nature of Buddhism..., on one hand, it is necessary to approach it with theoretical and empirical tools. Yet, on the other hand, practice from a position of faith and worship is also necessary. Therefore, [I will] pass beyond the ordinary bounds of the independent fields of science and religion, in order to include components of both.[25]

James Mark Shields has in a footnote suggested that Murakami's religious approach due to his "non-rational ground towards religion" is connected to the so-called "phenomenology of religion" found among twentieth century scholars such as Mircea Eliade and Rudolf Otto.[26] This, I believe, is a too hurried assertion. To me, Murakami's theoretical approach fits better in time and place with the ideas of Liberal Christianity as conveyed by the missionaries of the AEPM. More precisely, it resounds the methodology of the German *Religionsgeschichtliche Schule*, which also maintained the importance of faith in their historical study of Christianity. Within the *Religionsgeschichte Schule*, historical research on religion was understood not merely as a historical examination based on scientific evidence but also became intercorrelated with the faith on a search for a truth in all religions. As such, this approach was not problematic at the time. The German missionary Hans Haas published in 1900—a year before Murakami's publication of *Bukkyō tōitsuron*—an editorial essay in the Tokyo-based journal *Die Wahrheit (The Truth),* commenting on the relationship between faith and science: "There is no real contradiction between faith and science, between Christian conviction and the results of modern knowledge. True philosophy also, in the well-known words of Bacon, leads to God, and indeed to no God other than the true God... in him religious and the scientific claims finally agree"[27]

Murakami's interest in combining religious faith with science in an attempt to unearth those mutually shared points of truth within Buddhism in many ways resembled the comparative religious work of the AEPM explored in the previous chapter. It does therefore not surprise us that Murakami's work received the attention of the Swiss and German missionaries early on. In the article "Ventures through the Ethical Literature of Present-day Japan" (*Streifzüge durch die japanische ethische Literatur der Gegenwart*) published in the ZMR in 1893, the German scholar Leonard Busse analyzed Murakami's attempt in uniting Japanese Buddhism. Murakami was by Buss described as

> a modern Buddhist influenced by European philosophy. He is considered as a representative of the new Buddhism, but in fact he takes a middle position between the old and new Buddhism. He knows European philosophy but follows it only in the method of systematic representation, which he applies to Buddhism, while he does not change the content of the latter.[28]

Busse mentioned Murakami's latest publications such as *"Bukkyō ni tsuite Rinri wo soshisu"* (The systematization of Ethics in Buddhism,

1891) and labeled it "old wine in new bottles." Still, he recognized Murakami's inspiration from Europe:

> As far as his analysis of the substance of the doctrine is concerned, he does not go beyond Buddhism as such, but, just like Shaku,[29] he gives the doctrines of the Dharma a psychological foundation, develops them into a clear and coherent system, and submits them to a philosophical contemplation inspired by European philosophy and fills them with the conceptual terminologies. He fills, so to say, old wine into new bottles, applying the method of European philosophies to the content of Buddhist morality. As a result, the latter gains immense clarity and certainty.[30]

This account confirms how the ideas imported from Europe proved to be particularly well matched for the aspirations of Buddhist intellectuals who adopted them and integrated them into the context of Buddhism and gave them new meaning within the modern Buddhist movement. Murakami took the process one conceptual step further and expanded his understanding of comparative theory to its nationalistic extreme. In 1906, in his book *Nihon bukkyō no tokushoku* 日本仏教の特色 (Characteristics of Japanese Buddhism), Murakami wrote of three types of Buddhism, (*zazen* 座禅, *nembutsu* 念仏, and *Nichiren* 日蓮) in which one can understand the spiritual significance of the country of Japan: "There are so many nations that spread Buddhism, but I don't think there is a place in the world where Buddhism developed in so close contact with the nation from the beginning to the end as Japan."[31] Most definitely based on the understanding of critical historicism, Murakami universalized "Buddhism" as well as its uniqueness and, for that matter, nationality. In that sense, Buddhism for him had multiple meanings, and "Japanese Buddhism" was recognized as a religious system different from "foreign Buddhism." Although specific terminologies differ, the underlying idea remains the same as the writings of the AEPM discussed in the previous chapter. Murakami defined the historical narrative of Japanese Buddhism as one in which the people of Japan could recognize the hitherto spiritual right of Buddhism.

The concept of critical historicism thus functions as a flexible lens through which to accentuate the centrality of Japanese Buddhism in a variety of ways. In particular, it helped Murakami and others to emphasize the special significance of Buddhism for the future of Japan. Murakami furthermore utilized the ideas from Liberal Christianity as a kind of self-universalizing scheme, a way to characterize Japanese Buddhism's historical truth and right in Japan.

SHINRI, A CHRISTIAN JOURNAL

The ideas of a unified Buddhism founded on comparative studies could only gain so wide a recognition in Japan due to the broad publication of Christian journals at the time. During the period between the 1890s and 1900s, a number of Christian journals manifested themselves in the center of many debates among the Meiji intelligentsia and the public. The publication of the Japanese-language periodical *Shinri* 『眞理』 (Truth) by the AEPM from 1889 was hugely popular and had a great influence on the academic landscape of Meiji Japan. It attracted a great deal of attention due to it being an academic Christian periodical containing high-level and academically sound articles. How popular it was at the time can be seen from the following quote from Minami Hajime:

> While it is considered heresy in some quarters, "Shinri" has become so popular that it needs to be read—and wherever I ask, Shinri can always be found on the pastor's desk.[32]

As it can be seen, *Shinri* was hugely popular, especially among Japanese Christians, and played a major role in promoting liberal Christian ideas both inside as well as outside Christian circles. It was also instrumental in introducing rationalism into Christianity and several articles introduced the method of critical reading.[33] The articles also tapped into evolutionary theory, which previously had been considered incompatible with religion, and sought the ethnicization of religion free of the authority of the church and freed of superstition [34]

Through *Shinri*, the AEPM wrote for a general readership and explained Liberal Christianity's fundamental tenets in easy to-access language. For example, from 1890, Otto Schmiedel published in *Shinri* a series of articles surrounding the relationship between Darwin's theory of evolution and religion. In articles such as "Relationship between Darwin's doctrine and teleology" (*Daruwin gakusetsu to tetsugaku teki shūkyokuron no kankei* ダルウ井ン學説と哲學的終局論の關係),[35] "Is Darwin's theory on the competition for survival true?" (*Daruwinsetsu no seizon kyōsō to wa shin ka* ダルウ井ン説の生存競争とは眞歟), and "Darwin's human and monotheism" (*Daruwin no hito to isshinkyō*, ルウ井ンの人と一神教), Schmiedel explicated the scope of Christian faith and its compatibility with some of the most contentious topics of the time.[36]

As a project of its time, *Shinri*—like other magazines of the AEPM—analogously followed the societal modernization process founded on morality and religion and presented its case for a Liberal Christianity as the epitome of this. In several articles, Otto Schmiedel introduced and explained the philosophies of Kant, Hegel, and Schopenhauer, always as congruent with Christianity.[37]

The "modern European trend" of comparative religious studies, which Murakami had referred to above, was also introduced to Japan for the first time in *Shinri*. In September of 1890, the AEPM missionary Carl Munzinger published a 4-page article called "On the Necessity of Religion" (*Shūkyōgaku no hitsuyo wo ronzū* 宗教學の必要を論ず). In the article, Munzinger presented the field of comparative religious studies in Japan by using the word *shūkyōgaku* 宗教学 or "religious studies" and articulated its role in fashioning a comprehensive "religion" transcending the boundaries of sect and religion. Three years later in 1893, Minami Hajime wrote a similar essay in *Shinri* called "Comparative Religion and Christianity" (*Hikaku shūkyōgaku to kirisutokyō* 比較宗教學と基督教) explaining the sudden rise in research on Christianity that employed the comparative method. To him, religion was something vital to human nature and life itself. "Religion," he wrote, "is fundamentally made up of morality." Similar to Munzinger, Minami's article tapped into evolutionary theory, viewing "religion" as a movement towards the unification of religion.[38] According to Minami, modern sciences such as comparative studies and historical criticism of the Bible separated the historical facts from ignorant belief in fables and superstitions. Modern religious studies, he claimed, identified the falsities in religious texts: "higher criticism," Minami wrote, intended to point out the "true faith" in all religions.[39] But like the missionaries in the previous chapter, Minami remained biased by his own religion. This suggests an important argument of this book, that even while liberal Christians recognized that other religions were equally "religions," in the dialogue they established with other religions, they continued to assume the superiority or priority of their own religion.

The methods of comparative religious studies were most likely well-known among intellectual Buddhists such as Murakami given its frequent mention in publications at the time.[40] It is also significant that Munzinger and Minami chose to introduce comparative religious studies in the periodical *Shinri* written for a general Japanese-readership, as it implies that the AEPM regarded the theory as a central component of liberal Christian teachings.[41]

Munzinger and Minami's discussions on comparative religious studies resonates with arguments suggested by Murakami's book *Bukkyō tōitsuron* that viewed "critical studies" as a process toward the unification of Buddhism. In general, Christian journals such as *Shinri* allowed Buddhist readers to hand-pick theories and ideas that situated their Buddhism as the epicenter of Japan's transformative narrative. Not surprisingly, *Shinri* also played a leading role in developing Murakami's idea of a unified Buddhism as well.

In August 1894, Murakami published a short essay titled "Buddhism as seen in Christian journals" (*Kirisutokyō zasshi ni okeru bukkyō* キリスト教雑誌における仏教) in the Buddhist periodical *Bukkyō Shinrin* in which he mentioned the AEPM journal *Shinri* together with other Christian journals such as the Unitarian's *Rikugō zasshi* 六合雑誌 and the *Nichiyō sōshi* 日曜叢誌 (Sunday Magazine). In it he explained that these Christian journals are sources of inspiration for his wish to re-unify Buddhism.[42] Murakami furthermore stressed that he was open to suggestions by non-Buddhist intellectuals, which suggests that Murakami and his project on unifying or re-unifying Buddhism was a product of his immersion in the particular intellectual climate of the 1890s, where liberal Christian journals such as *Shinri* played a central role.

Shinri, Murakami, and Japanese Christians.

German Liberal Christianity and the concept of comparative religious studies, informed through the AEPM and *Shinri*, represents one example of how religious discourse in the late nineteenth-century became indigenized in Japan. Given the increasing prevalence of discourse on "Japan" and "the nation," by the end of the 1890s, it is not surprising that the scope of *Shinri* with time also became a platform for Japanese Christians to express their own opinions. As Munzinger noted in his book *Japan und die Japaner* in 1898 concerning *Shinri*: "The importance of the journal is seen in that speakers, writers, and other church figures among Japanese Christians now have a voice and have recognized that our journal is for their best."[43] In this sense, while *Shinri* managed to become local in its outlook, it was still fundamentally a propaganda tool for liberal Christian ideas, underpinning the importance of Christianity and missionaries in Japanese society. One example of this is Kozaki Nariaki's article "*Nihon ni okeru kirisutokyō no shikō*" 日本における基督教の思考 (Christian Thoughts in Japan) from 1892. Here Kozaki reminds his readers of the need for moral progress in a time of fast scientific progress:

> As the scientific method is the main characteristic of our modern age, it is also the feature of our present Japan as opposed to the closed and medieval Japan of 30 years ago. Now, nothing is too high and holy or too low and mean that it is not explored and pierced by the spirit of science. Like the spirits of our past, the latter knows no boundaries in space and

time; it changes the universe and does not care whether it frightens the spectators. And in Japan, where Kantian philosophy has not yet established its impermeable realm of inductive logic, scientific interest is the highest and most prevalent.[44]

For Kozaki, the modernization of the Japanese state went too fast, and the narrow focus on science had been too extreme. As he pointed out, in just thirty years Japan had passed through a development which had taken the Western nations two-hundred-and-fifty-years, but had failed to introduce the necessary humanistic philosophies in that process. He therefore encouraged his compatriots not to attack or reject the missionaries, but to listen to them for real guidance, to let them be their teachers in the progress of Japan becoming a modern state equal to any Western nation. Equally, another member of the AEPM, the Japanese Masaharu Sasaki, defended the missionaries in the article "Japanese National character and the Missionaries," stating the following:

> If you have once had the possibility to observe with your own eyes the life and activity of the missionaries in the Far East, you must have understood with which unselfish love they abandoned their more comfortable life at home to bring us their sacrifice. This vigorous proof of love has reopened the firmly closed hearts, and so we stand today with deep gratitude and admiration for the missionaries.[45]

Shinri's discursive move to be a forum for Japanese Christians to defend their Liberal Christianity proved to be an initial success. From 1889 to 1908 the periodical was published monthly.[46] Eight years after the periodical's inception Carl Munzinger reflected on the overall importance of *Shinri* in 1898:

> Without our journal, the Christian circles would in the last eight years have been under even more pressure. But Shinri stood guard, with its sharp sword of the spirit, it and its comrades held the brazen enemy in its place, allowing the Christian workers to continue building the kingdom of God.[47]

In *Shinri*, Liberal Christianity's privileged status as key to a universal religion legitimized the missionaries' claim that they were to be the unifier of the world. Under the openminded co-editorship of missionary Otto Schmiedel and the two students Maruyama Michikazu and Minami Hajime, the magazine went a long way towards meeting these goals.[48] The content of the journal was decided by a group of Japanese students and the editor in chief. The group would meet four times a month. Occasionally their meetings included scientific and philosophical lectures for its readers, and sometimes popular lectures were organized for the public. The young Japanese Christian editors and the missionaries recognized the mutual benefits of their cooperative efforts in stemming the tide of scepticism. The editors were emboldened by the missionaries' support, and correspondingly the missionaries began to publish translated content of *Shinri* in the ZMR.

The formulation of Liberal Christianity's special role as the universal religion unifying the world provided a doctrinal basis for the activities surrounding *Shinri*. It was not particularly paradoxical or contradictory for the AEPM to promote universal ideas while at the same time claiming the uniqueness and superiority of their own religion. For them, all countries, cultures, and religions shared the same essence and derived from the same source—that is, Christianity—and comparative studies of the world religions could prove this.

The analysis of this chapter so far shows that Buddhist intellectual ideas of a unified Buddhism or a modern Buddhism were intricately tied to the ideas of religion and universality proposed by Liberal Christianity. When examining Murakami's free interpretation of what the unity of Buddhism meant, for example, we find an argument similar to that of the AEPM. To Murakami, Buddhism and Japan held the key to a "universal "truth, resulting from the unique historical character of its imperial lineage. In other words, the combination of historical awareness and ethnocentrism served as the foundation of, or perhaps even facilitated, the reinterpretation of liberal Christian discourse in sweeping Buddhist terms.

Tada Kanae, a Buddhist reformist

The Shinshū Buddhist monk Tada Kanae 多田 鼎 (1875–1937) will serve as the second example illustrating the Buddhist intellectuals' appropriations of liberal Christian ideas. While Murakami Senshō above has received a lot of attention by scholars of modern Japanese Buddhism within recent years from both Western and Japanese scholars, the case is the opposite for Tada Kanae, who still remains largely unknown in contemporary scholarship.

Tada Kanae, originally named Tada Keigo 多田慶悟, was born as the third son into an Ōtani-branch temple in Aichi prefecture. Like many Buddhist monks at the time, Tada entered a scholastic education. He studied the classic texts and quickly learned to read Chinese. He moved to Tokyo at the age of seventeen to attend a vocational school, but later dropped out after about four months due to financial reasons. After leaving the school, he learned about the famous Japanese philosopher Kiyozawa Manshi 清沢満之 (1873–1949) from his brother-in-law, Murakami Senshō. Kiyozawa was a controversial figure. In the 1870s, Kiyozawa had traveled to Europe and he used the knowledge he had gained abroad to unite Protestant ideas of salvation with the teaching of his own Shinshū belief. Kiyozawa was interested not simply in Buddhism, but also in coming to understand religion in a deeper and more general, existential sense.[49]

In the fourth month of the twenty-ninth year of Meiji (1896), Tada moved to Kyoto and, like Murakami, entered Shinshū University. In the same year, he participated in a reform movement of the Higashi Honganji Temple led by his teacher Kiyozawa. As a consequence, Tada, together with Kiyozawa and several students, was expelled from the school but was allowed to return the following year. Tada, who was twenty-two at the time, followed the teaching of Kiyozawa, who acted as his direct mentor as well as disciplinarian, for the following 36 months. Later in his life, this idolization of his teacher would change, but during his school years, Tada was deeply inspired by Kiyozawa's reform Buddhism.[50]

Tada graduated from Shinshū University in 1900 and shortly after, he moved back to Tokyo where he became a leading member within a reformist youth community named Kōkōdō 浩々洞, literally, "the constantly moving water of a cave."[51] Kōkōdō was a controversial due to its "suspicious likeness to Christianity."[52] Lodged in Kiyozawa's house, he, together with the two young Buddhist students Akatsuki Karasuya 暁烏 敏 (1877–1954) and Sasaki Geshō 佐々木月樵 (1875–1926), formed a proximity that allowed frequent brainstorming sessions.

In 1902, Tada was appointed as professor at Shinshū University, which at that time had been relocated to Tokyo from Kyoto because of reforms within Nishi Honganji that had resulted in the closure of the normal school, but in November the same year, Tada resigned from this post. Some speculate that this resignation was due to fear among Tada's Shinshu colleagues that he was getting too radical in his reformism.[53] This also marked Tada's first turning point with Kiyozawa. Tada spent the following year away from the Buddhist intellectual world, before he in 1903 founded the school Chiba Gakuin 千葉教院 east of Tokyo. The establishment of Chiba Gakuin can be interpreted as a further attempt of Tada to move away from his Shinshū heritage. Tada proudly named the land surrounding the school "the no Shinshū land" (*Shinshū kaimu* 真宗皆無). This further marked Tada's shift away from Kiyozawa and other Shinshū Buddhists. He then began a scholarship and discussion of life centred around spiritualism and Evangelism. According to the German missionary Hans Haas, "Tada Kanae is an active Shinshū teacher who is… domiciled in Chiba, the prefecture's capital. Here he practices his influence over students of the local medizing school and the pupils of the teacher's collage as a preacher and a chaplain [*Seelsorger*]. Among his own, Mr. Tada is suspected of having a too close relationship to Christianity." Haas continued in his description of Tada further: "… he is clearly influenced by Christian missionaries. He organized his spiritual gatherings on Sundays, just like the Christians. He opens them with a prayer and readx out of the scriptures. He regularly preaches about the Tripitaka Canon or even non-canonical Japanese religious scriptures. What he preaches is not Buddhist heresies, although it is questionable whether the Shinshū and Jodōshū teachings he teaches still can be considered Buddhism."[54]

It is worth reiterating here the fact that, on the one hand, Tada's Chiba Gakuin was a Buddhist institution with a curriculum based purely on Buddhist scriptures such as the Tripitaka, and on the other hand, Haas's description of the school's activities as being "clearly influenced by Christian missionaries" can be interpreted as an obvious attempt to counterbalance the success of Christian youth associations.

Youth associations or so-called *seinen-kai* 青年会 run by Christians communities were in the mid–1890s, when Tada was studying in Tokyo, wildly popular. The AEPM's youth association Sol Oriens was flourishing and functioned as a center for experimenting with new modes of thinking. From an early stage, the missionaries of the AEPM had attracted a group of young students interested in philosophy, literature, and ethics, which likewise was functioned as a link between academia, journalism, and the general public. In September 1888, Wilfried Spinner had stressed the importance of such youth associations for the benefit of the whole society:

> [We want to give] the Japanese students at universities and university preparatory schools an opportunity to deal with presentations and discussions of ethical and religious issues in a scientific manner, in the belief that the solving of these questions helps the well-being of the individual as well as the whole society.[55]

The youth association of the AEPM was established by the Japanese student Kusama Jifuku originally under the name *Verein Deutsch verstehender Studierender zur Besprechung ethicher und religiöser Fragen*, which later was shortened to "Sol Oriens" (The Morning Sun).[56] It's purpose according to Spinner was "to further propagate the benefits of Christianity."[57]

Sol Oriens held seven different lectures annually spread over the year, with one lecture being given by Spinner, and the rest by the Japanese students at various workshops. These workshops had two purposes. First, they were to improve the relationship between the missionaries and their young students. Secondly, the lectures developed during these workshops were meant to communicate the benefits of Christianity for the modernization of Japan.[58] The latter was more easily achieved than the former. The group's youthful composition and the lack of sanctioned control in the classroom by the missionaries were both reflected at the opening of a workshop in 1888. Here Spinner writes of an incident in his diary:

Meeting of the "Verein zur Besprechung ethischer und religiöser Fragen." Kusama presided and presented the program which he and I had composed together. Mukō [Gunji], who continues his destructive tendencies, attends the meetings but does not visit the church. He chatted much uselessly, the similar [attitude] came from Maruyama [Michikazu]. Finally, as Mukō interrupted me with laughter, I corrected him sharply. His arrogance and [lack of] ambition does not make him suitable as a theologian. The same can be said of Kusama.[59]

Considering the uncooperative atmosphere between Spinner and his Japanese students, it is surprising that Sol Oriens managed to produce any significant results. But in a letter from 1889, Spinner could report that, as part of a lecture series organized by the Japanese students of Sol Oriens, the student Hattori gave a presentation on the topic "Which religion is the best for Japan?" Hattori, so Spinner reported, compared the religions of Japan, and argued for which suited a modern Japan. The conclusion was, perhaps not surprising given the context of the presentation, Christianity.[60]

The student members of the club belonged to a wider group of young Japanese who felt a discontent with the profane measures of the rational comprehension of morality. Instead, they were open to ideas which could address their individuality from within. The rapid development of Meiji Japan, as supported by historian Oleg Benesch, had left many Japanese feeling divided and rootless.[61] Youth groups and institutions such as Sol Oriens, which tended to caution against the rapid "materialistic" developments, quickly gained popularity among young Japanese students. They were places in which their questions and doubts could be voiced and discussed. In 1889, missionary Otto Schmiedel reported back to Switzerland: "The youth club, which Spinner says is blooming, is 'Sol Oriens.'"[62] From 1890 onward the ever-increasing success of Sol Oriens had the effect that Spinner could withdraw from the board and let the organization be solely run by Japanese students. The club ran for the next ten years. In 1891, according to a handwritten note from Spinner, the student board of Sol Oriens consisted of three Japanese students: Tsukui, Akanuma, and Mitari, all three of whom had previously attended the baptismal lessons of Spinner.[63]

When the board of Sol Oriens opened the doors to a workshop at the mission school in Hongo in the summer semester of 1891, they presented the following program:

- Friday, 29 March 1891: What religion is dangerous to the state?
- Friday, 4 April 1891: The influence of religion on society.
- Friday, 26 April 1891: Is modernization possible within Christianity, and if so, how should it be done?
- Friday, 10 May 1891: Should the choice of religion be left to the people or should it be prescribed by the state?[64]

As can be seen by the lectures of Sol Oriens, the students did not shy away from controversial discussions and through their activities, they set in motion an active campaign to propagate liberal Christian ideas to Japan.

Kanae's Chiba Gakuin worked in a similar fashion offering spiritual gatherings, scripture readings of the Tripitaka Canon, and brainstorming sessions for experimenting with new modes of thinking. It therefore does not surprise us that Tada's work in Chiba received extra attention from both the Shinshū clergy and the Swiss and German missionaries. According to Japanese scholar Ikama Yugaku, Tada was "by Ōtani scholars perceived as the Judas to Christ."[65] Similarly, Hans Haas could in his book *Amida Buddha unsere "Zuflucht*, report that: "Among his own, Mr. Tada is suspected of being too biased towards Christianity. But what they find offensive about him is not his dogmatic views, but his pastoral practice, which too clearly is influenced by Christianity."[66]

At the Gakuin, Tada cooperated with several students including the later leading Buddhists Miyamoto Masataka 宮本正尊 (1893–1983) and Shirai Shigekoto 白井成允 (1888–1973), while at the same time continuing his collaboration with Kōkōdō. The school, so Miyamoto later wrote, promoted a specific "religious mood."[67] However, running the Gakuin proved extremely difficult. The school lacked proper facilities for the students and living expenses was a constant burden. In 1911, a year after Haas had left Japan, Tada closed the school and returned to Aichi prefecture.

Kanae's integration of liberal christian ideas

Tada was not only prolific in his activities with youth forums, but he was also an avid writer and published several fascinating works in the 1900s. From 1900, Tada also worked as the co-editor for the Buddhist journal *Seishinkai* 精神界 (Spiritual World). It was from here that he also wrote the books *Shūdo kōwa* 修道講話 (Lectures of Practicing Religion, 1905), *Shōshinge kōwa* 正信偈講話 (*Shōshinge Lectures*, 1907), and *Onchō no shūkyō* 恩寵の宗教 (Religion of Grace, 1908). Especially Tada's second book, *Shōshinge Lectures*, received a lot of interest from the AEPM. *Shōshinge kōwa*, which refers to Shinran 親鸞 (1173–1263), the founder of Jōdo Shinshō's text *Shōshinge*, is a compiled series of seven lectures. In the lectures, Tada emphasized "the true meaning of the Buddhist ancestors." Influenced by Kiyozawa and Western spiritualism, Tada adopted the terms "introspection" (*naika* 内観) and "grace" (*onchō* 恩寵) to explain his understanding of Buddha. Introspection was a methodological premise of spiritualism at the turn of the century. In faith, it became important to adopt the method of "seeing the truth of yourself" (*jibun no shinsō o Miwa kuru* 自分の真相をみわくる). A personification of faith developed in Tada's teaching which mirrored liberal Christian ideas that saw faith as the decisive element in the constitution of "Persönlichkeit" or personality. Religious experience was for Tada understood as constitutive of the individuality of the individual, with "one's inner life" (reflecting the idea of Wilhelm Herrmann) as predominant. This line of thought is among others reflected in *Shōshinge kōwa,*, where Tada states: "I am at a loss when I look outside myself on the teachings. The way you choose [faith] should be decided directly from the inside."[68] To Tada, "introspection" was the self-reflective tool to gain awareness of one's finiteness, guilt and "grace." The idea "that man is covered with a darkness of guilt and only Amida Nyorai decides the pain and success of things."[69] As can be seen here, "introspection" and "grace" were for Tada inextricably linked. The awareness of oneself through introspection was the gift of Amida's grace, and Amida's grace could only be felt through introspection.

In 1910, Hass translated three of Tada's lectures from his first book *Shūdo kōwa* into German in his *Amida Buddha unsere "Zuflucht."* Here Haas noted on Tada's work: "As I read my translation of Rev. K. Tada's sermons, I felt that they sound so very Christian in thought that a reader might almost be attempted to suppose that I had made them up for purposes of my own, and that they were not translations at all."[70] What made Tada stand out in contrast to many leading Shin Buddhists at the time was, according to Haas, that he embraced a realization of a "union of the two major religions."[71]

In *Shūdo kōwa*, Tada discussed the idea of "grace," emphasizing the convergence of its principles with his own Buddhist movement, especially the notion of grace as God's mercy given to humankind because God desires humankind to have it was reflected in Tada's lectures. In the first of seven lectures which made up Tada's *Shūdo kōwa*, titled *byōjō shin kore-dō* 平常心是道 (The world that we have to go through), he summarized this idea of grace :

> We shall see even more clearly when we consider that the Father of Mercy willingly and abundantly forgives us of all our sins, sins which we tremble to contemplate, and that He accepts us as we are and saves us. But have we been forgiven; shouldn't we also forgive others? It is the Buddha's wish that forgives all people, so that we too should forgive as he has forgiven.[72]

In another passage, he carefully explained one of the principles of his belief:

> Put all people into one unity through the one name! Pray for all people to focus on the one and only Buddha! Let all seek their rest in the one and only paradise! That is the core and star of our faith.[73]

Although Tada does not use the word universality here in this context, he seemed fully aware of the implication of his description of bringing "unity through one name." Thus, when Tada mentioned "grace," it was in relation to his own project of reforming Buddhism itself. In other words, although Tada, as seen in the passage above, used similar terminology to Protestantism, it was with the goal of improving his own Buddhism.

Tada's *Shūdo kōwa,* in spite of its scattered nature and unstructured flow, constitutes an important source of understanding how liberal Christian ideas in particular were a good match for the aspirations of Buddhist reformers, as well as proving the burgeoning attraction of Buddhist intellectuals to create their independent belief.

On the side of the Swiss and German missionaries, the German missionary Emil Schiller provides an interesting example of how the missionaries equally were invested in participating in the debate on "personal religion." In 1903, in an article entitled "Das Heutige Japan und das Christentum" (*Contemporary Japan and Christianity*) published in the ZMR, Schiller noted that the reason why the Christian mission had difficulty settling in Japan was the "critical stance of Buddhists against all Christians."[74] Schiller believed that Shinshū Buddhists such as Tada Kanae and Murakami in many ways possessed a religious nature similar to Christianity, but that their understanding of the religion behind was different from that of the missionaries. In particular, he pointed out that many of them misunderstood the individuality of Christianity as "poisonous to the old social norms" by which people still ordered their lives.[75] According to Schiller, the strong chauvinistic pride among these Buddhist intellectuals made it difficult to establish a dialogue, as even the most fundamental ideas seemed to be lost in translation. One such idea was the Christian concept of the existence of God, "Dasein eines Gottes."

The historical development of "a polytheistic pantheism, Buddhist atheism and Confucian skepticism," Schiller argued, lay at the basis of the etymology of the Japanese word for the Christian God, Kami. It had been suffused with "a meaning of Ur- or all-encompassing power similar to the Confucian concept of *Ten* (heaven, 天), rather than an understanding of God as a personality as understood in Protestantism."[76] This mistranslation or misinterpretation, so Schiller argues, made many—and not only the intellectual Buddhists—feel that they did not need the foreign god of Christianity, as they already had one comparable on their own.

In another passage, Schiller carefully explained to his readers how the ideas of a single, personal God had entered Japan. "Without any exception, the concept of a single, personal God," he stated, "was new to Japan when the first Christian missionaries arrived in the sixteenth century." To Schiller, much of the Buddhist criticism of Christianity and the missionaries owed to misinterpretations and the difficulty in comprehending central Christian ideas such as sin and trinity. Hence, general teachings on "the existence of God, of his personality, and the like, are the first and foremost questions which the missionary work in Japan has to tend to."[77]

Mirroring his German article, the integration of liberal Christian concepts was introduced to Japanese cultural ontology through several Japanese publications. In 1901, Schiller published the book *Kami no kannen to kinsei tetsugaku* 神の觀念と近世哲學 (*The idea of God and Modern Philosophy*). In the book, Schiller highlighted the importance of teaching the Western ideas of God as a personality first, before exposing to the Japanese people the idea of Christ as a divine figure.[78]

Schiller addresses the same theme in the book *Kirisutokyō yōgi* 基督教要義 (The Essence of Christianity) from 1908. In it, he summarizes that the Christian message should begin with the explanation of God and not with Jesus Christ, because the Japanese language was not yet familiar with the strong individuality that had made God give Christ the role as savior of humanity.[79] A thorough introduction to the concept of God first, followed by an introduction of Jesus Christ: that was for Schiller the central aspect for the methodological sequencing of missionary presentations and teachings in Japan. Although not explicitly explained in this particular book, Schiller elsewhere in his writings identified the lack of "deeper understanding" and the focus on materialism as the main problems for Christianity in Japan, and feared that Christianity might become a movement of social work, which only emphasized practical work instead of developing a personal and rightful understanding of God.

The religious dialogue between Buddhism and Christianity at the time also led some of the missionaries to wonder whether the essence of Christianity genuinely was to be found in its ethical and philosophical teachings. And whether it therefore could live in co-existence with the other religions of Japan. One of the leading advocates for this approach was the German missionary, Hans Haas. Throughout his life, Haas made frequent use the comparative approach to promote a dialogue between the two religions. Haas played a major role in the prewar popularity of Shintsū Buddhism among German scholars through his network and literary skills. He was also instrumental in establishing the first sourcebook on the interrelationship between Buddhism and Christianity, *Bibliographie zur Frage nach den Wechselbeziehungen zwischen Buddhismus und Christentum* in 1922.[80] Haas also wrote for a general readership and explained Shinshū's fundamental similarities in

6. Buddhist Exposures to Liberal Christianity | 213

Missionarz Emil Schiller and Johannes Witte with Buddhist priests, Kyoto, 1924.
Photo: Zentralarchiv der Ev. Kirche der Pfalz.

Missionary Johannes Witte in a Buddhist temple, 1924.
Photo: Zentralarchiv der Ev. Kirche der Pfalz.

several articles written in the ZMR.[81] For example, in 1912, he wrote an article titled: "Christliche Klänge im japanischen Buddhismus" (Christian Sounds in Japanese Buddhism). In the article, Haas explicates the need for Christians to try to co-exist with Buddhists. As he pointed out in a remarkably self-critical way, Christianity's lack of success in Japan could not solely be blamed on the Japanese people, but rather the reasons might in fact be engrained in the nature of Christianity itself. He noted that the historical success of Buddhism in Japan was its capability to co-exist with Shintō. "Why then," he asked, "should Buddhism not also be able to co-exist with Christianity, especially if the latter had the audacity to compromise rather than conquer?"[82]

In a similar vein, Emil Schroeder, a German missionary stationed in Tokyo following Hans Haas, pleaded a more tolerant attitude towards Buddhism among Christians. In 1911, his short text "Aus der Mission der Gegenwart" (From the Mission of the Present), published in the ZMR, suggested adopting a Christian approach sympathetic to Buddhism which should not appear to condone compromise. Almost all the essential doctrines of Christianity, as Schroeder stated, were also to be found in Buddhist theology: "Buddhism has, apart from atonement, everything that Christianity has, including the incarnation and a trinity." The only difference between the two religions, Schroeder stated, was Jesus. It was "through the humanism of Jesus that the *Übermensch* was reached and that the creedal, the ecclesiastical, and the liturgical become valuable."[83] In his peculiar Nietzschean view, the religion of Christianity was no more acceptable nor finer than Buddhism, but Jesus was a better role model than Buddha and therefore needed to be propagated to the Japanese people.

For this chapter's study on Buddhist exposure to Liberal Christianity, the publications of Tada, Schiller, Haas, and Schroeder are significant in that they illustrate how in the beginning of the twentieth century, liberal Christian ideas played a role in one of the most massive Buddhist reformist movement in modern Japanese history. Through the works of Murakami and Tada, but also the Swiss and German missionaries, we see a new kind of circulation of ideas between Buddhists and Christians. Buddhist intellectuals' influence on expanding the scope of liberal Christian ideas thus became crucial for the cultural transfer of Liberal Christianity to Japan.

Summing up the Buddhist side of the encounter

Murakami Senshō and Tada Kanae both exemplified the modern Buddhist movement. Following developments of the time, they respectively occupied key positions and succeeded in establishing good repute among their peers and students. Moreover, both of their intellectual careers were, as shown, influenced, one way or another, by Japan's contact with Christianity, especially after the arrival of Liberal Christianity to Japan. It cannot be a historical coincidence that these two contemporaneous Buddhist figures both looked towards Christianity to reestablish their own belief in Buddhism.[84] Although the work of Murakami and Tada occurred under different circumstances, it is nonetheless possible to observe a few poignant commonalities. First, they both were products of an unstable time in which Buddhism was in crisis and sought to reform itself. Second, both implemented specific liberal Christian ideas in their writings on Japanese Buddhism. Murakami did so by adopting historicism and by arguing for the universality of religion. Tada achieved this more directly by adopting a Christian practice with lectures and Buddhist sermons in his youth association Kōkōdō, and by interpreting ideas of Grace and guilt into the works of Shinran. Third, neither Murakami nor Tada claimed to support the Christian mission; rather, they both fought the influence of Christianity and tried to increase the importance of Buddhism. These similarities between Murakami and Tada are striking and reflect once again the extent to which the missionary presence stoked unprecedented debates and how liberal Christian ideas of "historical truth" and "universalism" were utilized not only by missionaries who sought to promote their own cultural agenda, but also by Japanese Buddhists, who at the turn of the twentieth century appropriated and reformulated these ideas to suit their own religious and nationalistic ambitions.

It is worth reiterating here that, while on one hand, Buddhist intellectuals rejected missionaries and refuted their claims, on the other hand, some Buddhist intellectuals appropriated the ideas of Liberal Christianity to justify their own existence. This may seem contradictory, especially when thinking of the case of Murakami Senshō, who, as a teacher at one of the most prominent universities in Meiji Japan, was in a position to actively suppress the missionaries' ideas. However, by appropriating and reformulating liberal Christian ideas such as the "universalism" of religion into a Buddhist context, it becomes quite easy to see that in both cases, Liberal Christianity, despite its "universal claim," revolved around ethnocentric agendas. The universal claims and the scientific tools of Liberal Christianity could be utilized not only in Christianity, but also in other religions. The only difference was the name of the religion; the specific methods of achieving a "universal" claim remained ultimately the same.

This chapter on Buddhist intellectuals analyzed the Buddhist response to their encounter with Liberal Christianity. The examples of Murakami Senshō and Tada Kanae, although short, revealed that Buddhist individuals had contact with Liberal Christianity and its ideas. Murakami Senshō and Tada Kanae are not the only examples I have found in which Buddhist missionaries had direct or indirect contact to the concepts of Liberal Christianity and the missionaries of the AEPM. Buddhist intellectuals such as Shimaji Mokurai and Inoue Tetsujiro share stark similarities to the history of Murakami Senshō and Tada Kanae. Shimaji, for example, visited Berlin in September of 1872, where he was introduced to the later AEPM member Aoki Shūzō. Just like Aoki, Shimaji showed an interest in questions relevant to the relationship between the state and religion. Aoki also introduced Shimaji to the two liberal theologians and subsequent AEPM members Gustav Emil Lisco and Karl Heinrich Ritter.[85] Shimaji's later attempt to initiate a Buddhist reform by borrowing ideas from his discussions with the two liberal theologians is for example seen in the text *Kyōhō no gen* 教法の原 (Inquiry into Religion). Here he, for example, summarized Buddhism's missionary activities, its rejection of prayers, its monotheism, and the allowance of marriage in Shinshu Buddhism as clear similarities between Buddhism and Protestantism.[86]

However, the stark similarities between these Buddhist intellectuals suggest that German Liberal Christianity's influence on Buddhist intellectuals in Meiji Japan may be larger than previously thought, especially considering how many examples likely remain unknown. Regrettably, the limitations of this study make it difficult draw any firm conclusions. If similar examples in the future are located, it might be possible to gain more insight into this fascinating event of cultural transfer centered around the ideas of Liberal Christianity.

The following chapter will illuminate yet another phenomenon of cultural transfer. This time, however, we again pivot 180-degrees to look at the transfer of mission journals written in Japan directed at the Swiss and German youth readership.

7

Educating Youth at Home

Swiss and German Youth Missionary Literature

It was a chilly spring evening in April 1931 when 13-year-old Otto Schmitt and some of his friends hurried to the parish hall of his local church in Waldrach, near Trier, Germany. For the young Germans, it was a special day. Ever since the minister had announced that the church would be showing a film to the children, they had been filled with anticipation. The film was a silent movie about Japan produced by missionaries of the AEPM.

Avid readers of the youth magazines *Missionsblatt für die Kinder* and *Missionsblat für die Jugend* published by the AEPM, Otto and the other children regularly devoured reports and pictures portraying the adventures of the Swiss-German missionaries in Japan. However, on that special spring day, they met the missionaries and saw Japan for the first time in "living pictures." To them, it was as if they were transported to Japan: "We took the Siberian Railway to Kyoto in Japan. Once there, we visited the city. We saw countless temples of the Japanese religion. The dominant religion is Buddhism, but there are also other religions."[1] As if experiencing them firsthand, he described the peculiar customs and rites of the Japanese faiths. He observed that: "the carp are fed in large ponds. The Japanese believe carp are sacred animals. They are worshiped because they believe the carps are the souls of the deceased."[2] In addition to these religious customs, he also noticed something he knew from back home: the tuition in love for one's country: "The Japanese youth are educated in patriotism and love for their emperor. In the movie we saw boys dancing with their flags. Each boy had two Japanese flags and moved in chorus in accordance with their teachers' wishes."[3] After the film, the German missionary Emil Schiller presented his work at the Dōshisha University in Kyoto, as well as his broader involvement in the Christian communities, to the excited children. On small notes written down on a blackboard, he would tell them how the mission still had many challenges to face for the Christianization of Japan, and how they could help through prayers.[4] Clearly impressed by his experiences from the film, Otto Schmitt internalized the message, and concluded in an essay sent to the editors of the youth journal *Für die Jugend*: "The German mission is eagerly needed in Japan."[5]

The significance of youth mission journals

As young Otto Schmitt's insipient image of Japanese society grew, he was, at the same time developing his own self-image as a German in a globalized world. His observation that the missionaries were still "eagerly needed" to help the less civilized on their path towards modernity, as James Blaut argued, a central and unshakeable belief that existed in Germany and other European countries at the time.[6] And, by drawing from the lessons taught in his local parish hall, Otto Schmitt and his friends developed a conviction that Germany was a "blessed" land. This sentiment was revealed in the mission journals, as Germany was described as a "liberal, modern, and Christian society" to be contrasted with the "heathen" world, a world described and reconstructed for Otto and his contemporaries from the missionary point of view.

Young Germans like Otto grew up at a time when the world, according to German historian Jürgen Osterhammel, was getting ever smaller.[7] Through the youth mission journals,[8] the children were taught about the world's people and cultures, and how they could be categorized according to ambiguous but nonetheless generally understood hierarchies of civilization.[9] Germans could effortlessly differentiate between those at the top of the scale—namely "Europeans" or "Christians"—and those people still, like the Japanese, clinging onto superstitious beliefs and customs, and thus considered "less cultured." The ethnocentric discourse described in the previous chapters permeated the literature offered to the young Swiss and German readers. Children like Otto Schmitt, as Jeff Bowersox argues, were quite aware of their own superior position in the world.[10]

Academic research by post-colonial scholars such as John and Jean Comaroff, as well as Frederick Copper and Ann Laura Stoler, has claimed that central aspects of Europe's modern culture are products of its colonial relations with other parts of the world.[11] A genre that has often been used to demonstrate this thesis is youth missionary literature.[12]

In order to truly understand the formation of a German identity through a country's foreign relations, we must look beyond the study of the relationship of the missionaries and the people they interacted with abroad. First, as David Thelen argues, we can consider how the influence of the transnational encounters in the nineteenth and twentieth centuries not only shaped the *Weltanschauung* (worldview) of "one side," as traditional postcolonial theory argues, but in fact influenced "both sides" of the encounter.[13]

The exploration of the youth literature of the AEPM confirms this "two-sided" claim that the transcultural encounter worked both ways, and not only affected the Japanese people—as this study has hitherto shown. Rather, German and Swiss citizens were also affected by the encounter, which contributed significantly to the development of a particular self-image among children like Otto Schmitt. Schmitt's short essay gives us an insight into the meaning that church meetings, films, and missionary literature as primary sources had in the shaping of a particular image of Japan and its people. These educational and compelling missionary stories and films, of which Otto was a devoted user, are undoubtedly a good starting point into an analysis of how the use of stories and concepts from a widely different religious and cultural background functioned as means of educating and socializing children in Switzerland and Germany.[14]

Although books and magazines of this genre had occasionally been published earlier, youth missionary literature really blossomed in Switzerland and Germany in the decades after the turn of the twentieth century. During this period, a number of subject-related books and several different monthly magazines appeared on the Swiss-German market.[15]

The AEPM published various books and journals for children about the mission in East Asia. Typically, these books contained stories of the missionaries, their wives, children, or persons related to the foreign mission in one way or another. They themselves would often write a variety of articles, poems, and songs. Sometimes the texts included images of events and people, especially children, in the Swiss-German mission fields, primarily in Japan or China, but also in other parts of the "heathen world."[16] The majority of published texts were written in the form of letters. They were written by German missionaries abroad, or by people in Switzerland and Germany who supported the mission. A small number of the texts and publications were translations of British missionary publications.[17] Each of these different publications were addressed to the Swiss and German youth, mainly to children coming from church congregations supportive of the AEPM.

The reason why youth literature was important for the AEPM can be seen in a quote from mission helper Klara Gaedecke. In 1915, she stated that: "the love [for the mission] must be rooted deeply in every individual soul, and from there shine into the world."[18] In other words, similar to their Japanese students in the mission schools in Tokyo, explored in Chapters three and four, it was important for the missionaries to touch the Swiss and German children's mind, and positively influence them while their minds, opinions, and character traits were still pliable. Youth literature was therefore distributed to various schools, to children's mission clubs, and at festivities for children arranged by local Christian communities around the country in order to anchor the missionaries' messages in the children's souls.[19]

On the one hand, the youth literature aimed to provide moral and material support for missionary purposes, but at the same time it encouraged the children to pray for the mission work and the poor heathens, to join children's missionary clubs, to donate their own savings to the mission, to write letters to the missionaries, and to aspire to become missionaries themselves, or at least to become engaged in the plight of the heathens.[20]

The function of these texts, which were designed for a Swiss-German readership, was less about conveying precise facts and information about the Japanese people than it was to evoke the reader's affection and appreciation of his or her own position in a greater social and cultural world. They made the youth reader recognize the taxonomy of categories that established Christianity as the primary religion of the world, and thus carried a "feel good" factor. The literature functioned as an important medium through which the self-understanding of Swiss and German children would become closely tied to a certain perception of nationality, while religiously differing people overseas became the "religious other."

Through the two AEPM missionary youth journals *Missionsblatt Für die Kinder* and *Missionsblatt Für die Jugend*. one can identify the social truths and moral messages they communicated, and the images they painted: Which type of stories were mostly told? What motives were promoted? And what do these stories tell us about the role of missionaries as "cultural educators"?

Explaining the world in categories

The missionary literature directed at children was evidently organized around a set of categories that explained the world to the young readers. Each category was provided with a particular set of norms that upheld their own inductive potential.[21] The stories explored their subjects by appealing to the readers' categorizations of nationality, religion, and race.[22]

By far the most significant categories employed in the youth texts were those of the "heathen" (Heiden) and the "Christians," thus assigning the category of "religion" as the main value for differentiation between people. Heathens were depicted as daunting, unpredictable, emotional, and superstitious.[23] They were portrayed as inferior, uncaring of one another, deficient of human empathic capabilities, timid, and fearful, especially toward their own gods, such as in the article "Wer beten kann, ist selig dran" (He who Prays be Blessed) from 1917, which tells us:

> The heathens are all superstitious; they think that there are many evil spirits that bring bad luck to people. They even fear their own grandfather when he dies. The heathen people do not know that we will all go to heaven when we die.[24]

Being heathen also meant being treacherous. The texts often emphasized the need to keep an eye on Japanese servants, as they would steal money and use it for their own pleasure. Heathen Japanese men were often described as immoral and susceptible to drinking alcohol. Missionary Otto Schmiedel told his readers about his Japanese cook, who, after spending his own income and that of his wife, gaMBLed and drank alcohol, forcing his wife to ask the Schmiedels to intervene.[25] Another text describes the Japanese girl Umeko, who was abused by her heathen father: "Umeko's father was a reckless man who drank more sake than was good. Mostly he was not at home, and when he was, he was usually drunk."[26]

The undesirable characteristics associated with heathens were not limited to the binary category of "Christians" versus "heathen," but also flowed into other social categories such as gender, age, and family status. Heathen children were valued differently from heathen adults, and even among heathen women, there were distinctions. In a story from

1913, missionary Johannes Witte describes the baptism of an unnamed Japanese girl and emphasizes the despicable qualities of a mischievous aunt, stating that she threatened the young Japanese girl with physical abuse if she was baptized.[27]

Not unlike the fairy tales of the Brothers Grimm, with which most of the young Swiss and German readers must have been acquainted, heathen stepmothers or heathen aunts would be described as sinful and malevolent. By contrast, mothers were portrayed as more sympathetic. The category of "Christians," not surprisingly, radiated unequivocal positive qualities in the youth literature. The missionaries themselves usually had the role of the observant narrator, but if they brought themselves into the story, they were given characteristics such as self-sacrificing, kind, forgiving, and wise.[28]

Moreover, these positive portrayals were often told from the perspective of a heathen Japanese, thereby imbuing the statement with deeper meaning for the reader. An example of such a story is "Eine Glaubensschilderung in Japan" (A Story of Faith from Japan). Here, a young, believing Japanese Christian named Masuda falls ill with a "mysterious illness that was extremely painful."[29] Several doctors try to help her, but they all remain at a loss about the right treatment. By chance, two Western doctors appear and rescue her through surgery. However, throughout the surgery, Masuda endured extreme pain that would have usually been intolerable to any normal person. "All the Japanese present during the surgery, the article favorably states, were convinced that, "to endure such torment was not possible for anyone but a Christian." Only her devotion and firm belief in God made Masuda survive the painful operation. The author finally concludes for his readers, "There were heathens among the people [who witnessed the miracle] who now confessed that Christianity must surely be the best religion because it gives you so much courage and strength."[30]

In another story, Otto Schmiedel tells how he convinced a young Japanese woman to become a Christian. The woman initially visited Schmiedel to acquire knowledge about medicine and the medical profession in Germany. During their conversation, Schmiedel drew the topic of the virtue of the German Christian nurses who worked for peace during the First World War into the discussion, describing the aptitude of the German nurses as follows: "The delicate sense and gentle hand of a women is made to heal the wounds and diseases of war."[31]

By praising the abilities of these Christian nurses to heal people, Schmiedel—according to post-colonial scholar Helen Kanitkar—created an ideal image of universal values to which all women should strive.[32] According to Schmiedel's own accounts, the visiting Japanese woman was able to recognize the kindness and beauty of the work of the German nurses and began to cry: "The young woman's eyes became ever brighter until she finally shed tears. With these tears she was won for Christ," Schmiedel concludes in a satisfied manner.[33]

As these examples show, the categories of nationality and race were often more significant than the actual religious orientation. Categories such as "Christians" and "heathens" often took on a new meaning in the youth literature when put together with national and racial-ethnic categories, as in the case of the German nurses. For Schmiedel, the virtue of a German Christian was different from that of a Japanese Christian. Thus, the category "Christians" was dependent on nationality. While the mixed German-Christian category was considered desirable and virtuous, the Japanese-Christian composition was rather ambiguous. Most Japanese Christians were still described as superstitious and bound to Japanese religious beliefs, suggesting that they were not yet full Christians. In other contexts—especially when compared to the heathens—the Japanese Christian was again found to be as honest and respectable as any other Christian. In 1910, missionary Emil Schroeder wrote a small essay in *Für die Jugend* named "Christenkinder und Heidenkinder" (Christian Children and Heathen Children). The essay was, like many other stories in the journal, an ordinary story about the Japanese children in a missionary kindergarten: "How often do my wife and I agree on what a difference there exists between the Christian child and the other. In all things this is so."[34] In this quote,

Emil Schroeder clearly points out the sole category of "religion" as the main differentiator between the children in the kindergarten, where the Christian children are evaluated more positively in comparison to their "heathen friends."

The same can also be seen in another central category reoccurring in the youth missionary literature: age. When the missionaries wrote about children, the categories of nationality and religion seemed less important. Stories in which a Japanese child was the main character would typically relate to attributes such as youthfulness rather than heathenism. After all, being a child seemed, according to the youth literature, to be a universal right, whether one was Christian, heathen, German, or Japanese. As a child, you were generally considered good and innocent. Accordingly, a missionary wrote about the Japanese girl Kuniko:

> Kuniko was an orphan in Japan; her parents had been heathens, and she had not yet been baptized though she was fourteen years old. However, she had been attending a Christian school for some time and lived in the house of a missionary who taught her. Everyone liked her because she was diligent, friendly, and huMBLe; but she was also a very superstitious girl.[35]

As this example shows, the virtuous Christian was what the missionaries looked for in the Japanese Christians, and the Japanese Christian would always be deemed positive in comparison to the "non-Christian" Japanese. However, when put in contrast to the German or Western Christians, they would always be secondary.

Unlike their "blessed" Swiss and German friends, Japanese children and adolescents continued to be under the influence of their heathen Japanese culture. Despite her goodness, Kuniko was unable to detach herself from her heathen superstition. But in contrast to Japanese adults, Kuniko's docility and malleable nature allowed for the hope that, when given the right environment, she could become a good Christian. Gertrude Schroeder, wife of Emil Schroeder, expressed herself during her work in one of the many kindergartens established by the German mission in Japan in an article called "Kleine Japankinder" (Little Japanese Children) as follows:

> Every morning, the little ones come to play, jump, sing, and cheer. They learn beautiful stories, even from the Bible, and youthful prayers. They see how well-meaning our missionaries and their wives are with them. They trust us, the strangers. If they could, they would love to stay with us the whole day. The most beautiful activity in the kindergarten is the morning song. There is always one German and one Japanese song that is being sung. It sounds charming when the small children fold their hands and begin to sing.... Oh how well we can bring forward the good and drive back the evil! All the blessings for our mission![36]

In Gertrude Schroeder's story, the youthfulness of the Japanese children is at the center. The teaching of the Bible is bringing joy to the children, who, rather than going home to their heathen families, wish to stay in the kindergarten among the missionaries "the whole day." It is the purity in the children's nature rather than any category of heathenism that becomes their central attribute. In fact, as Carmaine Nelson points out, the child depicted in the youth literature often represented a universal category of itself—the category of innocence—that existed above all other categories.[37] Just as nationality or religious belief in the above-mentioned stories hardly played a role in the description of children in the Japanese mission field, the color of their skin also lost its meaning when put into the category of age. But still, as numerous scholars such as Franz Fanon tell us, the color white still imposed a meaning of superiority, and was considered by some to be the ideal skin color for a child.[38]

This can also be seen in missionary Adolf Wendt's article "Das bewunderte deutsche Kind" (The Admired German Child) which describes the Japanese fascination with his German child's skin color while traveling with his family in the Japanese countryside:

> Here, a foreign woman with a child had never been seen before. We therefore attracted the greatest attention; the child was admired like a

miracle and thought of as lovely and delightful, the color of its skin was compared to the color of the cherry blossom.[39]

Wendt's article on the admiration of his child not only imposes the superior meaning of white skin, but also appropriates the Japanese symbolism of "cherry blossom," while at the same time valorizing German ethnicity.

As a final category, gender was used as a factor of differentiation. In the stories, boys were consistently portrayed as being active and vigorous characters, while girls like Umeko were considered passive. This perhaps was a reflection of a European bourgeois expectation of qualities for boys and girls in nineteenth and twentieth century Germany. Being lively and vigorous was seen as a positive trait in boys, but when these attributes were given to girls, they assumed a negative meaning. In "Eine Geisteskranke Japanerin" (A Mentally Sick Japanese Girl), a "wild" girl is causing much grief and annoyance to her heathen family and their surroundings. To help her, a missionary takes her into his family and enrolls her in a mission school. The time in the school, however, is not easy, and the missionary in the story is many times close to giving up on her due to her "wild nature." Fortunately, as if by a miracle, she suddenly realizes the goodness of Jesus Christ and his teachings, and begins, so the essay tells us, improving into a well-behaved and modest Christian girl—all of course thanks to the teachings of God.[40]

On another level, this story also justified the work of missionaries among Japanese children, implying that missionaries were important factors in the civilizing of Japan. As the article shows, even the poorest Japanese soul could be helped as long as it was guided by the missionaries and Jesus Christ. The homiletic missionary texts in the youth missionary magazines thus contain and use—quite predictably—several different categories whose employment was prolific. On the one side, they mediated the modern European enterprise abroad, and on the other, they had a formative influence in educating their subjects in Europe. Thus, similar to what postcolonial scholar Gyan Prakash states, the youth missionary literature played a significant role in establishing a "concept of heathen natives, which helped European elites to discipline their working classes and peasants into modern subjects."[41]

Still, the youth literature did not just, as Prakash suggests, present Swiss and German youth with diffuse concepts of the "superstitious heathens out there." Rather, it fashioned a detailed and complex social stratum. It taught its young readers to think in a certain way not only about what was unfamiliar and alien to them, but also about their own social categories in Switzerland and Germany in relation to the Japanese people and rest of the world.[42]

The teaching of emotions: a transcultural experiment

In the descriptions of non-Christian Japanese, the youth texts generally emphasized negative characteristics. The literature reflected a common understanding of inferior heathens, irrational superstitious beliefs, childish and emotional anger, loose religious morality, and the unbearable fate of widows and children. Numerous stories dealt with social issues, neglect, alcoholism, forced marriages, persecution of Christians, and even prostitution as realities in Japan, and most often attributed these sufferings to heathen traditions and social customs influenced by the Japanese religions.

This negative representation of the "heathens" and their religions in the youth missionary literature was by no means limited to the German texts of the AEPM, but was also common in other Western countries. For example, in late nineteenth century America, according to Robin Bernstein, black children were not included in the "children" category because, she claims, they were unaffected by physical pain. "Pain," Bernstein argues, "functioned as a wedge that split childhood innocence, as a cultural formation into distinct black and white trajectories."[43]

The denial of heathen children's ability to feel pain, however, cannot be found in the Swiss-German literature. On the contrary: Japanese children are portrayed as full of innocence and as particularly sensitive to pain. To be sure, the depiction of their innocence is strengthened by the description of their reaction to pain and suffering. Such stories, as the four following examples from the AEPM's youth magazines show, were designed to evoke a specific emotional reaction in the reader.

One of these four examples is "O, die armen Kinder" (Oh, the Poor Children) written by the missionary inspector Johannes Witte, and published as a series of episodes in the missionary youth magazine *Für die Jugend* in the course of 1912. These were stories about suffering Japanese children. In one of these stories, Witte described the dark atmospheric setting of a Japanese peasant house belonging to a poor family with two children: a nameless boy and girl. The daily life of these children was sad and miserable, and every day before the parents left for work in the rice fields, they were locked in a cell and abandoned in the cold dark house. While the parents were out in the fields, the house was visited by a group of thieves. They searched the poor farmers' house for valuables but found nothing except for the children locked in the cell. The children were kidnapped and sold individually as slaves. Witte continued to describe the terrible experiences of the girl, who, separated from her brother, was forced to live as a prostitute in a brothel, where she was victim to a wide variety of sufferings and abuse. Only after years of violence and sexual abuse was the girl miraculously—as is typical for most of the youth literature—saved by a missionary who helped her escape the brothel and reunite with her brother.[44]

While such stories of suffering Japanese children seem unreal and overly horrifying, it is important to note that these stories originated in the contemporary conditions of children in Japan. Historian Patricia

E. Tsurumi has, in her book *Factory Girls: Woman in the Thread Mills of Meiji Japan*, for example noted similar instances of child abductions. Describing the poor conditions of many thread mill workers in the central region of Japan, she notes: "Kōfu and its environs were unsafe after dark; bands of thugs loitered about, ever ready to fight, rape, or relieve the unwary of their [the female workers' earnings]. There was always the possibility that the woman might be kidnapped and sold into prostitution."[45] Such stories of suffering and abuse would unquestionably have evoked horrifying images in the young German and Swiss readers' minds. Many similar horrific stories figured in the German youth literature. Another example of a story of suffering Japanese children is found in missionary Willi Hückel's article "Das Los der Mädchen und Frauen in Ostasien" (The Condition of Girls and Women in East Asia) from 1916. In this text, Hückel described in detail the horrendous conditions of a child marriage, the fate of a widow, and the agony of sick and neglected East Asian children. He depicted how girls' lives were permeated with injustice and cruelty from the very beginning, and how in most households, the birth of a female child caused grief instead of joy:

> The girls are so unwelcome that many of them are given away just after birth. The families want to show their ancestors that they wanted a son, a man (einen menschen); they wanted someone who could continue the family.[46]

Like the story above about the unfortunate life of the poor girl, this quote in a similar vein illustrates how the horrible stories of child abuse and dangerous customs were used to evoke a feeling of sadness and shock among its young readers. Unlike the German and Swiss children who lived in a "safe" and "civilized" Christian culture, they learned that some children, just due to the heathen superstitions of their parents, risked being given away and sold just after their birth. The horror of East Asian children was also reflected in another story published in the youth magazine *Für die Jugend*. Here, missionary Hans Haensel's "Ein

Besuch einer chinesischen Fabrik" (A Visit to a Chinese Factory) from 1929 looks at the harsh conditions of child labor at a sewing factory. Haensel asked his readers:

> How do these small tender hands work? How do these children look? Poor and ragged, tired and pale, many are already suffering from tuberculosis. And so, they stand day by day, at their long tables, and work and work. It is an unspeakably disturbing and sad picture to see all these poor little children for whom no one cares and for whom no joy fills their pale faces.[47]

By describing the inhuman conditions under which these children worked, the author underlined the generality of the problem of child labor. According to Haensel, a child was not meant to work but to play just like the Swiss and German children did. By evoking horrifying images and speaking to the readers' emotions, the story of the mistreated children provoked in the reader a feeling of empathy for the small factory workers. A last example found in the youth literature also took place at a sewing factory. In the "Trauriges Los eines japanischen Mädchens in einer Fabrik" (Sad Fate of a Japanese Girl in a Factory), missionary Emil Knodt described how a nameless twelve-year-old Japanese girl had been sent by her family to work in a silk factory in Tokyo. Together with nine other girls from her village, all the same age, she departed from the poor conditions in the countryside to the silk factory in the city. Day and night, the story tells us, the girls had to preform hard physical labor. At the same time, Knodt described how these poor girls were constantly harassed and sexually abused by the factory owner. Forced to live in a small room with nine girls, disease spread during the winter, killing four of the poor girls. Speaking in first person, the girl tells us:

> I cannot forget the sad feeling we felt when the bodies of the workers were taken out of the factory. These girls, who died so early, were 12 or 13 years old and all came from northern Japan. The most grievous, however, was that even after this tragic incident, the factory owner tried to seduce us into doing bad things all the time.[48]

The girl, according to Knodt, endured three years and eight months of hard labor and sexual abuse before she was allowed to leave the factory and return home to her family. Back home, away from the silk factory, her life, Knodt ensured his readers, was good. Still, the scars of the years in the silk factory would never leave her. What all these stories have in common is that they have been structured and written around an emotionally alluring theme, whose purpose it was to upset and engage its readers. Historian Danilyn Rutherford has argued that this was not done to evoke anger or to scare the young readers, but rather, the purpose of the sad stories was to develop empathy in order to appeal and excite them to feel for their young Japanese "brothers and sisters."[49]

At the same time, these stories fashioned a sense of gratitude in the readers for their own fortunate situation in Germany and Switzerland. There seems to have been a general belief among the writers of youth literature that by reading emotional stories about the pain and suffering of heathen children, the readers would inevitably acquire and develop a sense of empathy for others.

This can in particular be seen in a small essay from 1925, titled "Aus der japanischen Kinderwelt" (From the Japanese Children's World) written by missionary Willi Hückel. In this story, the young readers are encouraged to feel compassion for their heathen Japanese friends but are similarly reminded of how lucky and privileged they are:

> You will now feel that the Japanese children must be helped! Think of the horrible gods whom they worship, of the conditions of the girls working in the factories. And then, remember what you think of those children. You know God as a dear Father, you know Jesus as the friend of children who will lead you to heaven. How happy you must be, and how grateful you must be.[50]

Dipesh Charkrabaty has argued that once we read about suffering people, we automatically develop feelings of empathy, "because we, through the faculty of imagination, place ourselves in the position of the person suffering."[51]

When reading the missionary stories in the youth literature, the feelings of empathy are created through the immediate encounter between the subject and the object. Swiss and German children were able to imagine themselves in the often hopeless and abominable situations of children of the same age, and thus—according to Charkrabaty—could empathize with the feelings, ideas, and views of the people they read about. Furthermore, as with the examples above, most stories in the AEPM youth literature were told from the perspective of a single Japanese girl or boy, allowing the young reader to compare and relate with this individual.

To stimulate empathy, however, it was often not enough to put the reader in the position of the subject. Sometimes additional instructions from the missionaries were needed. For example, young German readers were encouraged to imagine that they themselves and their family were in the same position as the Japanese. Furthermore, the stories of suffering children were often visually accompanied by photographs of screaming, crying, homeless, and malnourished children in Japanese or Chinese slums—all with the intention of making those who saw these images feel the pain the people in the images were going through. Not infrequently, these portrayals of tales of suffering followed an invitation from the missionaries that the reader pray for a better future for their Japanese "friends":

> Shall we not think about the heathens, when we give the Lord's Prayer. Shall we not ask the good Lord to send them a great many missionaries, so that they may learn the truth.[52]

It is almost as if the missionaries played the role of the commanding teacher, telling their young readers what to do and feel. In some of the essays, the missionaries would even ask the children to include their parents: "If you have read this, go—and please make it fast—to your dear mother, greet her from me and ask her to read this too."[53] By doing this, the text created a sense of importance and superiority among the Swiss and German children. They were the ones with the knowledge to tell their parents about the suffering Japanese children. They were the ones with the power to improve the situation of the miserable youngsters. In other words, the homiletic technique used in youth missionary literature formed an understanding of empathy in the young readers, enabling them to fully identify with the suffering of the heathen children they were reading about, and react upon it.

Difference of empathy: a colonial structure of power?

In the most recent academic work on missionary activities abroad, postcolonial scholars have turned their attention to examining the development of empathy in the mission fields. Acknowledged experts in the field of post-colonial research have argued that while this evocation and mediation of empathy is to be understood as an honorable undertaking, the empathy depicted and taught in the mission literature often would contain antagonistic concepts of colonial power. Danilyn Rutherford has, for example, pointed out that the teaching of empathy is an important aspect of "colonial nation building."[54] Similarly, Amy Kaplan points out that the development of sympathy or compassion "across social divides could violently reinforce the very racial and class hierarchies that sentimentality claims to dissolve."[55]

Commonly, these scholars agree that missionaries, by provoking empathetic and compassionate feelings among their young readers, upheld a structure of power that resembled that of the colonial idea of superiority.[56] By conveying a feeling of empathy for the Japanese children, the youth literature taught its young readers to become aware of their own privileged position, and feel culturally and religiously superior.[57] As shown, empathy was taught through simple binary categories of religion, nationality, gender, and age. Japanese Christian children—usually girls—became subjects that deserved the readers' empathy. They were depicted as victims only able to change their sad circumstances by realizing the faith of God or by the last-minute intervention of a missionary. The stories in the journals, in other words, confirmed the existence of an asymmetric structure of power.[58]

In many of the stories, the depicted characters each represent one or more specific categories. The stories needed the "inductive potential" of these categories to convey the moral teaching of the text.[59] The locations of the stories in Japan mostly remained unclear, just as the main characters often were not mentioned by name. Instead, they were referred to as a "Japanese girl" or "Japanese boy." Within the stories, the content switched back and forth between descriptions of the suffering of individuals to more general observation of the degenerate customs and habits of the population. In the text "Das Knabenfest in Tokyo" (The Boys' Festival in Tokyo), written by missionary Johannes Witte, an objective and plain description of a Japanese festival for boys is transformed into a report on the malnutrition and illnesses of poor Japanese children in the slums of Tokyo:

> I saw many very, very unfortunate children. They looked muddy and miserable, and many had already as children lost their eyes. They do not have enough doctors who can help, and they are themselves too poor to go to the doctor. What a miserable life they live.[60]

The boys in Witte's story became an evocative example of the general community of suffering Japanese for whom all Swiss and German children were encouraged to feel, and were prompted to help, on the one hand by prayer, and on the other by financial support. Sometimes the young Japanese children were personified by a name. In Witte's "Was ich bei einer Taufe in Japan erlebte" (What I Experienced at a Baptism in Japan), a Japanese girl named Naoko is saved by the Swiss-German missionaries. Naoko, according to Witte, had decided to go against her family's wishes and wanted to convert to Christianity. Her religious commitment to Christianity had led the family to cut all bonds with her. Witte, who, according to the story, was present at the baptism wrote:

This young Japanese girl, who had been through so much to become a Christian, was wearing her best dress for her baptism.... One could see that she was deeply grateful and moved: now she was a Christian, now she was glad.[61]

Here the story becomes tangible and concrete, evoking in the Swiss-German readers a sense of involvement and of being in personal contact with the Japanese girl. As in other stories, Naoko's story was accompanied by a photo, presumably of Naoko, and a small text in which the reader was encouraged to feel as happy as Naoko felt during her baptism.

In this situation, a different meaning of empathy seems to appear. While empathy in the general portrayal of the Japanese children seemed to promote an emotional feeling of pity, the personified stories, in a much larger degree, encouraged the readers to feel an embodied joy and compassion for the Japanese subjects. Sometimes the stories prompted the readers to feel cheerful for their own situation by pitying the Japanese children, thus stimulating a feeling of pleasure in the readers' own situation. Other times, this feeling was less specific. The missionaries saw in empathy a supposedly Christian quality, and in some cases, even a universal human quality. Whether this included a sympathy towards Japanese traditions and customs is difficult to judge. For the most part, the stories in the youth literature were sceptical of Japanese "evil deeds" because, in the missionaries' eyes, these customs and traditions lacked moral and ethical development. Yet, at the same time, the children in Switzerland and Germany were encouraged through their reading to feel empathetic about the suffering of others, Christians or non-Christians. The youth missionary texts intended to sensitize the Swiss-German children to see and feel the pain and suffering of others, and to act on it in the correct fashion. Missionaries were determined to educate good people, and more importantly, good Christians. Their image of a good Christian included the ability to experience suffering and to be emotionally moved by the pain of others. The missionaries' project of moral and emotional education for the

Swiss and German youth proves an important point in this chapter; namely, that for the first decades of the twentieth century, youth missionary texts were part of a much larger transcultural setting. Within this setting was decided which objects were to become targets for the emotional feelings of the Swiss-German children.[62]

The study of youth missionary texts illustrates how missionaries taught a perception of the world as a place fashioned through a set of unevenly weighted relationships that were on the one hand, made by those who gave empathy, and on the other, by those who received it. In a broader context, the analysis of this particular case of Swiss and German youth missionary literature also illustrates how this disequilibrium was reflected and reinforced through general colonial structures of power existing in the mission field.

Social identity as cultural power

So far, this chapter has examined the ways that the youth missionary literature did more than just tell stories about heroic missionaries escorting heathen Japanese to the safe haven of Christianity or about unfortunate Japanese children being mistreated and abandoned by their own family. This literature also had an educational purpose that helped its young readers realize that the world was populated by many different cultures and people, and that these were defined by an elaborate classification based on religion and race. These characteristics of social identity defined for the reader what was to be expected of an individual and how he or she was to be judged.[63]

Inasmuch as the readers interpreted and defined their relationship with the Japanese, the missionary literature supported a specific structure of colonial power. In addition, Michel Foucault and others have argued that the missionary endeavor induced specific cognitive abilities in those who were Christianized. The analysis in this chapter indicates that the missionaries' work did more than just induce certain cognitive capabilities; it also created new ones.[64] The individual understanding and social identity fostered in the youth missionary literature was reliant on the establishment of a complex system of categories in which the young Swiss and German readers were given a special role.

According to Emil Durkheim's definition, the missionary youth literature functioned as a means of education, teaching its readers to "see, feel, and act on the norms and desires of their teachers."[65] It also effected an implicit awareness that these different aspects of education could not easily be re-learned.

Acquired knowledge, argues Ann Laura Stoler, therefore has a significant influence in forming a specific view of the world in the reader, and the youth missionary literature of the AEPM conveyed such a view to the young reader Otto Schmitt: a view of a world in which social categories were defined by asymmetric power relations.[66]

Conclusion

A critical reading of the two AEPM youth mission journals *Missionsblatt für die Kinder* and *Missionsblatt Für die Jugend* has provided insight into the missionaries' role as the cultural educators of their young Swiss and German readership.

The journals established social categories and emotions through the portrayal of the miserable fates of heathen children in the missionary youth literature which functioned as transcultural education for its readers at home. By reading the missionary magazines or by attending missionary events, the youthful readers themselves knowingly or unknowingly took on the worldview that the missionaries and other missionary sympathizers promoted. This mission enterprise, Jeff Bowersox argued, significantly influenced these German youth's own conception of the world around them.[67] Through youth literature, the missionaries of the AEPM presented an understanding of the heathen world in a powerful image: the image of Japan and other Asian countries as places that needed their help. It instilled in the young readers the feeling of being in a superior position to help others, which led to an asymmetric power relationship with others.

The youth missionary literature of the AEPM in the first decades of the twentieth century, in other words, constitutes an important source for understanding and bringing to light the different tolls and tactics used in educating Swiss and German youth about distant, unknown, and exotic people. By learning about the "heathen people," the young Swiss and German readers were concurrently meant to learn about themselves and their place in the world. They were expected to consider themselves as agents of Christian civilization. The literature also provides material needed to analyze the AEPM missionaries' larger role in the entangled transcultural history of the Swiss/German-Japanese relations. Despite geographical distance, the missionaries clearly effected the people at home. They taught the Swiss-German youth to become "imperial citizens," and to know their place in the global hierarchy. The missionaries functioned as transcultural agents educating the Swiss and German youth from abroad.[68]

In other words, the trans-cultural encounter between Swiss and German missionaries and the Japanese people in the late nineteenth and early twentieth centuries proves an interesting theoretical point, as their meeting with the Japanese culture influenced both sides of the encounter, and not just one side, as traditional colonial theorists often claim.

Conclusion

Our Mission Society was founded in 1884. Its activities span over a period of not even twenty years. Its conscription at home and its work in the distant world is still of modest magnitude. Every development takes time. We follow the principle of only sending out persons who are academically trained. It is only a limited number of missionaries, not large groups, who are employed by us in East Asia. We see our task in supplying heathen countries, through our literary work, with better and healthier air, the air of the Christian spirit. Outwardly, the success of such work is not easily noticeable, nor can it be measured in numbers. We are trying to win over individual souls and to gather them in communities. But we do not rush them. Better a few who are caught profoundly than many who are just baptized. God alone allows the growing, yet He does it when it suits Him. All mission work is a work of patience. Ours has to be so too.[1]

It was in these words in the year 1900, that mission director August Kind reflected on the end of the so called "Missionsjahrhundert" or mission century and the achievements of the *Allgemeiner Evangelisch-Protestantischer Missionsverein* in Japan. Kind had witnessed the enormous changes of the Japanese mission field over the previous 25 years. For him, Japan had changed from a country that could be fully Christianized "within the next few years" to a mission field that demanded an abundance of patience.[2] As the years passed and the difficulties accumulated, it had become ever harder to argue for the legitimization of the missionaries' own endeavor. Yet, in his essay, Kind continued to enthusiastically emphasize the importance of the missionaries still dedicated to the development of a Christian Japan.

In this book, I examined Swiss and German missionary prominence in Japan from the late nineteenth to early twentieth centuries. I contextualized the efforts of the AEPM in the Meiji and Taisho period as they reflected a greater undercurrent in Japan's modern religious landscape, which embraced Liberal Christianity and aimed to transform Japan from a practice-centered belief system of religion to one that was belief-centered.[3] The precise contours of their definition of a liberal Christian belief and their transformative potential attracted the attention of various Japanese communities who looked up to their modern mode of thought. In the 1890s, however, the Japanese Christian community took a more explicitly subversive and even rebellious characteristic, slowly moving away from the influence of the missionaries, first evident in the "Article 28 Protest," but mostly in the Ebina Danjō incident, the Unified Japanese church protest of 1905–1906, and the subsequently termination of the Fukyū Fukuin Kyōkai 普及福音教会 in 1909. Furthermore, among intellectual Buddhists, we saw the emergence of a movement of rational counter-argument against the missionaries' claim of truth.

As it was, the rise of Liberal Christianity in Japan was a significant development that interestingly came to mostly take place outside the confines of the missionaries' religious institutions, representing an example of a religious transfer of ideas that does not conform neatly to established boundaries or classification schemes. Despite their considerable importance for Japan's modern religious history, the AEPM remains a severely understudied topic due to the continuing influence of the traditional modality of research focusing on excellent Japanese Christians and the documents associated with them. This study has utilized documents ranging from local historical records to published magazines to personal diaries to investigate the history of the AEPM in a variety of contexts, and has suggested the effectiveness of a thematic approach that traces a particular religious idea or discourse over time. Such an approach provides an alternative avenue of analysis that highlights the transcultural encounter and illuminates vital aspects of the mission history that might otherwise have been ignored, marginalized, or simply forgotten.

An analysis of the continuing history of the AEPM in Japan during the difficult 1930s and into the postwar period is beyond the scope of this book. Kurt Suter's article (1984) on the unavoidable break between the Swiss and German partnership and its split into two independent mission societies following the rise of Nazi Germany and the new beginning of mission in Japan suggests that the mission society remained a particular niche in the Japanese religious world,[4] playing only a minor role in the Japanese Christian community of the 1940s and beyond.[5] Furthermore, the case of Akamatsu Renjō and the other intellectual Buddhists in chapter six suggests that Liberal Christianity was relevant in pre-war Japanese society, but not in a way directly related to what the missionaries offered. This book focused explicitly on the AEPM and their encounters with various groups within Japanese society, but different insights may emerge by examining the development of liberal Christian discourse through cases that did not necessarily involve the missionaries of the AEPM. Examining these cases may be necessary to trace the continuity of liberal Christian discourse into the post-war period, particularly in relation to the indigenous church movements of Nihon kumiai kirisuto kyōkai 日本組合基督教会 or the Kyoto School for Christian Studies (Kirisutokyōgaku キリスト教学).

One of the objectives of this book has been to illuminate the contradictions of Liberal Christianity that arise when it is put introduced to and propagated within a non-Christian society, such as the Japanese society of the late nineteenth and early twentieth centuries. I have highlighted these paradoxes by analyzing several independent incidents that occurred within the mission field over the period and attempted to do so without imposing various assumptions that have developed around the universal category of Liberal Christianity. As stated in the introduction, I am not necessarily against the philosophical approach to Liberal Christianity as a universal category. However, scholars should be aware of the practical use of the category, they should specify exactly how they intend to use the category as a historiographical tool, and they should remain mindful that Liberal Christianity has its own history, independent of its universal usage. Moreover, the use of Liberal Christianity as a scholarly category with a number of analytical agendas should not distort the concept of Liberal Christianity as found in the missionary sources and articulated by the missionaries themselves. The history of the AEPM as outlined here in this book leads one to ask which theologies can count as "liberal." What constitutes the difference between a liberal and a non-liberal theology? The paradoxes of Liberal Christianity in the case of the AEPM calls for further discussion on what criteria should be used to classify the programs and positions as "liberal." Theologians of the turn of the twentieth century understood Liberal Christianity as the religion of tolerance and individuality, and was regarded as the universal religion of modern culture. There were only very few liberal theologians who called into question the perceived superiority of their own traditions. This lack of self-reflection is what makes the case of the AEPM in Japan intriguing for further study.

Notes

Introduction

1. The long and tongue twisting name of the AEPM has in English research often been translated to *the Evangelical Protestant Mission Society*. See MULLINS 1997, 14. The official Japanese translation of the AEPM was 普及福音新教伝道会 Fukyū Fukuin Shinkyō Dendōkai. As a rule, we will adopt the scholarly abbreviation 普及福音教会 Fukyū Fukuin Kyōkai. Furthermore, in this book, I rely on the original German name and its acronym AEPM, which henceforth will be used when referring to the mission society.

2. A note on the term "modern" is necessary here as it can often have a variety of meanings. In this book, I use the designation "modern" to refer to the period from the opening of Japan to the West in 1868 until the early 1930s. This temporal understanding of "modern" also correlates with the Japanese translation for "modern" (*kindai* 近代) used to refer to the Meiji, Taishō, and Shōwa periods. See HOSHINO 2012, 4–5. Furthermore, in this book, I am careful not to use of terms like "modernist" or "modernization" as these often are more confusing than clarifying. Especially the term "modernization" is used with caution. In social science the concept of "modernization" is often placed in close connection to its twin "secularization," which assumes that modernization leads to the partition from religious thoughts and practices; see BERGER 1967. Yet, as Talal Asad argues, particularly in the modern age, "religion" should be understood as a part of the modernization project. According to Asad, religion did not vanish from sight with the arrival of modernity, but under the framework of secularism in the nineteenth century was perceived with a new understanding. It just ranked as a lesser concern than for example science or politics and became essentially transferred into the private sphere; ASAD 2001, 221. Still, one detects a problem in Asad's definition of "modernization" when it is applied in the context of the civilizing movement of the European missionaries in the nineteenth and twentieth century. How could religion be differentiated and marginalized in the modernization process when it seems to have been the overall motivating force of many of the missionary civilizing projects at the time? On the contrary, as has been shown by other scholars, in the missionaries' literature "religion" formed the pivotal parameter for "modernization." In fact, the "modernization" process became referred to as an evolutionary process from a non-Christian society to a Christian society. In other words, in the late nineteenth and early twentieth century Christianity (and "religion') became the definition of the modern. See also JANIEWSKI 1992 for a similar discussion on modernity in relation to the mission movement.

3. See SUZUKI 1979 and HAMER 2002.

4. The AEPM was founded on June 4, 1884 in Weimar, renamed Ostasianmission (OAM) in 1929 and split into two separate branches after the Second Wold War: Deutsche

Ostasienmission (DOAM) and Schweizer Ostasienmission (SOAM). The DOAM has been integrated into the Evangelical Mission Association of the Southwest Germany (EMS) since 1972 and the Berliner Missionswerk (BMW) since 1974. Of two remaining mission related organizations in Japan are the Tomisaka Christian Center 富坂キリスト教センター in Tokyo and the Haus der Begegnung (HDB) in Kyoto.

5. A short comment on the sources is necessary. The sources used in this study are based on material obtained from visits to the Zentralarchiv der Rheinland-Pfalz in Speyer (henceforth ZASP). The records kept there in the form of diaries, letters, and mission journals hold more than five decades of virtually unknown facets of Japanese-German history. Although letters and diaries will be included, the analyses presented in this book are predominantly based on the missionary journals published by the AEPM. This includes the journals *Zeitschrift für Missionskunde und Religionswissenschaft* (ZMR); *Das Missionsblatt* (MBL); *Missionsblatt für die Jugend und Kinder* (MJK), *Wahrheit*, and the Japanese language journal *Shinri* 眞理. The use of mission journals is important. To this date, however, the use of church and mission journals as a medium for historical research has for the most part been ignored. Although bibliographic overviews of mission journals have been available since the end of the seventeenth century, scholars' willingness to use these as historical sources still seems negligibly small. Friedrich Wilhelm Graf has, for example, complained that: "the extraordinary importance of the rich journal tradition for the study of the discourses, ideas, concepts, and mentalities which emerged in relationship to the religious cultures during the formation of modernity has so far hardly been taken seriously." GRAF 2005, 1825. In combination with the other primary sources, the missionary journals allow us to collect a detailed picture of the missionaries' possessive understanding of their encounter with Japanese people, their religions, cultures, and society. Furthermore, they can be used as a tool to show how the missionaries' own self-awareness and self-expression changed over time. ARNOLD & BICKERS 1996, 8. In other words, the emphasis on mission journals in this study is because they functioned as the most important public platform for discussions among the Swiss and German missionaries and therefore offer great insight into their self-perception, their social norms, and their culturally authorized views on practical matters. Still, while the missionary periodicals will be the main source for the analysis throughout this study, they will be accompanied by information obtained from unique letters and diaries accessed at ZASP. Their texts differ from the polished, repetitive style of the missionary journals, thus offering an alternative type of information to the published material, allowing an insight to the first-hand perspective of the missionaries' exchanges with the Japanese people. Connecting these differing sources opens numerous approaches and various views on the topics examined. In the following seven chapters, this book balances the need to faithfully provide first-hand accounts of the missionary experience while recognizing the potential one-sidedness of the sources. A similar characteristic of missionary texts has been given by Simon Gikandi in his book *Maps of Englishness: Writing Identity in the Culture of Colonialism*, GIKANDI 1996, xviii. See also, JONHSTON 2003 and PANESAR 2006.

6. For more on the study of the concept of Religious Universalism in modern Japan See MOHR 2014. For citation see MOHR 2014, 5.

7. On the difficulty of defining Liberal Christianity, see GRAF 1992B, 86–98.

8. GRAF 2002, 25.

9. The work of David Friedrich Strauss, *The Life of Jesus, Critically Examined* (*Das Leben Jesu, kritisch bearbeitet*), published in 1835, for example, shows how in a German-speaking context, Liberal Christianity developed as a historical theology using modern methodological instruments of research, which introduced critical questions of church history and the history of dogma to fields such as social history and "history of culture." See ZACHHUBER 2013, 73–80.

10. Or perhaps the even more important question, whether these liberal theologians were any more liberal than non-liberals at all? See GRAF 1992A.

11. ZACHHUBER 2013; BIRKNER 1976; OEXLE 1996; WOLFES 1999; Graf 1992B, 86–98.

12. See BIRKNER 1976, 33–42; MATHIEU 2010.

13. JENKINS 2003, 4.

14. CROUTER 2005

15. While Schleiermacher has been viewed with much suspicion for most of the twentieth century—with critiques that wove their way from Emil Brunner and Karl Barth—he is currently making a comeback in American scholarship. This is reflected in the recent works of Cathrine L. KELSEY (2003), Terrance RICE (2006), and most recently Ruth RAVENSCROFT (2019), just to mention a few.

16. The books and articles are too many to be listed here, but examples on recent Japanese translation on Schleiermacher are: FUKAI 2016, KUWAHARA 2014, and YASUKATA 2015.

17. The Department of Christian Studies (*Kirisutokyōgaku* キリスト教学) at the Imperial University of Kyoto was founded in 1922. The foundation of Christian Studies in Kyoto happened with a special political and educational goal in mind: It aimed to bridge the tense relationship between state universities and the religious communities as well as the claims of a tightly controlled national policy. The first leader of the department was one of the most prominent Japanese theologians at the time, Seiichi Hatano 波多野精一 (1877–1950). For Hatano there was no difference between theology and Christianity. He adopted historical methods he had learned from German theologians to research early Christianity. The *Religionsgeschichtliche Schule* had a particularly strong influence on him. As a philosopher, Hatano developed a religious philosophy based on the idea of personality. He shared a strong interest in developing research on the subject of "personality" which was central to the German missionaries. For a further exploration of into the development of Liberal Christianity at Kyoto University, see KOYANAGI 2020 and TSUDA 2020.

18. According to Friedrich Wilhelm Graf the term "Liberal Christianity" was first used by anti-liberals to criticize the tolerant and rationalist theological movement of late eighteen century Germany. See GRAF 2002, 25.

19. I am here listing the same commonalities as GRAF 2002, 29.

20. For a serious and well-documented attempt to answer this question, I refer to SEKIOKA 1985. In his article "About the Allgemeine Evangelisch Protestantische Mis-

sionsverein" (普及福音新教伝道会にっぃて), Sekioka ask whether the AEPM needs to be seen as belonging to the so-called *Tübingen School*, a school connected to the German theologian Ferdinand Christian Baur or the The *Religionsgeschichtliche Schule*. As far as I have been able to determine, the AEPM missionaries themselves claimed to belong to the latter. However, this does not exclude the other. In reality, as I mention in the text above, an important point about the missionaries was that they borrowed ideas and lines of though form many places. The wish to create clear categories, such as is attempted in Sekioka's article, is merely a product of what I like to call the inherent sickness of academics. The never-ending wish to find meaning and structures in things that are simply not there.

21. Both these American missions each by themselves played a significant role in introduction Liberal Christian ideas to Japan. In his work *Buddhism, Unitarianism, and the Meiji Competition for Universality*, Michel Mohr has recently written a history of the Unitarians mission between 1887–1922. Similarly, other books have pointed out the role of the Universalist and their first representative George L. Pering (1854–1921). For the Unitarians see MOHR 2014; for the Universalist, see HOWE 1993.

22. Aoki Shūzō went to Europe in 1868 to study in Berlin from 1869 to 1874. Between 1880 and 1894 he was named Japanese ambassador in Berlin three times, and from 1889–1892 and 1898–1900 Foreign Minister twice. Aoki played a decisive role in the revision of the so-called unequal treaties; AKASHI 1995, 13. The Iwakura Mission was a Japanese diplomatic expedition sent to the USA and Europe between 1871 and 1873. The members of the Iwakura Mission included Japanese statesmen and scholars who would later become well-known and define the development of the Meiji period. While it was not the only expedition of its type, the Iwakura Mission is by far the most renown and possibly the most significant in regard to the formation of modern Japan. See BREEN 2011.

23. Kozaki Hiromichi was a distinguished figure in Japanese Christian circles. Born in Kumamoto, he later became a student at the newly established Christian University Dōshisha. Belonging to the Congregational Church, Kozaki was an outspoken and public figure in Meiji Japan, particularly engaging in the debate about religion and government. See AOKI 1997 and BALLHATCHET 1998.

24. VOGT 1907.

25. The theory of cultural transfer is best described by Wolfgang Schmale who writes: "Cultural transfer research makes the rigid, linearly, delimited, and strictly systematic elements of each cultural phenomenon permeable, thereby revealing the hybrid and composite nature of cultural phenomena" See SCHMALE 2006, 2012.

26. Kanamori was one of the original members of the famous Kumamoto Band that also counted Ebina Danjō as one of its leading figure. Kanamori entered Dōshisha University, a Christian University founded by the Japanese Christian Nijima Jo. After graduating from Dōshisha Kanamori was "won over by Liberal Christianity". He published the book *Liberal Theology* (*jiyūshūgi shingaku*) which was a free translation of AEPM board member and theologian Otto Pfleiderer's book *Religionsphilosophie auf geschichtlicher Grundlage* (1892). For a deeper description of Kanamori's theology, see AOKI 1997, 22–4.

27. On the influence of the AEPM in Japan Aasulv Lande has commented: "This [German-liberal] school influenced the New Theology in Japan and is one of the challenging

influences behind the theology of Yokoi, Kanamori, and Ebina. [Their] modern thinking also gave an impetus to a social concern in the Japanese Christian church," see LANDE 1988, 60. Furthermore Japanese historian Kiyosage Naohiro has argued in a similar vein that "they [the AEPM] introduced biblical criticism approach of the Tubingen School... and had great influence not only on the church but on the wider society as well." See KIYOSHIGE 1983, 32.

28. According to Ebina, the personality or life of Christ constitutes the essence of Christianity and must be understood by believers as a matter of internal experience or consciousness. By positioning religious experience or mind as a place of theology, Ebina's theology on the essence of Christianity or religion, borrowed its ideas from liberal theologians such as Ernst Troeltsch and Tillich. See ASHINA 2016, 145–7.

29. SUMIYA 1962, 137.

30. MURAYAMA 1963, 5–6. For a more modern version of the same conclusion, see HOSHINO 2012.

31. Citation ASHINA 2016, 125.

32. Edward Said set in motion the precedence for the binary structured studies of the "white man's" encounter with the Orient in his book *Orientalism* (1978). Here Said pointed out the asymmetries of power structures inherent in most cultural dealings between the Occident and the Orient. This work, however, argues against such a clearly defined structure. Rather, as also pointed out by Richard King, the "[orientalist] discourse did not proceed in an orderly and straightforward fashion." In other words, one has to be careful in making this clear distinction between power of the Occident and Orient, Citation in KING 1999, 86. For a critical analysis of the binary structure of Orientalism, I refer to STOLER & COOPER 1997. For a more in-depth discussion on the missionaries' role in relation to this binary structure of colonialism and to the tremendous impact of Said's work in postcolonial studies, I recommend YOUNG 2001.

33. Citations in, JOSEPHSON 2012, preface; ISOMAE 2007, 93; OSTERHAMMEL 2014, 874–5.

34. An obvious question to ask is why these Western ideas drew such an intense interest during that specific period. But like the scholars Clinton G. Godart (2017) and Hoshino SEIJI (2012) state, the Meiji period has to be understood in terms of multidimensional discourses, where Japanese scholars not only defined themselves in relation to the new ideas from abroad, but also configured them in ways that would suit their respective agenda. See GODART 2017, 3–6; HOSHINO 2012, 6–7.

35. Here in particular, the letters kept at the *Zentralarchiv der Rheinland-Pfalz in Speyer* are the most significant resource. Likewise, the diaries of Swiss missionary Wilfried Spinner TB-SPINNER 1885–1892 and the German missionary Otto Schmiedel TB-SCHMIEDEL has contributed with insightful information to this study.

36. See HAMER 2002.

37. See MARBACH 1934, DEVARANNE 1934, BIELFELDT 1962, and HAHN 1984A.

38. For a sustained attempt to move the history out of its mission context and point to the larger developments of the AEPM in Meiji Japan, see WIPPICH 2001A. The author's sensitivity to the theological concerns works to the benefit of his general portrait of the

AEPM in the nineteenth century. A few other mentionable articles in German-language published within the last 30 years are RUST 1992 and WIPPICH 2001B.

39. MULLINS 2003.

40. When Karl Heinrich Ritter published his book on the Protestant Mission in Japan in 1890, it was the first of many historical reflections on the early Christian mission in Japan. Its influence also spread outside the German speaking boarders, which led to, in 1898 was, its translation and re-publishing under the English title *A History of Protestant Missions in Japan*. See RITTER 1890, 1898.

41. YUSAO 1997

42. Citation in THELLE 1987, 181.

43. Thomas Winburn does refer to the AEPM, but only in an overview of mission societies established in the period from 1883 to 1889. The list only includes the name of the AEPM and a short description in which the AEPM is compared to the Liberal Christian position of the American Unitarians. See WINBURN 1958, 81–3.

44. For a general overview of the early Protestant history in Japan including the developments of the liberal mission societies, see IGLEHART 1959, LANDE 1989, and DRUMMOND 1971.

45. Minami Hajime (1869–1940) from Ashikaga, first Japanese priest of the Japanese Christian community Fukyū Fukuin Kyōkai in Tokyo. He studied theology at the Theological Academy under the Swiss missionary Wilfried Spinner. From 1895 to 1900 editor of the Christian mission journal *Shinri* and as well as the Unitarian journal *Rikugū zasshi*.

46. See SABA 1976.

47. See SUZUKI 1979

48. See MIZUTANI 2010, 115–40.

1. A Universal Religion from the Swiss Highlands

1. Erst Friedrich Langhans, from Thun in Switzerland, was a pastor at Waldau (near Bern) from 1858 and worked as Professor of systematic theology and the history of religion at Bern University. Langhans's publication *Pietismus und Christenthum im Spiegel der äußeren Mission* was praised among liberals of his time but was also heavily criticized by more conservative groups and marked the growing discord between Protestant groups of nineteenth-century Germany.

2. OSTERHAMMEL 2016, 1105–55. On global colonialism and networks see OSTERHAMMEL & PETERSSON 2003, 16–23.

3. In the concept Interacktionsraüme, see OSTERHAMMEL & PETERSSON 2003, 19. On culture transfer within the colonial mission, see OSTERHAMMEL & JANSEN 2012, 101–7.

4. ZACHHUBER 2013, 1.

5. HAYMAN 2002, MURRAY 2002.

6. See GRAF 2002.

7. Citation from BUSS 1876, 244.

8. Buss quoted in ARENDT 1886, 194–5.

9. This is taken from Friedrich Wilhelm Graf's talk "Liberal Protestantism and Christian Studies at Kyoto University, held October 9, 2019.

10. BUSS 1886D, 169.

11. As will be discussed later, the connection between the critical approach to dogma and the liberal Christian movement was a major factor in the popularity of Liberal Christianity. At the turn of the century, many protestant liberals understood theology as the "Historische Kulturwissenschaft des Christentums", i.e., as a historical and hermeneutical science of Christian culture (GRAF 2002), which did not seek to produce dogmatic norms but rather sought to study faith as it was lived in history, and to understand popular religion. Scholars have attempted to discern to what extend the liberal Christian movement influenced German religious society during the nineteenth century. Graf (2002) has suggested that "German liberal academic theology developed in close dialogue with the other "Kulturwissenschaften" or cultural sciences." He points to Ernst Troeltsch as the most famous representative of this new interdisciplinary way of theology whose so-called "Historisismus" or Historicism changed the perception of language, religious traditions, cultural objects and much more. This is a valid point since the shift in the conception and understanding of "history," had the consequence that all groups of German protestant theologians who tried or wanted to be liberals became critical to the traditional patterns of authority and sought to critically revise traditional confessions of faith. See also GRAF 2006.

12. During the 1870s and 1880s, the society in Haag launched several competitions for books to defend Christianity and faith in the New Testament. Ernst Buss won the competition in 1874 with his submission Die christliche Mission, ihre prinzipielle Berechtigung und practische Durchführung, and the monograph was later published by Brill in 1876. In the year that Buss won the competition, the question was formulated as such: "What does the history of mission teach us concerning the purpose and ability of Christianity to become the universal religion of the world?" Within this question one could sense a fear, not necessarily because of the increasing reports from the colonies about the existence of other cultures and religions, but rather the fear of history's proven transitoriness and its influence on the Christian claim of being the absolute truth. For citation see HAHN 1984, 10, 18.

13. The Tübingen school is mostly associated with its leading figure Ferdinand Christian Baur. Inspired by the theology of Hegel and Schleiermacher, Baur managed to "embody the transition from eighteen-century 'pragmatic' interest in historical theology to nineteenth-century historicism." In the center of this school stood the goal of offering a *wissenschaftlicher* theology. The Tübingen schools with Baur set historical theology on the map in the 1840s. Citation ZACHHUBER 2013, 21.

14. Citation BUSS 1876, 123.

15. This is also mentioned in Otto Marbach's short biographical introduction to Ernst Buss. See MARBACH 1934, 1–15.

16. STÜBER 2009, 152.

17. In this respect their conservative critics, or anti-liberal theologians, did much better. Even in their hostile attitudes towards modernity, they managed to some degree to be more modern than many liberals. They did not demand a new homogeneity, but indirectly accepted the new world order of a pluralistic society.

18. The historical consciousness spread in Germany's theological circles at the time put an especially "profound leveling effect on all truth claims and values, including the truth claims of religion. It seemed to cut Christianity down to size, relegating it to the status of just one of the many religions around." This historical consciousness, in other words, prompted liberal Christians to look towards the inner religious life as a response to the increasing outer pressure. For citation see MAZUSAWA 2005, 312–13.

19. I borrow this phrase from Friedrich Willhelm Graf. See GRAF 1992.

20. Citation Meeting Protocol, in ZASP, DOAM 180.1.

21. Citation BUSS 1886A, 3.

22. Citation in HAHN 1984B, 13.

23. Citation in BUSS 1876, 1.

24. Citation in BUSS 1876, 5.

25. See BUSS 1876, 116–23.

26. Citation in BUSS 1876, 123.

27. Citation from BUSS 1876, 244.

28. STÜBER 2009, 167.

29. The letter from Friedrich Nippold to Buss said more precisely: "It's just what one needs today. Send it also to Max Müller in Oxford." Cited from a letter by Friedrich Nippold to Buss 12.04.1879, in ZASP vol. 1. In the archives in Speyer (ZASP), the letters of Buss are arranged, stored, and preserved. Along these letters the development of the AEPM through all its stages can be closely followed, from the first suggestions to the final formation. See ZASP vols. 1, 3, 6, and 7.

30. Müller replied in a letter back to Buss "I sent your book to Dr. Stanley and asked him to inquire whether a translation of the same by one of the English mission societies is possible." Letter from Müller to Buss in ZASP no. 1.

31. Friedrich Max Müller is, according to Otto Marbach, regarded as one of the precursors of the founding of the AEPM. In particular, in his two talks "Eine Missionsrede in der Westminsterabtei mit einleitender Predigt von A. P. Stanley;" held in Strassburg 1874, and "Zwei Essays," Strassburg 1876, he spoke highly of Buss's work and the idea of a liberal Christian mission. MARBACH 1934, 16; HAMER 2002, 278.

32. Pfleiderer, Otto (1835–1908), Professor in practical theology in Jena until 1875. Later moved to Berlin and worked as Professor for Systematic Theology. He was a distinct representative of Liberal Christianity and was associated with men like the Swiss theologian A. E. Biedermann and the Berlin based theologian G. Lipsius.

33. HAMER 2002, 280–1.

34. Handwritten letter from April 11, 1884 in ZASP no. 3. Citation, Letter from Prof. von Horn 18.dec. 1882 to Buss in Glarus. ZASP no. 1.

35. Following the "Protokoll über die vertrauliche Conferenz, zur Bildung eines AEPM," ZASP, no. 447, 5,30. According to Hayo Hamer, one-third of the 300 members

were Swiss nationals, while two-third were German nationalities. See HAMER 2002, 286.

36. Handwritten letter from the Grand Duke of Saxony-Weimar to Buss on July 1884, In ZASP no. 8.

37. Citation HESSE 1897, 71.

38. Citation, BUSS 1883, quoted from *Ostasien Jahrbuch* 1924, 72.

39. Citation from Protocol letter, ZASP, DOAM Nr. 180, 1.

40. Citation in ACMD 1883, 335.

41. The Halle Mission or Danish-Halle Mission was a pietist movement established in 1706 when the Danish King Frederik IV looked for missionaries to work in the Danish colony of South-East India. Two theologians from Halle followed his call and began what became the first German mission society. For the history of the Halle Mission, see LIEBAU 2006. Another pietist movement was the Herrnhuter Brüdermission. Established in 1732, the

Herrnhuter mission was heavily influenced by the Halle Mission, but chose to do mission work in South Africa. See MACK 2013, 42–3.

42. Handwritten letter from the first members meeting, January 3, 1883. ZASP vol. 3.

43. Citation in BUSS 1886D, 169.

44. Ibid., 169.

45. This assumption was particularly strong among scholars of the *Religionsgeschichtliche Schule*. It was the belief that through the critical study of the world religions (including Christianity), elements of a universal truth could be found. As we recall from above, Troeltsch himself argued that religion could not only be about individual conviction; there must be something intrinsic and inherent which makes it great. In his Christianity and the History of Religion, he states: "Christianity could not be the religion of such a highly developed racial group if it did not possess a mighty spiritual power and truth; in short, if it were not, in some degree, a manifestation of the Divine Life itself." As seen in the writings of Buss and other liberal theologians, this romantic sense of the truth existed among many nineteenth and twentieth century scholars of religion. For citation see TROELTSCH 1991, 26.

46. Citation in BUSS 1886A, 4.

47. At the meeting of the AEPM in Braunschweig in June of 1887, Richard Adelbert Lipsius gave the talk "Unsere Aufgabe in Ostasien" (Our task in East Asia) in which he asked the question "In what form should we bring the gospel to the pagan cultures?" I would like to quote three key sentences from the talk: (1) "We should not bring the gospel as human wisdom, but as divine revelation;" (2) "One must preach the gospel not as a new culture, but as help in moral need"; and (3) "But our messengers are not supposed to bring this message as a party matter, but as a testimony of the unified sanctuary." For citations see LIPSIUS 1894, 14, 17, 19.

48. Translated from the "geistigen Zeitmächten." See EGER 1981, 63.

49. Here the Gospel is understood to help the morally and mentally distressed, see also LIPSIUS & KIRMSS 1886.

50. See here Karl Heinrich Ritter's interpretation of the event that let up to the final decision, see RITTER 1884, 5–6.

51. See JAFFE 2019, 3; SUZUKI 1979, 27–8.

52. Citation in SABA 1976, 201.

53. Citation borrowed from HAMER 2002, 300.

54. Citation in RITTER 1884, 6.

55. The AEPM never went to India but hired the German missionary Ernst Faber to missionize in Tsingtau, China from 1885. Faber had previously worked for the Rheinische Mission in China but later quit due to disagreements over policy matters. He then saw his opportunity to join the newly established mission society of the AEPM. See STÜBER 2009, 157–62.

56. The AEPM stayed in close contact with the Deutscher Kolonialverein (German Colonial Association). There had been "personal discussions with a delegation of the mission board and the Deutscher Kolonialverein in Frankfurt whether to support the mission in Japan or not" See BUSS 1885, 40. Also primary sources reveal that from an early point there still were voices in the AEPM leadership who sought to establish a colonially supported mission. For example, in the AEPM journal ZMR from 1887, we find that the Berlin department of the AEPM met with the Neuguinea Kompanie to discuss an eventual mission field. Why this plan wasn't realized is difficult to say. See ZMR 1887, 64.

57. The missionaries' role in the colonies was, according to missionologist Gustav Warneck, clear. There existed a definite hieratical distinction where the mission was above the State. For example, in his mission statement Warneck wrote: "we are here dealing clearly with facts. Of course, it cannot be argued against by any sober person that the colonial policy… places itself directly at the service of the Kingdom of God…." For the full quote see WARNECK 1880, 24. The complicated mingling of the mission societies and the German colonial Government will only briefly be presented here. However, in the case of the AEPM, the distinction between mission and state was not as clear as it was in Warneck's case. The AEPM Mission Board was more interested in pursuing a mutual cooperation with the German Colonial Institutions than working independently from it. See BUSS 1885, 40. Monthly news about the religious development of Die Deutschen Kolonien was a constant feature in their publications up until 1918. Mission journals such as *Zeitschrift für Missionskunde und Religionswissenschaft* and *Das Missionsblatt* carried stories about the African colonies, the newest developments in Kaiser Wilhelm Land and Tsingtau in China. There, just like the AEPM in Japan, missionary work was seen as the "colonization of religion." See SCHMIEDEL 1891A; GRAUE 1887. The close connection between the mission society and government policy was valued by the missionaries of the AEPM: not only did they find in Grand Duke Carl Alexander von Saxon-Weimar a dedicated patron of the mission with close links to the diplomatic representatives of the German government in Tokyo, it also allowed them to establish a close link between the Japanese mission field and the political decision-making in Berlin. See HAMER 2002, 325–9. Lastly, the AEPM in Japan benefited from a political-national interest which underlaid the German cultural commitment in Meiji Japan economically as well. It received financial support from the German state. For a period, as much as 10,000 Marks a year was forwarded to finance

the projects of the AEPM in Japan. See Letter from Bismarck to Dörnhoff, 21/2, 1885, BA R 901/39191. For more on the discussion about the relationship of the German mission movement and the German government, see also BADE 1982, PORTER 1996, OSTERHAMMEL 1997, BARTH & OSTERHAMMEL 2006, and FITZPATRICK 2008. For quote, see HAMER 2002, 325–38; see also WIPPICH 2001A.

58. GRAF 2002, 29; NIPPERDEY 1990, 472.
59. Citation from AAGAARD 1967, 131.
60. Citation from ARNDT 1886, 194–5.

2. The Emergence of Liberal Christianity in Japan

1. See BUSS 1886C, 118.
2. See Introduction, Footnote 17 for a further biographical description of Aoki.
3. See AKASHI 1995, 13.
4. See HARADA 1935, 188. According to historian Anette Hack a total of 70 Japanese students were residents in Berlin in the 1870s and 1880s. They left a positive impression among their German teachers and distinguished themselves through their "diligence, love of truth, conscientiousness and courtesy." See HACK 1996, 11–12. For an excellent book on the Japanese impressions of Berlin See WADA 2006.
5. KRÄMER 2015, 97.
6. Citation from Aoki's autobiography *Aoiki Shūzō jiden*, AOKI 1970, 38.
7. See MICHAELIS 1922, 52. For citation, RITTER 1884, 6. See also HESSE 1885, 1050–1; ZMR 1886, 52.
8. There are a few other reasons why Japan became the first mission field of the AEPM. Firstly, the opening of Japan to German influence together with the 1883 interdenominational missionary conference in Osaka allowed for the belief among the members of the AEPM that Japan was a promising mission field. In 1885, for example, Gustav Warneck explicitly wrote about Japan: "All reports seem to agree that enormous religious changes are happening. It is a favorable sign of a not-too-distant Christianization of the Japanese islands." See WARNECK 1885, 195. See also RITTER 1890A and BEST 1966, 85. On Aoki's role in the decision for Japan, see RITTER 1884, 8. For Wadagaki's role in the decision of Japan, see RITTER 1890A, 105. For Citation in main text, MBL 1894, 95. For citation in quote, see RITTER 1884, 6.
9. See BUSS 1892A.
10. According to the German historian Heyo Hamer, the German community in Yokohama in 1879 encompassed a total of 160 persons characterized by two groups; a smaller group of "traders" and a larger group of "scholars." HAMER 2002, 365.
11. The German Studies Society School or Doitsugaku Kyōkai Gakkō was founded in 1881 by various liberal Japanese connected to Germany. These were the Christian scholars Nishi Amane and Katō Hiroyuki, and the diplomats Inoue Kaoru, Shinagawa Yajirō, Katsura Tarō, and Aoki Shūzō. Otto Bernhard Hering became a board member of the German Protestant Society in Tokyo. See HERING 1892; HAMER 2002, 444–7. For the

history of the phenomenon of foreign teachers in Meiji Japan, see Arthur Burks *The Modernizers: Overseas Students, Foreign Employees, and Meiji Japan*. BURKS 1985.

12. From Spinner's diary, we know that he stayed with Dr. Hering for 6 months until moving into his own rented house in the Tokyo area of Tsukiji. TB-SPINNER 8.9.1885.

13. Prince Kitashirakawa was a member of the Royal family. In 1867, he was appointed chief minister (*sōsei*) and later a cabinet member of the Japanese Government from 1870. He had an impressive military career, first fighting the *Tokugawa bakufu* in the Boshin War in 1868–1869, then against the famous Satsuma Rebellion in 1877, and finally in the Sino-Japanese War of 1894, where he contracted malaria and died the following year in Tokyo. See JANSEN 2000, 73–8.

14. This tactic was not just applied by the AEPM, but by all Christian denominations at the time. Richard H. Drummond has in his work *History of Christianity in Japan* estimated that "40 percent of the total body of Protestant Christians in Japan were of the samurai class, although the latter constituted only 5 percent of the total population. Among the Christians of Tokyo, nearly 75 percent belonged to this class." Citation in DRUMMOND 1971, 169.

15. In Spinner's diary we can see how important the contact and help of Aoki and Hering was for the initial establishment of Spinner's and AEPM's work in Japan. He, for example, states: "My birthday present today was the offer from the *Doitsu Gakkō* (aka Doitsugaku Kyōkai Gakkō) which I received from Dr. Hering. I have to teach 9 hours weekly (from February, 12 hours weekly) for 30 Yen a month and free accommodation in Surugadai (Kanda district of Tokyo). This allows me to 1) Get connected with the circles of leadership and thus be acquainted with some of the leading Japanese. 2) The school will be a very favorable point of contact for the missionary activity. 3) It allows for a partial change of scenery from our mission club. 4) It allows for the continuing communication with Aoki, who probably also is behind my employment at the school, as he intends to transform the school into a Christian one. 5). I can live in the city [Spinner until then lived with Dr. Hering in Yokohama]. 6) This is the best opportunity to learn about practices at a Japanese preschool and study the application of pedagogy among the Japanese youth. 7) I can learn why the school is filled with Catholic Austrian and anti-religious Germans. 8) In this case, I might be able to better direct the school into a true Christian direction." Citation from TB-SPINNER 12.10.1885.

16. Kozaki Hiromichi was a distinguished figure in Japanese Christian circles. Born in Kumamoto, he later became a student at the newly established Christian university, Dōshisha. Belonging to the Congregational Church, Kozaki was an outspoken and public figure in Meiji Japan, particularly engaging in the debate about religion and government. See BALLHATCHET 1998.

17. Quoted from KOZAKI 1893, 1012.

18. See MIZUTANI 2010, 124–9. On the influence of the AEPM in Japan, Aasulv Lande also comments: "This [German-liberal] school influenced the New Theology in Japan and is one of the challenging influences behind the theology of Yokoi, Kanamori and Ebina. [Their] modern thinking also gave an impetus to a social concern in the Japanese Christian church." Citation in LANDE 1988, 60; see also NIREI 2007.

19. HAMER 2002, 581.
20. See TB-SPINNER 01.07.1888.15.07.1888.
21. Kayama Shinjirō was baptized by Spinner in Tokyo in June 1886. We know from Otto Schimiedel's diary that Kayama moved to Kyoto and began working at the German School teaching German. He later joined the Nihon Kumiai Kirisuto Kyōkai in Kyoto. See TB-SCHMIEDEL 16.02.1891. Nakarai Sunao was a student of Spinner in the Hongo community. He traveled to Germany in 1889 and, among others, stayed in the house of Karl Heinrich Ritter in Berlin. Later he studied both at Tübingen University and in Jena. See HARADA 1935, 188.
22. TB-SPINNER. 17.07.1888.
23. See SPINNER 1890, 1893A, 1893B.
24. Statutes of the AEPM, § 3, in BUSS 1886D, 55.
25. TB-SPINNER 25.06.1888; TB-SPINNER 11.08.1888.
26. Shinshū Buddhism is a reformist movement within the Japanese Pure-Land tradition. It adopted many of the missionaries' and Western ideas and merged them with their Buddhist belief. The meeting between Jōdo Shinshū Buddhists and Wilfried Spinner during his visit in Kyoto 1888 will be discussed in-depth in Chapter six.
27. Letter from Spinner in PKZ 1889, 202–3.
28. ANONYMOUS, in MBL 1885; see also HORI 1978.
29. Already in 1886, Spinner realized that bringing about any cooperation and support of the mission work from the German community in Japan would be difficult. In a note from his diary, Spinner complained that the behavior of the Germans living in Yokohama had a negative effect on his mission plans: "My advancement towards the higher circles of Japanese has suddenly been put on hold and my school project may also be ruined. Our embassy suddenly became noticeably cooler towards me. God save me from my friends." Citation from TB-SPINNER 27.06.1886.
30. TB-SPINNER 03.14.1891
31. Spinner's criticism on the moral standards of the Christians living in Japan at the time was voiced in a news article written in the *Deutsche Kolonialzeitung* of 1886: "From Japan, Tokyo 12. February 1886.... A further difficulty of the mission lies in the life of the Christian foreigners living here. It is common among the native people in Japan to end a marriage with a contracted termination. The Japanese make abundant use of this open marital relationship; They often change their spouse, and if they do not morally prefer to divorce their wife, they take a *Musume* (concubine) or even visit the *Yoshiwara*, the red-light district (*Freudenviertel*).... Almost all of the unmarried foreigners make admissible use of this contractual life opportunity, except for a few, and they are "married like the Japanese,"... a bad habit with dangerous consequences because through these abuses, the Japanese skepticism is strengthened towards the Christians." DKO 3/1886, 285.
32. See BUSS 1886C, 125.
33. The AEPM would not build its own church until after Spinner's departure in 1892. See BUSS 1892B, 51–3.
34. Letter from Spinner 20.09.1886 See ZASP Nr. 180.1.
35. WIPPICH 2001B, 274.

36. Hamer 1998, 108.

37. Spinner 1891b, 4.

38. The school opened on August 1, 1888. On July 30, a clearly happy Spinner wrote in his diary "I had our Program for our theological school printed today. I myself will give lessons." Quote in tb-Spinner 30.07.1888.

39. See Harada 1935, 491.

40. Financial troubles in the mission work of the aepm were a constant concern. In a letter from missionary Max Christlieb (in Japan from 1892 to 1899) back home, he complains that "it is impossible to see any future for our theological academy if our money situation is not improved." Letter from Max Christlieb to Theodor Arndt, 6.7.1893 in zasp Nr. 180.1. doam vol. 185.

41. Chapter 3 and 4 will look further into the power struggles of the educational institutions of the aepm in Japan.

42. Mohr 2014, 38.

43. The second missionary of the aepm in Japan, Otto Moritz Schmiedel, arrived in 1887 and devoted himself mainly to teaching at Shinkyō Shingakkō and the administration of the journal *Shinri*. This allowed Spinner to focus on ministering to the German-Swiss Evangelical communities in Tokyo and Yokohama, as well as supervising the Japanese communities. When Carl Munzinger arrived in Japan in 1890, he became the third missionary of the society. He largely shared the work of Schmiedel during his stay. With only two exceptions (Friedrich Brinkmann and Georg Würfel), the missionaries usually stayed in Japan for at least five years: Max Christlieb for 7 years, 1892–1899; Hans Haas for 11 years, 1898–1909; Emil Schroeder for 12 years, 1908–1920; and the longest serving missionary of the aepm, Emil Schiller, for an impressive 36 years: 1895–1900 in Tokyo and 1900–1931 in Kyoto. For a full overview of the missionaries in Japan, see Appendix Nr. 1.

44. Citation from zmr 1889, 187; Schmiedel 1920a, 198.

45. Translated from Schmiedel 1920a, 198.

46. zmr 1889, 186–7.

47. Schmiedel 1920, 217; Schmiedel 1897, 13.

48. See Yanigata 1957, 50, Howes 2007, and Mullins & Nosco 2007.

49. By emphasizing the patriotic duty of the Japanese, the missionaries tried to link Christianity with the Japanese's duty towards the emperor. In this way, they hoped to overcome some of the difficulties they faced in the increasingly nationalistic climate of the 1890s, and to make Christianity look more suitable for proselytization in Japan. See Schmiedel 1891a, 13. Mark Mullins has made a similar analysis concerning Japanese Christian's relationship to State Shinto. See Mullins 1998.

50. I am borrowing Emily Anderson's term. See Anderson 2014, 66.

51. Anderson 2014, 64–8.

52. For a description of the similarities between Ebina Danjō and the aepm, see Terozono 1988.

53. Citation in Jahresbericht 1904/1905, 35.

54. Ibid., 35.

55. JAHRESBERICHT 1906, 20.
56. STOLER 2002.
57. Citation in SCHMIEDEL 1889A, 16.
58. While the house might have been Japanese, Spinner quickly had Western style furniture moved into his room. See TB-SPINNER 8.10.1885. For citation, see SCHMIEDEL 1889A, 8; Spinner in a letter 16.10.1885, ZASP Nr. 180.1.
59. Citation SCHMIEDEL 1920A, 54, 63. A picture of the mission house can be seen in ZASP, DOAM 180.8, vol. 8, 16.
60. SCHMIEDEL 1920A, 70.
61. Ibid., 72. It is worth mentioning that Kirin today is one of the largest beer brands in Japan.
62. Ibid., 89.
63. Emil Schiller in a letter to the AEPM 24.5.1901. In ZASP 180.1, DOAM vol. 224.
64. Citation from MUNZINGER 1898, 21.
65. Quote from LEHMANN 2009, 7.
66. In fact, they would write eagerly write essays of their life in Japan and published them in the missionary youth literature. See Margret SCHILLER, "Eine Vulkanbesteigung in Japan" (1915); Liselotte SCHILLER, "Ein japanischer Tempel" (1921); Elisabet SCHILLER, "Der Koyasan" (1922).
67. M. SCHILLER 1913A.
68. To run the school, the AEPM hired the teacher Johan Bolljahn. In contrast to the missionaries employed in Japan, Bolljahn did not have any proselytizing responsibilities. Instead he was put in charge of the Knabenschule with the sole purpose of teaching German children. Bolljahn stayed until 1898 before moving to Korea to set up a German school in Seoul. See BOLLJAHN 1889, 65–6; HAMER 2002, 413–19.
69. Note from ZASP 92 (§1).
70. Note from ZASP 92 (§11 & §17).
71. Note from ZASP 92 (§16 & §20).
72. We hear of this positive relationship in Otto Schmiedel's diary. Schmiedel reports in August 1890 that, "we are now contacting the Universalists, an American sect, whose [theological] approach is similar to that of the Unitarians as both are denying the eternal penalty of hell. We are trying to persuade the two gentlemen and two ladies to join us. They [the Universalists] are not as radical as the Unitarians." From TB-SCHMIEDEL 07.08.1890.
73. See TB-SPINNER 03.14.1891. Their close relationship went beyond theological work, extending into their private lives. Just three months after the arrival of the Universalists in 1890, Wilfried Spinner and Carl Munzinger received an invitation to the birthday celebration of George L. Perin, who seemed to have been able to communicate in German, TB-SP 14.07.1890. We also learn about the visit of Mrs. Perin and her two daughters in the house of the Schmiedel family in December 1891 TB-SPINNER 03.12. 1891.
74. On an invitation from Perin, Spinner, for example, joined Perin at a missionary convent in Tokyo on December 1, 1890. TB-SPINNER 01.12.1890.

75. Nevertheless, true inter-denominational work never gained momentum. Even within the so-called liberal groups, a consensus about a theological cooperation could not be achieved. The Unitarians, supported by the Japanese intellectual Fukuzawa Yukichi, were oriented towards Americans and had established their "own" school at Keio University, with three Unitarian missionaries hired as professors. The other liberal wing of intellectuals was oriented towards Germans and had the Doitsu Kyōkai Gakkō. Both schools were liberal and private enterprises, oriented towards Western education. And although they shared many similarities with the AEPM, to the representatives of the AEPM, a long-term cooperation with the more "orthodox" Universalist seemed just as meaningless as a cooperation with the syncretistic Unitarians. However, this did not preclude personal agreements between individual representatives of these three groups. An example of this are the friendships of several Swiss and German missionaries with the Perin family. See ZMR 1889, 2–3. For a deeper analysis of the Universalist enterprise in Japan, see Michel Mohr's excellent book *Buddhism, Unitarianism, and the Meiji Competition for Universality*, MOHR 2014.

76. According to Otto Schmiedel, most foreigners left Tokyo from the start of June until the end of September. See SCHMIEDEL 1920A, 79.

77. Citation from SCHMIEDEL 1920A, 80.

78. Ibid., 106.

79. Ibid., 81.

80. JAHRESBERICHT 1900, 33.

81. On liberalism and the impact on modern Japanese Christianity, see Nirei Yosuke article, "Towards a Modern Belief. Modernist Protestantism and Problems of National Religion in Meiji Japan," NIREI 2007.

82. YAMAMORI 1974.

83. Quoted from ZASP Nr. 180.8. DOAM vol. 135.

84. Max Christlieb and Carl Munzinger to the Business Committee 1.2. 1894. Translated from ZASP Nr. 180.1. DOAM vol. 91.

85. See also LANDE 1989, 83–9 for a similar description of the mission field.

86. MUNZINGER 1898, 376.

87. Citation from MUNZINGER 1891, 68.

88. As Mark Mullins has shown, the missionaries in Japan faced the problem of combining ancestral worship with Christian belief. Mullins argues that the Japanese religious pluralism needs to be considered as a syncretistic system of layered obligations which tends to stand in conflict with Christianity because of the latter's claim to be the only true religion. As a result, Mullins highlights the fact that most Japanese have been integrated into the system of household (Buddhist) and communal (Shinto) religious obligations, and then asserts that it is precisely this that made it exceedingly difficult for Japanese Christians to make a commitment to the Christian religion. MULLINS 1998, 168. This problem could also be seen in the missionaries' publications. In ZMR 1922, the Japanese Michi Kawai was quoted saying, "One of the main reasons why Buddhism has been so well integrated into the Japanese life is that it is a religion of the family and not of the

individual. You can ask many young leaders what their religion is, and the answer will be, 'My family belongs to this or that sect of Buddhism or Shinto." KAWAI 1922, 218.

89. The warning about a pantheistic interpretation of God was expressed in German missionary Emil Schiller's works. In his article "Contemporary Japan and Christianity" (*Das Heutige Japan und das Christentum*) published in ZMR in 1903, Schiller warned against the transformation of God from a personal and loving God to an all-encompassing divinity as it is known from Buddhism. See SCHILLER 1903. In his book, *The Idea of God and the Modern Philosophy* (*Kami no kannan to kinsei tetsugaku*), written in Japanese, Schiller repeated his argument, adding that this "misunderstanding" of the concept of God was due to the confusion of the Japanese translation of the word *Kami*. See SCHILLER 1901.

90. As Helen Ballhatchet has shown in her study, the Japanese Christian Kozaki Hiromachi symbolized a movement among Japanese Christians who sought to combine Confucian and Christian beliefs. See BALLHATCHET 1998. Although the missionaries encouraged the formation of a Japanese Christianity to "build on the seed of their indigenous religions," they were still afraid of some of the syncretic formations they saw occurring in some of the Christian communities.

91. Emil SCHILLER in letters from 24.5. 1901 ZASP Nr. 180.1 DOAM vol. 224.

92. Translated from Emil Schroeder 's letter to the Home Board, 9.9.1913 ZASP Nr. 180.1 DOAM vol. 250.

93. See CHRISTLIEB & MUNZINGER 1894.

94. Qouted from Max Christlieb, Letter from 24.11.1895 ZASP Nr. 180.1. DOAM vol. 91.

95. See VOGT 1907.

96. In NKRD 1988, 1198f.

97. KOZAKI 1933, 234.

98. HAMER 1984, 97.

99. Citation from ETHERINGTON 2005, 7.

100. For example, in 1929, the Japanese members of the Japanese Christian community would number as few as 124. See JAHRESBERICHT 1929, 65.

101. SATŌ 1998, 44.

102. The journal *Shinri* will be studied further in Chapter 6.

3. Internal Conflicts and External Challenges

1. Auguste Diercks (1862–1921), the first German female missionary in Japan, arrived on November 11, 1889. Until then only men had been sent out as missionaries of the AEPM. Diercks was followed by the second female missionary, Agnes Heydenreich (1898–1900), as there was an attempt to build on the successful tradition of the Anglo-Saxon female mission. Working among Japanese woman and children in domestic circles, the promising and—for the mission—rewarding initiative was sidelined due to a lack of funds, never to restart. Work among women and children would become the responsibility of

missionary wives and was supported by local Japanese nurses and helpers. Worth noting, among the female missionaries' contribution to the Japanese mission field is the creation of a social-welfare school for poor girls in 1893, which was started largely on the initiative of Käthe Christlieb, the wife of missionary Max Christlieb. See SCHMIEDEL 1891A, 30–2. Auguste Diercks herself stayed in Japan for five years until she had to return to Germany in 1894 due to health problems. In MBL 1892, 50–3.

2. Citation in DIERCKS 1892, 78.

3. Ibid. 79.

4. Citation DIERCKS 1893 58.

5. Simon Gikandi gives a similar characteristic of missionary texts in his book *Maps of Englishness: Writing Identity in the Culture of Colonialism*, GIKANDI 1996, xviii. Rita PANESAR (2006) also points out that missionary journals not only offered to inform and educate their readers about the mission work; they also served to bring about support for the mission work, to cultivate an increasing community of mission supporters in Switzerland and Germany, and to inspire potential future missionaries. Another central function of the journals was to increase the funding of the missions. Therefore, the missionaries had clear incentives to depict themselves and their work in the most positive way. The overall picture of a missionary as an unselfish and noble individual working to save sinful heathens for the kingdom of God was strong and persistent. Such portrayals were fashioned in cooperation with the missionaries abroad, the mission board in Switzerland and Germany, and the supporters, who edited, funded, and published the material. Anna Johnston's description of British missionary sources as "fundamentally and frankly propagandist in nature," also rings true for a big part of the equivalent Swiss-German publications. For citation, JOHNSTON 2003, 6. The propagandist nature of the genre meant that the missionaries portrayed their work as one of accomplishments and victories. When, as was frequently the case, they were faced with undeniable failures, they tended to justify their lack of success by referring to Japanese chauvinism and cultural resistance rather than their own insufficiencies or methods. According to Anna Johnson, the missionaries' texts "unsurprisingly.... always emphasize on positive evangelical achievements whilst limited successes or spectacular failures are rarely mentioned." See JOHNSTON 2003, 7. Further, however fruitless their efforts might at first seem, they continued to emphasize that victory could still be achieved in numerous ways. After a decade of declining numbers of Japanese members associated with the AEPM mission in Japan, for example, the missionaries would still write in their journals that "the victory of Christianity is only a question of time," See AEPM meeting report, ZASP 180.8 DOAM 1900. In short, the investment of the missionaries and their publishers to portray the missions as meaningful and profound strongly shaped the kind of narratives they told and the way in which they communicated them. In this analysis, it therefore seems particularly important to consider how these features of the genre might have influenced the missionary reports and, consequently, the way in which their understandings of historical realities were fashioned.

6. See ISHII 2004.

7. This has already been done to a certain extend by Heyo Hamer in his book *Mission und Politik*. See HAMER 2002.

8. See GLUCK 1985, 57.

9. An analysis of the students of Shinkyō Shingakkō will follow in Chapter 4.

10. A newsletter in the *Zeitschrift für Missionskunde und Religionswissenschaft* informs that a Sunday School was established in December 1887, see ZMR 1888, 250. In 1888, another newsletter, this time in the *Das Missionsblatt*, informs that the school had around 60 students, most of them children. See MBL 1888, 75. In 1889, it is stated that between 15 to 55 children are being taught in four classes, MBL 1889, 95. Symptomatically, there exist no sources about the Sunday Schools' closing; however, in another newsletter in *Das Missionsblatt* it says that the former Sunday School teacher, the Japanese Shimizu Saishirō, now is teaching at the Armenschule, MBL 1891, 91. We can therefore assume that the Sunday School either closed or was turned into a school for the poor around 1891–1892.

11. "Voluntary schools" are schools that in one way or another functioned without taking notice of the governmental education laws. As Roberta Wollons, a historian on child history, writes, "A series of education laws issued during the 1890s marked the shift from the importation of Western learning to the development of a national educational ideology. The laws not only chronicle the formation of national education policy but link the centrality of teaching the Japanese ethical system in schools to the fate of Christian education in Japan." In other words, the new governmental laws made it much harder for the missionaries to run their schools, and they therefore had to be more creative in the way they propagated their Christian teaching. With the establishment of evening schools and voluntary bible classes they sought to work around the laws of the Japanese government. For citation, see WOLLONS 1993, 14.

12. The change of religious schools in the 1890s was not only significant for Christian schools. Modern historian Tanigawa Yutaka has excellently shown how the educational laws of the Japanese government also affected the work of schools run by Japanese Buddhist sects. He states: "At the actual site of education, many monks doubled as public school employees due to the nationwide shortage of teachers… some decided to relinquish their status as monks in order to focus on their role as educators, while others privileged their duties as monks and did not take outside jobs." For citation see TANIGAWA 2014, 93.

13. One of these volunteering ministers was Yasukawa Tōru, a former evangelist and political friend of Aoki Shūzō. See, ZMR 1890, 244; TB-SPINNER 15-02.1889. In Otto Schmiedel's diary we learn of the first contact with Yasukawa: "We are now in contact with a Mr. Yasukawa, an earlier member of the Ministry, then preacher of the Ichi Kyokwai church community…. He introduced us to his home church, which statistically holds 60 members, but in fact consists of 20 more Christians. The community was abandoned by Ichi Kyōkai and has not been occupied by a pastor for 7 years. The community joined us last Sunday and Yasukawa, Kasuma, and Minami were out to inspect the village, which lies 4 Ri (app. 20 km) east of Tokyo and began their activities. The community will be visited by our pastors every 2–4 weeks, not by Spinner and me, 1. because it is a farming community, where we would be poorly understood, 2. because the tension with Buddhism is so great in the countryside now, that the appearance of Europeans in a peasant community would only hurt and bring about nothing good. 14 days ago, the two community leaders visited us. Energetic peasants with open, brave, and intelligent faces…. One

of them had fled at the beginning [early Meiji]... and had been hiding for months in the Russian consulate of Sendai. The community was originally Greek Catholic and then became Protestant. Another community member died in the dungeon because of his faith in Christianity." Citation in TB-SCHMIEDEL 21.03.1889. See also HAMER 2002, 497.

14. In 1892, the Shinkyō Shingakkō had only three students, as opposed to the Armenschule in 1889, which had 98 students. See JAHRESBERICHT 1899, 32.

15. At the mission station in Hongō in Tokyo, the male and female students performed different, often gender specific, types of work. The males would often teach other male students while the women would apply themselves to crafts and childcare. This gender separation can be observed in the establishment of the *Knabenschule,* which only allowed the teaching of boys. A similar gender distinction existed in the Armenschule, the youth group Seinen Dōmeikai 青年同盟会 and the women's school, or *Damenschule,* first established by Käthe Christlieb in 1895. All in all, the schooling regime that separated the male from the female student was meant to cultivate particular gender specific skills and susceptibilities suitable to contemporary German culture. Their liberal theological background encouraged the missionaries to engage in social welfare projects. One of them was the Lace School, which helped Japanese women to become economically self-sufficient through their lace work. Missionary Otto Schmiedel gives a detailed description of a newly established Lace School (*Klöppelschule)* for poor girls: "Fraulein Höhn, Dr. Hering and Maja [Ms. Schmiedel] are now setting up a lace school for poor girls, at hand for no more than 3–5, who can then provide for themselves. Frl. Höhn wants to teach them bobbins. This is going to start next week. The girls must be over 12 years so that they can be baptized afterwards." Citation in TB-SCHMIEDEL 17.01.1888; TB-SPINNER 01.10.1888." The goal of the school was "for poorer Japanese women to create profitable earnings, while avoiding time-consuming and costly training." Citation from the ZMR 1888, 250; ZMR 1889, 244;249. On the one hand, the training in needlework by German women provided vocational education and economic independence for the attending Japanese women and girls. On the other hand, it provided contact for German women associated with the Mission, through which Japanese girls could be introduced to Christianity. Needlework training combined with Christian education, as taught by the German women, was the holistic goal of the Lace School.

16. See SCHMIEDEL 1920A, 172.

17. See Auguste Diercks complaints above.

18. Citation ROHLEN 1983, 53.

19. An important law that constrained the freedom of missionary schools was the Educational Rescript of 1889. In 1896, the government introduced regulations that banned Christian education, and in 1899, the Japanese government ended the extra-territoriality rule, allowing free travel and residence of foreigners. While it gave more freedom to foreigners in some respects, it also placed foreigners under Japanese law, adding considerably to the degree of control the government could exercise over their activities. For more on the Educational Rescript, see GLUCK 1985, 57.

20. See RUBINGER 1986, 196.

21. GLUCK 1985, 103.

22. See ZMR 1893, 32–4. See also KETELAAR 1990, 132.

23. Inoue's comment stirred a heated discussion between Inoue's supporters, mostly Buddhist, and Christians, both Japanese and foreign missionaries. The AEPM also decided to engage in the discussion by publishing a harsh response to Inoue in the ZMR. See ZMR 1892, 32–6. For more on the conflict of Freedom of religious belief in Japan, THELLE 1987, 126–49 and BARAKA THOMAS 2019. According to historian Michel Mohr, the heated counterattacks on Inoue "were so strong that Dr. Inoue, who was slightly confused, asked [other Buddhists] for help." For citation MOHR 2005, 80.

24. Citation in RUBINGER 1986, 230.

25. Citation in SCHILLER 1900, 56–7.

26. Citation, ibid., 57.

27. In the context of colonial and missionary civilizing projects, scholar Heike Liebau has in his book *Faith and Knowledge* (2006) demonstrated how the complex process of the knowledge transfer which took place in the mission schools was meant to reproduce the order of the local society. See LIEBAU 2006. Catherine Hall also focuses on the nature of the civilizing mission in the nineteenth century. HALL 2002.

28. A similar argument about the nature of the mission schools has also been made by Nita Kumar in the context of India. See KUMAR 2000, 13.

29. For quote, see SCHILLER 1900, 56–63.

30. See WENDT 1901, 75.

31. This is among others reported in the two articles "Ausflug unserer Sonntagsschule in Kyoto (Japan)" and "Weinachten in Kyoto," see SCHILLER 1913A; SCHILLER 1913B.

32. See DIERCKS 1892.

33. Citation in VALLGÅRDA 2012, 93.

34. Warneck's attack summerized in SPINNER & ARNDT 1891, 189–91.

35. Citation SCHMIEDEL 1892A, 62.

36. In GENSICHEN 1984, 22.

37. See DALTON 1895; citations in ARNDT 1895, 131.

38. See here Wilfried Spinner's reply to Herman Dalton "Die Beurteilung deutscher Missionsarbeit in Japan durch D. Dalton" published in the ZMR 1895. See also SPINNER 1895, 151–2. An official letter was also published by the General Committee of the AEPM in 1896 entitled: "Zur Verteidigung gegen D. Dalton: Eine Widerlegung des Dalton'schen Angriffes" or "To defense against D. Dalton: A refutation of Dalton's attack. See CENTRALVORSTAND DES AEPM 1896.

39. Citation SPINNER 1895, 151.

40. Citation MBL 1896, 24.

41. Citation in HERING 1897, 93.

42. Ibid., 94.

43. This may have been one of the main reasons why the missionaries' educational projects kept being a subject of internal disputes throughout the period.

44. "Zentralvorstand-Konferenz am 9. April 1907, Abends 6 Uhr in Berlin." See JAHRESBERICHT 1907, 5.

45. "Außerordentliche Zentralvorstands-Konferenz am 5. Februar 1908, vormittags 9 Uhr, in Berlin," See JAHRESBERICHT 1908, 4.

46. See JAHRESBERICHT 1908, 17.

47. Ibid., 6.

48. A similar characterization of the mission literature is also made by Rita PANESAR (2006).

49. Mark Mullins argues that the faith of Jesuits in the sixteenth century "undoubtedly shaped the Japanese perception of Christianity [in the nineteenth century]" Citation in MULLINS 1994, 262.

50. Citation in RITTER 1892A, 31–2. Reports of Japanese hostility appeared frequently in the missionaries' publications. Missionary Carl Munzinger, for example, in 1906 tells of an incident that occurred in 1889 when the liberal Minister of Education Mori Arinori was murdered by a "fanatic patriot." Munzinger writes: "Upon entering the famous Shinto Temple *Kōtaijingū* 皇大神宮 in the province of Ise, Mori had not noticed the warning "Take off your shoes; the place on which you stand is holy land;" and inside the temple he had, with his walking stick, knocked back the curtain which protects the most holy part of the temple. In the eyes of the people, this was a misdeed against the most sacred customs of the fatherland which, according to the feelings of patriotic zealots, only blood could avenge. In order not to fall into the hands of the police, the murderer committed suicide after his act. The tomb of Mori, who, despite some quirks, was one of the richest Japanese members of parliament, was deserted from day one. Thousands of good Japanese pilgrims, however, went to the murderer's resting place every day, covered the grave with flowers, lit incense, decorated it with written prayers, and happily took some crumbs of the consecrated earth from the grave with them home. This fanatic has become the martyr of the Japanese, a national saint. The love for the fatherland has turned into an obnoxious enthusiasm of madness." Citation in MUNZINGER 1906A, 157–8.

51. Citation RITTER 1892B, 106.

52. Citation in Spinner's diary, TB-SPINNER 12.02.1890.

53. Citation SCHILLER 1899, 181.

54. Citation from SCHMIEDEL 1889A, 12.

55. Japanese scholar Noriko Kawamura Ishii has in her study on American female mission schools in Kobe, for example, shown how high-standing families who sympathized with Christianity often let only their girls be baptized. The remaining part of the family stayed Buddhist due to fear of persecution See ISHII 2004, 74. Aoki Shūzō, an important supporter of the AEPM, also kept his baptism a secret while he was in office at the Foreign Ministry of Japan. This still did not stop the nationalist from injuring him in the attempted assassination of 1893.

56. TANIGAWA 2014, 94–5.

57. Citation in DIERCKS 1893, 191.

58. Citation in WOLLONS 1993, 29.

59. ISHII 2004, 122–9.

60. See JOHNSTON 2003, 66–7.

61. Nita Kumar has made a similar argument about the mission schools in India. The schools functioned not only as arenas of disputes between the colonial rulers and the local Hindu cast, but were also points of contention between the missionaries and the parents of the children attending the mission schools. See KUMAR 2000, 13.

62. In the mission literature, the indigenous religions were in most cases defined as "the heathen religions" and we cannot simply assume their social or religious position. However, in a few cases, as in the example above, they were specifically categorized as either "Buddhist priest," "Shintoist" or "national patriots."

63. Citation in WITTE 1913B, 2–3.

64. This has been the forceful argument suggested by Pierre Bourdeui's theory of Cultural Changes and adopted in the postcolonial scholarship. See for example DIRKS 1996, ELBOURNE 2008, and GARTMAN 2002.

65. Citation from ISOMAE 2011, 95.

66. Citation in FASS 2003, 964.

67. Education is as Pierre Bourdieu and Jean-Claude Passeron also have argued, essential to the social reproduction of society. See BOURDIEU & PASSERON 1977.

68. Citation in WENDT 1910A, 1.

69. Citation in IRSCHIK 1994, 9.

70. See SCHEINER 1970, 133.

71. Such depictions often follow the line of Edward Said's groundbreaking work *Orientalism*, see SAID 1978. Here, the modern colonizing project is portrayed as highly effective, and as reaching the heart of the colonized societies. Despite efforts to maintain a resistance, the colonized cannot help but be sucked into a westernized mentality, because the resistance itself is seen to take place on the colonizers' terms. Examples of this are SCOTT 1999 and DIRKS 1992.

72. This is arguably the image painted by the Comaroffs in their seminal work *Of Revelation and Revolution: Christianity, Colonialism, and Consciousness in South Africa*. See COMAROFF & COMAROFF 1991.

73. Citation in ELBOURNE 2003, 459.

74. Gertrude Schroeder's article on "Kleine Japankinder," in the mission journal *Für die Jugend* is an example of a positive description of the Japanese kindergartens. In her essay, she tells how her kindergarten in Kyoto almost overflowed with happy and excited children waiting for her in the morning to open the kindergarten. See SCHROEDER 1910, 4.

75. In 1890, we know that the AEPM had in total 42 students in its bible school and 46 members in its Sunday School. The numbers stayed constant throughout the whole period until its closure in 1893. Similarly, throughout the 1890s, the Armenschule had a stable number of students ranging from 30 to 55. "Statistik der protestantischen Mission in Japan 1890, Anlage 1 zum Bericht der Kaiserlichen Gesandtschaft in Tokyo vom 2. Nov. 1890." See ZAB 390/87; JAHRESBERICHT 1900, 18.

76. Citation from SCHMIEDEL 1920A, 218–19.

77. Agnes Heydenreich was sent to Japan in 1898 as the second female missionary where she was to continue the work of Auguste Diercks in the women's and children's

mission. She mainly cared for Japanese women and children in the Sunday School and led various women and household circles. She left Japan two years later in 1900.

78. Citation from HEYDENREICH 1900, 120.
79. Citation in SPINNER 1885A.
80. Citation in GONZÁLEZ 2007, 7.
81. Citation in CHRISTLIEB 1898, 29.
82. WOLLONS 1993, 15–26.
83. Letter from Mumm to Bülow, 27.5 1907, PAAA R 18663.
84. A similar argument has been made by Japanese historian Namikawa Yoko. See NAMIKAWA 2009, vii.

4. A Class Dispute

1. Minami Hajime (1869–1940) from Ashikaga. First Japanese priest of the Japanese Christian community Fukyū Fukuin Kyōkai in Tokyo. Studied theology at Shinkyō Shingakkō under Swiss missionary Wilfried Spinner. From 1895 to 1899 editor of the journal *Shinri*.

2. Reconstruction of the event based on Tamao Harada biography on Minami Hajime, *Nihon ni okeru jiyú kirisitokyō to sono senkusha*「日本に於ける自由基督教と其先駆者」, HANADA 1935, 174.

3. Mukō Gunji (b. 1869) was born the same year and in the same prefecture as Minami. He was a student at the Doitsugaku Kyōkai Gakkō, and participant in Spinner's baptism classes. From 1887, he also studies at the theological academy, followed by a stay with the Hongō community until 1894, before finances and a sick mother forced him to take a teaching position at Kansai University.

4. TB-SPINNER 29.09.1885

5. Spinner's first meeting with Minami Hajime is interesting, because we also get a sense of what kind of young Japanese Spinner was looking for in building his mission. In his diary he writes of the first meeting: "This afternoon two students from Dr. Hering's school (Doitsugaku Kyōkai Gakkō) visited us. They came to inquire about my mission: Minami and Odaka. Both had received Christian teachings from the Albrecht Brothers missionary Vögelein [an American-based Evangelical Church founded by German immigrants]. It was beautiful, as Minami told me, that among the Japanese there are many like Nicodemus (hereby referring to the willingness of the Japanese to learn from Christianity). Minami had been baptized, while Odaka had turned away from Vögelein. The former gives me the impression of a pure Johannes nature. He wishes very much to study theology. Maybe we can send him to Germany. Both students promised to visit me more often and to bring others with them. So then, with God's help, a beginning has been made. God bless the progress!" Citation from TB-SPINNER 29.09.1885. Odaka was one of the five students who followed Spinner's teachings at Doitsugaku Kyōkai Gakkō and who stayed in contact with the AEPM after the classes as well. But in contrast to Minami, he never became a part of the Shinkyō Shingakkō. See TB-SPINNER 28.03.1886.

6. Citation in JANIEWSKI 1992, 3.
7. The term "total institution" is borrowed from Bourdieu and Passeron. See BOURDIEU & PASSERON 1977, 44.
8. Citation in HAMER 2002, 470.
9. Scheiner 1970.
10. This legitimization was, as was also argued by Catherine Hall, based on an assumption that the missionaries, through their teaching, helped lead non-Christians towards "modernization." See HALL 2002. See also JANIEWSKI 1992. This relationship between religion and modernity will be further discussed in the following chapter.
11. Citation in ARNDT 1886, 194.
12. The main reason was, as Spinner points out it in his diary: "the education of students in the schools can lead the way for Christianity." Citation in TB-SPINNER 11.10.1885.
13. Citation in TB-SPINNER 28.31.121890.
14. While Spinner in the quote states that the founder of Hai Kinshiu was unknown, this is in fact untrue. The religion was founded by Takahashi Yoshio 高橋養雄 in 1886–1887 when he published his English titled doctrine *The Worship of Almighty Money*. As explained in the quote by Spinner, it was the purpose of the religion to worship money like one worshiped the gods and Buddha. For citation see SPINNER 1887, 232.
15. Citation SPINNER 1886A, 3.
16. Citation TB-SPINNER 24.09.1885.
17. This has been argued by Heike Liebau, among others, in her book *Faith and Knowledge*. Here she argues that in order to understand the transformational processes that took place in the mission fields in the nineteenth and twentieth centuries, one needs to investigate the implicit or explicit teaching of social knowledge which took place in the mission schools and led to the adaption of particular religious habits and to the development of specific Christian beliefs. See LIEBAU 2006.
18. Citation TB-SPINNER 05.10.1886.
19. Citation in CHRISTLIEB 1898, 29.
20. Over the course of the past three or four decades, scholars of colonial and missionary civilizing projects have documented how Christianity played an important role for many colonizing projects throughout East Asia and elsewhere, especially in the late nineteenth century and the start of the twentieth century. They have argued that the mission schools often were designed to change the overall order of society. See JOLLY 1998, CROOK 1996, and BROWN 1998.
21. Citation in MUNZINGER 1897, 75.
22. See SCHILLER 1922. Similar assessments were also made by other missionaries of the Mission. See for example also; SCHMIEDEL 1898, 5; SPINNER 1885B, 18–19.
23. This despite, as shown in the previous chapter, their relative lack of success.
24. Citation in LIPSIUS 1898, 13.
25. According to statistics provided by Heyo Hamer (2002), the school, which began in 1881, had 83 students in 1883 divided into two programs. And two years later the school would register 470 students. In 1888, the German teacher, Georg Michaelis reported that the school continued its explosive growth with the number of students totaling 561. In

1890, the introduction of the Imperial Rescript of Education affected the numbers of new students and the school could only report 440 students. See MICHAELIS 1887, 1; HAMER 2002, 454.

26. Otto Bernhard Hering. Dr. Phil from Thuringia; took his doctorate in Jena. Encountered Wilfried Spinner in Jena, Germany before Spinner traveled to Japan, see TB-SPINNER 08.02.1885. The encounter probably also introduced Hering to Aoki Shūzō, who suggested that he teach in Japan at Doitsugaku Kyōkai Gakkō. Today the school is known as Dokkyō University, an abbreviation of its original name. For more on the establishment on the school, see HAMER 2002, 451–4.

27. For a list of curricula see HAMER 2002, 451.

28. From 1883, the German Emperor officially donated 2,400 yen annually over a ten-year period. In 1886, another donation of 10,000 yen was made by the cultural minister. In 1887, a donation of 20,000 yen annually by the German Finance Minister began. One yen was by the late nineteenth century equivalent to three Deutsch Mark. The German government's support of the mission schools continued up until the First World War. See FESTSCHRIFT 100 JAHRE 1983, 106–8; FESTSCHRIFT 75 JAHRE 1958, 144.

29. From letter in ZASP no. 91, 51.

30. Citation BHABHA 2004, 122.

31. See FOUCAULT 1978. See also STOLER 1995, 3.

32. In his book *Refashioning Futures Criticism after Postcoloniality*, David Scott demonstrates how modern concepts of political representation, community, rights, justice, obligation, and the common good did not apply universally but were entangled in a net of various power battles and thus require reconsideration, see SCOTT 1999.

33. Citation in THOMAS 1992, 385.

34. Protocol letter in ZASP no. 91, 50.

35. Ibid, 51.

36. Letter from Home Board in ZASP no. 91, 51.

37. Noticeable also is that Spinner, against former historical interpretations, did not start with the schooling of students, and thereafter establish a Japanese Christian community. Instead, neither of these seemed to happen before the other, as both were attributed to Spinner's wish to enable liberal Christian identities. This chance seemed to have come to Spinner with the expulsion of Minami and Mukō from the Doitsugaku Kyōkai Gakkō. See also WIPPICH 2002, 273.

38. Minami and Mukō met Spinner through Otto Hering, a teacher at the school, in September of 1885, and in the following year, the two students would become Spinner's first students of his theological academy, the Shinkyō Shingakkō. See TB-SPINNER 29.09.1885; see also HARADA 1935, 480.

39. For citation TB-SPINNER 28.03.1886.

40. Letter from Spinner to the Home Board in ZASP 91, 51.

41. The three students of the newly established Shinkyō Shingakkō are also included in these numbers. See ARNDT 1888, 238–9.

42. Spinner mentions this in his diary for the first time, see TB-SPINNER 04.03.1886.

43. Citation from TB-SPINNER 30.10.1887.

44. See BUSS 1888B, 249.
45. Overview from BUSS 1889, 248.
46. The students taught by Spinner at Shinkyō Shingakkō were Minami Hajime 1887–1890; Mukō Gunji 1887–1889 and 1891–1892; Maruyama Michikazu 1888–1892; Kasuma Jifuku 1888–1889 and 1891; Akikusa Jūzo, Miyoshi Atsuyoshi, and Sekiya Yūnosuke 1889; Fujita Sutematsu 1890–1894). For list see also HAMER 2002, 475.
47. Citation in SPINNER 1893C, 244.
48. Citation from SPINNER 1889A, 62.
49. Citation from SPINNER 1891C, 92.
50. For citation see SCHMIEDEL 1892B, 57.
51. Citation in BASSERMANN 1886, 69.
52. These classes of the theological schools were held regularly during the weekdays and on Sundays after the normal Sunday School from 2pm. For an overview, see SCHMIEDEL 1920A, 219. For citation, see BASSERMANN 1886, 70.
53. Otatsume was supported by the AEPM through a one-year scholarship for students of Protestant theology, "in order to be in the service of our association in the future." See the newsletter in the ZMR 1887, 188.
54. Spinner mentions the visit of Mukō's mother in TB-SPINNER 26.06.1888.
55. Citation in TB-SPINNER 21.06.1888.
56. Report from Wilfried Spinner in ZASP 1888/1889, 5.
57. Citation from TB-SPINNER 25.06.1886.
58. Report from Wilfried Spinner in ZASP 1888/1889, 10.
59. Ibid., 10.
60. Ibid., 10.
61. Ibid., 11.
62. Citation in TB-SPINNER 15.09.1888.
63. Citation from TB-SPINNER 17.10. 1888.
64. Citation in MICHAELIS 1922, 119.
65. Ibid., 115–16.
66. Citation in SPINNER 1886C, 161.
67. Describing one of his Japanese students, Carl Munzinger, for example, writes in his book *Japan und die Japaner* (1898): "Among his German teachers at the University.... I always heard praise and recognition. "Oh he belongs to you?!" they asked, "you should be proud of that." And I was also proud of him.... But in our small community, he never managed to perform excellently [as he did in the school] and not once did I see him begin a prayer." Citation MUNZINGER1906A, 187.
68. The first shipment of 1,200 books arrived at the Shinkyō Shingakkō, allowing the school to open its first library for its students. See TB-SPINNER 10.21.1887; SPINNER 1891B, 2.
69. About the Japanese students, Schmiedel more concretely notes: "The Japanese student is talented." He is, however, Schmiedel also notes "not a scientific genius. He does not reflect critically on problems. Many of my students understand very well how to introduce

a critical thought here and there and make a lot of clever insinuations to their reading, but these remarks often remain shallow." Citation in SCHMIEDEL 1920, 112.

70. In a curious case, missionary Wilhelm Hückel, in his book *Aus der Japanischen Kinderwelt* (1925) writes how, in Japan, not only day and night are opposites, but also how cultural habits such as taking your shoes off instead of your hat are antipodal to what he knows from Germany. He concludes inquisitively about the Japanese: "According to our terms their world is upside down!" Citations from HÜCKEL 1925, 3.

71. Citation in MUNZINGER, 68.
72. Ibid., 68.
73. Ibid., 67.
74. Ibid., 67.
75. Ibid., 70.
76. Citation from SÁNCHEZ-EPPLER 1996, 206.
77. Citation in BHABHA 1997, 453.
78. The missionaries' publications on the youth of Japan will be further scrutinized in Chapter 7.
79. This occurs among others in SPINNER 1885B, 19; SPINNER 1886C, 58; SPINNER 1889C.
80. See among others ANONYMOUS 1906A, 109; ANONYMOUS 1917A, 1–4.
81. The term "Japanese Christian" was frequently used, not only in the German and Swiss missionary literature, but also more generally in the British and American missionary discourse. In the missionary use it was an indication of the impurity of their Christianity, in other contexts, it could express the more eclectic nature of religious identity in Japan. The meaning of this construct will further be examined in Chapter 5.
82. Citation in SPINNER 1891B, 4.
83. Robert Wright, for example, provides an excellent illustration of this in his historical study of the Canadian Protestant mission. See WRIGHT 1991, 158–9.

5. Christian Magazines and Religion in Meiji Japan

1. Citation in RITTER 1886, 142.
2. See ŌTANI 2014B, 99–100.
3. The lack of research in Christian journals is also mentioned by HOSHINO 2014, 100.
4. In fact, many religious denominations were claiming to be "truer" than others. The AEPM was no exception in this. Chapter 6 will look further into the Buddhist intellectuals' discussion of truth and into the responses of the missionaries to these claims.
5. Citation in BUSS 1886A, 5.
6. Citation in MÜLLER 1888, 23.
7. KISALA 2006, 3–4.
8. SMITH 1998, MASUZAWA 2006, JOSEPHSON 2012.
9. ASAD 1993, FITZGERALD 2000, MASUZAWA 2006

10. ISOMAE 2011, xvi-xvii.

11. See JOSEPHSON 2012, 71–3. See also THOMAS 2019, for a newer interpretation of the same problem.

12. Although Darwin's *On the Origin of Species* was already written in 1859, Clinton G. Godart has shown that his theories were first introduced to Japan by the American zoologist Edward S. Morse in 1877. See GODART 2017, 26–31.

13. This movement has commonly been termed *Social Darwinism*. Herbert Spencer was one of the leading Social Darwinists who combined theories of religion with the ideas of social developments. Clinton G. Godart has excellently shown how the ideas of Darwin and Spencer were readily adapted in nineteenth century Japan. Especially the American biologist Ernst Fenollosa's lectures on Spencer's *The Principles of Sociology* in 1878 allowed for the first phase of evolutionary theory to seamlessly be accepted by the religious elite of Japan, including Buddhist and Shinto scholars. See GODART, 72–3.

14. JOSEPHSON 2012, 4.

15. It has also been noted by Japanese religious scholar Isomae Jun'ichi that "liberal theology tended to promote the conversion of religion into a system of ethics." Thus, promoting a conversation between religion and society. See ISOMAE 2011, 51. For citation please see RÜETSCHI 1887, 193.

16. The missionaries' Protestant understanding of religion as an important part of the inner life of the individual and as a requirement for a moral and ethical human life differed, as Jason Ānanda Josephson also has demonstrated, majorly from the ordinary Japanese's idea of the concept. Yet, even though the new word for religion never entered directly into the everyday conversations of the Japanese people, its very existence was used by the missionaries as a tool to differentiate between "uncivilized" and "civilized" habits. See JOSEPHSON 2012.

17. The AEPM was not alone in depicting this understanding of Confucianism. As Galen Amschutz has shown in his book *Interpreting Amida*, many missionaries stationed in Japan in the late nineteenth century made similar efforts to dismiss Confucian thought. See AMSCHUTZ 1997, 63–4.

18. Citation in AHLERS 1887, 2.

19. See AMSCHUTZ 1997, 14.

20. See KRANZ 1903 and KIND 1910.

21. Helen Ballhatchet has demonstrated how Japanese Christians, such as Kozaki Hiromichi, attempted a harmonizing of their Christian beliefs with "Confucian" ideas in order to create a Christianity fitting for Japan. See BALLHATCHET 1998.

22. Citation in BUSS 1886A, 1.

23. Ibid., 2.

24. Ibid., 1.

25. Ibid., 1.

26. Ibid., 1.

27. Ibid., 1.

28. This is taken from Friedrich Wilhelm Graf's talk "Liberal Protestantism and Christian Studies at Kyoto University, held 9 October 2019.

29. Citation in BUSS 1886A, 2.
30. Ibid., 2.
31. Ibid., 2.
32. Ibid., 2.
33. Citation in BUSS 1888A, 55.
34. Ibid., 56.
35. Citation in BUSS 1876, 34.
36. Citation in PFLEIDERER 1906, 1.
37. The Church's obligation to engage in social welfare centers like that of *Die Gesellschaft für Zimmerleute* was, as we saw with Buss above, a core belief among many liberal Protestants. They saw it as the responsibility of the church to provide welfare services, or more generally to serve as a watchdog for social ills within the society. These ideas about social programs for people in need also spread to the mission field in Japan, where schools such as a Lace School or *Klöppelschule* for poor girls, briefly explained in Chapter 3, were established. Wilfried Spinner referred to the Klöppelschule as a "vocational school [*Arbeitsschule*] for lacework" and defined the goal to be a school that provides "for poorer Japanese women to create profitable earnings, while avoiding time-consuming and costly training." (Spinner quoted from the curriculum from 18 May 1888 in ZASP 91.1). For Spinner, the school's main concern was the alleviation of suffering and hunger through work, rather than actual learning. In the spirit of "learning by doing," courses were established to develop the lace working skills and abilities of its students. From 8 February 1888 onward, they were based on a solid organizational framework with courses held on a weekly basis. See SPINNER 1889B, 90; ANONYMOUS 1890, 72.

Overall, the female schools gave their students an education that enabled them to become well versed in the domestic realm, which—in accordance with the European custom of the time—the liberal missionaries considered the appropriate place for women. At the same time, the female school functioned as a social institution that supported the women to earn their own money. They were given sewing training, and they were, like the male students, taught and encouraged to become closely associated employees of the Mission, see JAHRESBERICHT 1900, 31. In the late nineteenth century, female schools, and lace schools in particular, were a normal phenomenon among European missions in Japan. As argued by Noriko Kawamura Ishii, the mission societies used the girls' schools to prepare young women for their role as Bible women who could reach out into the women's quarters of Japanese homes and proselytize there. See here ISHII 2004, 33.

Because of the successful example of the needle school, the missionaries did encourage proposals for further similar ventures, like nursing schools and kindergarten training to educate Japanese girls beyond the normal schooling. Many of these activities were led and organized by the wives of the German missionaries, who physically worked and culturally interacted with poorer Japanese women and girls and thereby actively committed to the Mission's liberal and social outlook. These attempts at educating Japanese women were not limited to the poorer sectors of Japanese society. In fact, by teaching the girls lacework and other skills at the Mission school, the Swiss and German missionaries were simultaneously able to convey Christian liberal ideas of the German middle and upper class about female respectability to the corresponding classes in Japan. However, in the Lace School in Tokyo, where the girls usually came from underprivileged sections of society, it is very likely that many of these young girls would have had to find paid work to (help) support their families.

38. Citation in RÜETSCHI 1887, 193.

39. That the field of comparative religious studies is a direct offspring of Protestantism is well documented; the works of Wilfred Cantwell Smith and Jonathan Z Smith have long demonstrated how the study of comparative religion until the mid-twentieth century was a distinctly Christian science. See SMITH 1962, 1998). Citation in MÜLLER 1882, 14.

40. Citation in RÜETSCHI 1887, 199.

41. Ibid., 199.

42. Ibid., 198.

43. Ibid., 206.

44. Ibid., 206.

45. Ibid., 208.

46. Ibid., 208.

47. See THELLE 1987, 153–4; OKUYAMA 2019.

48. RÜETSCHI 1887, 208.

49. When looking at how history unfolded for Japan during the years up to the Second World War, one must admit that Rüetschi's analysis in this case was accurate.

50. RÜETSCHI 1887, 207.

51. See ADAS 1989 and PENNY 2002.

52. Citation in RÜETSCHI 1887, 206.

53. See LOPEZ 1995. See also ŌTANI 2013 for a similar analysis.

54. Citation in PFLEIDERER 1906, 3.

55. On Schleiermacher's influence on the theology and mission enterprise in Germany, see Spinner's talk "Theology and Religion in Modern Germany" to the mission assemBLy in Tokyo, SPINNER 1886D, 1–3. On the reception and introduction of Schleiermacher's theology to Japan, see the study "Die Problematik der Rezeption der "Reden" in Japan" of Mizutani Makoto, see MIZUTANI 1999.

56. Citation DEVARANNE 1934B, 16.

57. JOSEPHSON 2006.

58. For the development of the concept of "religion" in Meiji Japan, see ISOMAE 2003, HOSHINO 2012, and JOSEPHSON 2006, 2012.

59. For example, in the journal *Wahrheit*, Haas takes up Inoue Enryō's discussion of philosophy as the "king of sciences" See HAAS 1900, 55–61. I borrow the term "Buddhist intellectuals" from Hayashi Makoto's article "Four Buddhist Intellectuals in Late 19th Century Japan," see HAYASHI 2019.

60. KLIMKEIT 1997, 9.

61. In his article on Tenrikyō, Haas also discusses the interrelationship between Tenrikyō and Christianity. See HAAS 1910B.

62. Citation in HAAS 1912A, 45

63. Ibid., 12.

64. Citation from Haas 1910a, 7.

65. Christoffer Kleine, in "Der 'protestantische Blick' auf Amida: Japanische Religionsgeschichte zwischen Orientalismus und Auto-Orientalismus," has excellently explored how Amida Buddhism was interpreted from a Western/Christian perspective throughout much of the modern period. See Kleine 1996, 7–11.

66. Citation in Haas 1910a, 5.

67. Ibid., 142.

68. See for example, Ahlers 1887, Dorner 1904, and Bornemann 1914.

69. Citation in Munzinger 1906a, 85.

70. Citation in Christlieb 1899, 23.

71. Citation in Steiner 2006, 47–8.

72. See Christlieb 1902a; Christlieb 1902b; Christlieb 1904a; Christlieb 1904b.

73. As Christlieb writes: "Here [among the Kulturvölker] the missionary encounters a theoretical worldview, which is based on strong principles, ideals, concepts of virtue; everything has been firmly placed in a rigid system and been literarily edited to fit the way of the peoples' national ideal." Citation in Christlieb 1899, 4.

74. Citation in Christlieb 1899, 5–6.

75. Ibid., 15.

76. Ibid., 16.

77. With "reform-Buddhism" Christlieb is referring to the religious sect of Jōdo Shinshū. Just like Haas above, Christlieb's writings on Japanese Buddhism seemed only to deal with this one Buddhist sect. Other Buddhist traditions such as the Nichiren or Tendai sects were mostly ignored. First around the 1930s, we see a Western academic interest in the study of other sects. The explanation for this one-sided focus on Jōdoshū and Jōdo Shinshū among Western scholars at the turn of the century was, as Amstutz also points out, their similarity to Christianity. For quote see Christlieb 1899, 16.

78. Ibid., 16–17.

79. Ibid., 17.

80. Ibid., 18.

81. Citation in tb-sp 16.12.1890.

82. See Munzinger 1891b.

83. For more on Munzinger's interpretation of the Japanese People, see Petersen 2020.

84. See Munzinger 1897 and 1898.

85. Munzinger 1906a, 158.

86. The consequences of article 28 and the Educational Rescript on the mission field have been discussed in Chapter 4.

87. Munzinger 1906a, 121.

88. Ibid., 123.

89. Ibid., 120–1.

90. Like the other missionaries, Munzinger also characterized the popular belief of the Japanese as being a combination of the two religions Shintō and Buddhism. See MUNZINGER 1906A, 84.

91. Citation in MUNZINGER 1906A, 91.

92. Ibid., 105.

93. Ibid., 169.

94. See MUNZINGER 1976.

95. The essay was published in the ZMR as a series throughout the year. See HAAS 1907B, 1907C, and 1907D.

96. Citation in HAAS 1907B, 106.

97. Ibid., 110.

98. Citation in HAAS 1907D, 273.

99. Ibid., 270.

100. Ibid., 296.

101. Ibid., 274.

102. Itō Hirobumi is known as the first statesman and founding father of modern Japan. He traveled to the United States already in 1870 and was together with Kido Takayoshi, the leading diplomat of the Iwakura mission. From 1885, Itō was the Prime Minister of Japan. In 1909, while in Manchuria, Itō was assassinated by a Korean independence activist. Kido Takayoshi is considered one of the most influential persons during the Meiji Restoration, having a major role in laying out the new Meiji constitution. Together with Itō and Aoki he joined the Iwakura mission in in Europe 1871. For the discussions among the three on a future Christian state, see BREEN 2011.

103. Quoted in BREEN 2011, 158.

104. See AOKI 1970, 32.

105. One of the more significant contributions was Rudolf Schulke's *Die Religion*, written in 1901. In this long article, which stretches over more than fifty pages, Schulke discussed everything from the origin of religion to its ethical composition. See SCHULKE 1901.

106. Citation from Munzinger 1906B, 260.

107. The writings on Japanese superstition continued throughout the years. In an article called "Sitten und Gebräuche in Japan" from 1895, Robert Lange writes how superstitious beliefs such as *kitsunetsuki*—being possessed by a fox—were still practiced in Japan. Lange, for example, wrote: "[The believe in the] "Osaki-fox," the animal god that practices magic still exists to a large degree in Japan." Citation in LANGE 1895, 65.

108. See SCHILLER 1902.

109. See BUSS 1886A, 2.

110. Citation in BUSS 1879, 17.

6. Buddhist Exposures to Liberal Christianity

1. The Jōdo Shinshū sect (浄土真宗) is comprised of ten main branches, among which two predominate in size. The first is the Ōtani-branch (Shinshū Ōtani-ha 真宗大谷派), so renamed in 1881 after having been known as the Higashi Honganji-branch between 1877 and 1881. Its main temple is Higashi Honganji 東本願寺 (the Eastern temple, located on the east side of Kyoto). The other branch is the Nishi-Honganji branch (Jōdo Shinshū Honganji-ha), whose main temple is the Nishi Honganji 西本願寺 (the Western temple, located a few blocks to the west of the other Honganji). The split between these two branches is the result of the Tokugawa policy of dividing to rule.

2. Akamatsu Renjō, is a monk and religionist belonging to Jōdo Shinshū. He visited Europe and the United States for the first time with Shimaji Mokurai 島地黙雷 (1838–1911). After two and a half years abroad, he returned to Japan, where he began working on the separation of Shintō and Buddhism and advocated for a better education of monks from his Shinshū sect. See AMSTUTZ 1997, 62.

3. Akamatsu Renjō, due to his English language ability, received many visits from interested foreigners over the years in Kyoto. In his diary, Spinner wrote: "Visited high priest Akamatsu, who knew me from Holleben (Theodor von Holleben, German diplomat in Tokyo from 1886–1892). The temple is a majestic construction. A Monk showed me around. Magnificent painted parlor. I was curious and opened the [sliding-]walls a bit. Akamatsu spoke a little bit of English; some years ago [he] stayed 2 years in England. Knew Brahmo Somadsh [Brahmo Somaj, a Hindu monk leader of a syncretistic movement in India]. He belongs to the northern Buddhism [Jōdo Shinshū]." Citation in TB-SPINNER 02.07.1888. On Brahmo Somaj see SABA 1976, 201.

4. SPINNER 1891A, 1–2.

5. This is at least the impression one gets from reading Spinner's diary of the encounter TB-SPINNER.02.07.1888.

6. Reconstruction of the event described in TB-SPINNER 02.07.1888. Here Spinner further paints a critical picture of Akamatsu, writing: "He calls the Unitarian Knapp who visited him too liberal. When the missionaries are too narrow [minded], he also becomes narrow, when too liberal, he also becomes liberal. He does not like it when the missionaries write simplified reports in their newspapers after their visit."

7. In 1879, Akamatsu published a short paper written in English titled *A Brief Account of "Shinshū."* In the short text, Akamatsu argued that Jōdo Shinshū possessed characteristics in parallel with Protestantism which made it agreeable and ready for modernization and enlightenment. The small account by Akamatsu was the first non-Japanese language account on Jōdo Shinshū doctrine and received a lot of interest from foreigners. Japanese theologian Takizawa Katsumi has argued that Akamatsu, in his role as the upper priest at the Nishi Honganji temple, contributed significantly to establishing a dialogue between Buddhism and Christianity, see TAKIZAWA 1978. Akamatsu's writings inspired many Europeans, and in the twentieth century, the analogy between Buddhism and Christianity was prominently discussed by the German protestant theologian Karl Barth in his *Kirchliche Dogmatik*, published in 1935. Barth—whose main source was Hans Haas' Ger-

man translation of Akamatsu's paper—agreed with Akamatsu's comparison of the two religions and wrote about Shinshū Buddhism, stating that it is "the most precise, most comprehensive, and most plausible 'pagan' parallel... of the reformed shape of Christianity." Citation BARTH 1935, 372. See also HAAS 1910A; AKAMATSU 1879.

8. Citation TB-SPINNER 02.07.1888

9. I use the term "modern Buddhist" here in the same sense that Hayashi Makoto did when he coined it "Modern Buddhism" as it refers to the developments during the almost-one-hundred-year period (1868–1945) within traditional Buddhism, the thought and activities of Buddhist reformers, new religious Buddhist movements, and folk Buddhism." Citation HAYASHI 2014, 2.

10. Today, scholars agree on the use of the term "Buddhist intellectuals." There is general consensus that these individuals represented a new way of thinking about the relationship between the West and Buddhism. However, some scholars still warn that the category is not entirely clear. Swiss scholar Michel Mohr, for example, questions the term and notes that the category does not apply to all Buddhist intellectual thinkers of the period. See MOHR 2014, 64. See also OMI 2014, 11–14; ŌTANI, YOSHINAGA & KONDŌ 2016.

11. See HAYASHI, ŌTANI & SWANSON, 2014.

12. YUSAKATA 1979, BLUM 2011A.

13. I am here referring to ŌTANI 2016, 4–5; For further details on the formation of the universal term on "Buddhism", see LOPEZ 1995, 2 and ISOMAE 2011, 98–103.

14. Citation from KLAUTAU 2012, 84.

15. Citation from MURAKAMI 1914, 270–1.

16. It is worth observing in this regard that out of the forty-eight mission societies, 22 were from America, 10 from Britain, 5 from Canada, 4 from France, and 1 from Russia, Finland, and Swiss/Germany. For a full table check MULLINS 1998, 14–15.

17. SUEKI 2005, 16.

18. ŌTANI, YOSHINAGA and KONDŌ 2016, 5.

19. Referring to James Mark Shields description of the movement *hihan bukkyō* 批判仏教. See SHIELDS 2005.

20. Citation MURAKAMI 1901, 3–4.

21. GENSICHEN 1984, 22.

22. Anesaki was well aware of—and indeed, emphasized—the fact that his reinterpretation of Japanese Buddhism's connection to the original Buddha was one based on faith, and this only confirmed his belief in the necessity of unifying world religions.

23. Murakami quoted in OKADA 2005, 34.

24. See MOHR 2014, 69.

25. Murakami quoted from an English translation, SUEKI 2005, 13.

26. SHIELDS 2005, 124.

27. HAAS 1900, 2

28. Quoted in BUSSE 1893, 82–3.

29. Shaku Unshō 釋雲照 (1827–1909) was similar to Murakami; a Shinshū Buddhist intellectual who argued for a centralization of Buddhist denominational governance and the creation of centres for clerical education similar to those of the mission societies.

30. Citation in BUSSE 1893, 83.
31. Citation MURAKAMI 1906, 34
32. Minami quoted in HARADA 1935, 370.
33. See here the SCHMIEDEL 1888B; SCHMIEDEL 1888C.
34. This can among others be seen in Minami Hajime's article 「日本に於ける自由派神學の進步」The progress of Liberal Christianity) published in *Shinri* in 1890, see MINAMI 1890.
35. SCHMIEDEL 1891B.
36. SCHMIEDEL 1891C. See also Schmiedel's "Protestantism as the foundation of Modern science" (*shingaku wa kagaku nari* 神學は科學なり), SCHMIEDEL 1892C. Interestingly, Schmiedel was not the only missionary to write about Darwin. For the influence of Darwinism in Meiji Japan, see Clinton Godart's excellent book *Darwin, Dharma, and the Divine: Evolutionary Theory and Religion in Modern Japan*, GODART 2018.
37. Some of the articles from Shinri were written by Georg Landor PERIN 1891, "*Bunmei no genso* 文明の原素" (The Elements of Civilization); Otto SCHMIEDEL 1893 "*Gōri-ron to shin-shingaku to no kubetsu* 合理論と新神學との區別" (Distinction between rationalism and liberal theology). Kodō Saturo's "*Kinsei no kagaku kenkyū to kirisutokyō no michi go* 近世の科學研究と基督教の道碁" (Modern Science and the Study of ethical Christianity). See KODŌ 1891. MUNZINGER 1890.
38. MINAMI 1893, 162–8.
39. MINAMI 1893, 162.
40. According to Isomae Jun'ichi, the Buddhist intellectual Inoue Tetsujirō established the first class for comparative religion and Eastern philosophy at Tokyo Imperial University just one year after Munzinger's article had been published in Shinri.
41. This can also be seen in several other articles such as Murayama Michikuzu's 「再び神道の處置を論ず」(Again on the Treatment of Shinto) Murayama 1891A;「神の概念より基佛南教の論ず」(Discussions about the Concept of God in Christianity and Buddhism) Murayama 1891B;「基督教曾拜像歷史」(Historical and Religious observations of Christian worship) Murayama 1892.
42. See MURAKAMI 1894. Michel Mohr (2014) has made a similar analysis of the essay focusing on Murakami's reading on the Unitarian journal *Rikugō zasshi*. See MOHR 2014, 77–8.
43. Citation in MUNZINGER 1898, 405.
44. Citation from KOZAKI 1892, 33.
45. Citation in SASAKI 1909, 172
46. *Shinri* ran for twenty years (1889–1908). During that time, it managed to publish almost 1200 articles in which most of them attempted to introduce German theology and philosophy. See MIZUTANI 2010, 117–8.
47. Munzinger 1898, 405.
48. Otto Schmiedel and Maruyama Michikazu began as editors of the journal and were later joined by Minami Hajime in 1891. In 1892, Maruyama dropped out of the theologian academy, which also ended his editorial work for Shinri. Following Maruyama's exit, Minami remained the only editor of the journal. In addition to his editing work,

Minami also contributed numerous articles himself. The number of essays listed under Minami's name is eighty-two. In any case, Minami was the only person who was present from the beginning of the publication of Shinri to the end. See MIZUTANI 2010, 120–1.
49. See BLUM 2011B.
50. HARUCHIKA 2017, 51–3.
51. The name is a play on words and is difficult to translate into English. *Dō* 洞 can also be referred to as "community," while Kōkōdō 浩々 also can mean "wave of spirituality." So, the Kōkōdō 浩々洞 can also be understood as a community of constantly moving spirituality.
52. This is the interpretation of the German missionary Hans HAAS 1910A, 35.
53. HARUCHIKA 2017, 51–3.
54. Cited in HAAS 1910A, 35.
55. ME, DOK–13, digit no.1.
56. See ZMR 1890, 73.
57. See TB-SPINNER 18.09.1888.
58. See SCHMIEDEL 1888A.
59. Citation from TB-SPINNER 15.10.1888.
60. Leavings of letters from Wilfried Spinner in ZASP, 180.8.
61. See BENESCH 2014, 42–3.
62. Citation from TB-SCHMIEDEL 02.12.1889.
63. Leavings of letters from Wilfried Spinner in ZASP 180.8.
64. Handwritten letter from Spinner in ZASP 242.37.
65. IKAMA 1992, 102.
66. Citation in HAAS 1910A, 35.
67. HARACHIKA 2017A.
68. Citation TADA 1907, 456.
69. Tada quoted in HARUCHIKA 2008, 399.
70. Citation in HAAS 1910A, 35–6.
71. Citation in HAAS 1899, 280.
72. Tada quoted in HAAS 1910A, 146.
73. Ibid. 147.
74. Citation SCHILLER 1903, 310.
75. IBID., 304.
76. IBID., 309.
77. IBID., 309.
78. See SCHILLER 1901, 3.
79. Citation in SCHILLER 1908, 8.
80. HAAS 1922.
81. For more on Hans Haas's work on Buddhism, see PETERSEN 2021.
82. Citation in HAAS 1912A, 45.
83. Citations SCHROEDER 1911A, 90; 92.
84. In fact, historian James Ketelaar in this context speaks of the Japanese Buddhist response as a "strategic Occidentalism." KETELAAR 1991.

85. Karl Heinrich Ritter and Gustav Lisco housed several Japanese in Berlin during the 1870s and 1880s and their contact with Aoki Shūzō and Shimaji Mokurai was just two of many encounters with Japanese students at the time. See also MBL 1887, 61. The close connection between Lisco's office in Berlin and the AEPM can be seen in a note in the Zeitschrift für Missionskunde und Religionswissenschaft. Here his office is mentioned as the head office of the AEPM branch in Berlin. See ZMR 1887, 128. The connection between Lisco and the Japanese students is also briefly mentioned in a 2014 book chapter by Mick Deneckere called "Shin Buddhist Contributions." DENECKERE 2014, 25. Minami Hajime mentions in the book *Nihon ni okeru jiyū kirisitokyō to sono senkusha* (1935) that Ritter and Lisco baptized several Japanese students during their stay in the German capital, among them the Lord Kashimura, Aikawa Katsuko, Yamakawa Yukio and Nakarai Sunao in 1870s and 1880s. See MINAMI 1935, 188. See also AOKI 1970, 32. The relationship between Lisco and Shimaji has also carefully been investigated by German scholar Hans Martin Krämer's *Shimaji Mokurai and the Reconception of Religion and the Secular in Modern Japan*. See KRÄMER 2015, 97–102.

86. SCHULZER 2019, 25–6.

7. Educating Youth at Home

1. Citation in SCHMITT 1932, 2
2. Ibid., 4.
3. Ibid., 4.
4. The movie *Der Japan Film* still exists today in the mission archives of ZASP, 180.18.
5. Citation in SCHMITT 1932, 4.
6. BLAUT 1002, 130.
7. OSTERHAMMEL 2009, 13.
8. With "youth" are also those generally referred to as so-called "pre-adults." Because contemporary ideas of childhood, adolescence, and adulthood first were designed in the early twentieth century, it is difficult to draw precise lines that define the terminologies of each other's difference. In general, the accepted age of adulthood started from one's eighteenth year, yet this would vary differently depending on the child's class, gender, educational background, and occupation.
9. See MACK 2013. 126–8.
10. Just as Chapter 5 looked at the German missionaries' categorization of religions, this chapter looks at the categorized hierarchies established in the missionary youth literature. For the general tendencies of hieratic categorization in the nineteenth and twentieth centuries, see, e.g., PENNY 2002 and RECKWITZ 2006. For citation, see BOWERSOX 2013, 3.
11. See COMAROFF & COMAROFF 1991, STOLER & COOPER 1997, and HALL 2002.
12. For the importance of youth literature in Germany, see BOWERSOX 2011.
13. "One-sided" theory applies to the classical oriental scholarship of Edward Said and others. It only works from the relationship of power played out by the "colonizer" towards

the "colonized." See SAID 1984 and BEHDAD 1994. "Both-sided" theory, on the contrary, denotes that the transfer of power and knowledge went not in one direction (from colonizer to colonized), but that the encounter at the same time also sent new knowledge and power back to the colonizers. This idea is among others illustrated by THELEN 1999, 968.

14. For a study of children's place in the missionary movement, which also looks at the youth missionary publications, see PROCHASKA 1977, 103–18; BOWERSOX 2015. For a brilliant analysis of English missionary children's magazines reprinted in the US, see the works of SÁNCHEZ-EPPLER 1996, 2005.

15. Along with the early youth magazine *Das Missionsblatt für Kinder*, from the mid-nineteenth century, German language youth magazines started their publications in the first decades of the twentieth century. This included *Aus Nord und Süd* (1904); *Für die Kinder*; *Für die Jugend* (1926); *Das Jugendmissionsblatt Mission-Glöcklein, Nachrichten aus der Heidenwelt für unsere Kinder,* (1923) and, *Ajo! Ein Missionsbuch für deutsche Jugend* (1926).

16. The focus here is on the texts and images mainly about Japan and its people, excluding the stories from other parts of the world. In content and style, the stories about Japan do not differ markedly from the other stories, but focusing the reading this way allows for more in-depth study of this part of the genre.

17. This analysis does not differentiate between German and translated texts. The fact that a text was translated was not mentioned but could only be assumed from its subject and substance, so the contemporary youth readership may not even have noted that it was. More significantly, translated and non-translated texts had the same moralizing and informative function in relation to Swiss and German children.

18. Citation in GAEDECKE 1915.

19. This certainly seems to have been the case with *Für die Jugend*, as the title itself indicates, but it was probably the case with some of the other magazines as well. Some, for example, mentioned exercises which could be done in school or encouraged the readers to ask their teacher for information about this. The magazine could, for example, be purchased at a discounted rate to be distributed at children's parties, Christmas parties in school, or to be used in school lessons. How widely these publications were distributed is difficult to ascertain, but in 1910, *Das Missionsblatt* had a print run of 25,000 copies, and in its best years, this had proved to be an insufficient number as they were quickly sold out and the mission often asked its readers to re-order it. Moreover, since the publications were shared among siblings, among children in Sunday school, and not least in the local missionary clubs for children, the number of readers is likely to have been much higher.

20. The children's contributions to the mission were not insignificant. In 1902, the different missionary clubs for children collected 2,487.38 Marks, and the amount increased steadily over the years. In 1911, the number had reached 5,785. Marks.

21. By inductive potential is meant the type of logical thinking which, based on the experiences and observation, forms the generalized knowledge of the readers and enables them to know what to be true or false. See ROTHBART & TAYLOR 1992.

22. Julia Ulrike Mack has in her book *Menschenbilder: Anthropoligische Konzepte und stereotype Vorstellungen vom Menschen in der Publizistik der Baslermission 1816–1914*

from 2013 characterized similar categories. Here her main source is the investigation of the Basler Mission Magazines. See MACK 2013.
23. See ANONYMOUS 1906A; ANONYMOUS 1906B; SCHROEDER 1910, 2–3.
24. Citation in ANONYMOUS 1917B, 2–3.
25. SCHMIEDEL 1920A, 64–5.
26. ANONYMOUS 1911, 1–2.
27. WITTE 1913B, 1.
28. See for example, KNODT 1917B; SCHMIEDEL 1920B, 1–2; M. SCHILLER 1913A, 1–4.
29. Citation in ANONYMOUS 1889, 41.
30. Ibid., 44.
31. Citation in SCHMIEDEL 1920B, 1.
32. Helen Kanitkar has identified the same stylistic device in British youth fiction in the period from 1909–1919. See KANITKAR 1996
33. Citation in SCHMIEDEL 1920B, 1.
34. Citation in SCHROEDER 1910, 2–3.
35. Citation in ANONYMOUS 1917A.
36. Citation in G. SCHROEDER 1917, 2.
37. See NELSON 2014, 403.
38. See FANON 1967. For examples in a German colonial context, see SOBICH 2006 and KUNDRUS 2003.
39. Citation in WENDT 1910B, 1–2.
40. Citation in ANONYMOUS 1890–1893.
41. Citation in PRAKASH 1999, 13. A similar argument has been made by Ann Laura Stoler in STOLER 2005.
42. A similar point is also made by Jeff BOWERSOX 2013, 0
43. Citation in BERNSTEIN 2011, 33.
44. See WITTE 1912.
45. Citation in TSURUMI 2009, 53.
46. Citation in HÜCKEL 1916, 9.
47. Citation in HAENSEL 1929, 1–2.
48. Citation in KNODT 1917A.
49. On the methods and motivations behind the development of empathy and sympathy, see RUTHERFORD 2009.
50. Citation in HÜCKEL 1925, 32–3.
51. Citation in CHARKRABARY 2000, 126.
52. Citation in ANONYMOUS 1917B, 4.
53. Citation in WITTE 1913A.
54. See RUTHERFORD 2009.
55. Citation in KAPLAND 1998, 281. Similarly, Susan Thorne has in her investigation in the British missionaries' discourse about abuse in heathen societies argued that, while the stories "expressed without doubt the genuine sympathy on the part of many missionaries and their home supporters," the stories would at the same time argue the abuse to be rightful as the heathens, due to their religion, were "deservedly damned." Empathy for

heartens, thus for Throne, is ambiguous. It is a positive feeling but is compromised by its union with the concept. See THRONE 1999, 52–3.

56. This is an argument made by, among others, Ann Laura Stoler in her work *Race and the Education of Desire: Foucault's History of Sexuality and the Colonial Order of Things*. See STOLER 1995.

57. According to Amit Rai, empathy for non-Europeans came to function as a key discourse of gender and race in the 18th and 19th century evangelical social movements. He argues that empathy is a "paradoxical mode of power." The classification of racial, gender, and class inequalities became increasingly divided through the agent of empathy. This paradoxical mode of power, Rai concludes, transformed many of the ways in which people came to think of "the other" in the nineteenth century. See RAI 2000.

58. The literature also had another function. Much of the missionary literature sees the poor condition of women as evidence of the backwardness of the Japanese compared to the West. The writings of the missionaries therefore help to strengthen the image of Christianization as a morally valid, even sometimes as a necessary enterprise. The German-Swiss stories of Japanese domestic terror undoubtedly provided some of the moral foundations that legitimated missionary work in Japan.

59. Here again referring to the term as used by ROTHBART & TAYLOR 1992.

60. Citation in WITTE 1924, 3.

61. Citation in WITTE 1913B, 1.

62. Moreover, a second important point in the investigation into the Swiss and German missionary youth literature further exposes the insight that emotions can be constructed and artificially created in a variety of situations. This means that our seemingly honest and real feelings of pain or compassion for others are often created and exist only within a framework of certain power relations. To feel good also implies a sense of superiority.

63. By "judged" I here refer to Robert Solomon's definition of emotions as essentially a type of judgment that are affectively constituted. See SOLOMON 1988.

64. As Michel Foucault has phrased it, the idea of productive power is that: "It operates on the field of possibilities in which the behavior of active subjects is able to inscribe itself. It is a set of actions on possible actions; it incites, it induces, it seduces, it makes easier or more difficult... in the extreme, it constrains or forbids absolutely, but it is always a way of acting upon one or more acting subjects by virtue of their action or being capable of acting. A set of actions upon other actions." Citation in FOUCAULT 1994, 326.

65. According to Durkheim, "all education is a continuous effort to impose on the child ways of seeing, feeling, and acting which he could not have arrived at spontaneously." Citation in DURKHEIM 1982, 6.

66. Ann Stoler makes a similar point in her book *Along the Archival Grain: Epistemic Anxieties and Colonial Common Sense*. See STOLER 2009.

67. See BOWERSOX 2011.

68. Term borrowed from Karen SÁNCHEZ-EPPLER 1996.

Conclusion

1. KIND 1901, 5.
2. Citation in MUNZINGER 1891, 1.
3. See here ISOMAE 2014, xv-xix.
4. These two were SOAM and DOAM. For further explanation, see reference 4 in the Introduction.
5. SUTER 1984

Acknowledgments

I was able to write this book due to the many acts of kindness and generosity offered to me by teachers, colleagues, and friends. First and foremost, I would like to thank the people at the Nanzan Institute for Religion and Culture. Throughout the years they patiently listened to many of my unstructured and inchoate ideas and encouraged me to think bigger. Their insightful guidance and steadfast support carried me through my doctoral studies allowing me to publish this book. I will always strive to emulate their example in my own academic career.

My gratitude also goes to Dr. Markus Wriedt, Dr. Martin Kessler and Dr. Catharina Wenzel, all of whom served as my advisors during my time in Germany at the Goethe University in Frankfurt am Main and offered numerous helpful suggestions on the project. I also benefited from working with other scholars, who in one way or another passed my way, particularly, Or Porath, Paride Stortini, Justin Stein, Jolyon Baraka Thomas, Alena Govorounova, Joseph O'Leary, and Niklas Södermann. I would also like to thank Harald Greve, Renate Greve, and the people of SOAM and DOAM for their constant kindness and support throughout the years.

I have been blessed with supportive colleagues and friends. Special thanks to Or Porath, Ben Dorman and Tomoko Dorman for helping me to settle in and navigate Nagoya when I first moved here. I also learned immensely from my conversations with Saitō Takashi, Haruka Goto, Tim Graf, Jørn Borup, Christian Hermansen, and Yoshiya Yoshimitsu. Many more friends from both Europe and Japan—too many to thank individually—helped me expand my horizons and have given me many fond memories.

I have been a beneficiary of kind suggestions and guidance from the thoughtful inputs of Matthew McMullen on early drafts of individual chapters. Furthermore, I am indebted to Mizutani Makoto for hosting me at Doshisha University's Theological Department in 2015.

A special thanks is due to Jim Heisig at the Nanzan Institute for Religion and Culture for guiding me through the publication process and giving me the opportunity to publish through Chisokudō Publications. I would also like to thank Zachary Smith and Robert Roche for promptly reading my manuscript and offering suggestions for improvements. My research would not have been possible without the support of librarians and staff at various institutions, mainly the Zentralarchiv der Evangelischen Kirche im Rheinland-Pfalz who kindly granted permission to use their images for enhancing this book. I would also like to thank the Canon Research Foundation and the Japanese Ministry of Education for providing financial support for my research.

My colleagues at the Department of German Studies at the Nanzan University provided me with a supportive and collegial environment to work on this book in. As a result, My thoughts on the subject of German and Swiss missionaries depended on numerous conversations with people in and outside of Nanzan University.

Finally, I would like to thank my family. My mother, Bodil, who always supported my decision to pursue an academic career and encouraged me throughout the process of writing this book. My father, Thies and his wife Kicki, who not only provided the excellent cover photo for this book, but were a constant source of inspiration and help throughout all the years. My sister, Kathrine, who was always there for me, ready to engage in a Skype conversation on the other side of the world, no matter the time of day. Thank you all for always being there for me and believing in me.

Bibliography

AAGAARD, Johannes
1967 *Mission, Kirche. Die Problematik ihrer Integration im 19. Jahrhundert in Deutschland* (Lund: Studia Missionalia Upsaliensia).

ADAS, Michael
1989 *Machines of Measure of Man: Science, Technology, and Ideologies of Western Dominance*. (Ithaca: Cornell University Press).

AHLERS, Heinrich
1887 "Buddhismus und Christentum," *Zeitschrift für Missionskunde und Religionswissenschaft* 2: 1–20.

AKASHI Shigetarō 赤司繁雄
1995 『自由基督教の運動―赤司繁太郎の生涯とその周辺』[The movement of Free Christianity: The Life of Shigetarō Akashi and his Surroundings] (Tokyo: Asashi Shorin).

AKAMATSU Renjō 赤松連城
1879 「真宗略説」[A Brief Account of ^p]『興隆雑誌』[Rejuvenation journal] 3. Reprinted in AKAMATSU 1982–1984, vol. 3: 577–79.
1982 「赤松連城資料」[Amamatsu Renjō Materials] (Kyoto: Honganji, 1982–1984), 3 vols.

AKIO Dohi 昭夫土肥
1997 "The First Generation: Christian Leaders in the First Period," in Yasuo Furuya ed., *A History of Japanese Theology* (Grand Rapids, Michigan: William B. Eerdmans Publishing Company), 11–42.

AMSTUTZ, Galen
1997 *Interpreting Amida: History and Orientalism in the Study of Pure Land Buddhism* (New York: SUNY Press).

ANDERSON, Emily
2014 *Christianity and Imperialism in Modern Japan: Empire of God* (London: Bloomsbury Press).

ANONYMOUS
1885 "Die Gründung der deutsch-evangelischen Gemeindein Tokio," *Das Missionsblatt des Allgemeinen Evangelisch-Protestantischer Missionsverein* 1/12.
1889 "Eine Glaubeschilderung in Japan," *Missionsblatt für Kinder* 5/4: 41–4.
1890 "Nachrichten," *Das Missionsblatt des Allgemeinen Evangelisch-Protestantischer Missionsverein* 5/5.
1891 "Die Schulanstalten: Die Handarbeitsschule," *Das Missionsblatt des Allgemeinen Evangelisch-Protestantischer Missionsverein* 6/11.
1893 "Ein Sonntag in Hōwoden," *Das Missionsblatt des Allgemeinen Evangelisch-Protestantischer Missionsverein* 8/4.
1906a "Heidnischer Aberglauben," *Missionsblatt für Kinder* 22/10: 109.
1906b "Ein Brief aus Japan," *Missionsblatt für Kinder* 22/10: 121–7.
1911 "Ein wahre Geschichte aus Kanagawa," *Missionsblatt für Kinder* 27/10: 1–2.
1917a "Warum Kuniko sich so sehr vor dem Donner fürchtete," *Für die Jugend. Missionsblatt des Allgemeinen evangelisch-protestantischen Missionsverein* 17/5: 1–4.
1917b "Wer beten kann, ist selig dran," *Für die Jugend. Missionsblatt des Allgemeinen evangelisch-protestantischen Missionsverein* 17/9: 1–4.

AOKI Shūzō 青木周藏
1970 『青木周蔵自伝』[Biography of Aoki Shūzō] (Tokyo: Hebonsha).

ARNDT, Theodore
1885 "Die Mission als Vermittlerin der Kultur," *Protestantische Kirchenzeitung für das evangelische Deutschland* 32/52: 30.12.1885.
1886 "Die Mission als nationale Aufgabe," *Zeitschrift für Missionskunde und Religionswissenschaft* 1: 193–207.
1888 "Missionsrundschau: Statistik der Mission in Japan für das Jahr 1887," *Zeitschrift für Missionskunde und Religionswissenschaft* 3: 238–9.
1895 "Zur Abwehr wider Dalton (1)," *Zeitschrift für Missionskunde und Religionswissenschaft* 10: 11–16.

ARNOLD, David & Robert A. BICKERS
1996 "Introduction," in R. Bickerts & R. Seton, eds., *Missionary Encounters: Sources and Issues* (Richmond: Surrey), 1–10.

ASAD, Talal
2001 "Reading a Modern Classic: W. C. Smith's The Meaning and End of Religion," *History of Religions* 40: 205–22.

ASHINA Sadamichi 芦名定道
- 2016 『近代日本とキリスト教思想の可能性―二つの地平が交わるところにて―』[The possibilities of modern Japan and Christian thought-at the intersection of the two horizons] (Tokyo: Kirisutokyō Kenkyū Sōsho).

BADE, Klaus Jürgen
- 1982 *Imperialismus und Kolonialmission. Kaiserliches Deutschland und koloniales Imperium (Beitrage zur Kolonial- und Überseegeschichte*. (Wiesbaden: Franz Steiner).

BALLHATCHET, Helen
- 1998 "Confucianism and Christianity in Meiji Japan. The Case of Kozaki Hiromachi," *Journal of the Royal Asiatic Society of Great Britain and Ireland* 2: 349–68.

BARTH, Boris & Jürgen OSTERHAMMEL
- 2006 *Zivilisierungsmissionen. Imperiale Weltverbesserung seit dem 18 Jahrhundert* (Konstanz: Uvk Verlag).

BARTH, Karl
- 1960 *Die Kirchliche Dogmatik* (Zürich: Evangelische Verlag, 1935), 4 vols.

BASSERMANN, Heinrich
- 1886 "Die christliche Pflicht der Heidenmission," *Zeitschrift für Missionskunde und Religionswissenschaft* 1: 65–77.

BEHDAD, Ali
- 1994 *Belated Travelers: Orientalism in the Age of Colonial Dissolution*. (Durham: Duke University Press).

BENESCH, Oleg
- 2014 *Inventing the Way of the Samurai: Nationalism, Internationalism and Bushidō in Modern Japan* (Oxford: Oxford University Press).

BERGER, Peter L.
- 1967 *The Sacred Canopy: Elements of a Sociological Theory of Religion*. (Garden City, NY: Doubleday).

BERNSTEIN, Robin
- 2011 *Racial Innocence:. Performing American Childhood from Slavery to Civil Rights* (New York: New York University Press).

BEST, Ernest Edwin
- 1966 *Christian Faith and Cultural Crisis: The Japanese Case* (Leiden: Brill).

BHABHA, Homi K.
- 1997 "World and the Home," in A. McClintock, A., A. Mufti & E. Shohat, eds., *Dangerous Liaisons: Gender, Nation, and Postcolonial Perspectives* (Minneapolis: University of Minnesota Press), 445–55.
- 2004 *The Localization of Culture* (London: Routledge).

BIELFELDT, Johannes
- 1962 "75 Jahre Ostasienmission," *Nackauer Hefte* 10 (Heidelberg: Evang. Verlag).

BIRKNER, Hans-Joachim
- 1976 "Liberale Theologie," in M. Schmidt, & G. Schwaiger, eds. *Kirchen und Liberalismus im 19. Jahrhundert* (Göttingen: Vandenhoeck & Ruprecht), 33–42.

BLAUT, James Morris
- 1993 *The Colonizer's Model of the World* (New York: The Guilford Press).

BLUM, Mark L.
- 2011A "Shin Buddhism in the Meiji Period," in M. Blum, & R. Rhodes, eds., *Cultivating Spirituality: A Modern Shin Buddhist Anthology* (New York: State University of New York Press), 1–54.
- 2011B "Kiyozawa Manshi: Life and Thought," in ibid., 55–66.

BOLLJAHN, Johannes
- 1889 "Die Knabenschule in Tokyo," *Zeitschrift für Missionskunde und Religionswissenschaft* 4: 65–77.

BORNEMANN, Daniel
- 1914 " Geschichte und Christentum in buddhistischer Beleuchtung," *Zeitschrift für Missionskunde und Religionswissenschaft* 33: 161–171.

BOURDIEU, Pierre & Jean-Claude PASSERON
- 1977 *Reproduction in Education, Society and Culture* (London: Sage Publications).

BOWERSOX, Jeff
- 2011 "Boy's and Girl's Own Empires: Gender and the Uses of the Colonial World in Kaiserreich Youth Magazines," in M. Parraudin & J. Zimmerer, eds., *German Colonialism and National Identity* (New York: Routledge), 57–69.
- 2013 *"Raising Germans in the Age of Empire: Youth and Colonial Culture 1871–1914* (Oxford: Oxford University Press).

2015 "Classroom Colonialism, Race Pedagogy, and Patriotism in Germany," in G. Eley & B. D. Naranch, eds., *German Colonialism in a Global Age* (Duke: Duke University Press), 170–86.

BREEN, John
2011 "Earnest Desires: The Iwakura Embassy and Meiji Religious Policy," *Japan Forum* 10/2: 151–65.

BROWN, Kathleen M.
1996 "Brave New World: Woman's Gender History," *William and Mary Quarterly* 50/2: 311–28.

BURKS, Ardath W.
1985 *The Modernizers: Overseas Students, Foreign Employees, and Meiji Japan* (Boulder: West View Press).

BUSS, Ernst
1876 *Die christliche Mission, ihre principielle Berechtigung und praktische Durchführung* (Leiden: Brill).
1885 "Das AEPM und die Deutsche Kolonial Verein," *Kirchen und Schulblatt in Verbindung* 35/3: 38–40.
1886A "Programm," *Zeitschrift für Missionskunde und Religionswissenschaft* 1: 1–10.
1886B "Statuten des allgemeinen evang.-protestantischen Missionsverein," *Zeitschrift für Missionskunde und Religionswissenschaft* 2: 55.
1886C "Vereinsnachrichten. 1: Missionar Spinners Reise und Anfangsthätigkeit," *Zeitschrift für Missionskunde und Religionswissenschaft* 1: 169.
1888A "Neue Missionsbestrebungen," *Zeitschrift für Missionskunde und Religionswissenschaft* 3: 55–59.
1888B "Vereinsnachrichten – Vierter Jahresbericht des Allgemeinen evangelisch-protestantischen Missionsverein," *Zeitschrift für Missionskunde und Religionswissenschaft* 3: 241–52.
1889 "Vereinsnachrichten," *Zeitschrift für Missionskunde und Religionswissenschaft* 4: 248.
1892A "Über die Tätigkeit unserer ersten Missionarin," *Zeitschrift für Missionskunde und Religionswissenschaft* 7: 248.
1892B "Die deutsch-evangelische Kirche in Tokyo," *Zeitschrift für Missionskunde und Religionswissenschaft* 7: 51–3.

CARY, Otis
1982 *A History of Christianity in Japan* (Tokyo: Tuttle Company Reprint).

CENTRALVORSTAND DES AEPM
1896   *Zur Verteidigung gegen D. Dalton. Eine Widerlegung des Dalton'schen Angriffes* (Berlin: Arnold von Haack).

CHARKRABATY, Dipesh
2000   *Provincializing Europe. Postcolonial Thought and Historical Difference* (Princeton: Princeton University Press).

CHRISTLIEB, Max Heinrich
1898   "Junger Samurai," *Das Missionsblatt des Allgemeinen Evangelisch-Protestantischer Missionsverein* 8/4.
1899   "Die moderne Kultur und die Aufgabe der evangelischen Mission in Japan," *Neunte Flugschrift des AEPM* (Berlin: Allgemeiner Evangelisch Protestantischer Missionsverein), 3–24.
1902A   "Moderne Missionsprobleme," *Zeitschrift für Missionskunde und Religionswissenschaft* 16: 65–75.
1902B   "Der Kampf um die Sprache in der Mission," *Zeitschrift für Missionskunde und Religionswissenschaft* 16: 353–60.
1904A   "Politik und Mission in den Kolonien (I)," *Zeitschrift für Missionskunde und Religionswissenschaft* 18: 330–48.
1904B   "Politik und Mission in den Kolonien (II)," *Zeitschrift für Missionskunde und Religionswissenschaft* 18: 352–68.

COMAROFF, Jean & John COMAROFF
1986   "Christianity and Colonialism in South Africa," *American Ethnologist* 13: 1–22.
1991   *Of Revelation and Revolution. Volume 1: Christianity, Colonialism, and Consciousness in South Africa* (Chicago: Chicago University Press).

CROOK, Nigel
1996   "The Control and Expansion of Knowledge: An Introduction," in N. Crook, ed., *The Transformation of Knowledge in South Asia: Essays on Education, Religion, History and Politics* (Oxford: Oxford University Press), 1–27.

CROUTER, Richard
2010   *Friedrich Schleiermacher: Between Enlightenment and Romanticism* (Cambridge, MA.: Cambridge University Press).

DALTON, Hermann
1895   *Auf Missionspfanden in Japan* (Bremen: C. E. Müllers Verlagsbuch).

DENECKERE, Mick
2014 "Shin Buddhist Contributions to the Japanese Enlightenment Movement of the early 1870s," in HAYASHI, ŌTANI, & SWANSON 2014, 17–51.

DEVARANE, Theodore
1934A *50 Jahre evangelischer Arbeit im Fernen Osten 1884–1934* (Berlin: Ostasien-Mission).
1934B "Neubesinnung und Rückblick: Von Zinzendorf zu Buß," in T. Devarane, ed., *50 Jahre evangelischer Arbeit im Fernen Osten 1884–1934* (Berlin: Ostasien-Mission), 10–21.

DIERCKS, Auguste
1892 "Missionsnachrichten," *Das Missionsblatt des Allgemeinen Evangelisch-Protestantischer Missionsverein* 4/4.
1893 "Aus Japan. Unsere Missionarin Auguste Diercks," *Zeitschrift für Missionskunde und Religionswissenschaft* 8: 78–80.

DIRKS, Nicholas B.
1992 *Colonialism and Culture* (Ann Arbor, MI: University of Michigan Press).
1996 "Foreword," in B. Cohn, ed., *Colonialism and Its Forms of Knowledge* (Princeton: Princeton University Press), ix–xvii.

DORNER, August Johannes
1904 "Der Buddhismus," *Zeitschrift für Missionskunde und Religionswissenschaft* 19: 193–210.

DRUMMOND, Richard
1971 *A History of Christianity in Japan* (Grand Rapids-Michigan: Eerdmans).

DURKHEIM, Emil
1982 *The Rules of Sociological Method* (New York: The Macmilian).

EGER, Wolfgang
1981 "Zur Geschichte der Deutschen Ostasien-Mission," *Blätter für Pfälzische Kirchengeschichte und religiöse Volkskunde* 48: 61–70.

ELBOURNE, Elizabeth
2003 "Word Made Flesh: Christianity, Modernity, and Cultural Colonialism in the Work of Jean and John Comaroff," *The American Historical Review* 108/2, 435–59.
2008 "Religion in the British Empire," in Stockwell, S.E., ed., *The British Empire: themes and perspectives* (Malden: Wiley-Blackwell), 131–51.

ETHERINGTON, Normann
  2005 "Introduction," in N. Etherington, ed., *Missions and Empire* (Oxford: Oxford University Press), 1–18.

FANON, Franz
  1967 *Black Skin, White Masks* (London: Grove Press).

FASS, Paula S.
  2003 "Children and Globalization," *Journal of Social History* 36/4: 963–77.

FITZPATRICK, Matthew P.
  2008 *Liberal Imperialism in Germany: Expansionism and Nationalism 1848–1884* (New York: Berghahn Books).

FOUCAULT, Michel
  1978 *The History of Sexuality* (New York: Pantheon Books).
  1994 "The Subject and Power," in J. Faubion, ed., *Power: Essential Works of Foucault 1954–1984* (London: Penguin Publishers), 326–49.

FUKAI Tomoaki 深井智朗
  2016 『ドイツ的大学論 (転換期を読む)』[German University Theory (Reading the Transition] (Tokyo: Miraisha).

FURUYA Yusuo 古屋安雄
  1997 *A History of Japanese Theology* (Grand Rapids, MI: William B. Eerdmans Publishing Company).

GAEDECKE, Klara
  1915 "Weihnachten in Japan," *Für die Jugend. Missionsblatt des Allgemeinen evangelisch-protestantischen Missionsvereins* 15/11: 1–2.

GARTMAN, David
  2002 "Bourdieu's Theory of Cultural Change: Explication, Application and Critique," *Sociological Theory* 20/2: 255–77.

GENSICHEN, Hans-Werner
  1984 "Theologische Wandlungen der Ostasien-Mission in die deutsche Missionswerke des 20. Jahrhunderts," in F. Hanh, ed., *SPUREN… Festschrift zum hundertjährigen Bestehen der Ostasien-Mission* (Stuttgart: Quell Verlag), 19–37.

GIKANDI, Simon
  1996 *Maps of Englishness: Writing Identity in the Culture of Colonialism* (New York: Columbia University Press).

GLUCK, Carol
1985 *Japan's Modern Myths: Ideology in the Late Meiji Period* (Princeton: Princeton University Press).

GODART, Clinton G.
2017 *Darwin, Dharma, and the Divine: Evolutionary Theory and Religion in Modern Japan* (Honolulu: University of Hawai'i Press).

GRAF, Friedrich Wilhelm
1992A "Kulturprotestantismus," in H. M. Müller, ed., *Beiträge zu einer Geschichte des modernen Christentums* (Gütersloh: Kohlhammer Verlag), 21–77.
1992B "Liberale Theologie," in E. Fahlbusch, ed., *Evangelisches Kirchenlexikon* (Göttingen: Vandenhoeck and Ruprecht), 86–98.
2002 "What has London (or Oxford or Cambridge) to do with Augsburg? The Enduring Significance of the German Liberal Tradition in Christian Theology," in M. Chapman, ed., *The Future of Liberal Theology* (London: Routledge), 18–38.
2005 "Zeitschriften," *Religion in Geschichte und Gegenwand* 8: 1822–7.
2006 *Geschichte Durch Geschichte Überwinden. Ernst Troeltsch in Berlin* (Berlin: De Gruyter).

GRAUE, Heinrich
1887 "Gott will, dass allen Menschen geholfen werde; Festpredigt, gehalten bei der dritten Jahresfeier des Allgemeinen evangelisch-Protestantischen Missionsvereins," ZASP No. 18.08.624.

GONZÁLEZ, Odina
2007 "Introduction," in O. González & B. Premo, eds., *Raising an Empire: Children in Early Modern Iberia and Colonial Latin America* (Albuquerque: H-Atlantic), 1–16.

HAAS, Hans
1898 "Das Leben Jesu und die Buddhalegende," *Zeitschrift für Missionskunde und Religionswissenschaft* 13: 129–42.
1899 "Buddhismus und Christentum," *Zeitschrift für Missionskunde und Religionswissenschaft* 14: 277–80.
1900 "Der Köning der Wissenschaften," *Wahrheit. Erste Deutsche Zeitschrift in Japan* 1: 55–61.
1905 "Die Japaner in der neuesten (III) Auflage der Religionsgeschichte von Chanteoie de la Saussane," *Zeitschrift für Missionskunde und Religionswissenschaft* 19: 359–67.
1907A *Japans Zukunftsreligion* (Berlin: K. Curtius).

1907b "Das Seelenleben der Japaner (i)," *Zeitschrift für Missionskunde und Religionswissenschaft* 21: 104–15.
1907c "Das Seelenleben der Japaner (ii)," *Zeitschrift für Missionskunde und Religionswissenschaft* 21: 210–22.
1907d "Das Seelenleben der Japaner (iii)," *Zeitschrift für Missionskunde und Religionswissenschaft* 21: 258–79.
1908 *Annalen des japanischen Buddhismus* (Tokyo: MOAG).
1910a *Amida Buddha unsere "Zuflucht." Urkunden zum Verständnis des japanischen Sukhavati-Buddhismus* (Leipzig: Dieterich'sche Verlagsbuchhandlung).
1910b "Tenrikyo," *Zeitschrift für Missionskunde und Religionswissenschaft* 25: 129–45.
1912a "Christliche Klänge im Japanischen Buddhismus," *Zeitschrift für Missionskunde und Religionswissenschaft* 27: 34–45.
1912b "Die japanische Umgestaltung des Buddhismus durch Honen Shonin und Shinran Shonin," *Zeitschrift für Missionskunde und Religionswissenschaft* 27: 129–45.
1922 *Bibliographie zur Frage nach den Wechselbeziehungen zwischen Buddhismus und Christentum* (Leipzig: J. C. Hinrichs).

HAACK, Annette.
1992 "Die Deutsch-Japanischen Gesellschaft Wa-Doku-Kai (1888–1912)," in G. Haasch, ed., *Die deutsch-japanischen Gesellschaften 1888–1996* (Berlin: Ed. Colloquium), 11–66.

HAENSEL, Hans
1929 "Ein Besuch einer chinesischen Fabrik," *Für die Jugend. Missionsblatt des Allgemeinen evangelisch-protestantischen Missionsverein* 29/3: 1–4.

HAHN, Ferdinand
1984a *SPUREN... Festschrift zum hundertjährigen Bestehen der Ostasien-Mission* (Stuttgart: Quell Verlag).
1984b "Das theologische Programm von Ernst Buss," in ibid., 10–18.

HALL, Catherine
2002 *Civilising Subjects: Metropole and Colony in the English Imagination 1830–1867* (Chicago: University of Chicago Press).

HAMER, Heyo
1984 "Missionsarbeit in Japan 1885–1945," in Hahn, F., ed., *SPUREN... Festschrift zum hundertjährigen Bestehen der Ostasien-Mission* (Stuttgart: Quell Verlag), 79–105.

1988 "Zur Geschichte der Fremdlinge in Japan," in H. Knobeloch, ed., *Freiheit und Verbindlichkeit. Fescschrift für Matthias Kohn* (Aachen: Rader-Publischer), 263–90.
1992 "Die Elementarschule der Hongō-Gemeinde in Tokyo 1891–1909," in Maiwald, R., ed., *Erziehen – Unterrichten – Ausbilden*. (Frankfurt am Main: Peter Land AG), 239–70.
1998 *Mission und Politik, 3 Teile auf Mikrofiches* (Frankfurt am Main: Verlag der Deutschen Hochschulschriften).
2002 *Mission und Politik* (Aachen: Verlag-Mainz).

HAMISH, Ion
1993 *The Cross and the Rising Sun: The Canadian Protestant Missionary Movement in the Japanese Empire, 1872–1931* (Waterloo-Ontario: Wilfrid Laurier Press).

HARADA Tamao 原田瓌生
1935 『日本に於ける自由基督教と其先駆者』[Free Christianity and its Pioneers] (Tokyo: Bunshōin Shuppanbu).

HARUCHIKA Takashi 春近敬
2008 『多田鼎の信仰変容に関する一考察』[A study on the transformation of Kanae Tada's faith], in『現代と親鸞/親鸞仏教センター』[Hyundai and Shinran/Shinran Buddhist Center] 16: 26–54.
2017 『「みどりご」誌にみる後期多田鼎の信仰理念』[The Late Tada Kanae and his Philosophy of Faith in "Midorigo" Magazine], in 『武蔵野大学仏教文化研究所紀要』[Bulletin of Musashino University Institute of Buddhist Culture] (Tokyo: Musashino University Institute of Buddhist Culture), 49–69.

HAYASHI Makoto 林 淳
2014 "Editors' Introduction," in HAYASHI, ŌTANI, & SWANSON 2014, 1–16.
2019 "Four Intellectual Buddhist in 19th Century Japan," *Numen* 66: 185–206.

HAYASHI Makoto 林 淳, ŌTANI Eiji 大谷栄一, & Paul L. SWANSON
2014 *Modern Buddhism in Japan* (Nagoya: Nanzan Institute for Religion and Culture).

HAYMAN, Paul D.
2002 "Postmodern Theology: The Apotheosis or Scourge of Liberalism?," in M. Chapman, ed., *The Future of Liberal Theology* (London: Routledge), 191–207.

HERING, Otto
- 1889 "Urteile des modern 'gebildeten' Japans über Religion und Moral(I)," in *Zeitschrift für Missionskunde und Religionswissenschaft* 4: 1–9.
- 1892 "Das modern japanische Unterrichtswesen," *Zeitschrift für Missionskunde und Religionswissenschaft* 7: 215–19.
- 1897 "Die Armenschule der deutschen Mission," *Zeitschrift für Missionskunde und Religionswissenschaft* 12: 140–143.

HESSE, Bernhard
- 1885 "Japan und der AEPM," *Protestantische Kirchenzeitung für das evangelische Deutschland*: 1049–55.
- 1897 *Erinnerungen aus dem amtlichen Leben* (Frankfurt am Main: Diesterweg).

HEYDENREICH, Agnes
- 1900 "Von unseren Arbeitsfeldern aus Japan," *Zeitschrift für Missionskunde und Religionswissenschaft* 15: 120–23.

HORI Masao 堀光男
- 1978 『独逸普及福音新教伝道会の成立からその日本伝道開始までの事情について』[On the Circumstances of the Foundation of the Allgemeiner Evangelisch Protestantischer Missionsverein to the Beginning of its Work in Japan] (Tokyo: Tokyo Daigaku Kyōyō Kateihen).

HOSHINO Seiji 星野靖二
- 2012 『近代日本の宗教概念 宗教者の言葉と近代』[The Concept of Religion in Modern Japan] (Tokyo: Yūshinsha).
- 2014 「キリスト教メディアの近代」[Christian Media and Modernity], in 『宗教研究』, 100–1.

HOWE, Charles
- 1993 *The Larger Faith: A Short History of American Universalism* (Boston: Skinner House Books).

HOWES, John E.
- 2007 "Christian Prophecy in Japan: Uchimura Kanzō," in *Japanese Journal of Religious Studies* 341: 127–50.

HÜCKEL, Willi
- 1916 *Das Los der Mädchen und Frauen in Ostasien!* (Berlin: Hutten Verlag).
- 1925 *Aus der japanischen Kinderwelt* (Berlin: Verlag d. Ostasien-Mission).

IGLEHART, Charles W.
  1959   *A century of Protestant Christianity in Japan* (Tokyo: Charles E. Tuttle).

IKAMA Yugaku 伊香間祐学
  1992   『「精神主義」を問い直す』[Re-questioning" Spiritualism], (Tokyo: Hokuriku Monpō Dōjō Sōsho).

ISHII NAKAMURA Noriko 中村典子
  2004   *American Woman Missionaries at Kobe Collage, 1873–1909: New Dimensions of Gender* (New York: Routledge).

ISOMAE Jun'ichi 磯前純一
  2003   『近代日本の宗教言説とその系譜：宗教・国家・神道』[Religious Discourse in Modern Japan and its Genealogy: Religion, State, Shintoism] (Tokyo: Iwanami).
  2007   "State Shinto, Westernization, and the Concept of Religion in Japan," in Fitzgerald, T., ed., *Religion and the Secular: Historical and Colonial Formation* (London: Equinox), 93–102.
  2011   *Religious Discourse in Modern Japan: Religion, State, and, Shinto* (Leiden: Brill).

JAFFE, Richard M.
  2019   *Seeking Sākyamuni: Formation of Modern Japanese Buddhism* (Chicago: Chicago University Press).

JANIEWSKI, Dolores
  1992   "Learning to Live 'Just Like White Folks': Gender, Ethnicity and the State of in the Inland Northwest," in D. O. Helly & S. Reverby, eds., *Gendered Domains. Rethinking Public and Private in Women's History* (Ithaca: Cornell University Press), 167–82.

JANSEN, Marius B.
  2000   *The Making of Modern Japan* (Cambridge Mass.: Harvard University Press).

JOHNSTON, Anna
  2003   *Missionary Writing and Empire, 1800–1860* (Cambridge: Cambridge University Press).

JOLLY, Margaret
  1998   "Introduction. Colonial and postcolonial plots in histories of maternities and modernities," in M. Jolly & K. Ram, eds, *Maternities and modernities: Colonial and Postcolonial Experiences in Asia and the Pacific* (Cambridge: Cambridge University Press), 1–25.

JOSEPHSON, Jason Ānanda
2006 "When Buddhism Became a "Religion": Religion and Superstition in the Writings of Inoue Enryō," *Japanese Journal of Religious Studies* 33/1: 143–68.
2012 *The Invention of Religion in Japan* (Chicago: University of Chicago Press).

KANITKAR, Helen
1996 "Imaging the Self at the Expense of the Other: Stereotypes in Juvenile Imperialist Fiction on India," in N. Crook, ed., *The Transmission of Knowledge in South Asia: Essays on Education, Religion, History, and Politics* (Oxford: School of Oriental and African Studies), 229–44.

KAPLAND, Amy
1998 "Manifest Domesticity," *American Literature* 70/3: 581–606.

KAWAI, Michi
1922 "Individualismus, Familie und Religion im Japan", *Zeitschrift für Missionskunde und Religionswissenschaft* 36: 218–19.

KAYSSER, Christian
1926 *Ajo! Ein Missionsbuch für deutsche Jugend* (Nürnberg: Glocken Verlag).

KELSEY, Catherine L.
2003 *Thinking about Christ with Schleiermacher* (London: John Knox Press).

KETELAAR, James E.
1990 *Of Heretics and Martyrs in Meiji Japan: Buddhism and Its Persecution* (New York: Princeton University Press).
1991 "Strategic Occidentalism: Meiji Buddhist at the World's Parliament of Religions," *Buddhist-Christian Studies* 11: 37–56.

KIND, Auguest
1901 "Introduktion," in A. Kind, ed., *Jahresbericht* (Berlin: Ostasien-Mission), 1–6.
1910 "Pfarrer Wilhelms Gespräche des Konfucius," *Zeitschrift für Missionskunde und Religionswissenschaft* 36: 227–35.

KING, Richard
1999 *Orientalism and Religion: Postcolonial Theory, India and "The Mystic East"* (London: Routledge).

KISALA, Robert
2006 "Japanese Religions," in P. L. Swanson & C. Chilson, eds., *Nanzan Guide to Japanese Religions* (Honolulu: University of Hawai'i Press), 3–13.

KIYOSHIGE Naohiro 清重尚弘
1983 "Jesus in Japanese Christian Thought," *The Japan Christian Quarterly* 49: 31–37.

KLAUTAU, Orion
2012 『近代日本思想としての仏教史学』[Buddhist History and Modern Japanese Thought] (Tokyo: Hōzōkan).

KLEINE, Christoph
2003 "Der protestantische Blick auf Amida. Japanische Religionsgeschichte zwischen Orientalismus und Auto-Orientalismus," in M. Schalk, O. Freiberger, & C. Kleine, eds., *Religion im Spiegelkabinett. Asiatische Religionsgeschichte im Spannungsfeld zwischen Orientalismus und Okzidentalismus* (Uppsala: Uppsala Universitet), 145–93.

KLIMKEIT, Hans-Joachim
1997 "Preface," in C. Steineck, ed., *Quellentexte des japanischen Amida-Buddhismus* (Wiesbaden: Harrassowitz), 9–10.

KNODT, Emil
1917A "Trauriges Los eines japanischen Mädchens in einer Fabrik," *Für die Jugend. Missionsblatt des Allgemeinen evangelisch-protestantischen Missionsverein* 17/9–10: 1–4.
1917B "Durch," *Für die Jugend. Missionsblatt des Allgemeinen evangelisch-protestantischen Missionsverein* 17/9–10: 5–6.

KUWAHARA Shunsuke 桑原俊介
2016 「シュライアマハーの解釈学: 近代解釈学の成立史」[Schleiermacher's Hermeneutics: History of Modern Hermeneutics] (Tokyo: Ochanomizu Shobō).

KOYANAGI Atsushi 小柳敦史
2020 "Liberal Protestantism and Christian Studies at Kyoto University: A Case Study of Seiichi Hatano," *Journal for the History of Modern Theology/Zeitschrift für Neuere Theologiegeschichte* 27/1: 4–11.

KOZAKI Nariaki
1892 "Christliches Denken in Japan," *Zeitschrift für Missionskunde und Religionswissenschaft* 7: 32–36.

Kozaki Hiromichi 小崎弘道
- 1893 "Christianity in Japan: Its Present Condition and Future Prospects," in Barrows, J.H., ed., *The World's Parliament of Religions* (Chicago: Parliament Publishing), 1012–15.
- 1933 *Reminiscences of Seventy Years, The Autobiography of a Japanese Pastor* (Tokyo: Kyōbukan).

Kranz, P.
- 1903 "Konfuzius und Christus nicht Feinde, sondern Freunde," *Zeitschrift für Missionskunde und Religionswissenschaft* 17: 268–79.

Krämer, Hans-Martin
- 2015 *Shimaji Mokurai and the Reconception of Religion and the Secular in Modern Japan* (Honolulu: University of Hawai'i Press).

Kumar, Nita
- 2000 *Lessons from Schools: The History of Education in Nanaras* (New Delhi: Sage Publication).

Kundrus, Birthe
- 2003 *Moderne Imperialisten. Das Kaiserreich im Spiegel seiner Kolonien* (Colonge: Böhlau Köln).

Lande, Aasulv
- 1989 *Meiji Protestantism in History and Historiography* (Frankfurt am Main: Verlag Peter Lang).

Lange, Robert
- 1895 "Sitten und Gebräuche in Japan (III)," *Zeitschrift für Missionskunde und Religionswissenschaft* 9: 65–73.

Langhans, Ernst Friedrich
- 1865 *Pietismus und Christentum im Spiegel der äußeren Mission* (Lepzig: Verlag von Otto Wigand).

Lash, Nicholas
- 1996 *The Beginning and End of "Religion"?* (Cambridge: Cambridge University Press).

Lehmann, Jürgen
- 2009 *100 Jahre Deutsche Schule Kobe 1909 bis 2009. Eine Chronik als vorläufige Geschichte dieser kleinen deutschen Schule in Japan* (Tokyo: Iudicium Verlag).

Liebau, Heike
- 2006 "Faith and Knowledge: The Educational System of the Danish-Halle and English-Halle Mission," in A. Gross, V. Kumaradoss,

& H. Liebau, eds., *Halle and the Beginning of Protestant Christianity in India,* vol III (Halle: Verlag der Franckeschen Stiftungen), 1181–2214.

LIPSIUS, Richard Adelbert & Paul KIRMSS
1886 "Unsere Aufgabe in Ostasien," *Flugschrift des Allgemeinen Evangelische-Protestantische Missionsverein* (Berlin: Haack), 4 vols.

LIPSIUS, Richard Adelbert
1887 "In welcher Form sollen wir den heidnischen Kulturvölkern das Evangelium bringen?" *Zeitschrift für Missionskunde und Religionswissenschaft* 2: 129–39.
1898 "Missionspredigt II," *Das Missionsblatt des Allgemeinen Evangelisch-Protestantischer Missionsverein.* 13/2.

LOPEZ, Donald S.
1995 *Curators of the Buddha: The Study of Buddhism under Colonialism* (Chicago: The University of Chicago Press).

MACK, Julia Ulrike
2013 *Menschenbilder. Anthropologische Konzepte und stereotype Vorstellungen vom Menschen in der Publizistik der Basler Mission 1816–1914* (Zürich: Theologische Verlag Zürich).

MARBACH, Otto
1934 *50 Jahre Ostasien-Mission, ihr Werden und Wachsen* (Berlin-Steglitz-St. Gallen: Ostasienmission).

MARUYAMA Michikazu 丸山道一
1891A 「再び神道の処置を論ず」[Again on the Treatment of Shinto], 『眞理』2/11: 77–81.
1891B 「神の概念より基佛南教の論ず」[Discussions on the Concept of God in Christianity and Buddhism], 『眞理』2/11): 85–7.
1892 「基督教會拝像歴史」[Historical and Religious Observations of Christian Worship], 『眞理』2/20: 365–9.

MASUZAWA Tomoko
2005 *The Invention of World Religions, or, How European Universalism was Preserved in the Language of Pluralism* (Chicago: Chicago University Press).

MATHIEU, Edward C.
2010 "Public Protestantism and Mission in Germany's Thuringian States, 1871–1914," *Church History* 71/1: 115–43.

MICHAELIS, Georg
- 1887 "Aus Japan," *Deutsche Kolonialzeitung: Organ der Deutschen Kolonialgesellschaft* 4.
- 1922 *Für Staat und Volk* (Berlin: Severus Verlag).

MINAMI Hajime 三並 良
- 1890 「日本に於ける自由派神學の進歩」[The Progress of Liberal Christianity],『眞理』2/13: 4–15.
- 1893 「比較宗教學と基督教」[Comparative Religion and Christianity],『眞理』4/42: 162–8.
- 1935 『日本に於ける自由基督教と其先驅者』[Free Christianity and its Pioneers] (Tokyo: Bunshōin Shuppanbu).

MIZUTANI Makoto 水谷 誠
- 1996 「プロテスタンティスムスとリベラリスムス：普及福音新教伝道会の日本宣教を事例にして」[Protestantism and Liberalism: The Work of the Allgemeiner Evangelisch Protestantischer Missionsverein], in 『キリスト教研究』58/1: 1–25.
- 1999 "Die Problematik der Rezeption der "Reden" in Japan. Ein geschichtlicher Überblick und einige Problempunkte," in U. Barth, U. & C. D. Osthövener, eds., *200 Jahre Reden über die Religion Akten des 1. Internationalen Kongresses der Schleiermacher-Gesellschaf* (Berlin; New York: DeGruyter), 928–43.
- 2010 「三並長のキリスト教：その生涯と信仰」[The life and faith of Minami Hajime], in M. Mizutani, ed.,『日本におけるドイツ：日本におけるドイツ宣教史研究会論』[Germany in Japan: 125 Years in the German Mission] (Tokyo: Shinkyō Shuppansha), 115–40.

MOHR, Michel
- 2005 "Murakami Senshō: In Search for the Fundamental Unity of Buddha," *The Eastern Buddhist* 37/1–2: 77–105.
- 2014 *Buddhism, Unitarianism, and the Meiji Competition for Universality* (Cambridge, Mass: Harvard University Asia Center).

MULLINS, Mark R.
- 1994 "Ideology and Utopianism in Wartime Japan: An Essay on the Subversiveness of Christian Eschatology," *Japanese Journal of Religious Studies* 212–3: 261–80.
- 1998 *Christianity Made in Japan: A Study of Indigenous Movements* (Honolulu, University of Hawai'i Press).
- 2003 *Handbook of Christianity in Japan* (Leiden, Brill).

MULLINS, Mark R. & Peter NOSCO
- 2007 "Christians in Japan," *Japanese Journal of Religious Studies* 34/1: 1–7.

MUNZINGER, Carl
- 1890 「宗教學の必要を論ず」[On the Necessity of Religion], 『眞理』2/13: 25–9.
- 1891A "Das zukünftige Christentum Japans in Lichte seiner Gegenwart," *Zeitschrift für Missionskunde und Religionswissenschaft* 5: 1–15.
- 1891B "Die Missionsgemeinde und ihr inneres Leben," *Zeitschrift für Missionskunde und Religionswissenschaft* 5: 65–78.
- 1897 "Das Geistesleben des Japaners und die christliche Mission," *Zeitschrift für Missionskunde und Religionswissenschaft* 11: 65–79.
- 1898 *Die Japaner. Wanderungen durch das geistige, soziale und religiöse Leben des japanischen Volke* (Berlin, Verlag von A. Haack).
- 1906A *Japan und die Japanern* (Stuttgart, D. Gundert).
- 1906B "Unser recht und unsere Pflicht zur Mission," *Zeitschrift für Missionskunde und Religionswissenschaft* 20: 257–67.
- 1934 "Die ersten zehn Jahre unsere Mission," in T. Devaranne, ed., *50 Jahre evangelischer Arbeit im Fernen Osten 1884–1934. Ostasien Jahrbuch 1934. Im Auftrage des Zentralvorstandes herausgegeben von Missionsdirektor Devaranne* (Berlin: Ostasien-Mission), 15–20.
- 1976 『ドイツ宣教師の見た明治社会』[Meiji Society as seen from a German Missionary], transl. by B. Ikuma (Tokyo: Shinjinbutsu Ōraisha).

MURAKAMI Senshō 村上専精
- 1914 『六十一年：一名赤裸裸』[Year 1868, One person, exposed] (Tokyo: Heigo Shuppansha; 1993 reprint by Ōzorasha).

MURRAY, Paul
- 2002 "A Liberal Helping of Postliberalism Please," in M. Chapman, ed., *The Future of Liberal Theology* (London: Routledge), 208–20.

MÜLLER, Friedrich Max
- 1882 *Introduction to the Science of Religion. London: Four Lectures delivered at the Royal Institute in February and May 1870* (London: Longmans, Green and Co.).
- 1888 "Der christliche Missionar in seiner Beziehung zu anderen Religionen," *Zeitschrift für Missionskunde und Religionswissenschaft* 3: 231–7.

NAMIKAWA Yōko 並河葉子
2009 "Missionary Women during the Late 19th Century and the Early 20th Century in Japan," in Y. Namikawa, ed., *Japan as Seen by British Woman in Christina Mission* (Tokyo: Eureka Press), i–xii.

NELSON, Caramaine
2014 "Innocence Curtailed: Reading Maternity and Sexuality as Labor in Canadian Representations of Black Girls," in G. Campbell & E. Elbourne, eds., *Sex, Power, and Slavery* (Athens; Ohio University Press), 401–23.

NIPPERDEY, Thomas
1988 *Religion im Umbruch. Deutschland 1870–1918* (München: C. H. Beck).

NIREI, Yosuke
2007 "Towards a Modern Belief: Modernist Protestantism and Problems of National Religion in Meiji Japan," *Japanese Journal of Religious Studies* 34/1: 151–75.

OEXLE, Otto Gerhard
1996 *Geschichtswissenschaft im Zeichen des Historismus: Studien zu Problemgeschichten der Moderne* (Göttingen: Vandenhoeck & Ruprecht Gmbh & Co).

OKADA Masahiko 岡田正彦
2007 "Revitalization versus Unification: A Comparison of the Ideas of Inoue Enryō and Murakami Senshō," *The Eastern Buddhist* 34/1: 28–38.

OKUYAMA Michiaki 奥山倫明
2019 "Rethinking "State Shinto" in Past and Present," *Numen* 66: 163–84.

OSTERHAMMEL, Jürgen
1997 *Colonialism: A Theoretical Overview* (Princeton, NJ: Markus Wiener Publishers).
2009 *Die Verwandlung der Welt. Eine Geschichte des 19. Jahrhunderts* (München: C. H. Beck).
2014 *The Transformation of the World, A Global History of the Nineteenth Century* (Princeton, NJ: Princeton University Press).

OSTERHAMMEL, Jürgen & Jan JANSEN
2012 *Kolonialismus: Geschichte, Formen, Folgen* (München, C. H. Beck Verlag).

OSTERHAMMEL, Jürgen & Niels PETERSSON
2003   *Geschichte der Globalisierung Dimensionen, Prozesse, Epochen* (München, C. H. Beck Verlag).

ŌTANI Eiichi 大谷栄一
2012   「プロテスタント仏教 概念を再興する」[Rethinking the concept "Protestant Buddhism"], 『近代仏教』41: 107–22.
2014A   "The Movement called "New Buddhism" in Meiji Japan," in HAYASHI, ŌTANI, & SWANSON 2014, 57–62.
2014B   「明治仏教史における雑誌と結社」[Magazines and Associations in the History of Buddhism in the Meiji Period] 『宗教研究』87: 99–100.

ŌTANI Eiichi 大谷栄一, YOSHINAGA Shin'ichi 吉永進一, & KONDŌ Shuntarō 近藤俊太郎
2016   『近代仏教スタディーズ: 仏教からみたもうひとつの近代』[Modern Buddhist Studies: Another Buddhist view on Modernity] (Tokyo: Hōzōkan).

PAILIN, David A.
1984   *Attitudes to Other Religions: Comparative Religion in Seventeenth- and Eighteenth-Century Britain* (Manchester: Manchester University Press).

PERIN, George L.
1891   「文明の原則」[The Elements of Civilization] 『眞理』11: 12–18.

PETERSEN, Esben
2020   "Meiji Japan as Seen by a German Missionary: Carl Munzinger's Book Die Japaner," *Bulletin of the Nanzan Institute for Religion and Culture* 44: 11–31.
2021   "Hans Haas, The Songs of Buddha, and their Sounds of Truth: A German Missionary's Interpretation of Pure Land Buddhism," *Journal of Religion in Japan* 10/2: 161–94.

PFLEIDERER, Otto
1892   『自由新学』[Liberal Theology], transl. by T. Kanamori (Tokyo: Kanamori Tsūrin).
1906   "Die Bedeutung der Religionsgeschichte in der Gegenwart," *Zeitschrift für Missionskunde und Religionswissenschaft* 20: 1–8.

PORTER, Andrew
1996   "Mission and Cultural Imperialism," in A. Lande & W. Ustorf, eds., *Mission in a Pluralist World* (Frankfurt am Main: Peter Lang), 65–80.

PRAKASH, Gyan
  1999 *Another Reason: Science and the Imagination of Modern India* (Princeton: Princeton University Press).
PROCHASKA, Frank K.
  1977 "Little Vessels: Children in the Nineteenth Century English Missionary Movement," *Journal of Imperial and Commonwealth History* 6/2: 103–18.
RAI, Amit
  2000 *The Rule of Sympathy. Sentiment, Race, and Power, 1750–1850* (New York: Palgrave).
RAVENSCROFT, Ruth Jackson
  2019 *Das hybride Subjekt. Eine Theorie der Subjektkulturen von der bürgerlichen Modern zur Postmoderne* (Weilerwist: Velbrück).
RECKWITZ, Andreas
  2006 *The Veiled God: Friedrich Schleiermacher's Theology of Finitude* (Leiden: Brill).
RITTER, Karl Heinrich
  1884 "Die Grundsätze und Ziele des allgemeinen evangelisch-protestantischen Missionsvereins," in *Mitteilungen des AEPM Januar*.
  1886 "Die Religiöse Entwicklung des Japanische Volkes in den Zusammenhängen mit Seinen politischen Wandlungen," *Zeitschrift für Missionskunde und Religionswissenschaft* 1: 121–47.
  1890A *Dreißig Jahre protestantischer Mission in Japan* (Berlin: Verlag A. Haack).
  1890B "Geschichte der Protestantischen Mission in Japan," *Zeitschrift für Missionskunde und Religionswissenschaft* 5: 38–64.
  1892A "Japanisches: Nach dem Attentat auf dem russischen Thronfolger," *Zeitschrift für Missionskunde und Religionswissenschaft* 7: 31–32.
  1892B "Deutschlands Missionsberuf in Ostasien, insbesondere in Japan," *Zeitschrift für Missionskunde und Religionswissenschaft* 7: 98–108.
  1893A "Japanisches: Gegenströmung gegen das Christentum und Zeichen beginnender Unterströmung," *Zeitschrift für Missionskunde und Religionswissenschaft* 8: 89–93.
  1893B "Japanisches: Neuer Buddhismus in Japan," *Zeitschrift für Missionskunde und Religionswissenschaft* 8: 93–8.
  1898 *History of Protestant Missions in Japan* (Tokyo: Methodist Publishing House).

1899 "Mission bei den gebildeten Völkern," *Zeitschrift für Missionskunde und Religionswissenschaft* 14: 1–9.

ROHLEN, Thomas
1983 *Japan's High Schools* (California: University of California Press).

ROTHBART, Myron & Marjorie TAYLOR
1992 "Category Labels and Social Realities: Do We View Social Categories as Natural Kinds?," in G. Semin & K. Fielder, eds., *Language and Social Cognition* (London: Sage Publications), 11–36.

RUBINGER, Richard
1986 "Education from One Room to One System," in M. Jansen & G. Rozman, eds., *Japan in Transition from Tokugawa to Meiji* (Princeton: Princeton University Press), 195–231.

RUDOLF, Kurt
1969 "Die Bedeutung von Hans Haas für die Religionswissenschaft," *Zeitschrift für Religions- und Geistesgeschichte* 21/3: 238–52.

RUST, Arnold
1992 "Karl Munzinger. Ein pfälzischer Pfarrer und Missionar in Japan," *Blätter für pfälzische Kirchengeschichte und religiöse Volkskunde* 59: 101–17.

RUTHERFORD, Danilyn
2009 "Sympathy, State Building, and the Experience of Empire," *Cultural Anthropology* 24/2: 1–29.

RÜETSCHI, Albrecht Rudolf
1887 "Die Vergleichende Religionsgeschichte und das Christentum," *Zeitschrift für Missionskunde und Religionswissenschaft* 2: 193–208.
1905 "Das Christentum die einzige Weltreligion: Vortrag gehalten in der Generalversammlung," *Zeitschrift für Missionskunde und Religionswissenschaft* 20: 22–8.

SABA Wataru 佐波 亘, ed.
1979 「日本におけるドイツ神学の影響」[The Influence of German Missionaries], in SABA 1979, 12–18.
1979 『植村正久と其の時代』[Uemura Masahisa and His Times] (Tokyo: Kyōbunkan).

SAID, Edward
1978 *Orientalism* (New York: Pantheon Books).
1984 "Orientalism Reconsidered," *Race and Class* 27/2: 1–15.

SÁNCHEZ-EPPLER, Karen
- 1996 "Raising Empires like Children: Race, Nation, and Religious Education," *American Literary History* 83: 399–425.
- 2005 *Dependent States: The Child's Part in Nineteenth-Century American Culture* (Chicago: Chicago University Press).

SASAKI Masaharu
- 1909 "Der japanische Volkscharakter und die Missionare von einst und heute," *Zeitschrift für Missionskunde und Religionswissenschaft* 24: 169–73.

SATŌ Toshio 佐藤敏夫
- 1997 "The Second Generation," in Yasuo Furuya., ed., *A History of Japanese Theology* (Grand Rapids, Michigan: William B. Eerdmans Publishing Company), 43–82.

SCHREINER, Irwin
- 1970 *Christian Converts and Social Protest in Meiji Japan* (Berkeley: California University Press).

SCHILLER, Emil
- 1899 "Vereinsnachrichten. Von unseren Arbeitsfeldern in Japan," *Zeitschrift für Missionskunde und Religionswissenschaft* 14: 180–181.
- 1900 "Vereinsnachrichten. Von unseren Arbeitsfeldern in Japan," *Zeitschrift für Missionskunde und Religionswissenschaft* 15: 56–63.
- 1901 『神の觀念と近世哲學』 [The Idea of God and Modern Philosophy] (Tokyo: Shinrisha).
- 1902 "Berührungspunkte und Gegensätze zwischen Christentum und Japanischem Charakter," *Zeitschrift für Missionskunde und Religionswissenschaft* 17: 33–42.
- 1903 "Das Heutige Japan und das Christentum," *Zeitschrift für Missionskunde und Religionswissenschaft* 18: 289–312.
- 1908 『基督教要義』 [The Essentials of Christianity] (Tokyo: Shinrisha).
- 1922 "Missionsarbeit unter der Jugend," *Für die Jugend. Missionsblatt des Allgemeinen evangelisch-protestantischen Missionsverein* 18/12: 1–4.
- 1924 "Die Erdbeben-Katastrophe in Japan," *Ostasien Jahresbuch. Jahresbericht des Allgemeinen Evangelisch-Protestantischen Missionsverein* (Berlin: Ostasienmission).

SCHILLER, Elisabet
- 1922 "Der Koyasan," *Für die Jugend. Missionsblatt des Allgemeinen evangelisch-protestantischen Missionsverein* 22/4: 1–3.

SCHILLER, Liselotte
1921 "Ein japanischer Tempel," *Für die Jugend. Missionsblatt des Allgemeinen evangelisch-protestantischen Missionsverein* 21/3–4: 1–3.

SCHILLER, Magarete
1913A "Ausflug unserer Sonntagsschule in Kyoto (Japan)," *Für die Jugend. Missionsblatt des Allgemeinen evangelisch-protestantischen Missionsverein* 13/5: 1–4.
1913B "Weinachten in Kyoto," *Für die Jugend. Missionsblatt des Allgemeinen evangelisch-protestantischen Missionsverein* 13/2: 1–4.
1915 "Eine Vulkanbesteigung in Japan," *Für die Jugend. Missionsblatt des Allgemeinen evangelisch-protestantischen Missionsverein* 15/5: 1–4.

SCHLEIERMACHER, Friedrich Ernst Daniel
2010 *Über die Religion: Reden an die Gebildeten unter ihren Verächtern* (Stuttgart: Phillip Reclam jun).

SCHMALE, Wolfgang
2006 "Erkenntnisinteressen der Kulturtransferforschung," in W. Schmale & M. Steer, eds., *Kulturtransfer in der jüdischen Geschichte* (Frankfurt am Main: Campus Verlag), 23–41.
2012 "Culture Transfer," *European History Online*, http://ieg-ego.eu/en/threads/theories-and-methods/culturaltransfer.

SCHMIEDEL, Otto Moritz
1888A 「批評的歴史的及道徳的青年の聖書」[Critical Reading of the Bible for Young Men]『眞理』1/4: 21–7.
1888B 「福音書評論の法如何」[Way of Reading the Gospel Critical], in 『眞理』1/4: 20–3.
1888C 「聖書創世記の事果たして眞乎」[Is the Genesis True?], in 『眞理』1/5: 5–11.
1889A *Eine Woche in der Japanische Christengemeinde zu Tokyo* (Berlin: A. Haack).
1889B "Unsere Institute in Japan. Die Klöppelschule," *Das Missionsblatt des Allgemeinen Evangelisch-Protestantischer Missionsverein* 4/10.
1891A "Kultur- und Missionsbilder aus Japan," *Flugschrift des allgemeinen evangelisch-protestantischen Missionsvereins* 2 (Berlin: A. Haack).
1891B 「ダルウ井ン學説と哲學的終局論の關係」[The Relationship between Darwin's Doctrine and Teleology]『眞理』1/9: 66–9.
1891C 「ダルウ井ンの人と一神教」[Darwin's Human and Monotheism]『眞理』1/11: 8–10.

1892a "Antwort auf Dr. Warnecks Urteil über unsere Missionare," *Zeitschrift für Missionskunde und Religionswissenschaft* 7: 60–63.
1892b "Vereinsnachrichten. Von unseren Arbeitsfeldern," *Zeitschrift für Missionskunde und Religionswissenschaft* 7: 56–58.
1892c 「神學は科學なり」[Protestantism as the Foundation of Modern Science]『眞理』3/25: 5–11.
1897 *Kultur und Missionsbilder aus Japan* (Berlin: A. Haack).
1898 *Was lehrt und lernt der Missionar in Japan?* (Berlin: A. Haack).
1920a *Die Deutschen in Japan. Nach eigenen Erlebnissen und Beobachtungen geschildert* (München: Verlag Carl Kuhn).
1920b " Aus unserer Japan-Missionsarbeit," *Missionsblatt für Kinder* 35/7–8.

Schmitt, Otto
1932 "Der Japan Film," *Missionsblatt für Kinder* 47/2.

Schroeder, Emil
1910 "Christenkinder und Heidenkinder," *Für die Jugend. Missionsblatt des Allgemeinen evangelisch-protestantischen Missionsverein* 10/7: 2–3.
1911a "Aus der Mission der Gegenwart," Zeitschrift für Missionskunde und Religionswissenschaft 15: 88–94.
1911b "Der Kindergarten," in A. Kind, ed., *Jahresbericht 1910* (Berlin: Ostasienmission), 88–94.

Schroeder, Gertrude
1910 "Kleine Japankinder," *Für die Jugend. Missionsblatt des Allgemeinen evangelisch-protestantischen Missionsverein* 10/2.
1917 "Aus unserer Arbeit in Japan," *Für die Kinder: Missionsblatt des Allgemeinen evangelisch-protestantischen Missionsverein* 32/10: 4.

Schulke, Rudolf
1911 "Die Religion," *Zeitschrift für Missionskunde und Religionswissenschaft* 15: 286–305, 335–65.

Sekioka Kazushige 關岡一成
1985 「〈普及福音新教伝道会〉につて」[On the Allgemeine Evangelische Protestantische Missionsverein]『神戸外大論叢』36: 1–12.

Scott, David
1999 *Refashioning Futures. Criticism after Postcoloniality* (Princeton: Princeton University Press).

SHIELDS, James Mark
    2005   "Parameters of Reform and Unification in Modern Japanese Buddhist Thought: Murakami Senshō and Critical Buddhism," *Eastern Buddhist* 37: 106–34.
SHIMAZONO, Susumu 島薗進 & TSURUOKA Yoshio 鶴岡賀雄
    2014   『宗教再考』[Rethinking Religion] (Tokyo: Perikansha).
SMITH, Wilfred Cantwell
    1962   *The Meaning and End of Religion: A New Approach to the Religious Traditions of Mankind* (New York: Macmillan).
SMITH, Jonathan Z.
    1998   "Religion, Religions, Religious," in M. Taylor, ed., *Critical Terms for Religious Studies* (Chicago: University Chicago Press), 269–84.
SOBICH, Frank Oliver
    2006   *Schwarze Bestien, Rote Gefahr. Rassismus und Antisozialismus im deutschen Kaiserreich* (Frankfurt am Main: Campus Verlag).
SOLOMON, Robert
    1988   "On Emotions and Judgement," *American Philosophical Quarterly* 25/2: 183–91.
SPINNER, Wilfried, & Theodore ARNDT
    1891   "Warnecks Angriff," *Zeitschrift für Missionskunde und Religionswissenschaft* 6: 89–91.
SPINNER, Wilfried
    1885A   "Missionar Spinners bericcht aus Japan," *Das Missionsblatt des Allgemeinen Evangelisch-Protestantischer Missionsverein* 1/1.
    1885B   "Aus Japan," *Das Missionsblatt des Allgemeinen Evangelisch-Protestantischer Missionsverein* 1/1.
    1886A   "Briefe aus Japan," *Das Missionsblatt des Allgemeinen Evangelisch-Protestantischer Missionsverein* 2/2.
    1886B   "Der erste Missionsversuch der evangelischen Kirche," *Das Missionsblatt des Allgemeinen Evangelisch-Protestantischer Missionsverein* 2/2.
    1886C   "Aus Japan von Pfarrer Spinner," *Das Missionsblatt des Allgemeinen Evangelisch-Protestantischer Missionsverein* 2/2.
    1886D   "Theology and Religion in Modern Germany," *Japan Gazette*, 22.05.1886, 9pages.
    1887   "Aus Japan von Pfarrer Spinner in Tokyo," *Zeitschrift für Missionskunde und Religionswissenschaft* 2: 231–2.

316 | Bibliography

1889A "Aus Japan," *Das Missionsblatt des Allgemeinen Evangelisch-Protestantischer Missionsverein* 4/3.
1889B "Büge aus dem Leben des japanisches Volkes," *Das Missionsblatt des Allgemeinen Evangelisch-Protestantischer Missionsverein* 4/10.
1889C "Warum ein japanischer Jüngling Theologie studieren will?," *Das Missionsblatt des Allgemeinen Evangelisch-Protestantischer Missionsverein* 4/8.
1890 "Moderner Shintōismus," *Zeitschrift für Missionskunde und Religionswissenschaft* 5: 1–14.
1891A *Unsere Aufgabe in Ost- und Südasien* (Berlin: A, Haack).
1891B "Die Studenten in Japan," *Das Missionsblatt des Allgemeinen Evangelisch-Protestantischer Missionsverein* 7/1.
1893A "Götterfest in Japan," *Zeitschrift für Missionskunde und Religionswissenschaft*, 8: 1–10.
1893B "Shinto-Totenfeier und Ahnenkultur," *Zeitschrift für Missionskunde und Religionswissenschaft* 8: 168–75.
1893C " Zweiter Teil: Unser Missionswerk in Ostasien," *Zeitschrift für Missionskunde und Religionswissenschaft* 8: 239–47.
1895 "Die Beurteilung deutscher Missionsarbeit in Japan durch D. Dalton," *Zeitschrift für Missionskunde und Religionswissenschaft* 10: 151–2.

STEINER, Rudolf
2006 *Autobiography: Chapters in the Course of My Life 1861–1907* (New York: Steiner Books).

STOLER, Ann-Laura & Frederick COOPER
1997 "Between Metropole and Colony: Rethinking a Research Agenda," in A. Stoler, & F. Cooper, eds., *Tensions of Empire. Colonial Cultures in a Bourgeois* (Berkeley: University California Press), 1–56.

STOLER, Ann-Laura
1995 *Race and the Education of Desire: Foucault's History of Sexuality and the Colonial Order of Things* (Durham: Duke University Press).
2002 *Carnal Knowledge and Imperial Power. Race and the Intimate in Colonial Rule* (Berkeley: University of California Press).
2009 *Along the Archival Grain. Epistemic Anxieties and Colonial Common Sense* (Princeton: Princeton University Press).

STÜBER, Gabriel
2009 "Liberalismus und Mission am Beispiel der Ostasienmission. 1884–1900," *Blätter für pfälzische Kirchengeschichte und religiöse Volkskunde* 76: 151–71.

SUEKI Fumihiko 末木文美士
2005 "Building a Platform for Academic Buddhist Studies: Murakami Senshō," *The Eastern Buddhist* 37/1–2: 8–27.

SUZUKI Norihase 鈴木範久
1979 『明治宗教思潮の研究：宗教学事始』[Studies on the Religious Trends of the Meiji Period] (Tokyo: Tokyo Daigaku Shuppankai).

TADA Kanae 多田 鼎
1905 『修道講話』[Lectures on Practicing Religion] (Tokyo: Bummeidō).

TANIGAWA Yutaka 谷川 穣
2014 "The Age of Teaching: Buddhism, the Proselytization of Citizens, the Cultivation of Monks, and the Education of Laypeople during the Formative Period of Modern Japan," in HAYASHI, ŌTANI, & SWANSON 2014, 85–11.

TERAZONO Yoshiki 寺園喜基
1988 "Die Wirkungsgeschichte des Allgemeinen Evangelisch-Protestantischen Missionsvereins (AEPM) und der Allgemeinen Evangelischen Gemeinde in Japan," in Y. Terazono, & H. Hamer, eds., *Brennpunkt in Kirche und Theologie Japans* (Neukirchen-Vluyn: Neukirchener Verlag), 93–102.

THELEN, David
1988 "The Nation and Beyond: Transnational Perspectives on United States History," *Journal of American History* 86/3: 965–75.

THELLE, Notto R.
1987 *Buddhism and Christianity in Japan. From Conflict to Dialogue, 1854–1899* (Honolulu: University of Hawai'i Press).

THOMAS, Baraka Jolyon
2019 *Faking Liberties: Religious Freedom in American-Occupied Japan* (Chicago: The University of Chicago Press).

THOMAS, Nicholas
1992 "Colonial Conversations: Difference, Hierarchy, and History in Early Twentieth-Century Evangelical Propaganda," *Comparative Studies in History and Society* 34: 366–89.

TROELTSCH, Ernst
1907 "Missionsmotiv, Missionsaufgabe und neuzeitliches Humanitätschristentum," *Zeitschrift für Missionskunde und Religionswissenschaft* 21: 129–39.
1991 "Christianity and the History of Religion," *Religion in History* 21.

TSUDA Kenji 津田謙治
2020 "Liberal Protestantism and Tetsutaro Ariga," *Journal for the History of Modern Theology/Zeitschrift für Neuere Theologiegeschichte* 27/1: 12–19.

TSURUMI, Patricia
1990 *Factory Girls: Woman in the Thread Mills of Meiji Japan* (Princeton: Princeton University Press).

VON MOHL, Ottmar
1904 *Am japanischen Hof* (Berlin: Verlag Dietrich Reimer).

WADA Hirobumi 和田博文
2006 『言語都市・ベルリン 1861–1945』 [Berlin, a City in Words, 1861–1945] (Tokyo: Fujiwara Shoten).

WARNECK, Gustav
1880 *Warum ist das 19. Jahrhundert ein Missionsjahrhundert?* (Halle: Julius Fricke).
1885 "Missionsrundschau," *Allgemeiner Missionszeitschrift* 12: 193–202.

WENDT, Adolf
1901 "Aus Japan," *Zeitschrift für Missionskunde und Religionswissenschaft* 16: 74–6.
1910A "Isaburos Tod," *Für die Jugend. Missionsblatt des Allgemeinen evangelisch-protestantischen Missionsverein* 10/11: 1–4.
1910B "Das bewunderte deutsche Kind," *Für die Jugend. Missionsblatt des Allgemeinen evangelisch-protestantischen Missionsverein* 10/4: 1–2.

WINBURN, Thomas
1959 *Protestant Beginnings in Japan: The First Three Decades 1859–1889* (Tokyo: Charles E. Tuttle Company).

WIPPICH, Rolf-Harald
2001A "Christliche Mission und Kulturimperialismus. Aufbau und Entwicklung der deutschen protestantischen Missionstätigkeit in der Meiji-Zeit," in H. Gössmann & A. Mrugalla, eds., *11. Deutschsprachiger Japanologentag in Trier 1999* (Münster: Lit Verlag), 51–61.

2001B "Wilfried Spinner: Eine Art Heimweh nach Japan: Ein Porträt des ersten Japanmissionars des Allgemeinen Evangelisch-Protestantischen Missionsvereins," *OAG Notizen* 2: 5–16.

2002 "Die Deutsche Missionstättigkeit in Meiji Japan," in M. Krebs, *Japan und Preusen* (München: Stollfuß Verlag Bonn), 267–86.

WITTE, Johannes
  1912 "O, die armen Kinder," *Für die Jugend. Missionsblatt des Allgemeinen evangelisch-protestantischen Missionsverein* 12/3: 1–3.
  1913A "Die Nähmaschine," *Für die Jugend. Missionsblatt des Allgemeinen evangelisch-protestantischen Missionsverein* 13/5: 4.
  1913B "Was ich bei einer Taufe in Japan erlebte," *Für die Jugend. Missionsblatt des Allgemeinen evangelisch-protestantischen Missionsverein* 13/9: 1–4.
  1924 "Das Knabenfest in Tokyo," *Für die Kinder: Missionsblatt des Allgemeinen evangelisch-protestantischen Missionsverein* 39/3: 1–4.

WOLFES, Matthias
  1999 *Protestantische Theologie und Moderne Welt* (Berlin; New York: de Gruyter).

WOLLONS, Roberta
  1993 "The Black Forest in a Bamboo Garden: Missionary Kindergartens in Japan, 1868–1912," in *History of Education Quarterly* 33/1: 1–35.

WRIGHT, Robert
  1991 *World Mission: Canadian Protestantism and the Quest for a New International Order 1918–1939* (Quebec City: McGill-Queen's University Press).

YANIGATA Tomonobu 柳田友信
  1957 *A Short History of Christianity in Japan* (Sendai: Saisho Tosho Kankokai).

YAMAGUCHI Teruomi 山口輝臣
  1999 『明治国家と宗教』[Religion and the State in Meiji Japan] (Tokyo: Tokyo Daigaku Shuppansha).

YAMAMORI Tetsunao 山森鉄直
  1974 *Church Growth in Japan: A Study in the Development of Eight Denominations 1859–1939* (South Pasadena: William Caray Library).

YAMAMOTO Hideteru 山本秀煌
  1929 『日本キリスト教会史』[History of the Christian Church in Japan] (Tokyo: Nihon Kyōkai Jimusho).

YUSAKATA Toshimasa 山本秀煌
  1979 『神々の明治維新：神仏分離と廃仏毀釈』[The Meaning of Gods in Meiji Japan: The Separation of Shinto and Buddhism and the Dismissal of Buddhism] (Tokyo: Iwanami Shoten).

YUSAMARU Yoshio 安酸敏眞
  2015 『シュライアマハー『キリスト教信仰』の弁証：『信仰論』に関するリュッケ宛ての二通の書簡』[Schleiermacher's "Christian Faith" Defense: Two Letters to Rücke on "Faith Theory"] (Tokyo: Chisen Shokan).

YOUNG, Robert
  2001 *Postcolonialism: An Historical Introduction* (Malden: Wiley-Blackwell).

ZACHHUBER, Johannes
  2013 *Theology as Science in Nineteenth-Century Germany: From F. C. Baur to Ernst Troeltsch (Changing Paradigms in Historical and Systematic Theology)* (Oxford: Oxford University Press).

General Index

Adas, Michal, 160, 275
AEPM. *See* Allgemeine Evangelisch Protestantische Missionsverein.
Ahlers, Heinrich, 147, 273, 276
Aikawa Katsuko, 282
Akamatsu Renjō 赤松連城, 164, 187–9, 193, 243, 278–9
Akikusa Jūzo, 271
Albrecht Ritschl, 6–7, 31
Alexandrovich, Nicholas, 99
Alleinherrschaft, 154
Allgemeine Conservative Monatsschrift für das Christliche Deutschland, 41
Allgemeine Evangelisch Protestantische Missionsverein (AEPM), 1–4, 7, 9–20, 26–8, 31, 33–4, 36–52, 54–7, 59–60, 62–6, 71–7, 82–6, 88–101, 103, 105–6, 108–11, 113–5, 117–20, 122–3, 125–7, 129, 131, 136, 142, 144, 148, 156, 163, 171–2, 175, 182, 185, 188, 191, 193–202, 205, 208, 216, 218, 220–2, 229–30, 234, 239–40, 242–50, 252–62, 265–8, 271–3, 282
Allgemeingültigkeit, 34–5
American Union Hall, 58
Amida (Buddha). A. Buddhism; 133, 164–5, 167, 208, 273, 276; A. Grace, 209; A. Nyorai; 168, 209
Amitabha, 167. *See also* Amida
Amschutz, Galen, 273
Anderson, Emily, 258
Anesaki Masaharu 姉崎正治, 193, 279
animism, 158, 160
Anknüpfungspunkte, 44, 170, 193
anti-dogmatic, 6

Aoki Shūzō 青木周藏, 10, 51–4, 59, 99, 119, 182, 216, 248, 255–6, 263, 266, 270, 277, 282
Arbeitsschule, 274
archival grain, 285
Arisugawa Takehito 有栖川宮威仁, 53
Armenschule, 86, 90–2, 95, 105, 263–4, 267
Arndt, Theodor, 255, 258, 265, 269, 270
Asad, Talal, 245, 272
Astrid Schiller, 69

Ballhatchet, Helen, 248, 256, 261, 273
Basler Mission, 32, 41, 284
Bassermann, Heinrich, 43, 143, 271
Baur, Ferdinand Christian, 7, 31, 65, 156, 248, 251
Berlin University, 51
Berliner Missionswerk, 246
Bern University, 37, 250
Bernstein, Robin, 229, 284
Bhabha, Homi, 120, 136, 270, 272,
Bible lessons, 92, 134
Bible School, 267
Birkner, Hans-Joachim, 6, 247
Bismarck, Otto von, 255
Blaut, James, 219, 282
Blum, Mark, 190, 279, 281
Bolljahn, Johan, 259
Boshin War, 256
Bourdieu, Pierre, 267, 269
Bowersox, Jeff, 220, 239, 282–5
Brahmo Somaj, 45–6, 278
Brinkmann, Friedrich, 258
Buddhist Protestantism, 188
Bülow, Hans, 268

bunmei kaika 文明開化, 145
Buss, Ernst, v, 14, 18, 25–44, 47–8, 55–6, 58–9, 121, 124, 127, 143, 148–57, 161, 171, 174, 183, 185, 195, 250–5, 257, 271–4, 277
Busse, Leonard, 195, 279–80

Cambridge University, 51
Cary, Otis, 15
Chiba Gakuin 千葉教院, 204–5, 207
China, 45–6, 64, 176, 193, 221, 254
Christian. C. civilization, 178, 240; C. culture, 30, 33, 35–6, 40, 43, 70, 127, 140, 231, 251; C. ethics, 138–9, 147
Christlieb, Käthe, 262, 264
Christlieb, Max Heinrich, 72, 74, 108–9, 118, 124, 169, 171–5, 177–9, 182, 185, 258, 260–2, 268–9, 276
colonialism, 120, 161, 246, 249–50, 262, 267
Comaroff, Jean, 106, 220, 267, 282
Comaroff, Jeff, 106, 220, 267, 282
comparative religious studies, 55, 194, 198–200, 275
Confucianism, 12, 73, 90, 133, 144, 146, 148, 159, 177, 184–5, 273
Congregational Church, 75, 248, 256
conservative, 28, 41, 47, 250; c. critics, 252
Copper, Frederick, 220
Crouter, Richard, 7, 247
Culture Protestantism, 4
culture transfer (*Kulturtransfer*), 11, 26, 120, 215, 217, 248, 250

Dalton, Herman, 94–5, 265
Damenschule, 264
Danish-Halle Mission, 253
Darwin, Charles, 145, 198, 273, 280
Dasein, 211
Deneckere, Mick, 282
Deutsche Kolonialzeitung (DKO), 257
Deutsche Ostasienmission (DOAM), 245–6, 252–3, 258–62, 286

Deutscher Kolonialverein, 254
Deutscher Protestantverein. *See* Protestant Union
Devaranne, Theodore, 14, 162, 275
dharma, 196, 280
Deutsche Schule, 163
Diercks, Auguste, 81, 82, 84, 101, 261–2, 264–7
DKO. See *Deutsche Kolonialzeitung*
DOAM. *See* Deutsche Ostasienmission
doctrine of faith, 29
dogma, 6, 29, 31–3, 44, 157, 165, 184, 247, 251
Doitsugaku Kyōkai Gakkō 獨逸學協會學校, 53, 58, 60, 86, 92, 113, 119, 121–4, 126, 255–6, 268, 270
Doitsugaku Kyōkai, 獨逸學協會, 119
Dokkyō University, 270
Dōshisha University, 54, 76–7, 219, 248, 256
Drummond, Richard H., 15, 250, 256
Duke of Saxony-Weimar, 38, 46, 253
Durkheim, Emil, 239, 285

Ebina Danjō 海老名弾正, 1, 11, 64–6, 72, 242, 248–9, 256, 258
Educational Rescript, 177, 264, 276
Eliade, Mircea, 194
empathy, 151, 232–235, 237–8, 284, 285
Emperor worship, 73
EMS. *See* Evangelical Mission Association of the Southwest Germany
Ernst Troeltsch, 7–8, 33, 48, 77, 143, 249, 251, 253
essence of Christianity, 29, 35, 202, 212, 249; e. of faith, 194; e. of God, 151; e. of religion, 11, 30, 32, 152
Evangelical Mission Association of the Southwest Germany (EMS), 246
evolutionary theory, 197, 199, 273, 280

Fanon, Franz, 227, 284
fetishism, 158, 160

Flensburger Pils, 67
Flensburger, 120, 238, 270, 285
Foucault, Michel, 120, 238, 270, 285
Frederik IV, 253
free theology, 4
Fukyū Fukuin Kyōkai 普及福音教会, 10, 15, 49–1, 58, 62–6, 72, 74–5, 242, 245, 250, 268
Fukyū Fukuin Shinkyō Dendōkai 普及福音新教伝道会, 245

Geistesleben, 146, 176
Gesellschaft für Zimmerleute, 156, 274
Gikandi, Simon, 246, 262
González, Ondina, 108, 268
Gottfried, Johan, 65
grace, (Amida's grace), 115, 208–10, 215
Graf, Friedrich Wilhelm, 6, 30–1, 47, 152, 246–7, 250–2, 255, 273

Haager Gesellschaft, 31
Haas, Hans, 97, 162–3, 170, 173–4, 178–83, 185, 195, 204–5, 208–9, 212, 214, 258, 275–9, 281
Haensel, Hans, 231–2, 284
Hahn, Ferdinand, 14, 34, 249, 251–252
haikinshū 拝金宗, 116
Halle Mission, 253
Hamer, Hayo, 2, 14, 47, 85, 245, 249, 252–5, 257–9, 261–2, 264, 269–71
Harada Tamao 原田瓊生, 15–6, 255, 257–8, 268, 270, 280
Harnack, Adolf von, 7–8, 43, 48, 77, 143
Hatano Seiichi 波多野精一, 1, 77, 247
Haus der Begegnung (HDB), 246
Hayashi Makoto 林 淳, 275, 279
Hayman, Gavin, 27, 250
HDB. See Haus der Begegnung
Hegel, Georg Wilhelm Friedrich, 198, 251
Heidelberg University, 53
Hering, Otto Bernhard, 53, 95–6, 124, 126, 255–6, 264–5, 268, 270

Hermann, Wilhelm, 7, 166
Herrnhuter Brüdermission, 253
Hesse, Bernhard E., 39, 253, 255
Heydenreich, Agnes, 107, 261, 267–8
hierarchies of civilization, 220
Higashi Honganji 東本願寺, 203, 278
historical theology, 11, 26, 31, 35–6, 47, 247, 251
historicism (Historisismus), 196–7, 215, 251
Höhn, Fraulein, 264
Holleben, Theodor von, 278
Hongō church, 64–5
Hongō community, 66, 86, 105, 107, 268
Hoshino Seiji 星野靖二, 245, 249, 272, 275
Hückel, Willi, 231, 233, 272, 284

Imperial Rescript, 10, 88, 270
Imperial University of Kyoto, 247
inner life, 176, 209, 273
Inoue Enryō 井上円了, 164, 189, 191, 275
Inoue Tetsujirō 井上哲次郎, 88, 216, 265, 280
Interacktionsraüme, 26, 250
Irshick, Eugene, 104
Ishihara Ken 石原 謙, 77
Islam, 158
Isomae Jun'ichi 磯前純一, 13, 102, 249, 267, 273, 275, 279–80, 286
Itō Hirobumi 伊藤博文, 52, 182, 277
Iwakura mission, 52, 248, 277

Japan Daily Mail, 64, 89
Japanese Unification Church. See Nihon Kumiai Kirisuto Kyōkai
Jean-Claude Passeron, 267, 269
Jenkins, Jennifer, 6, 247
Jesuits, 98, 266
jiyūshugi shingaku 自由主義神学, 2, 49, 248

Jōdo Shinshū (Pure Land Buddhism), 46, 64, 162–4, 166–8, 187, 189–90, 257, 276, 278
Jōdoshū, 276
Josephson, Jason Ānanda, 13, 144, 249, 272–3, 275
Jugendmissionsblatt Mission-Glöcklein, 283

Kaiser Wilhelm Land, 254
Kanitkar, Helen, 225, 284
Kant, Immanuel, 5, 198
Kasawara Kenjū 笠原研寿, 46
Katō Hiroyuki 加藤弘之, 119, 255
Katsura Tarō 桂 太郎, 255
Kawamura Noriko, 川村典子, 83, 266, 274.
Kayama Shinjirō, 55, 128, 257
Kazushige Sekioka 關岡一成, 247–248
Kesselring, Karl Heinrich, 38, 42, 45, 55
Ketelaar, James, 265, 281
Kido Takayoshi 木戸孝允, 52, 182, 277
Kind, August, 241, 273, 286
Kitashirakawa Yoshihisa 北白川宮能久, 53, 256
Kiyozawa Manshi 清沢満之, 203–4, 208
Klautau, Orion, 190, 279
Kleine, Christoffer, 227, 267, 276
Klöppelschule, 264, 274
Knabenschule, 69, 259, 264
Knodt, Emil, 232–3, 284
Kodō Saturo, 280
kokka shintō 国家神道, 12. *See also* State Shinto
Kōkōdō 浩々洞, 204, 208, 215, 281
Kozaki Hiromichi 小崎弘道, 10, 53–4, 59, 75, 248, 256, 261, 273, 280
Kozaki Nariaki, 200–1
Kulturmission, 43
Kulturtransfer. *See* culture transfer.
Kulturvölker, 172, 276
Kumar, Nita, 265, 267

Lace School, 91, 264, 274–5
Lande, Aasulv, 15, 248–50, 256, 260
Lange, Robert, 277
Langhans, Friedrich, 25, 250
Liberal Theology, iii, 4, 15, 47, 49, 54, 59, 72, 158, 248, 273, 280
Liebau, Heike, 253, 265, 269
Lipsius, Richard Adelbert, 43, 118, 143, 252, 253, 269
Lisco, Gustav Emil, 43, 51–2, 216, 282
logos spermatikos, 161
logos, 36, 43
London Missionary Society, 101

Mack, Julia Ulrike, 253, 282–284
Māhāyana, 193–4
Manchuria, 277
Marbach, Otto, 14, 249, 251–2
Maruyama Masao 丸山眞男, 12
Maruyama Michikazu 丸山通一, 60, 74, 127, 202, 206, 271, 280
Masuzawa Tomoko, 32, 144
MBL. *See Missionsblatt, Das*
Meiji Restoration, 190, 277
Michaelis, Georg, 52, 131–2, 255, 269–1
Michitomo Kanamori 金森通倫, 11, 248, 256
Minami Hajime 三並 良, 15, 17, 60, 74, 113–4, 119, 122–4, 126–7, 138, 197–9, 202, 250, 263, 268, 270–71, 280, 282
Missionsblatt, Das (MBL), 40, 95, 108, 117, 118, 126, 246, 254–5, 257, 262–3, 265, 282–3
Missionsblatt für die Jugend, 218, 222, 225, 230–1, 239, 246, 267, 283,
Missionsblatt für die Kinder, 218, 222, 239, 283
Missionsjahrhundert, 241
Miyoshi Atsuyoshi, 271
Mizutani Makoto 水谷 誠, 16–7, 54, 250, 256, 275, 280–1
Modern Buddhism, 12, 46, 202, 279

Mohr, Michel, 3, 62, 194, 246, 248, 258, 260, 265, 279, 280
Mukō Gunji 向軍治, 60, 113–4, 119, 122–4, 126–8, 130, 138, 206, 268, 270–1
Müller, Friedrich Max, 37–8, 42–3, 45, 143–5, 157, 163, 166, 191, 193, 252, 272, 275
Mullins, Mark, 245, 250, 258, 260, 266, 279
Munzinger, Carl, 11, 61, 68, 72–4, 118, 124, 134–5, 168–9, 175–9, 182–3, 185, 198–201, 258–61, 266, 269, 271–2, 276–7, 280, 286
Murakami Senshō 村上専精, 1, 189–200, 202–3, 211, 215–6, 279, 280
Murray, Paul D., 27, 250

Nakarai Sunao, 55, 128, 257, 282
Nanjō Bunyū, 南条文雄 46, 55
nationalism, 5, 15, 174, 176
nationhood, 185
nenbutsu 念仏, 196
Nichiren 日蓮, 196, 276
Nichiyo Sōshi 日曜叢誌, 199
Nihon Kumiai Kirisuto Kyōkai (Japanese Unification Church), 75, 243, 257
Nipperdey, Thomas, 47, 255
Nippold, Friedrich, 37–8, 42, 252
Nishi Honganji 西本願寺, 187, 204, 278

OAM. *See* Ostasianmission
Odaka Naoyoshi, 268
Oexle, Otto Gerhard, 6, 247
Okuma Shigenobu 大隈重信, 62
Ostasianmission (OAM), 245
Osterhammel, Jürgen, 13, 26, 219, 249–50, 255, 282
Ostwald, Martin, 75, 96–98
Ōtani Eiichi 大谷栄一, 190, 272, 275, 279
Ōtani University (Shinshū University), 190, 203–4
Ōtani-ha 大谷派, 164, 189, 203, 278
Otto, Rudolf, 194

Oxford University, 55

PAAA. *See* Politische Archiv des Auswärtigen Amtes

Panesar, Rita, 246, 262, 266
Perin, George L., 70, 259–60, 280
Persönlichkeit, 209
Petersson, Niels P., 26, 250
Pfleiderer, Otto, 38, 43, 77, 143, 154, 161, 248, 252, 274, 275
philology, 163
Philosophical Academy (Tetsu-gaku-kan), 191
PKZ. *See* Protestantische Kirchenzeitung für das evangelische Deutschland
pluralism (religious pluralism), 6, 28, 33, 150, 157 184, 260
Politische Archiv des Auswärtigen Amtes (PAAA), 268
Prakash, Gyan, 229, 284
Presbyterian, 65
Protestant Union (Deutscher Protestantverein), 6
Protestantische Kirchenzeitung für das evangelische Deutschland, (PKZ), 257
Pure Land Buddhism. *See also* Jōdo Shinshū, Jōdoshū

Rai, Amit, 285
Ravenscroft, Ruth, 247
Religionsgeschichtliche Schule, 6, 195, 247, 248, 253
religious pluralism. *See* pluralism
Rennyo 蓮如, 167–8
Rheinische Mission, 254
Rikugō zasshi 六合雑誌, 199, 280
Ritter, Karl Heinrich, 14, 46, 52, 99, 141, 216, 250, 254–5, 257, 266, 272, 282
Rubinger, Richard, 85, 88, 264, 265
Rudolph, Kurt, 163
Rüetschi, Rudolf, 148, 155–61, 171, 174, 185, 273, 275
Russo-Japanese War, 50, 64–5, 175–6

Saba Wataru 佐波亘編, 16, 250, 254, 278
Said, Edward, 249, 267, 282
Śākyamuni, 193
Sánchez-Eppler, Karen, 272, 283, 285
Sanskrit, 45–6, 163, 191
Sasaki Geshō 佐々木月樵, 201, 204, 280
Satō Shigehiko 佐藤繁彦, 77
Satō Toshio 佐藤敏夫, 261
Scheiner, Irwin, 105, 114, 267, 269
Schiller, Emil, 68–70, 74, 89–90, 97, 99, 118, 183, 210–4, 219, 258–9, 261, 265–6, 269, 277, 281, 284
Schiller, Margret, 59, 259, 284
Schleiermacher, Friedrich, 4–5, 7–8, 29, 32, 48, 65, 150, 162, 247, 251, 275
Schmale, Wolfgang, 11, 248
Schmiedel, Otto Moritz, 57, 62, 67–8, 70–1, 86, 93–4, 100, 123–4, 127, 134, 171, 175, 198, 202, 207, 223–5, 254, 258–60, 262–7, 269, 271–2, 280–1, 284
Schmitt, Otto, 218–220, 239, 282
Schopenhauer, Arthur, 198
Schroeder, Emil, 74, 214, 225–6, 258, 261, 281
Schroeder, Gertrude, 226–7, 267, 284
Schulke, Rudolf, 277
Schweizer Ostasienmission, (SOAM) 246, 286
secularization, 245
Seinen Dōmeikai 青年同盟会, 264
Shaku Unshō 釋雲照, 279
Shields, James Mark, 194, 279
Shimaji Mokurai 島地黙雷, 189, 216, 278, 282
Shinagawa Yajirō 品川弥二郎, 255
Shinkyō Shingakkō 新教神学校, 10, 59–61, 73–4, 76, 81, 86, 105, 112, 119, 123–8, 130–1, 136, 139, 163, 258, 263–4, 268, 270–1
Shinran 親鸞, 165–7, 208, 215
Shinri 眞理, 2, 15, 49, 77, 197–202, 246, 250, 258, 261, 268, 280–1
shinshū kaimu 真宗皆無, 204

Shinshū University. *See* Ōtani University
State Shinto (*kōkka shintō*), 10, 12, 63, 66, 258
Shirai Shigekoto 白井成允, 208
shōbai no susume, 116
Shūdo kōwa 修道講話, 208–10
Smith, Jonathan Z, 144, 275
SOAM. *See* Schweizer Ostasienmission
Sol Oriens, 205–7
Spencer, Herbert, 145, 273
Spinner, Wilfried, 9–10, 14–5, 38, 45–6, 49, 52–62, 67, 69–70, 74, 81–2, 86, 92, 99, 108, 113–7, 121–34, 138, 171, 175, 187–9, 205–7, 249–50, 257–9, 265, 268–72, 274–5, 278
Strauss, David Friedrich, 5, 247
Sunday School, 69, 86, 263, 267–8, 271, 283
Suzuki Norihase 鈴木範久, 2, 16, 245, 250, 254
Swanson, Paul, 279
sympathy, 21, 235, 237, 284

Tada Kanae 多田 鼎, 164, 189, 203–5, 207–11, 214–6, 281
Tagebuch Schmiedel (TB-Schmiedel), 249, 256–7, 259, 264, 281,
Tagebuch Spinner (TB-SPINNER), 249, 256–9, 263–4, 266, 268–71, 276, 278–9, 281
Tenrikyō, 165–6, 275
Tetsugakkan 哲学館, 191. *See also* Philosophical Academy
theologia liberalis, 4
Thorne, Susan, 284
Tiele, Cornelis, 153
Tillich, Paul, 7, 249
Tomisaka Christian Center 富坂キリスト教センター, 246
Tōsuke Hirata 平田東助, 53, 119
Tripitaka, 46, 56, 165, 205, 207
truth (*Warhheit*), 6, 20, 32, 35, 44–5, 47, 150–4, 157–8, 185–6, 189, 193, 209, 234,

242, 252–3, 272; absolute t., 44, 152, 185, 251; divine t.. 41, 147; elements of t., 10, 25, 140, 165, 169; historical t., 197, 215; love of t., 255; religious t., 21, 162; seeds of t., 147, 161–2, 169; sounds of t., 144, 162, 169–70; universal t., 44, 106, 169, 195, 202, 253
Tsingtau, 254
Tübingen School, 6, 31, 156, 248, 251

Uchimura Kanzō 内村鑑三, 64, 88; U. incident, 63
Unitarianism, 248, 260
Unitarians, 9, 15, 248, 250, 259–60
universal religion, v, 25, 31, 150, 158, 160, 184, 201–2, 244, 250–1
universalists, 9, 15, 70, 259

Vallgårda, Karen, 92, 265
Vögelein, 268
Volksreligionen, 158–60

Wadagaki Kenzō 和田垣謙三, 51–2, 255
Wahrheit, 44, 185, 195, 246, 275. *See also* truth.
Warneck, Gustav, 93–4, 254–5, 265
Weiss, Johannes, 77

Wendt, Adolf, 91, 104, 227, 228, 265, 267, 284
Werner, Micheal, 11
Winburn, Thomas, 15, 250
Wippich, Rolf, 59, 249–50, 255, 257, 270
Witte, Johannes, 101–2, 213, 224, 230, 236, 267, 284–5
Wollons, Roberta, 101, 109, 263, 266, 268
Wright, Robert, 272
Würfel, Georg, 75, 96–8, 258

Yamakawa Yukio, 282
Yasukawa Tōru, 263
Yoshinaga Shin'ichi 吉永進一, 279

Zachhuber, Johannes, 26, 247, 250–1,
ZASP. *See* Zentralarchiv der Rheinland-Pfalz
zazen, 196
Zeitschrift für Missionskunde und Religionswissenschaft (ZMR), 20, 33, 43, 55, 88, 141, 184, 186, 246, 254, 263, 282
Zentralarchiv der Rheinland-Pfalz, (ZASP), 42, 46, 246, 252–3, 257–62, 270–1, 274, 281–2
ZMR. *See Zeitschrift für Missionskunde und Religionswissenschaft*

Printed in Poland
by Amazon Fulfillment
Poland Sp. z o.o., Wrocław